THE PRACTICE OF SURVEY RESEARCH

For our students, colleagues, and friends, who join us on this journey . . .

THE PRACTICE OF SURVEY RESEARCH

Theory and Applications

Erin E. Ruel
Georgia State University

William E. Wagner III
California State University, Channel Islands

Brian Joseph Gillespie
Sonoma State University

Los Angeles | London | New Delhi
Singapore | Washington DC | Boston

Los Angeles | London | New Delhi
Singapore | Washington DC | Boston

FOR INFORMATION:

SAGE Publications, Inc.
2455 Teller Road
Thousand Oaks, California 91320
E-mail: order@sagepub.com

SAGE Publications Ltd.
1 Oliver's Yard
55 City Road
London EC1Y 1SP
United Kingdom

SAGE Publications India Pvt. Ltd.
B 1/I 1 Mohan Cooperative Industrial Area
Mathura Road, New Delhi 110 044
India

SAGE Publications Asia-Pacific Pte. Ltd.
3 Church Street
#10-04 Samsung Hub
Singapore 049483

Acquisitions Editor: Vicki Knight
Associate Editor: Katie Bierach
Editorial Assistant: Yvonne McDuffee
Production Editor: Olivia Weber-Stenis
Copy Editor: Cate Huisman
Typesetter: C&M Digitals (P) Ltd.
Proofreader: Sue Irwin
Indexer: Scott Smiley
Cover Designer: Anupama Krishnan
Marketing Manager: Nicole Elliott

Cataloging-in-publication data is available from the Library of Congress.

ISBN 978-1-4522-3527-1

15 16 17 18 19 10 9 8 7 6 5 4 3 2 1

BRIEF TABLE OF CONTENTS

TABLE OF CONTENTS

PREFACE

Our purpose in writing this text is to create a comprehensive survey research book that incorporates survey design, survey implementation, data management, and data analysis. Most existing books are particularly weak in this last dimension. It's not just textbooks that are weak in that area, however. Research methods courses tend to cover only the collection of data using surveys, while statistical courses cover data analysis only for perfectly clean data. Nowhere do students see the effort needed to prepare collected data for analysis, nor do they learn how to do it.

This survey textbook is based in sociological research; the book provides breadth and examples suitable for survey expertise for both graduate students and advanced undergraduate students. One or two of the chapters are more advanced than others, and instructors may decide not to include them in an undergraduate survey course. This text can be used to supplement a research methods course or can be used as a standalone text in a survey course. We attempted to break up the chapters in such a way that the text can be used in a variety of ways.

Survey research is one of the most utilized methods in the social sciences. Students may think that this means the method is pretty well standardized. But this is not the case. Each research question is distinct and raises special concerns that need to be addressed. For example, the research topic could entail having to write challenging questions. Alternatively, the topic could involve a population that is hard to find or hard to convince to participate in the research. Or, the way the survey is administered may be important given the traits or characteristics of the population. We wrote this book with the uniqueness of each research topic in mind. We are constantly having to make decisions about the many unique situations we face while trying to answer our research questions. Each chapter is framed with a list of decisions that need to be made, depending on the various challenges that may arise as the survey study is developed.

We were also driven by the desire to bring a more applied approach to the survey process. Over the course of teaching students for many years, we have found that a disconnect can occur between what is learned in the classroom and what students do outside the classroom for their undergraduate honors papers and MA theses. Therefore, the data analysis chapters include write-ups for policy reports and articles to demonstrate how to interpret and use the data to communicate findings.

At the end of each chapter we provide a list of terms that students should learn. We also include a set of critical thinking questions that students can answer to help ensure they have learned the material. We provide many real life research examples throughout the text. In addition, we provide the oh-so-important checklists that survey researchers live by to make sure they have comprehensively addressed all the decisions that need to be made.

Research ethics are an important part of any methods course. Rather that introduce ethics once in a single chapter, we added an "ethics corner" to many of the chapters, starting in Section III, Implementing a Survey. In each ethics corner, issues specific to the chapter topic are raised and discussed. In this way, students can see that ethical decisions come up throughout the survey process. Ethics become less abstract.

ACKNOWLEDGMENTS

The authors wish to thank the editorial team at SAGE for their efforts and help in making this book a reality. In particular, we would like to thank Vicki Knight for her support throughout the process. Our thanks also extend to those who worked hard to provide critical reviews of the drafts that were fashioned into the chapters that lie ahead.

We also wish to acknowledge and thank the graduate students and former graduate students who worked so hard on the Urban Health Initiative at Georgia State University, and who worked with many of the materials that made up the third and fourth parts of this book: Angela Anderson, Chris Pell, Elton Wilson, Nia Reed, Renee Skeete Alston, Amanda Dorrington Powell, Robert Maddox, Brandon Attell, Erin Echols, Angie Luvara, and Leah Kozee.

Our thanks and acknowledgements extend also to the following for their inspiration, advice, and contributions: Stefan Malizia for his editorial expertise and assistance, Kevin Austin for his patience, Janet Lever for her guidance, the Ruel family for all their support, and ultimately, Vic Arcabos, who very sadly is no longer among us (R.I.P., 5/18/2013), but whose love and inspiration have changed the lives of so many.

SAGE Publications wishes to thank the following reviewers: Richard E. Adams, Kent State University; Carol A. Angell, University of Wisconsin–La Crosse; Silvia K. Bartolic, University of British Columbia; Andrew M. Burck, Marshall University; Jon R. Norman, Loyola University Chicago; Sharon Sharp, California State University, Dominguez Hills; Lihua Xu, University of Central Florida; Kenneth C. C. Yang, University of Texas at El Paso; and Diane Zosky, Illinois State University.

SAGE
50
YEARS

ABOUT THE AUTHORS

Erin E. Ruel is Associate Professor of Sociology and Director of Graduate Studies at Georgia State University in Atlanta. She received her PhD in sociology at the University of Illinois at Chicago in 2003. While there, she worked at the Health Research and Policy Center as the data collection manager of the Impacteen Project. In 2003 Ruel took a postdoctoral position at the University of Wisconsin–Madison in the Center for Demography of Health and Aging, working on the Wisconsin Longitudinal Study.

Soon after arriving in Atlanta to take an assistant professor position at Georgia State University in 2005, Ruel and colleagues began the Urban Health Initiative, a longitudinal survey study of public housing residents facing involuntary relocation. Ruel was principal investigator of the National Institutes of Health study on the health outcomes of relocated public housing residents, and she was coinvestigator on two National Science Foundation studies examining social disorganization and social support for public housing residents. She employs quantitative and mixed methods to examine health disparities and the health consequences of racial residential segregation, neighborhood disadvantage, housing, and socioeconomic status. She has published in numerous journals, including *Demography, Social Forces, Social Science Research, Health and Place, Journal of Housing Studies, Cities, Sociology Compass, Journal of Adolescent Health,* and *Journal of Urban Health.*

Dr. Ruel can be located on the web at: http://www2.gsu.edu/~wwwsoc/2747.html.

William E. Wagner III, MA, MPH, PhD, is Professor of Sociology at California State University, Channel Islands. Prior to coming to CSU Channel Islands, he served as a member of the faculty and Director at the Institute for Social and Community Research, California State University, Bakersfield. While there, Dr. Wagner was principal investigator on over $2 million worth of research grants and contracts. He completed his PhD in sociology at the University of Illinois at Chicago; during that time he held positions at both the University of Illinois Survey Research Laboratory and at SPSS, Inc. (now IBM SPSS). Dr. Wagner also holds an undergraduate degree in mathematics from St. Mary's College of Maryland, as well as an MPH degree (Master of Public Health) from CSU Northridge. He has published in national and regional scholarly journals on topics such as urban sociology, homophobia, academic status, sports, and public health. Dr. Wagner has authored or coauthored two other SAGE titles: *Adventures in Social Research,* forthcoming in its ninth edition (Babbie, Wagner, and Zaino 2015) and the fifth edition of *Using SPSS Statistics for Research Methods and Social Science Statistics* (Wagner 2014).

Dr. Wagner can be located on the web at http://faculty.csuci.edu/william.wagner.

Brian Joseph Gillespie, PhD, is Assistant Professor of Sociology at Sonoma State University. He received his PhD at University of California, Irvine in 2012. His primary research interests are in demography, family, migration, and the life course. He is trained in quantitative and qualitative research methods and has published research in these areas using sophisticated statistical modeling, ethnographic research, in-depth interviews, and narrative analysis. His research has been supported by the American Sociological Association Section on Methodology, the National Science Foundation, the regents of the University of California, and the Center of Expertise on Migration and Health.

Dr. Gillespie can be located on the web at http://www.sonoma.edu/sociology/faculty/brian-gillespie.html.

SECTION I

Decisions to Make Before Conducting the Survey

1

Introduction to Survey Research

WHAT IS SURVEY RESEARCH?

Survey research is a highly effective method of measurement in social and behavioral science research. Well-designed surveys can be extremely efficient and very effective in generalizability. Survey research is particularly flexible given the numerous options available for instruments and data collection.

In the past, surveys were implemented primarily over the phone or using pen-and-paper questionnaires. E-mail and the web have now emerged as a primary vehicle for questionnaire distribution and data collection. Surveys are, however, much more than just the questionnaire. A survey also relies on proper design, representative sampling, and appropriate and effective administration of the questionnaire.

Survey research has become pervasive in the modern Western world and beyond. It can be seen as a crucial research tool in academia, government, and the private sector. In the United States it is virtually impossible to avoid surveys; they have become a staple for information gathering by people in different positions within many fields. Questionnaires can be long or short; difficult to comprehend or easy to understand; delivered in person, by mail, or over the Internet. Sometimes the questionnaires are highly structured, while other times they are simple and might seem to have been thrown together in just a few minutes.

Keep in mind that surveys do not always look like surveys. Consider college or university course examinations, particularly multiple-choice exams. These fixed response questions, testing your knowledge of information from all or part of the course, are actually surveying your knowledge and understanding of course content.

Brainstorming: Can you think of other things that are not called surveys but in fact are surveys?

Who develops surveys? Just about anyone! With the great power and potential afforded by e-mail and software such as Survey Monkey, Fluid Surveys, or Qualtrics, the tools to develop and implement a survey are widely available. While that is, no doubt, a good thing, surveys that are developed without considering the concepts covered in this book may not produce the results that one would expect. In fact, a poorly designed survey may provide incorrect information upon which a person or organization may act, and this could have serious consequences.

HOW DO YOU KNOW IF A SURVEY IS GOOD?

In some cases, even the uninitiated survey respondent can tell that a questionnaire does not meet muster. For example, consider the question in Mini Case 1.1.

MINI CASE 1.1

Problematic Sample Survey Question

There should be a tax cut and a new national health insurance program:

agree or disagree

This question is confusing and highlights a problem for many, if not most, readers of the question: What if you agree with one aspect of the question, but not the other (tax cuts, national health insurance)? "Neither agree nor disagree" is an appropriate response for that likely significant proportion of respondents. Also, since neither a neutral category (neither agree nor disagree) nor an overt missing-response category is presented (such as an option for the respondent to report "don't know"), some respondents are likely to select agree (or disagree) when that is not a correct representation of their opinions. See Chapter 3, "The Cover Letter and Survey Instrument," for more detailed information.

More often, however, most respondents regard the questionnaire as scientific and proper. That does not mean that the survey was well designed: Survey respondents, themselves, are not necessarily the appropriate evaluators of a survey, and the survey is a process that includes much more than just the questionnaire.

Have you ever received an e-mail survey from someone in the executive office or communications office of the organization where you work or attend school? Have you ever wondered to yourself why particular questions were asked and others were not? Did you feel that, perhaps, the questionnaire could have been easier to understand, more applicable to you, or maybe even more applicable to the stated objective of the survey? Did you ever think that one of these surveys was rather poorly constructed? You might very well have legitimate concerns about the survey you received.

It is widely thought that survey research is something that is easy to do, and that a researcher with a short amount of time and few resources can produce significant actionable results. Relatively speaking, survey research is a highly efficient way to gather data in a number of settings for a variety of purposes. Unfortunately, the responsibility of "taking a survey" in many organizations is often delegated solely to administrative assistants (who may have a variety of titles, ranging from secretary to office manager to program analyst and beyond) who may have little or no formal education in the development and implementation of surveys. That is not to say that some administrative assistants are not highly skilled in this area and that some organizations do not provide the necessary time and other resources to carry out the survey. However, that tends not to be the norm, particularly as public and private organizations alike strive to reduce costs and still produce the same or increasing outputs. So even with something as seemingly innocuous as an employee opinion survey, which ultimately might result in some changes in organizational culture or structure, the endeavor's result can be anything but innocuous, since it may yield incorrect information upon which potentially important decisions are made. In such a case, it might have been better to not use the survey at all!

SURVEYS ABOUT TEACHERS: ARE THEY "GOOD" TEACHERS?

Surveys take on many names and forms. For instance, consider student teaching evaluations carried out at most colleges and universities. At the end of a course, students are often presented with a questionnaire seeking evaluative information about the course they have just taken as well as the instructor. Which questions were chosen, which were not included, and in what order they are presented, among other things, can impact the results. The results can impact the future development of a course, including content, style, and so on. They can also impact the career of the teacher, positively or negatively. So, naturally, one would expect that these surveys are designed by experts in the area of survey research to ensure that curriculum and careers are not being impacted willy-nilly. Perhaps it will surprise you to learn that many of these "evaluation instruments" are not designed by survey researchers. Experts in the area of teaching and pedagogy might have great insight into what types of information could be useful, but may have very little expertise in methods to properly collect useful data.

If you are going to carry out a survey, do it right. Otherwise it is at best a waste of time, and at worst detrimental to the cause of those whom it was intended to benefit. Take Mini Case 1.2, for example, where an error in sample selection has ruined the opportunity for any meaningful results in the survey.

MINI CASE 1.2

Is a ten-year-old boy the right respondent for a survey about diet soda?

Ten-year-old Billy was with his mom while she was shopping in a women's clothing store at the mall. He asked if he could go to the toy store in the mall while his mom shopped for clothes, and she agreed, provided that he go directly to the toy store and remain there. On the way to the toy store, Billy was accosted by a well-dressed woman carrying a clipboard. She asked if he liked soda and if he would like to try some samples. While a child should not talk to strangers offering sweets, Billy did. He loved soda and could not resist the opportunity, particularly since his parents carefully rationed his soda intake to just a few glasses per week. So, he followed the stranger into the long eerie hallways behind the mall stores that ultimately led to a small office.

In the office, the woman put several six-packs of bottled soda into bags; the six-packs were differentiated only by unique colored caps. Each colored cap represented one flavor variation. She asked Billy some demographic questions, and then she handed Billy several survey sheets and asked that he fill out and return one for each pack of sodas. As Billy labored to carry the heavy bags back out to the mall, the lady mentioned that these were diet sodas. Billy was disappointed but figured that maybe he could trade the sodas to his mom for regular sodas. It turns out that his mom was not

(Continued)

(Continued)

thrilled to learn about his adventure and did not provide him with any regular soda. She drank the diet sodas and filled out the survey sheets later, after she had drunk all of the sodas and did not remember which was which.

It is hard to imagine that the soda company was at all interested in surveying a very thin 10-year old boy about his opinions on variations of diet sodas that were under development. So why did this happen?

After all, you would not survey a dog about cat food, would you? In fact, you would not (or should not) give a pen-and-paper questionnaire to a dog at all. The data yielded from Mina, the dog above, on such a questionnaire will be similar in quality to the data in the example described above!

Whether a survey is implemented by a firm for market research purposes, by university faculty for academic research, by pollsters looking to predict voting outcomes, or by a firm seeking to measure employee satisfaction, there are always limited resources in terms of time and money (labor, supplies, and so on). There are always decisions that must be made relative to the feasibility of completing the project, no matter how large or small. These decisions are sometimes subject to individual preferences, (also known as unconscious bias) or time constraints. Obtaining "perfect" information is rarely, if ever, a viable option, since infinite resources simply do not exist. It is crucial, however, to be absolutely certain that decisions about how to limit costs or time do not compromise the quality of the survey to the point that, for instance, skinny 10-year-old boys are being surveyed about diet sodas. Therefore these decisions cannot be left to unconscious thought or to the whims of those involved.

In the case of 10-year-old Billy's soda survey experience from Mini Case 1.2, it is likely that the staff who were administering the questionnaires were under a deadline to get a particular number of surveys completed. Surely, there was a sampling frame that required certain demographics, and it is reasonable to assume that these demographics did not include 10-year-olds. If the demographics were accurately coded, then this case would need to be omitted from the results and would end up being a waste of resources for the company. What is actually more likely is that Billy was recorded as an adult filling needed quotas in the sampling frame. As a result of this false coding, the data from Billy's questionnaires would be included in the overall analysis and ultimately would taint the results. If this practice was anything more than a one-time fluke, it is clear that the results of the entire survey effort are not correct, and all of the resources that went into the project were ultimately wasted. Other, less egregious problems with this survey also emerge from this Mini Case; those specific issues will be discussed later in this book.

Does this mean that a survey needs to be perfect in order for it to be useful? No. In fact, a survey may not even be the best way to collect the richest data on a particular subject. However, given the versatility of survey research, a survey may offer insights into how better to conduct research to obtain those richer data. Also, it may not be fiscally feasible to engage in some of the other types of research in which one might wish to engage. Survey research can often provide useful and actionable information with fewer resources than would be required using most other effective methods.

APPLICATIONS OF SURVEY RESEARCH

Opinion polls, whether related to political elections or not, are pervasive in modern society and a prominent example of survey research. The ability to measure attitudes or opinions of a population through a relatively small representative sample is a powerful tool.

Surveys can be used in experimental research or causal research. With causal research, the goal of the survey is usually to determine factor(s) that influence a dependent variable. Survey research can be intertwined at various levels with experiments. Questionnaires are often used as pretests, posttests, and/or as follow-up inquiries.

The methodological design of a survey can be cross-sectional or longitudinal (see Table 1.1). A political voting survey or opinion poll is a prime example of a cross-sectional survey, one that takes a snapshot of opinions at one point in time. Longitudinal surveys can ascertain change over periods of time. The longitudinal variety of survey takes on these common forms: repeated cross-sectional design, fixed-sample panel design, or cohort study. As expected from the name, surveys of repeated cross-sectional design administer the same questionnaire at more than one point in time to make a comparison. The fixed-sample panel design follows a sample of individuals over several time points and can measure change over time. A cohort study is a special case of the panel design that follows people over time who have experienced a common event or starting point. For more information on methodological design of the survey, see Chapter 2, "Types of Surveys."

Table 1.1 Cross-Sectional Versus Longitudinal Surveys

Cross-Sectional	*Longitudinal*
Snapshot of opinions at one point in time	Repeated cross-sectional
	Fixed-sample panel design
	Cohort study

TECHNOLOGY AND SURVEY RESEARCH

Technology related to survey research used to be restricted to such things as telephones and CATI (computer assisted telephone interview) software. Advances in computer hardware technology, Web browser capabilities, iPads/tablets, iPhones/smartphones, and other devices are transforming the scope of survey research and how it is done. Software such as Survey Monkey and Qualtrics allows for sophisticated survey design that, on the front end, can be graphical and interactive in nature and that flows seamlessly and effortlessly as the respondent points and clicks. The user is not burdened with seeing extraneous material, having to navigate skip patterns, or having to worry about whether answers are marked properly. This enables the instrument to collect far more information far more accurately than a traditional pen-and-paper mail survey, or even a telephone survey, would feasibly allow. We spend a great deal of time integrating these technologies into the chapters ahead, because modern surveys regularly require technology and innovations to collect data in a timely and accurate way.

THE ETHICS OF SURVEY RESEARCH

Since survey research involves human subjects, it is important to consider the ethical treatment of subjects. The principles of the *Belmont Report* (National Commission for the Protection of Human Subjects of Biomedical and Behavioral Research, 1979) are widely accepted as the standard for this type of research. The report was created in response to numerous research studies that were seen as crossing the line with regard to the rights of subjects. The major principles put forth in this report are justice, beneficence, and respect for persons. The report and its ideals are often the underpinnings for many organizations' and associations' codes of ethical conduct, such as that of the American Sociological Association. Institutional review boards (IRBs) were developed at universities and other organizations as a self-regulating safeguard to guarantee the protection of subjects. In such institutions, survey research should always follow ethical protocols and be submitted to an appropriate IRB. Specific ethical concerns are addressed in this book as they arise throughout the process of survey research.

KEY DECISIONS IN SURVEY RESEARCH: WHAT'S AHEAD

Throughout much of this book, we will explain the process of survey development and the decisions that must be made along the way. As you develop the survey, sampling frame, questionnaire, and so on, you will be presented with many options at each level.

The choice of an appropriate, yet feasible, option is not always as obvious as it might seem. Good selections can improve and maintain the ultimate quality of the data you collect and analyze through the survey. Poor selections can reduce or destroy the credibility of your data. With our guidance, you will choose wisely!

Section I: Decisions to Make Before Conducting the Survey

These decisions are covered in the current chapter, Chapter 1.

Section II: Questionnaire Design

In Chapter 2, the general characteristics of a survey are discussed along with the decisions you will need to make about the design of the research. Consider the scale of the survey: Will it be a specific topical survey, or will it be combined with other questions as part of an omnibus survey? You will need to consider whether an interviewer will administer the questions or whether respondents will respond on their own. Then, there are numerous types of survey formats to choose from: mailed pen-and-paper questionnaires, face-to-face interviews, face-to-group interviews, telephone (CATI) interviews, written questionnaires delivered via the Internet, or some mixture of these. Among those formats, there is a variety of technology that can be employed as well. In this chapter you will also learn about how to make these decisions based on your research questions, the target population, and the resources at your disposal.

Chapter 3 introduces the cover letter as an important part of the survey process. The survey instrument and how it should be organized as a whole is also presented. In Chapter 4, we discuss how to develop appropriate questions that will measure the concepts you intend to measure. Validity and reliability of the measurements are considered in Chapter 5. Chapter 6 introduces types of pretesting—ways to assess questionnaires prior to putting them to use.

Section III: Implementing a Survey

Chapter 7 details how to select an appropriate probability sample, including considerations of sample size and sampling techniques. Nonprobability samples and populations that are difficult to sample are examined in Chapter 8, with considerations of how to effectively sample in those potentially troublesome cases. Chapter 9 addresses sampling errors and strategies that can be used to minimize those errors. Chapter 10 will focus on the technologies referenced throughout the book that can be used to facilitate and improve survey research. In Chapter 11, the issue of data collection is discussed, with emphasis on the individuals directly collecting the data and how they must be trained, as well as on how data will be stored and accessed.

Section IV: Postsurvey Data Management and Analysis

In Chapter 12, attention is given to issues surrounding how data goes from the survey instrument (questionnaire) to the data file that will ultimately be analyzed (e.g., coding, data entry). Data cleaning, which will not require any bleach, is covered in Chapter 13. Chapter 14 introduces the concept of basic or univariate and bivariate data analysis, while Chapter 15 covers more advanced forms of data analysis, such as multiple regression. Finally, Chapter 16 introduces data archiving to ensure that data are preserved properly for future use.

SECTION II

Questionnaire Design

Designing a questionnaire is a multistage process that involves much more than simply preparing questions. A number of issues, detailed in Chapter 2, "Types of Surveys," have to be considered with respect to how the survey will be delivered and by whom. The mode of delivery might use advanced technology, such as web-based software, or a face-to-face ask-and-answer mode may be used. A survey might stand alone or might be combined with the work of other researchers to form a larger multipurpose omnibus survey. Some of these issues will be determined by the research questions, target population, and available resources.

It is also important to consider principles of questionnaire construction, as addressed in Chapter 3, "The Cover Letter and Survey Instrument." For instance, how should the questions be generally organized? What special considerations are there, given the nature of the research questions and the target population? How complex should questions be? There are ways to obtain complex information from a series of carefully crafted simple questions, which may include the use of gateway questions and skip patterns. Overall, one must assess the task burden on the respondents and be sure that this burden does not exceed the threshold over which the respondents will either (a) not complete the questionnaire or (b) not complete the questionnaire with care to provide correct answers.

Chapter 4, "Survey Question Construction," introduces the use of survey questions to measure simple and complex concepts at both the person level and at an aggregate or macro level. (For example, "Were you laid off from a job during the Great Recession?" is a person-level question, whereas "What percentage of employees were laid off between 2008 and 2012" is a macro- or firm-level question.) Vignette forms of questions are introduced. Open-ended items are discussed. Prospective versus retrospective issues are examined. The chapter closes with a look at creating variables from concepts and a discussion of levels of measurement.

Concerns about validity and reliability are addressed in Chapter 5, "The Quality of Measurement: Validity and Reliability." In particular focus are internal (causal) validity, measurement validity, and reliability. The basics of these issues will be addressed and discussion will then be extended to cross-comparative and open-ended questions.

Requirements of survey instrument testing prior to actual administration are detailed in Chapter 6, "Pretesting and Pilot Testing." Among the topics introduced are cognitive interviews, behavior coding, and the use of a panel of experts.

2

Types of Surveys

INTRODUCTION

In determining the scale of the survey project to undertake, there are a number of considerations. You might produce a survey to collect the data necessary to answer your research questions, or you may be interested in participating in a larger survey that collects data on a number of topics and is, in turn, used by multiple researchers to address various research questions. Regardless, the way the survey is administered needs to be addressed: Will you interview individuals in person, by phone, by mail, over the Internet, or in some combination of these? In addition, will respondents self-administer the questionnaire, or will staff administer the questionnaire? A **survey** is the overall systematic procedure to collect data from different individuals. A **questionnaire** is a tool used to collect information from respondents and is part of the larger survey process. The questionnaire can also be referred to as a **survey instrument**. Regardless of who administers the survey instrument, it is important to familiarize yourself with available technology to make the data collection process more efficient and more accurate. In fact, technology can allow for the collection of additional data, without losing efficacy, while making the survey process less taxing for the respondent—thus allowing additional questions to be added to the survey instrument.

OMNIBUS SURVEYS

Surveys in which multiple data on a wide variety of subjects are collected are referred to as **omnibus surveys**. Usually multiple researchers contribute different questions to the instrument and demographic questions benefit most or all of the research. While the instrument will be more cumbersome than a smaller questionnaire, the economy of scale often allows additional pooled resources resulting in a larger sample size. The General Social Survey (GSS) is among the most pervasive ongoing omnibus surveys, as detailed in Mini Case 2.1.

MINI CASE 2.1

About the GSS Data

The National Opinion Research Center (NORC) at the University of Chicago administers the General Social Survey (GSS). The GSS was started in 1972 and continues today. The data used for the examples in this book come from the latest available completed version of the GSS; they were collected in 2012. According to NORC, with the exception of the US Census, the GSS is the most frequently analyzed source of information in the social sciences. NORC acknowledges that there are at least 14,000 instances where the GSS has been used for articles in scholarly journals, books, and doctoral dissertations. Furthermore, it is estimated that more than 400,000 students annually use the GSS in their work.

The GSS contains many demographic and attitudinal questions as well as questions on rotating topics of special interest. A number of core questions have remained unchanged in each survey since 1972. This allows for rich longitudinal research about the attitudes, opinions, and demographics in the United States. Topical questions appear sometimes for just one year; other times, they can appear for a period of years. Therefore, the GSS is versatile as a longitudinal data resource and a relevant cross-sectional resource.

To maximize the amount of information that can be collected in this massive interviewing project, the GSS uses a *split ballot design*, in which NORC asks some questions in a random subsample of the households and asks other questions in other households. Some questions, including demographic items, are asked of all respondents. If you examine some of the GSS data, you will notice that some data items have a substantial number of respondents for whom data are marked as missing. For the most part, this refers to respondents who were not asked that particular question as a result of the split ballot design.

Although many items were asked of only a subsample of respondents, you can still take the responses as representative of the US adult non-institutionalized population, subject to normal sampling error. For more information about how the GSS data were collected, see Appendix B, "Field Work and Interviewer Specifications," and Appendix C, "General Coding Instructions," in the *General Social Survey 1972–2012 Cumulative Codebook* (Smith et al. 2011). Also, visit the GSS website: http://www3.norc.org/GSS+Website/.

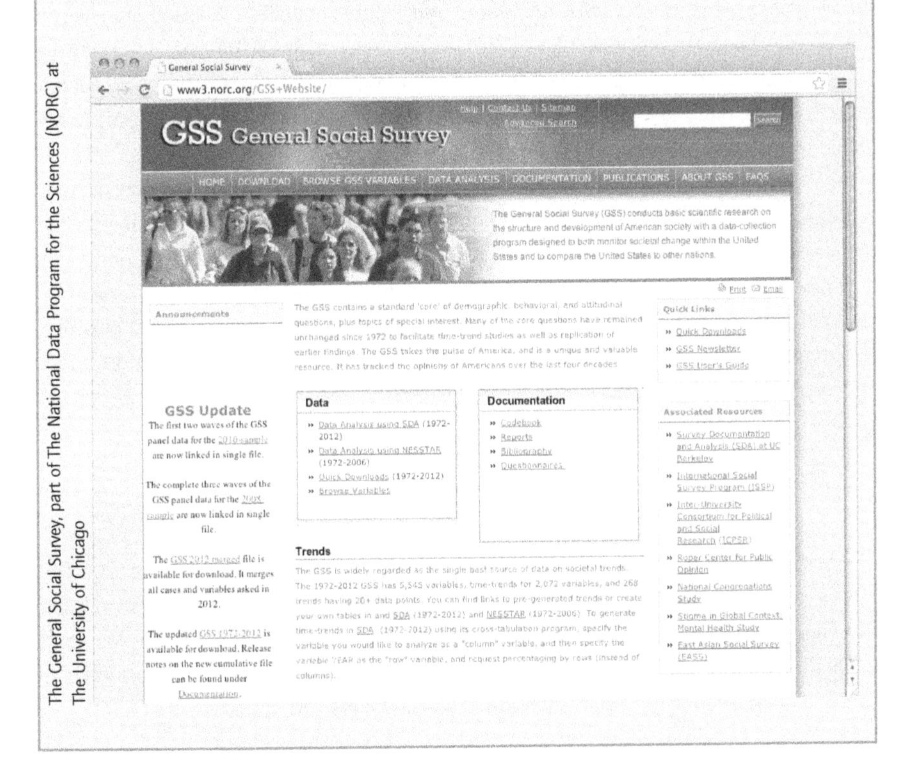

The General Social Survey, part of The National Data Program for the Sciences (NORC) at The University of Chicago

Very large omnibus surveys have to contend with the problem of respondent fatigue, but there are ways to deal with that problem so that the quality of data will not be undermined. For instance, the GSS, described in Mini Case 2.1, uses a split ballot design. In the split ballot design, all respondents are asked demographic and basic questions, while the remainder of the questions are split into two or more *ballots*, and each respondent is asked only questions from one ballot. Since the sample size of an omnibus survey like the GSS is generally large, the random subsample answering each ballot is typically sufficient. It is critical that the method used to determine which respondents are assigned to each ballot is random or entirely representative.

ADMINISTRATION

A questionnaire can be self-administered by respondents, or it can be administered by a trained member of the research team or staff. Of the two, self-administered questionnaires require a greater degree of careful wording, layout, and explanation. The reason for the even higher standard is that each respondent will be expected to understand not only the questions, but also the instructions and context for the questionnaire, in the same manner as all of the other people who complete that questionnaire. Self-administered survey types are mail surveys that are sent to participants to be filled out and returned to the research team. Online or web-based surveys are accessed on the Internet. Interviewer-administered survey types include a telephone survey, a face-to-face survey, and even a survey administered to a group. In each case, the survey questions are read to the participants by an interviewer who then directly collects and saves all the responses.

Why might a researcher want to use a self-administered questionnaire format rather than an interviewer-administered one? There are a number of good reasons. The two most pressing reasons tend to be cost and potential accessibility of population, both of which are of paramount importance in the implementation of survey research. Dillman, Smyth, and Christian (2009) call this the tailored design method, meaning researchers should tailor their survey designs to the population, the research question, and availability of resources.

Cost

The costs tend to be lower when questionnaires are self-administered, given that the number of staff required is lower, since there is not a need for interviewers or related training. Also, if the self-administered instrument uses survey software on the web, such as Qualtrics or Survey Monkey, data entry costs will be saved (though this cost savings can also be realized using direct software entry protocols with interviewers.)

Accessibility

For certain populations, it will be easier to reach members of the sample using a self-administered format. Here, it is very important to know and understand the target population well. The **target population** represents all of those from whom the sample to be surveyed will be drawn; the target population is the complete group, collection, or population that the research is studying and about whom the research is ideally intended to generalize. The term **intended population** can be used synonymously with target population. The **accessible population**, however, is the population that the researcher is actually reasonably able to measure. Various constraints, such as the hidden or semihidden nature of some populations (e.g., gay men), necessarily require the accessible population to be smaller than the target or intended population. The **sampling frame**, then, is generally thought of as the "list" of accessible elements of the population from which the researcher conducts the draw of the sample. It need not be a physical list, but there must exist some systematic way to enumerate this list so that a sampling mechanism may be used to randomly (or at least representatively) select elements for the sample.

In some cases, interviewer-administered questionnaires may provide more access (such as with a population of nursing home residents). If, however, the intended population is composed of those with access to the web, who tend to be either employed full-time or enrolled in school full-time (or some combination of the two), then the self-administered methods may offer greater access, provided that you are able to reach the population about the questionnaire and provide incentive to engage in it. Also, for research involving "anonymous" populations, the self-administered option offers best access and response rates. The drawback is that it may be more difficult to recruit respondents to help with snowball sampling or respondent-driven sampling (Heckathorn 1997) as described in Chapter 8, "Nonprobability Sampling and Sampling Hard to Find Populations." Table 2.1 summarizes these pros and cons.

Table 2.1 Pros and Cons of Self vs. Interviewer Administered Surveys

	Self-Administered	*Interviewer-Administered*
Least expensive	X	
Best response rate for Internet/electronically engaged populations	X	
Best response rates for non- or partially non-Internet engaged populations		X
Best response rates for "anonymous" populations	X	

IMPORTANCE OF PROPER TRAINING OF INTERVIEWERS

If the questionnaire is to be administered by interviewers, it is absolutely critical that the interviewers all go through the same comprehensive training. Failure to have them do this may invalidate the data that are collected. Interviewers need to know how to handle questions, concerns, or problems experienced by respondents, and the interviewers all must handle those issues in a consistent way. Inconsistent interviewer performance effectively alters the experience of some respondents, weakening or even destroying the generalizability of the survey results. The key to success in this regard is that interviewers need to be trained to administer the survey *consistently*. It can be tempting to save money in the overall survey endeavor by cutting back on the caliber of interviewers and the time and depth of trainings for them, but that would be ill advised. We are able to test how consistent interviewers have been by examining inter-rater reliability and intra-rater reliability, as discussed in Chapter 5, "The Quality of Measurement: Validity and Reliability."

TYPES OF SURVEYS

Surveys vary in numerous ways. The variation can be affected not only by whether the questionnaire will be self-administered or administered by trained interviewers, but by other delivery and methodological factors. The questionnaire may be mailed, administered by phone, administered in person, delivered by e-mail, accessed on the Web, or even accessed on a tablet (such as an iPad) or smart phone (such as an iPhone). The technology and resources available may shape the delivery of the questionnaire, as well as the availability of the target population.

Mail Surveys

Mail surveys are surveys printed on paper, copied, and mailed to participants' home addresses along with (preferably) a self-addressed stamped envelope for easy return to the research team. Participants take the survey at home by themselves and answer questions as best they can. Questionnaires need to be highly structured and easy to follow. Instructions for the survey need to be well written and at a reading level that is appropriate for the general population.

Mail surveys are appropriate when resources are a constraint. They are one of the cheaper forms of surveys. They are also good to use with a geographically dispersed population, as it is cheaper to mail a survey than to hire an interviewer. A drawback is that response rates are very low with mail surveys, meaning that people are less likely to complete and return them.

Questionnaires delivered by mail used to be far more popular than they are now. The obvious reason is that they have been supplanted, first by telephone survey administration and now by increasing use of Internet surveys, since much of the population to whom a mail survey would have been targeted now has access to the Internet.

Face-to-Face or Group Interviews

With a mail survey, participants are responsible for reading and understanding the questions, marking the appropriate answer, and returning the survey to the research team. With face-to-face or group interviewing, participants interact with a trained interviewer who can assist with the answering of the questionnaire by providing definitions, where allowed, and by marking answers. Additionally, the questionnaire can be less structured and far more complex, as the interviewer goes through the questionnaire rather than the participant.

Both face-to-face and group interview surveys have very high response rates, meaning few participants will say no to an interviewer's face when asked to complete a survey. Interviewer-assisted surveying is very expensive, as interviewers need to be hired and trained. Face-to-face interviews take more resources than a group interview, as in a group interview there can be quite a few participants for each interviewer and interview scenario. Using interviewers adds a potential problem known as interviewer effects. If interviewers are not well trained, it is possible that each interviewer will handle the survey differently and thereby influence how participants answer questions. To minimize this problem, interviewers need to be trained to handle the interviews in as standardized a manner as possible. By standardized is meant that all questions, interviewer behaviors, and interactions with participants are all handled exactly the same across interviewers.

Telephone Surveys

Telephone surveys are surveys administered over the phone by an interviewer. Sometimes a researcher has information about a predetermined sample and uses phone numbers to reach members of the sample. Other times, researchers used a random digit dialing apparatus to select a sample. (The issue of sampling will be covered in detail in Chapter 7, "Selecting a Sample: Probability Sampling.") Regardless of sampling arrangements, the telephone was once ubiquitous as a survey tool, since it was the only common way to reach people while they were in their homes. It was especially cost effective at reaching a geographically dispersed sample.

As you can imagine, a researcher or staff member could read survey questions to respondents and record the answers just as they would during a face-to-face interview. Since the telephone allowed greater access to respondents, and in turn larger samples, there emerged an extra incentive to make the process more efficient.

The Role of Technology in the Type and Delivery of Surveys

What was once typical in survey research was the use of telephone calling as a means to reach respondents. Over time, the availability of technology has guided the means of engaging in survey research. As technology has evolved, so has the ability to implement surveys quickly and effectively. However, with new technology comes new challenges; if not addressed properly, those challenges can limit the usefulness of survey research results.

CATI (computer assisted telephone interviewing) was developed to automate part of the data collection process for survey research. While a human was still involved, the computer program provided the questions, one by one, to the interviewer, who would read them to the respondent. After acknowledging the response, the interviewer could select the choice made by the respondent on the computer screen. This not only created efficiency by eliminating the need to eventually enter hand-written responses into the computer but also improved accuracy of data collection by eliminating the opportunity to mark responses incorrectly.

Advanced and well-programmed CATI software allowed for seamless *skip patterns* (see Mini Case 2.2). With these patterns, the interviewer sees only questions intended for one particular respondent. So, for instance, for a respondent who answered "no" to the question in Mini Case 2.2, the interviewer would be presented with the text of Question 19 and not need to manually follow the skip pattern and either scroll or click past the questions in between.

MINI CASE 2.2

Sample Question in Skip Pattern

12. Have you ever been enrolled in a college- or university-level course?
    a) Yes [default, go to next question]
    b) No [skip to question 19]
    c) Not Sure [skip to question 19]

Note that the instructions [in brackets] are not read to the respondent but are used by the interviewer to determine the next question to present. Alternatively, those instructions are coded into the software and not seen by the interviewer. In that case, the computer will present the next appropriate question based on the respondent's choices.

In the early days of CATI, one of the most pervasive software programs for designing CATI surveys was known as the Computer Assisted Survey Execution System (CASES), developed at the University of California at Berkeley. While that software is still available and in use for CATI, it is also available for developing web surveys, though it is not as commonly used for that as some other commercial software packages, such as Qualtrics or Survey Monkey.

BOX: CASES (Computer Assisted Survey Execution System)

Developed and maintained by the CSM (Computer-assisted Survey Methods) Program at the University of California at Berkeley. Visit http://cases.berkeley.edu for more information.

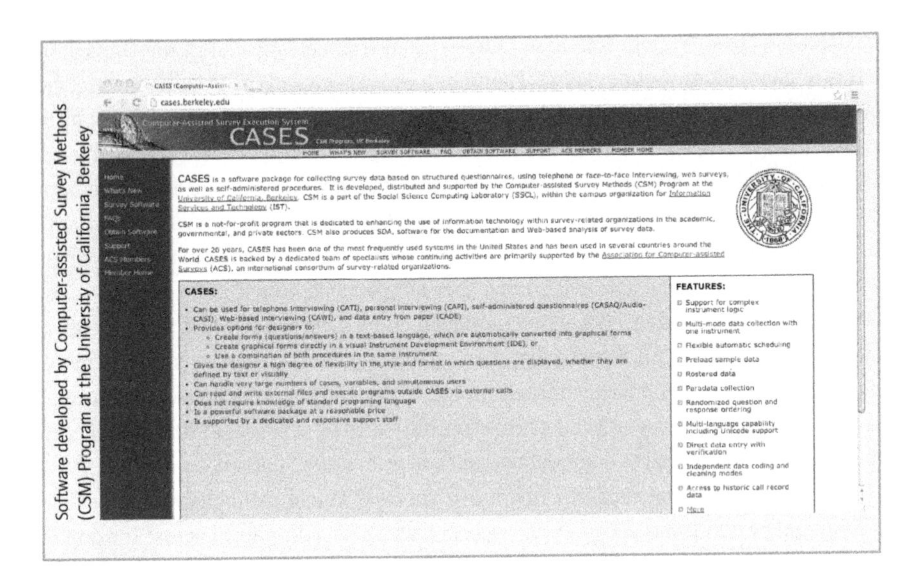

Software developed by Computer-assisted Survey Methods (CSM) Program at the University of California, Berkeley

The Use of the Internet to Facilitate Survey Administration

Ultimately, widespread access to the Internet now allows access to respondents in their homes (or elsewhere) via computer, tablet, or smartphone (Sue and Ritter 2007). E-mail surveys are delivered as messages to the respondents' e-mail addresses. Respondents can indicate their answers in a reply message. This type of survey is generally effective only for short questionnaires, as it starts to get confusing, and different e-mail clients use different formatting parameters that can make anything other than the simplest format difficult to standardize. In variants to this type of e-mail survey, the survey can be sent as an attachment (e.g., as an MS Word document or even as a fillable PDF document). However, the response rate will be reduced whenever a message requires a respondent to open a document or attachment in another program; this is true for a number of reasons. First, opening an e-mail attachment and completing a form is usually perceived as a much more complicated endeavor by the respondent. Also, some of the respondents' computers may not automatically open the attachment, which will almost certainly end those respondents' interest in participating. Moreover, many respondents simply will not open an e-mail attachment due to computer virus/worm/malware concerns.

More versatile than e-mail surveys, web-based surveys have emerged as very effective instruments. For web-based surveys, the respondent must go to the URL or website where the survey is housed. Along with other methods of both traditional and more modern recruitment, an e-mail can be sent to potential respondents to alert them that the survey is available. There are many commercial software packages (as well as CASES, described earlier in this chapter) that can be used to develop and program a web-based survey.

Due to advances in technology, web-based surveys can be designed to be interactive, nimble, and attractive. Skillful survey programming can reduce survey fatigue and increase accuracy of data collection. Web-based surveys as instruments are almost unmatched in terms of possibilities (Couper 2008). The web questionnaire can incorporate interactive question mapping, photographs, videos, and other media where appropriate. It can also include a considerable amount of information and yet seem like a much shorter document; one way that this is possible is through the use of pull-down menus for fixed-response questions, particularly those with numerous possible choices. Additional information, such as definitions or proper noun descriptions (which can be provided in text as well as graphically) can be made available so that they are provided only when requested—this might be designed so that information is shared about a term when the term is either moused over or clicked on. Beyond that, web surveys tend to be less expensive than more traditional surveys. Also, as with most electronically designed questionnaires, a big advantage of a web-based survey is that data collected are stored electronically on the server, and therefore there is no need to enter data or hire and train staff to enter data.

So, what is the downside to web-based surveys? While technology is spreading quickly, not everyone has access to the web, and access is not uniform across the population in the United States. Recruitment needs to be done through traditional methods for most types of social science research. In addition, it might be necessary to bring mobile devices (laptops, tablets, etc.) to some respondents, or to reach them by phone and enter information for them. It will be necessary to verify that those respondents have questionnaires that are equivalent to those that others are responding to, since this effectively becomes a **multimode survey**, combining two or more different types of survey methodologies into one complex implementation.

Multimode Surveys

Using more than one type of survey has the advantage of optimally leveraging survey design possibilities to fit different components of data collection or of the target sample. For instance, if part of the sample of respondents is unable to experience the survey as it was primarily designed, a multimode survey enables you to prepare one or more alternate platforms to deliver the equivalent instrument to that part. This has the effect of maximizing the likelihood of collecting data from various types of respondents within the target population. However, the key is to demonstrate that the alternate platform(s) are truly equivalent.

Determining the Type of Survey

When designing a survey, it is important to consider the primary research question, the target population, and available resources. Each of these matters and plays a role in making choices that will produce a survey that best fits the situation. No one type is always best.

The nature of the primary research question largely affects the way that questions should be delivered to respondents and how answers should best be recorded. More sensitive topics, for instance, may require greater care, detail, and interactivity. In those cases, it may be best to deliver the questionnaire in person with trained interviewers.

The size and accessibility of the target population are important considerations in recruitment and mode of delivery. When a target population is not easily reached by the Internet (e.g., an elderly population), use of a web-based survey is not recommended. Face-to-face or phone interviews work better in those situations.

Obviously, available resources play a role in determining anything. This is, of course, true for survey research. However, it is important to recognize that you cannot expect the same results when you cut back on resource allocation: This is a false economy. If you cut necessary sample size or proper questionnaire administration, the results will be inadequate or inaccurate and ultimately not generalizable. To save resources, it might be necessary to scale back on facets of the target population or the depth of the research questions under study. Cutting the budget, for example, may lead to a more surface-level analysis of a given topic, but that is preferable to a poorly executed survey on a deeper topic.

How does this advice play out in deciding what form of survey administration to use? If the material is sensitive, a mail survey might be best. However, it is possible in a face-to-face survey for the interviewer to step away and allow the participants to input answers privately for portions of the survey. Determine who the population is and what access to technology is generally available. Those populations who are not good candidates for a survey using Internet technology may not be good candidates for a mail survey, and may be best reached through a phone survey or face-to-face interview. If the population is geographically dispersed, a web-based survey, mail survey, or telephone survey will be more feasible than a face-to-face survey. Response rates for mail surveys are much lower than rates for face-to-face surveys, and telephone interviews are increasingly having lower response rates. If the goal is to maximize response rates, a face-to-face or group administered survey is best. Last, if resources are a major issue, the Internet provides lower costs and faster access as well as greater efficiency and accuracy, and if the population is internet savvy, this is the best option. The costs to carry out a mail survey are far less than the face-to-face interviews.

CONCLUSION

There is no one single way to use survey data to answer important research questions. A survey can be undertaken to achieve that end, or it can be combined with other surveys to produce an omnibus survey. Of course, it is sometimes possible to draw from existing omnibus surveys, such as the GSS. While that is not always a feasible option, it can save a lot of time, money, and other resources. When doing survey research, it is important to remember that there are many options to select from before embarking on the fun of collecting data from respondents. For example, the researcher will need to determine whether the questionnaire will be self-administered or be administered by an interviewer. If it is self-administered, will it be done in person, by mail, or over the Internet? If it is administered over the Internet, will this be done through a web server or via direct e-mail? Some of these decisions may be impacted by the sampling method, the way that members of the target population are chosen (see Chapter 7, "Selecting a Sample: Probability Sampling"). Ultimately, the type of survey and the fashion in which it is administered will be determined by more than one factor. Among those factors, one must consider the available resources and the accessibility of the target population.

KEY TERMS

Survey 13
Questionnaire 13
Survey instrument 13
Mail survey 16
Face-to-face survey 16
Telephone survey 00
Online survey 00
Web based survey 16
Omnibus survey 14
Target population 16
Intended population 16
Accessible population 16
Sampling frame 17
Multimode survey 22
CATI 20

CRITICAL THINKING QUESTIONS

Below you will find three questions that ask you to think critically about core concepts addressed in this chapter. Be sure you understand each one; if you do not, this is a good time to review the relevant sections of this chapter.

1. What are the advantages and challenges of using an omnibus survey to answer your individual research questions?
2. What problems does the use of a multimode survey overcome? What problems does the use of a multimode survey introduce, and how should you mitigate such problems?
3. What are the advantages and disadvantages of using interviewers versus self-administration in surveys?

3

The Cover Letter and Survey Instrument

INTRODUCTION

The quality of the data you get from a survey is only as good as the survey that produced them. Thoughtful design and formatting of the survey instrument is essential to reduce error as much as possible. This chapter outlines the key elements to consider in creating a survey that is clear, accurate, and easy to work with, both for respondents and for the researchers who collect the data. We begin with a description of the cover letter used to introduce your survey and encourage respondent participation. We then move on to the instrument itself, detailing strategies to produce clearly presented content, an intuitively organized sequence, and a visually appealing layout. The chapter concludes with a summary checklist. The overall goal is to produce a survey that neither intimidates nor confuses the respondent and that lends itself to facile interpretation later on by the researcher.

THE COVER LETTER

The cover letter is a formal invitation to participate in a research project, and it is an essential part of survey research design. This is the first exposure that respondents will have to the study, so it is important to make it count. An effective cover letter can make the difference between a high response rate and a low one because it gives the researcher an opportunity to persuade respondents to participate in their study (Yammarino, Skinner, and Childers 1991). The cover letter should briefly discuss the importance of the research and outline the important components of the study in a friendly yet professional tone. It should also highlight the potential benefits of the research to respondents, who are being asked to invest their time, energy, and trust in your project. To this end, it is important to be clear about the nature of the survey—how long it will be, what type of questions will be asked, whether the responses will be anonymous or confidential (as described in Box 3.1), and whether there will be follow-up plans. The letter must also cover important logistical concerns such as the due date and means of returning the survey (Shuttles and Bennett 2008).

BOX 3.1

Anonymity and Confidentiality

The difference between anonymity and confidentiality depends on whether respondents will need to provide personal and identifying information about themselves as part of the study. When researchers ensure the **confidentiality** of responses, this means they are collecting personal information about respondents (e.g., name, address, birth date, medical history) but this information will not be provided to anyone outside of the project.

In contrast, when a researcher ensures **anonymity**, this means that respondents are not asked to provide any personal information. When collecting anonymous data, it is often useful to remind respondents not to include any personal information, such as their name or other identifying information, in open-ended responses. A researcher may also detail what will be done with the data to ensure its anonymity, such as aggregate it and destroy hard copies, and emphasize that no individual responses will be shared. When conducting anonymous research, it is important to create a unique identifier, such as an identification number, for each respondent that is anonymous.

When sending these materials out, remember to allow enough time for respondents to complete the survey and/or to ask more people to participate (if necessary). It is also important to note that some organizations, universities, or institutional review boards (organizations that ensures that research is conducted ethically) may have particular guidelines for the information presented in the cover letter in addition to that described here.

Where possible, the survey letter should include three types of information. First is information relating specifically to the respondents and the importance of their role. Show your consideration for their perspective by including

- Why they were chosen for the survey.
- How their contact information was obtained.
- The voluntary nature of the participation you are requesting.
- The anonymity or confidentiality of their responses.
- The token of appreciation you are offering for participation, if any.

Second, if it is possible to do so without compromising the responses, discuss the study itself. Explain the importance of the work both in terms of your goals and in the potential benefits it could provide for respondents. Inspire their interest, excitement, and participation by emphasizing the valuable role they will play in your project. You may mention benefits like

- The opportunity for respondents to voice their opinions on a topic.
- How the results have the potential to influence policy in a certain area.
- How results will improve our understanding of a specific issue.

Third, include the necessary logistical concerns: what respondents will want to know about the survey up front, and what they need to know to deliver their completed survey to you, on time. Be clear and direct in providing

- An estimate of the amount of time the survey will take for them to complete.
- Any completion deadline or due date. (Use a due date that is a day or more prior to your anticipated date in case respondents are late to respond.)
- A link to the survey (if you are using a web-based survey).
- Directions for completing and returning the questionnaire (if you are using a mail-in survey). Also, include a self-addressed stamped envelope.
- Contact information, in case there are any questions.
- An offer to provide summary findings of the research (but ask for contact information to be sent separate from the survey, to ensure anonymity).
- A reminder not to put any identifying information on the survey.

In addition to content, the formatting of the cover letter is extremely important.

- Be straightforward. Do not attempt to sweet-talk the respondent.
- Try to keep the letter to a single page, and use normal font and margins.
- Use bullet points when listing items.

- Personalize the cover letter only when privacy and anonymity are not at issue. (This largely depends on what you are studying). Do *not* auto place respondents' e-mail addresses in the greeting (e.g., "Dear bgillesp@uci.edu").
- Sign the cover letter (or include a copy of a digital signature) and include your title and affiliation information.
- For e-mail cover letters, include the cover letter in the body of the e-mail *and* as an attachment—some respondents will want to read and save the file, while others may not look at attachments at all.
- For web-based surveys, use an organization-based or university-affiliated e-mail address whenever possible.
- For pen-and-paper surveys, use official organizational or departmental letterhead.
- For e-mails, use a trustworthy and legitimate subject line.
- Do not include video, pictures, flash, or JavaScript in the e-mail.

Many people will have spam guards on their computer to filter out unsolicited bulk e-mails (Kaye and Johnson 1999; Scriven and Smith-Ferrier 2003). Be sure not to use spam language in the subject line or body of the e-mail. You can check the spam rating for the e-mail at http://www.contactology.com/check_mqs.php. Box 3.2 lists some spam trigger words, phrases, and symbols.

BOX 3.2

Spam Triggers

money symbols

exclamation points (especially multiples, e.g.,!!!)

make money, earn extra cash, etc.

prize/prizes

urgent

click here, click below

opportunity

offer expires

important information regarding

you have been selected . . .

Reducing Attrition

Attrition takes place when respondents refuse to participate in later rounds of a longitudinal survey study. Researchers using longitudinal panel surveys have developed strategies to maintain respondents across many rounds of a survey conducted over several years. For instance, the Longitudinal Study of Generations has a newsletter that lists developments in the study and publications based on the research (Bengtson 2000). The respondents are also provided with a refrigerator magnet with contact information, which keeps the survey on their minds. If you intend to collect follow-up information, mention any such bulletins, et cetera, in your cover letter.

Keeping Track and Following Up

A **respondent inventory**, also known as an audit, is a researcher's way of keeping track of respondents. This will vary based on the mode of data collection. For pen-and-paper surveys, the researcher can simply number each survey and use this as the identification number for the respondent. For web-based surveys, researchers can give a unique URL to each respondent. They can also provide each respondent with a unique key/password that is needed in order to access the full survey. Some type of inventory should be taken in order to safeguard against a respondent filling out a survey more than once (Bauermeister et al. 2012). Thus, keeping a record of respondents is important and helps avoid multiple responses from the same individual.

On the other hand, if a respondent does not reply immediately, you may want to contact him or her again to make sure you are recruiting all the willing participants you can. If you do follow up, it is appropriate only to send a single follow-up letter or e-mail to individuals who did not respond to the original message—do not send more than that.

In order to maintain an up-to-date mail/e-mail list and avoid sending unsolicited requests, remove respondents from lists if they are expressly unwilling to participate, if you are notified that an e-mail address is old, or if you have received no response after a single follow-up attempt.

Keeping all of these guidelines in mind will help you craft a cover letter with the best chance of attracting respondents' attention, encouraging their participation, and preventing subsequent frustration and attrition by being honest and straightforward from the very start. Box 3.3 shows an example of such a letter, which you may want to use as a starting point for your own projects.

BOX 3.3

Sample Cover Letter

Dear *(First Name of Respondent)*,

I am writing to request your assistance with an important research project, "*(Project Title)*," being conducted by *(Researcher Name)* at *(Organization/Institution)*. As part of a larger program to evaluate *(brief description of research)*, we are conducting a survey of *(sample population)* to ask about *(research topic)*.

You were selected to be part of this project because *(selection method)*. I can imagine this is a busy time of year for you, but I hope you will take some time to participate in our very brief survey. The questionnaire will require only *(liberal window of time)* to complete.

To complete the survey online, please access the URL below. Enter the respondent key that appears at the bottom of this letter, and then follow the online survey instructions. If you do not have dependable Internet access, or prefer to answer the questionnaire on paper, you may request a paper survey by sending an e-mail to *(e-mail address)* or calling *(phone number)*.

As a token of our appreciation for your participation in this important study, upon receipt of your completed questionnaire, we will enter your name in a series of lotteries in which respondents are eligible for *(possible compensation/incentive)*.

There is no risk involved, and your answers will be completely confidential. Moreover, the results of the survey will be reported in a summary format, so that no one will be able to associate you with your responses on this survey. Text responses will be reported word for word, so please do not include your name or provide any identifying information in your comments. Participation is strictly voluntary, and you may refuse to participate or discontinue participation at any time.

Completion and return of the questionnaire will indicate your willingness to participate in this study. Thank you in advance for your participation in this important research. If you have any questions about the administration of the survey, please contact our research offices at *(phone number)* or *(e-mail address)*.

Sincerely,
(Researcher Signature)
(Title, Name, Affiliation)
(Link to Survey)

THE SURVEY INSTRUMENT

In addition to a well-crafted cover letter, the style, organization, and content of the survey instrument itself will influence the return and completion rate (Dillman 2007; Bradburn, Sudman, and Wansink 2004). Respondents initially interested in your project may still change their minds at any point if they become frustrated, confused, or bored with the survey itself. And even those who complete and return the survey may find reason to rush through questions without concern for providing the best or most accurate answers, or misunderstand instructions or questions and provide responses they did not really intend. In the sections that follow, we address some of the potential pitfalls in survey design that may impede the collection of quality data, and we provide guidelines to ensure the clarity and accuracy of your survey instrument.

The guidelines that follow are based on a common premise: that the most effective instrument is the one most attuned to the needs of the respondent. Your goal of collecting detailed and comprehensive data will not be served by a questionnaire that appears overly burdensome or otherwise off-putting to the person who has volunteered their time to complete it. Thus, before we address the mechanics of survey design, we must first note the common concern that underlies all of the strategies to follow: respondent burden and fatigue.

Respondent Burden and Fatigue

The degree to which a survey is stressful, complex, and perceived as time consuming is known as **respondent burden** (Biemer and Lyberg 2003). In addition to all the time and energy required to complete the survey, certain items may place a heavier burden on respondents than others. For example, some questions involve sensitive topics that a respondent may be reluctant to provide information about, even after assurances of anonymity or confidentiality have been made. Other items might require respondents to reference past events that they cannot easily recall, requiring a high degree of concentration they did not expect or intend to exert (Graf 2008).

It is important to avoid adding the unnecessary burden imposed by asking respondents to answer long and tedious questions, to maintain information across a number of items, or to recall events in the distant past. Such demanding questions can quickly cause **respondent fatigue** and limit the efficacy of your survey. High respondent burden usually leads to higher nonresponse or else effortless guessing and lower quality data.

It is therefore important to strive for the simplest questions and layouts possible, throughout the entire survey design process. Much undue burden can be easily avoided simply by making the effort to view your survey through the eyes of the respondent. Beyond this, once you have completed the design stage, **pretesting** the finished product is one of the best ways to make a more objective assessment of potential respondent burden (Babbie 2014). Pretesting gives researchers a valuable opportunity to identify and target problem areas before expending the time and money required to widely circulate the survey, so that modifications may be made ahead of time to significantly reduce burden and improve the quality of the data collected. (Specific methods for pretesting your survey are discussed in Chapter 6.)

For now, note that several of the guidelines suggested to encourage participation also serve to alleviate respondent burden and prevent fatigue:

- Remember to utilize the cover letter to emphasize the importance of participation in your study. Establishing a strong base of interest in the respondent is a good start toward avoiding respondent burden and fatigue later on.
- Be sure to sincerely thank respondents for their time at the beginning of the survey. Let them know you appreciate their position.
- Do not downplay the length and complexity of the survey. Offer a window of time it might take to complete the survey in the cover letter or introduction. Respondents may allot a certain amount of time to take the survey, and they are more likely to leave the survey if the survey takes longer than they were told.
- Again, emphasize anonymity and confidentiality—this will reduce the amount of time respondents spend wondering whether or not they should answer a sensitive question, how they should answer it, et cetera.

The remainder of this chapter outlines more new strategies for effective survey design that help to avoid respondent burden and fatigue and ensure that the time and effort of researchers and respondents alike are used well. First we address the overall organization of the instrument—including general sections, optimal ordering of questions, presentation of response options, and more advanced items like **contingency questions** and **screener questions**. Then we turn to the visual layout of the instrument—ways to best present your items and instructions for the greatest clarity and ease of use. Finally, we end the chapter with a look at some issues specific to web-based versus pen-and-paper surveys, concluding with a summary checklist you may wish to use as a quick reference to help evaluate your finished product.

WELCOME MESSAGE AND INTRODUCTION

In addition to your cover letter, you should include some introductory material at the beginning of the survey itself (Newman 2012). Start with a brief and interesting title, no more than one line long (e.g., "Sex, Love, and Money Survey") and printed in boldface text. Follow the survey title with a welcome message thanking the respondent for participating. Respondents will be more likely to provide open, honest responses when you acknowledge their participation. You may also include a little bit of general information about the survey here, although if you have already introduced details in the cover letter, it is not necessary to repeat yourself in the introductory message. Do reiterate here, however, that respondents' information will be kept anonymous or confidential.

Think of this introduction as one more opportunity to persuade respondents that this survey is worth their time and to assure them that data will be handled professionally—this can help reduce stress and prevent them from skipping sensitive questions or even abandoning the survey altogether. This introduction is also a useful place to give *general* instructions about how to progress through the survey and how to think about responses. Any more specific instructions for questions in specific sections should be added into their respective sections, immediately preceding the questions to which they apply; avoid front-loading the questionnaire with an imposing array of rules that will likely be forgotten anyway. See Box 3.4 for a sample introduction that is deferential, informative, and appropriately brief.

BOX 3.4

Sample Introduction

Thank you for taking the time to complete this survey. Your honest answers are appreciated, and the survey should take no longer than 20 minutes to complete. All responses will be completely anonymous, and they will be combined with many other responses to learn about *(study topic)*. When your responses have been reported, please click "continue" at the bottom of each page.

ORGANIZATION AND QUESTION SEQUENCE

Following your introduction, think about arranging the rest of your survey instrument with the most intuitive layout—the manner in which the survey is formatted, designed, and presented to respondents. In order to reduce measurement error, it is important to design an instrument that respondents find easy to understand and that researchers find intuitive for the later process of data entry. A poorly designed questionnaire may lead to skipped questions, an abandoned survey, and data-processing errors. From the outset, researchers must keep their audience in mind, tailoring the wording and flow of survey items so as to best meet the expectations of the targeted respondents. How this is done largely depends on the mode of survey data collection (i.e., pen-and-paper, computer assisted interview, or web-based questionnaire), but there are also some common concerns that inform instruments of all types.

Question Order

It is important to logically organize the questions within the survey, typically by clustering questions according to topic. Inconsistent and careless ordering will seem jumbled and can easily confuse respondents. To further ensure that the questions are grouped logically into intuitive subgroups, use simple headings for individual sections, including section-specific directions when applicable.

Start the survey with the most engaging or easy questions in order to encourage completion (Dillman 2007). Avoid placing any sensitive or private questions at the beginning, where they may set the wrong tone for the overall instrument and give your respondent second thoughts. Move them instead toward the middle of the survey, so respondents will already be comfortable and familiar with the tone before they reach these slightly more burdensome items. Even if such items still give the respondent pause, the time and energy they have already invested in the survey will help motivate them to continue to the end.

Leave your demographic questions (e.g., respondent's age, gender, income, education) until the end of the questionnaire. These items will probably not raise concerns about privacy and confidentiality, but they are also not the most exciting or engaging for the respondent. Exceptions to this rule are any "screener" demographic questions (see section below for more details) that qualify (or disqualify) individuals for inclusion in the survey, based on some characteristic that you are interested in studying. For example, many researchers limit their surveys to people in certain age groups. These questions must be located near the beginning of the instrument, to save the time of both the respondent and the researcher, should the respondent not meet your study qualifications.

In addition to these general guidelines, the ordering of other more specific questions can affect the results of your survey by cueing certain ideas or mindsets for respondents that they otherwise might not have brought to bear on subsequent questions (Schwartz and Hippler 1995). For example, if an item were to ask respondents about their religion, and then follow up with a question about the kinds of people they admire, they might be more inclined to identify a religious figure as being highly admired. In such a situation, it could be hard for a researcher to tell if the respondents really did admire that figure above others, or if the respondents said so only under the influence of the previous question on religion.

Another issue related to question order is **habituation.** Habituation occurs when respondents are confronted with a series of questions similar enough that they might appear redundant, so respondents stop paying attention to differences and answer each similar item in the same way (Schuman and Presser 1981). Even if it is only the response categories that remain the same across questions, this is enough to pose a risk of habituation and inaccurate responses. For example, in a customer satisfaction survey, satisfied customers might simply select "very pleased" for every question possible to save themselves the time of reading each question or option. To reduce the risk of habituation, phrase similar questions in unique ways, rather than merely switching a single word from one question to the next.

Order of Response Options

Respondents are more likely to select answers that are presented at the top of a list. This is especially true when respondents are confused or conflicted about the best way to answer a question. This becomes more likely when they are asked to consider a long list of possible responses, to choose between responses they perceive to be similar, or when items in the question or responses are ambiguous or otherwise confusing (Yzerbyt and Leyens 1991).

For example, if you are interested in knowing about the sources of stress in peoples' lives, you might ask respondents something like, "Which of the following causes you the most stress?" You would then be compelled to offer several responses to cover the wide range of potential stressors, and would likely observe a strong tendency among your respondents to simply select the first item of the list. This problem can sometimes be overcome through randomization of the order of responses. For web-based surveys, software has been developed for just this purpose. You may also consider approaching the issue differently, such as allowing multiple responses, or avoiding the list altogether by using an open-ended item in which respondents write in their own responses.

Advanced Logic

Some surveys require a more complex organization, beyond a simple linear progression from the first to last item. You may need to use questionnaire items to filter out ineligible respondents, to guide some respondents past irrelevant items, or to divide your respondents into groups and direct them to different subsets of relevant questions. The sections below on contingency questions and screener questions elaborate on some strategies and guidelines for dealing with these organizational issues and more.

Contingency Questions

A **contingency question** is a survey item that applies only to some respondents: those who have provided a specific answer to a previous question. Should the answer qualify them as some specific type of person the researcher is particularly interested in—individuals who attend church regularly, for example, or have school-age children—then they can be directed to a follow-up question or questions soliciting more details related to that subject—questions about their parents' religiosity, for example, or attitudes about the local school system, respectively. Respondents who do not fit the criteria are instructed to skip the follow-ups to save them time and confusion. Contingency questions and subsequent skip patterns allow respondents to bypass certain irrelevant questions, thereby guiding everyone through to only the relevant portions of the survey, and reducing the chances of respondent burden and fatigue.

Contingency questions thus allow the researcher to elicit more detailed and nuanced information on a particular topic without frustrating and alienating respondents who are not in the relevant subgroup. Alternatively, if researchers are interested in following up on *both* (or *all*) of the subgroups defined by a contingency question, they can include a slightly more complex skip pattern after the question to redirect one subgroup to a particular set of questions, and another subgroup to a different set. For example, questions about work satisfaction apply only to individuals who are employed, but the researcher may want to gather information about unemployed people as well. Respondents who indicate they are currently employed would be instructed to answer the next question about work satisfaction, and then instructed to skip the following question about job search strategies. Respondents who indicate current unemployment would be instructed to skip the next question about work satisfaction, and then instructed to resume answering on the following question about their job search.

These questions need specific instructions in pen-and-paper surveys. Survey researchers typically write instructions detailing the skip logic next to the relevant response option to ensure they are not overlooked. In web-based surveys, skip patterns for contingency questions can be built into the survey design, an advantage that further reduces respondent burden.

Screener Questions

For some studies, it will be necessary to ask respondents **screener questions** to determine if they are eligible to participate in the entire study itself (and not just a portion of it, as described in the previous section on contingency questions) (Adler and Clark 2015). For example, if the researcher is interested only in studying married couples, then the respondent's marital status should be the subject of the very first question asked; this should be followed by instructions for married individuals to continue to the next survey item, and for nonmarried individuals to cease answering any further questions. When this is the case, screener or filter questions should present ineligible respondents with something like the following message: "We're sorry but you do not meet the qualifications to participate in this study. We are very thankful for your time and participation."

A different version of the screener question can be helpful in alerting the researcher to discard a completed questionnaire, even if the respondent did not self-identify with any criteria suggesting ineligibility. The issue in this case is not the relevance of the questions to the respondent, but the quality of the data the respondent has supplied. There is always a risk that respondents are clicking through or checking off responses without paying sufficient attention to the questions. To guard against this, different screener questions can be inserted into the survey (e.g., into a matrix question) to assess whether or not an individual is truly paying attention to the questions. Such an item is one that does not necessarily have to do with any research interests, but is simply a question for which there is only one obvious response, a response of which any attentive respondent would be well aware. For an example, see Box 3.5.

BOX 3.5

Screener Question

The president of the United States is elected every four years.

☐ True ☐ False

Any respondent paying even minimal attention should be able to answer the above item correctly.

Use such screener questions sparingly. At best, these items have the latent consequence of increasing the survey's length and completion time, thereby adding to respondent burden; at worst, such questions may be so obvious as to discourage attentive respondents, who might feel their responses are not being taken seriously.

Concluding the Survey

After you have guided respondents through all of the relevant items on your survey instrument and have collected all the data you need to address your research interests, there are still some brief considerations to keep in mind as you conclude your questionnaire. Rather than letting the survey come to an abrupt end or closing with a hasty valediction, take a moment to consider the opportunities presented by this final communication with your respondent.

Just as pretesting your survey can be a highly valuable tool to reflect on your organizational and design skills, the inclusion at the end of your questionnaire of a postsurvey assessment can help you better tailor this or a future survey instrument to the needs and expectations of potential respondents. It may thus be useful to allow participants who have finished the survey to briefly describe their overall impressions, critiques, and concerns in response to the undertaking they have just completed. Consider adding a few more items about the survey experience itself, and/or an open-ended prompt for respondents' "Additional Comments on the Survey Experience" followed by several blank lines. With the substantive questions already answered, there is no more risk here of fatigue: Respondents may leave this blank if they choose, or they may provide some insights of value to your subsequent research and professional development.

Finally, at the very end of the survey, include a page thanking respondents for their time. This is especially important if you plan to follow up with respondents, but at the very least it is a courteous recognition of the voluntary effort they have expended on your behalf.

This concludes this chapter's discussion of the organization, ordering, and other substantive aspects of your survey's presentation. However, these are not the only concerns you will need to address. The substance of your survey instrument still needs to be translated into a concrete visual product, whether in web-based or pen-and-paper form. Herein lie some final issues of presentation: appearance, formatting, and design—all of which can either simplify the survey process and encourage participation or else add to respondent burden and fatigue. It is to these issues we turn now.

APPEARANCE, FORMATTING, AND DESIGN

General Concerns

It is important to design your survey so that it appears professional, visually appealing, and interesting to the respondent. A clean and clear design not only makes your survey appear user-friendly; it underscores your professionalism as well. This is important for recruiting respondents, gaining their trust, and encouraging their most thoughtful and attentive participation. To this end, you should avoid peppering the survey with irrelevant pictures, graphics, and other distractions, and focus instead on a presentation that is crisp, clean, and to the point.

By the same token, irrelevant, redundant, or otherwise inefficiently designed questions can also clutter the survey design and, worse, add unnecessarily to its length. Long surveys are problematic—too many pages or a very slow moving progress bar will deter respondents from taking or completing the survey. Be conservative about questions, and make sure that they are absolutely necessary for inclusion in the survey. Discard any questions that are not directly related to the research you are conducting for this specific project. It is sometimes tempting to add questions that are interesting or might be helpful in future projects, but may not be relevant or necessary. Avoid this practice, and make sure to include only necessary items.

Once you have trimmed extraneous items and graphics, focus on the clean and crisp presentation of the remaining survey items. Make sure the text is perfectly legible and questions are phrased in simple, concise language, and check grammar and spelling personally in addition to using computer spell-check functions. Use a normal, common font (Times New Roman, Courier, etc.) that is appropriate for the method of administration (e.g., surveys taken on smartphones may need larger fonts). A white website background or paper color is preferred. Judicious use of varied font types, colors, and sizes can be useful, helping respondents distinguish among instructions, questions, and response options (e.g., questions in bold and response options in normal font, emphasized words underlined). But unnecessary font variations are distracting and undermine professionalism.

The use of space in a survey is also important (Dillman 2007). To avoid confusion, use a separate line for each question and for each response choice, and allow enough room for open-ended responses. Do not clutter the items or response options in overly compact configurations just to cut down on survey length—this can make the survey appear more complex and daunting, and also difficult to read. At the same time, do not overuse space—the survey will appear "inflated" and longer than it actually is. Look for a happy medium that is legible and conservative without appearing crowded.

Designing Web-Based Surveys

Technological advances have revolutionized how survey research is conducted. Use this to your advantage. Web-based surveys have simplified skip patterns, contingency questions, filters, screening, and randomization. They also introduce the potential for drop-down menus, which are helpful for conserving space. At the same time, making use of this new platform entails some additional concerns to guard against respondent burden and to ensure data quality. This section details some of the opportunities web-based surveys offer and some of the pitfalls to avoid.

A **progress indicator** is a graphic bar, typically located toward the bottom of the respondent's computer or device screen that gradually fills as the respondent progresses through the survey. The filled portion of the bar thus represents the percentage of the survey that a respondent has completed. Depending on the size of the survey, this may or may not be a useful tool (Crawford, Couper, and Lamias 2001). A slow-moving progress bar may discourage respondents from completing the survey, while a quick-moving one may well increase respondents' enthusiasm and encourage completion.

Survey length aside, not all survey instruments lend themselves to the use of this tool. Keep the following in mind when considering including a progress bar:

- If progress is based on the number of questions completed, note that some questions are obviously more complex and time-consuming than others.
- Since use of contingency questions will vary the length of a survey across subgroups of participants, it may be impossible to measure the true completion progress in such surveys.
- Respondents may fixate on the progress bar, becoming distracted from questions to the point of slowing progress (and thereby risking fatigue) or providing careless answers.
- Intermittent progress bars on every other page are also possible and may be more useful than consistent reminders of progress (or lack thereof).

An additional challenge with web-based surveys is that the design process is more complex than it is with pen-and-paper surveys—computer-aided design is a long way from white paper and black ink! The aforementioned criteria for visual appeal still apply. Avoid abusing the potential provided by web-based designs by keeping simplicity and clarity in mind. The following guidelines will help you develop a design for your web-based survey that is both appealing to the eye and easy and intuitive to use:

- Do not use excess color or varying font sizes.
- Use only *relevant* videos, graphics, and visual cues. Keep in mind that these may take longer to load than plain text, so use them judiciously.
- Aim for a minimal number of pages. Do not include unnecessary "interludes" with pictures or headers, and avoid devoting entire, separate pages to sets of instructions.
- Avoid using distracting background images or bright background colors. Bright colors make concentration difficult, and background images may make text difficult to read.
- Different font colors can help differentiate between sections and among questions, instructions, and responses—just remember to be consistent and judicious in their use.
- Do not allow questions or responses to flow onto the next page.

New formatting options can be helpful, but also entail new considerations to make them user-friendly for your respondent:

- Make sure that text fits the width of the screen (wrap the text) and does not require the respondent to scroll back-and-forth horizontally to read the ends of lines—this is both time consuming and frustrating.
- Avoid drop-down lists that require scrolling down to view all the items they contain. Respondents may not see the options available at the bottom.
- Do not use a single page for all survey questions, unless the survey is extremely short. Group question sets together on individual pages. (This is especially necessary for contingency questions, since responses will call up or skip items on a separate page.)
- Make sure respondents cannot complete the survey more than once. (Software has been developed to prevent this.)

A final, but very important, consideration is that people are increasingly using their smartphones and other devices for Internet activity. Make sure surveys can be read and completed on such devices without requiring too much effort to zoom in and out.

For some purposes or target audiences, web-based surveys may simply not be feasible or advisable. The following section details guidelines for the more traditional pen-and-paper surveys that you still may find advantageous or necessary.

Designing Pen-and-Paper Surveys

For many purposes, traditional pen-and-paper surveys are still in use. This format too requires some specific considerations to encourage participation, ensure the quality of data collected, and reduce respondent burden and fatigue. Observe the following guidelines:

- Avoid clutter, use a legible font, and keep directions concise.
- Print the survey on quality paper, and check the quality of copies to make sure there are no smudges, lines, et cetera.
- Use 1-inch margins with single-spaced text for the question itself, but use 1.5 line spaces between the question's response options.
- Add a *Q* to each question number (e.g., Q1, Q2) to distinguish numerical response options from question numbers.
- Indent response options to set them off from questions and instructions.
- Use arrows for skip instructions.
- For open-ended responses, ask respondent to "please print clearly."
- Include enough lines for open-ended responses and enough space between lines. Bear in mind that respondents' styles of handwriting can vary widely, and some handwriting will consume much space on the page.
- To reduce the need for flipping pages back and forth, do not let questions continue from the bottom of one page to the top of the next.

Consider as well the added actions required for the respondent to return the survey instrument to you as well as your need to keep track of the physical surveys and the pages they contain:

- Include detailed instructions for returning the questionnaire, both on the instruction page (up front) and at the very end of the questionnaire.
- Include a self-addressed and stamped envelope with the mailing.
- Include the return address on the survey in case the envelope is lost.
- Print a number unique to each survey on the back of the very last page. This will be used for respondent inventory.
- Number each page of the survey (except the first).
- Ultimately, the way you design your survey will depend on a working knowledge of the type and amount of information you want to collect. Nevertheless, survey design is one of the most important components of survey research. Given how much error is reduced with a properly designed survey, it is well worth the time, effort, and trouble to ensure a high response rate and reduce confusion and measurement error. Consider the checklist in Box 3.6 when designing your survey.

CHECKLIST: THE COVER LETTER AND SURVEY INSTRUMENT

COVER LETTER

- ☐ Introduction of researcher and organization
- ☐ General description of the nature of the study (and its importance)
- ☐ Statement of time commitment for the survey
- ☐ Due date for completion
- ☐ Contact information
- ☐ Assurance of respondent anonymity/confidentiality
- ☐ Thank you
- ☐ Single page
- ☐ Web-based survey: No spam language
- ☐ Mail survey: Official stationary or departmental letterhead

SURVEY DESIGN

- ☐ Introduce the survey.
- ☐ Make sure pages are uncluttered.
- ☐ Use boldface, italics, and underlining consistently and judiciously.
- ☐ Avoid distracting images and bright colors.

SURVEY ORGANIZATION

- ☐ Logically group question subsets.
- ☐ Order questions in intuitive sequence.
- ☐ Avoid separate items that appear too similar.
- ☐ Lead with interesting/intriguing questions.
- ☐ Locate sensitive questions toward the middle.
- ☐ Save demographic questions for the end.

OTHER

- ☐ Thank respondents.
- ☐ Mail survey: Include a stamped envelope and clear directions for returning the survey.
- ☐ Check spelling and grammar.

KEY TERMS

Anonymity 26
Confidentiality 26
Respondent inventory 29
Respondent burden 31
Respondent fatigue 31
Pretesting 31
Habituation 34
Contingency question 32
Screener question 32
Habituation 34
Progress indicator 39

CRITICAL THINKING QUESTIONS

Below you will find three questions that ask you to think critically about core concepts addressed in this chapter. Be sure you understand each one; if you don't, this is a good time to review the relevant sections of this chapter.

1. Briefly sketch an outline for a survey on individuals' attitudes regarding same-sex marriage. Which topics would you cover in such a survey? Is there a particular order for different types of questions that is both consistent and intuitive?
2. How might a contingency question be worked into the above survey?
3. Why is it important to avoid respondent burden in survey-based research? Provide several examples of how researchers can avoid unnecessary respondent burden.

4

Survey Question Construction

INTRODUCTION

In order to test a hypothesis or answer a research question, survey researchers must measure the concepts they reference as precisely as possible, striving always for the least amount of error. In testing hypotheses, researchers use variables to represent specific concepts. Survey questions tie the **variables** (traits or characteristics about the population that vary from person to person) to the theoretical concepts of interest. This involves paying careful attention to the design of each questionnaire item and response option, so the survey instrument is as valid and reliable as it can be for the job it must do. This chapter elaborates some practical guidelines to aid in this important task. The chapter begins with a discussion of the types of concepts you may wish to measure. We then turn the focus to question development, including several topics and examples that will help you generate precise and unbiased survey items. Following this, we address issues in the crafting of appropriate response categories for multiple choice questions, and when to use open-ended responses instead. Finally, we conclude the chapter with some closing remarks on sources of error in survey research and a summary checklist of major points to aid in the design of your own survey research projects.

The types of measures developed for the survey instrument should ideally produce relevant, unbiased, error-free data. Therefore, the first step is to set concrete research goals at the outset of the design process. Make sure you can clearly answer the key questions: What are you trying to accomplish? What information needs to be collected in order to do so? How are you going to collect this information? And how are you going to analyze the information collected? Next, make sure you can translate these needs into unambiguous questions and concepts that communicate clearly and directly with the wide range of respondents on whom you will rely for your data (Bradburn, Sudman, and Wansink 2004). It is absolutely necessary that all respondents share a common interpretation of the meaning of each question, and furthermore, that this interpretation mirrors your intent as a researcher.

The importance of the above questions cannot be overstated. Each element—research goals, data collection, and methods of analysis—shapes and constrains the others. For example, the design of questions and response options depends largely on the mode of delivery of the questionnaire—telephone interview, online survey, pen-and-paper mailer, or face-to-face interview. Furthermore, the format of individual questions—such as open- versus closed-ended—informs the type of analyses you can later perform. For example, an open-ended response to a measure about one's attitudes toward abortion would not lend itself easily to the tight quantification required for a statistical analysis. The researcher must thus always be mindful of the optimal coordination of all of these elements for the most successful survey design.

CONCEPT MEASUREMENT: TRAITS, ASSESSMENTS, AND SENTIMENTS

The primary goal of survey research in the social sciences is to gather data on individuals' demographics, behaviors, personal details, attitudes, beliefs, and opinions. This might seem like an easy task—akin, perhaps, to asking people questions in everyday, real life—but there are actually a number of measurement issues that must be considered in order to develop a high-quality questionnaire.

The first issue relates to the complexity of the concepts about which you would like to ask. Many measures are well established by previous survey research—such as asking one's age and gender—and relate to relatively *simple* (i.e., easily measured) concepts. Other concepts—perhaps those that are more novel, complex, abstract, or unobservable—require a more cautious and carefully strategized approach in order to avoid bias while eliciting accurate responses. Developing questions that are phrased correctly will help lead to more reliable and valid data collection efforts.

Simple Concepts

As mentioned above, some questions are more easily answered than others, such as asking a respondent's age and gender. While referencing a slightly more complicated concept than these, **single construct** measures such as, "What is your religious preference?" similarly tap into a single, well-understood concept and are likewise typically unproblematic when encountered in a questionnaire. Such straightforward and well-established measures and questions tap into **unidimensional** or **simple concepts**: concepts that reflect a single idea, attitude, or behavior.

Complex Concepts

Unobservable and Multidimensional Concepts

A survey question is a measurement tool, describing your respondent by reference to a singular concept (like age or gender), in something of the same way that a tape measure is a tool that singularly describes an object by its height. However, at times the concept you wish to measure may be something that is not so easily observable, something that lacks an established, singular metric to describe it. Depending on your research goals, a more complex and multidimensional measure may be necessary to describe this obscure construct, just as some purposes might suggest the combination of a tape measure *and* a scale to take a multidimensional measurement of an object's height and weight.

A **multidimensional concept** is one that combines multiple singular constructs or attributes of an object in order to compose some new, abstract attribute that cannot be directly observed or measured. It is only by combining multiple questions that measure related singular concepts that this composite, multidimensional concept can be indirectly described. However, this is not to say that merely asking multiple questions about a single topic automatically produces a multidimensional concept. A group of related questions that yield similar answers aggregated into a single score are still considered to be unidimensional if they ultimately reflect the same underlying concept. On the other hand, multidimensional constructs require researchers to ask questions that span *multiple* concepts, from which combination a more complex and novel concept actually *emerges*.

For example, a researcher might ask various questions all related to particulars of respondents' religious practices: what church they attend, what religious texts they use, the particular rites and practices they observe, et cetera. Yet each of these questions, and even the aggregate score resulting from their combination, aims at describing the same concept: their religious affiliation.

But perhaps rather than a taking simple measure (or measures) identifying an individual's religious affiliation, a survey researcher might want to assess an individual's religious spirituality, behavior, *and* attitudes for a more comprehensive assessment of an individual's *religiosity* (i.e., a person's unobservable, overall level of religiousness). See Figure 4.1 for an example of how a researcher might take measurements across the various facets composing this multidimensional concept.

Here, religiosity is a multidimensional concept, because it measures *not only* spirituality *but also* religious behaviors *and* religious attitudes—all similar but separate components of an individual's level of religiousness. Of course, religious attitudes, religious behaviors, and spirituality are probably closely associated with one another, so the responses on each question in Figure 4.1 may be similar. However, the responses related to religious *behaviors* would likely be more closely associated with one another than with responses related to spirituality or attitudes—evidence of the essential independence of the composite dimensions.

Figure 4.1 Multidimensional Measures for Religiosity

	Strongly Agree	*Agree*	*Neutral*	*Disagree*	*Strongly Disagree*
Religion is important in my life. *(attitudinal dimension)*	1	2	3	4	5
I regularly attend religious services. *(behavioral dimension)*	1	2	3	4	5
I feel connected to a higher power. *(spiritual dimension)*	1	2	3	4	5
Religion is the one true path to eternal life. (*attitudinal dimension)*	1	2	3	4	5
I frequently read religious literature . . . (*behavioral dimension*)	1	2	3	4	5
I believe that religion is sacred. *(spiritual dimension)*	1	2	3	4	5

QUESTION DEVELOPMENT

Certain types of questions produce more accurate data than others (Schwarz 1999). As mentioned above, questions about the unidimensional concepts of age and gender tend to produce highly accurate results. But other questions—especially those measuring behaviors, opinions, and attitudes—may yield less precise responses. This is why survey research questions require careful calibration. Questions about behaviors, opinions, and attitudes must be carefully worded, so researchers can obtain responses that might be difficult for a respondent to communicate and express.

Guidelines for Developing Questions

Aim for Simplicity

Be concise; use simple, clear language; and avoid vague, abstract terms.

Recall the lessons proffered in chapter three about respondent burden and fatigue. When a question is too long or too complex, or it contains abstract language (Converse and Presser 1986), respondents may be unwilling or unable to complete the survey, may stop paying attention to the question, and/or become annoyed—possibly *more* annoyed—with the entire process. Limited attention or annoyance may lead respondents to provide rushed and potentially incorrect responses or to drop out altogether, further affecting the quality of the data you are able to collect. Thus, the best way to collect high-quality data is to keep survey items short, simple, and clear. Use as few words as possible to ask questions that everyone will understand *in the exact same way*. The examples below will lead you through this (and subsequently other) issues in question design by comparing some improperly worded sample questions with their improved, more efficient counterparts.

1a. When did you move from Philadelphia to Los Angeles?

This is an unclear question that does not indicate exactly what type of answer is required. For example, an individual could answer "after high school," "when I was 17," "in 1999," or in another way. In contrast, a more clearly articulated question would read,

1b. In what year did you move from Philadelphia to Los Angeles?

2a. Do you favor or oppose the systemic reform of immigration policies that will assist lawmakers with adequately addressing delays in visa processing and the enforcement of contemporary immigration laws?

This question is just too long and too complex. (In fact, it was difficult to even *write* it without losing interest!) If a question requires a second, third, or fourth read to be completely understood, this is a surefire sign that it is too long or too complex to include in a survey. The following question is much more concise and effective:

2b. Do you favor or oppose immigration reform policies in the United States?

3a. How important are family values to you?

The problem with this question is that *family values* could mean a number of different things to different people. Could family values be related to spending time with one's family? In that case, exactly how much time spent with one's family would constitute "family values?"

For some socially conservative individuals, family values may mean opposition to premarital sex, same-sex marriage, and reproductive rights. For many socially liberal individuals, family values might imply accepting same-sex partnership adoptions, embracing nontraditional family forms, and providing financial assistance for underprivileged families. Thus in many respects, this question is not adequately measuring a single construct that is *interpreted the same way by all respondents.* A better idea is to remove the guesswork by phrasing the question to clarify exactly what you mean:

3b. How much do you enjoy spending quality time with your immediate family?

4a. Do you favor or oppose the use of assisted reproductive technology?

Researchers should avoid using technical language and jargon in their surveys. *Assisted reproductive technology,* a term commonly used by fertility specialists, may not be easily understood by all respondents. Although the practice of using technical language may appeal as a way to sound more professional, it can easily make questions appear unclear and confusing to respondents unfamiliar with the concept or phrasing. In other words, although the survey may sound less formal, using a conversational tone can sometimes yield higher quality data:

4b. Do you favor or oppose the use of fertility treatments in order to conceive children when an individual is unable to do so through sexual intercourse?

Be Specific

5a. Are you a "social drinker?"

This question is vague, because not all respondents will interpret the term *social drinker* to mean the same thing. For some people, social drinking could simply refer to enjoying a few drinks with friends once or twice a week. For others, casual drinking with friends might entail multiple drinks across several hours, possibly extended across several nights per week. In the latter case, you might have classed respondents as *heavy drinkers* rather than agreeing with their own interpretation and identification as social drinkers. A more direct question might ask exactly how many drinks an individual consumes in a given time period:

5b. In the past 30 days, how many alcoholic beverages have you consumed?

Avoid Double-Barreled Questions

There are times when you must ask multiple questions about a topic to obtain the information you desire; this requires the separation of these questions into completely distinct survey items. Failing to do this creates **double-barreled questions**, "two-in-one" questions that are problematic because a respondent might be willing or able to answer only a single part of the question:

6a. How important are family get-togethers to you and your family?

This two-part question is really asking two questions: How important are family get-togethers for you, *and* how important are family get-togethers for your family? The researcher's assumption here that these two answers are always in agreement may confuse, discourage, or mislead a respondent and lead to lower quality data. In addition to this, the latter half of the question is asking the respondent to report on *someone else's* feelings toward something—a task that is virtually impossible to do! In most instances, this type of question can be easily broken out into two separate questions. For this particular example, however, it is better just to eliminate the second, highly speculative component altogether:

6b. How important do you think family get-togethers are?

7a. Do you favor or oppose the use of fertility treatments in order to conceive children when an individual or couple is unable or unwilling to do so through sexual intercourse?

☐ Favor ☐ Oppose

This question introduces two additional confounding variables (individual vs. couple, unable vs. unwilling), each of which is problematic on its own. What if a respondent favors treatments for couples but not individuals? Or for people unable to conceive, but not those who are merely unwilling? In combination, this creates the potential for multiple different answers (technically, 16!) that are hardly served by the two response options provided. The researcher needs to decide whether all of these variables are truly of interest and then separate the question into multiple, more precise items:

7b. Do you favor or oppose the use of fertility treatments in order to conceive children when a couple is unable to do so through sexual intercourse?

7c. Do you favor or oppose the use of fertility treatments in order to conceive children when an individual is unable to do so through sexual intercourse?

8a. Do you think that capital punishment is an archaic form of discipline and that the federal government should abolish it?

This is another example of a double-barreled question—it assumes the respondent is going to respond to both parts of the question in the same way, either affirmative or negative across the board. However, if respondents do *not* feel that capital punishment is an outdated form of punishment, but *does* nevertheless have some other reason to oppose it (or perhaps even vice-versa, approve of archaic discipline), they may be conflicted about how to answer, adding burden and frustration. A more appropriate design for a question of this sort is to separate elements, or use a skip pattern if you are truly only interested in respondents who agree that capital punishment is archaic:

8b. Do you think that capital punishment is an archaic form of discipline? (And then, depending on response):

8c. Do you think that the federal government should abolish capital punishment?

Misleading Single-Barreled Questions. Certain phrases may appear to be double-barreled (because the word *and* appears) when they are simply using established terminology that refers to a single construct. For example, "Do you own your home free and clear?" is a question that may seem to be asking two questions in one. However, "free and clear" is a term in property law that indicates that property is owned outright (without an outstanding mortgage or lien). It is important to understand and be mindful of these terms when crafting survey questions with the simplest and clearest possible terminology.

Avoid Biased and Leading Questions

Designing questions with accurate, unbiased, and simple phrasing, especially when measuring complex, multidimensional, and intangible concepts, is one of the most difficult parts of designing a survey. A significant problem related to question phrasing in survey research design is that researchers may bias their results by "leading" respondents to answer questions in a specific way. **Leading questions** often use strong, biased language and/or contain unclear messages that can manipulate or mislead a respondent to answer in a specific way. Even the most ethical researchers can still do this unintentionally, if they are not attentive enough to this common pitfall. Consider the following questions:

9a. In the wake of the largest economic downturn since the Great Depression, did you support our Republican-led Congress's 2013 decision to shut down the government?

The use of the phrases "largest economic downturn since the great depression" and "Republican-led congress" makes it difficult to disentangle whether the responses you receive are reactions to the strong language or even the unnecessary detail about our current congressional profile. Instead, consider the following:

9b. Did you support Congress's 2013 decision to shut down the government?

10a. You wouldn't say that you support affirmative action in California, would you?

This question is judgment laden, suggesting strong disapproval of affirmative action that encourages a respondent to answer "no." Questions like this make too clear the intentions of the researcher and color the resulting data to the point that it is useless. A less biased question might ask this:

10b. Do you agree or disagree with affirmative action in the state of California?

11a. Did our president, Barack Obama, make a mistake when he enacted the Patient Protection and Affordable Care Act, which forces individuals into universal health care?

This question uses emotionally suggestive language such as "make a mistake" and "forces individuals" that may bias an individual toward taking a specific stance. There is an even more subtle bias in this example: With the word *our* before *president,* the question may appeal to nationalism and pressure respondents to answer favorably. (To be fair, the word *our* in this example is unlikely to create much confusion; nevertheless, it is certainly possible.) Such a subtle bias shows how survey respondents are influenced in many indirect and complex ways. It is, therefore, important to be vigilant and consistently use the most balanced, inoffensive, and unbiased language possible. Consider this less biased (and much simpler) alternative to our previous example:

11b. Tell us how much you agree or disagree with the following statement: Enacting the Patient Protection and Affordable Care Act benefited Americans.

12a. Do you favor or oppose the use of fertility treatments in order to conceive children when an individual is unable to do so through more traditional means?

Though it is commonly used, the word *traditional* can potentially be a very loaded term, implying that something is deep-rooted and established. Respondents may be influenced to respond based on their general attitudes toward tradition and change, rather than on careful consideration of the specific issue at hand. For example, people who are resistant to or unnerved by change might be more inclined to oppose fertility treatment simply because it bears the marker of something unconventional or conceptually foreign. A better question avoids introducing this potential bias while also adding greater specificity:

12b. Do you favor or oppose the use of fertility treatments in order to conceive children when an individual is unable to do so through sexual intercourse?

13a. The tragedy in Newtown, Connecticut, has motivated Americans to enter the debate on gun control. What do you believe is the root cause of gun violence in America?

This question is appealing to respondents' emotions by referencing the "tragedy in Newtown" before asking a question about gun control. A less biased question will instead get to the point without sensationalism:

13b. What do you believe are the primary causes for gun violence in America? (Please mark all that apply.)

Weighing Bias Against Straightforwardness. Offensive and biased terms are occasionally difficult to avoid, such as when such terms are part of widely recognized colloquialisms to which no clear alternative is available. For example, a question probing whether or not an individual supports "partial birth abortion" is likely easier to answer than a question asking about "abortion in the instance of intact dilation and extraction." Although "partial birth abortion" may seem like a biased (and possibly even offensive) term, it may still elicit a more valid response than "intact dilation and extraction," a phrase likely to be unfamiliar to the vast majority of respondents. However, even in such cases, the inclusion of such potentially loaded terms and questions in your work will surely be identified and criticized by readers and peers. Be aware of this potentiality, and carefully weigh all phrasing options so that you can defend your choices later.

Avoid Making Assumptions

Premising a question on a controversial assumption can be just as problematic as the use of such biased language as described above. Consider the question below:

14a. In your opinion, does the increase in work hours among employed mothers have an influence on the lack of respect children now have for their families?

This question makes two assumptions that might introduce error into the responses. First, the question proclaims that there has been an increase in work hours among employed mothers. The respondent may or may not even agree with this assertion. Second, the question assumes that the respondent agrees that youth have lost respect for their families. Therefore, even if respondents have no opinion on this issue and accept that there has been an increase in work hours among employed mothers, they are still unable to answer accurately, because they do not agree that children have a lack of respect for their family. As is typically the case, simplicity and brevity can reduce the burden on respondents and improve the precision and quality of their responses:

14b. Has there been an increase in work hours among employed mothers recently?

Carefully Ask Personal and Sensitive Questions

Often, researchers need to ask for personal and sensitive information that respondents may be hesitant to provide out of concerns for their privacy. **Item nonresponse** (i.e., skipping questions) is normally higher for these questions (Tourangeau and Yan 2007). Try to reduce the potential sensitivity regarding such personal questions with careful phrasing and question/response structures that make items quicker and easier to answer. Some common examples of sensitive questions include those relating to income, voting behavior, and the more intimate details of peoples' private lives.

Sensitive questions may be more successful when possible responses are presented as **bracketed categories**, in which each response choice encompasses a range of numbers or categories defined in relevance to the question (Tourangeau and Yan 2007). For example, asking respondents to report their number of sexual partners may elicit a greater number of responses when followed by a range of choices like the following: 0, 1, 3–5, 6–10, and 11 or more. Identifying a category may feel less like a revelation of specific, personal information, and may thus encourage a higher response rate at the expense of a little bit of precision. This approach is helpful in another way, since some respondents might not remember their *exact* number of sexual partners—and the longer they think about it, the more burdensome the question becomes.

Above all, do not force respondents to answer any questions. Respondents who feel they are being coerced into answering a personal question may skip the question at best, or abandon the survey altogether at worst. Simply adding a response option of "decline to state" can make the difference between a skipped item and an abandoned survey, and preserve respondents' trust in the sensitivity of the researcher.

Social Desirability. **Social desirability** refers to the inclination for respondents to overreport socially acceptable behaviors and underreport socially undesirable behaviors (Krumpal 2013). For example, it is not socially desirable to express homophobic or racist attitudes, so respondents may be apprehensive about admitting these behaviors. This tendency is especially marked in face-to-face interviews, where the presence of an interviewer can magnify respondents' perceptions of being judged. In the same vein, respondents will underreport socially undesirable behavior, such as illegal substance abuse; again, this is even more likely in a face-to-face setting. In addition, earlier advice about avoiding bias is especially relevant here, as desirability effects can easily be triggered by loaded words like *illegal* or *abuse* (when referencing substance use; other topics will entail different linguistic sensibilities).

Privacy and social desirability are important concerns that should be taken seriously so that respondents feel comfortable answering fully and truthfully.

Emphasize Anonymity and Confidentiality. Again, it is important to emphasize that survey responses will remain anonymous or confidential at the outset and, if necessary, reiterate this assurance when touching on sensitive subjects.

Choose Delivery Mode Carefully. There is more response bias and social desirability in face-to-face interview surveys.

Organize Sensitive Questions Strategically. Do not start a survey with personal or sensitive items or questions prone to social desirability. When respondents begin a survey, their level of commitment is usually quite low, and personal questions early on may deter them from continuing. Also, placing these questions at the end of the survey is ill-advised, because this might lead to respondents feeling apprehensive, unpleasant, or offended, as though they are being manipulated. This may even introduce selection bias into future results when follow-up surveys are necessary and respondents are unwilling to participate. It is best to include personal and sensitive questions in the middle of the survey, so those respondents who have committed time and energy to completing the survey will still want to complete it.

Additional Guidelines for Question Development

In addition to the general concerns detailed above, there are a number of minor details that, left unaddressed, may add to overall respondent burden and discourage participation and attention to quality answers. Many of these details are presented here, with positive and negative examples to illustrate each one:

- Avoid abbreviations; spell out the entire phrase instead. If the abbreviation is absolutely necessary (which is rare), define it for the respondent.

  Incorrect: How do you feel about the GOP?

  Correct: How do you feel about the Republican Party?

- Avoid slang and contractions.

  Incorrect: How many kids live in your household?

  Correct: How many children live in your household?

- Avoid ambiguous phrases, even those that are common in everyday talk.

  Incorrect: Do you agree that abortion should be illegal most of the time?

  Correct: Do you agree or disagree that abortion should be illegal under X circumstance? Do you agree or disagree that abortion should be illegal under Y circumstance?

- Avoid negatively phrased questions.

  Incorrect: How frequently do you not attend church?

  Correct: How many times in the last month did you attend religious services?

- Avoid double negative questions.

  Incorrect: Should the Supreme Court not have opposed the right of same-sex couples to marry?

  Correct: Do you favor or oppose the Supreme Court's ruling on the Defense of Marriage Act?

- Use a realistic time frame when asking about attitudes and behaviors.

  Incorrect: How many cigarettes have you smoked in your entire life?

  Correct: In the past month, how many cigarettes have you smoked?

- Make sure all questions are absolutely necessary.

One of the most important ways to elicit high-quality responses to survey questions is to have an organized questionnaire with questions that are clearly and impartially articulated. Verification that questions are relevant and do not contain (potentially inaccurate) assumptions will also safeguard against measurement error.

Once you are satisfied that you have included all the relevant questions you need for your research purposes, excluded irrelevant and unnecessary items, and arrived at question wording that is clear, concise, and unbiased, the next step is to focus on the response options you provide for the respondent to these questions. It is to this area of survey design that we turn our attention in the sections that follow.

RESPONSES TO QUESTIONS

Types of Responses

There are many options to consider in the way you allow respondents to answer your survey questions. For some purposes you may wish to allow them to speak freely in their own words; other times, it will be more effective and efficient to provide them a range of responses from which to choose. The type of response you solicit will depend on the nature of the concept you wish to measure (and the research question or hypothesis that underlies it) as well as the subsequent analysis you intend to perform with the data collected. The sections below outline the strengths, weaknesses, and special considerations of the various response options, to help you choose the ones best suited to your specific research needs.

Closed-Ended Questions

Closed-ended questions are questions formatted such that the response possibilities are limited ("closed") to a specific list from which the respondent must choose—they are also referred to as **fixed-choice questions**. There are several different types of closed-ended questions, and depending on the concept being measured, some are more appropriate than others. Your questionnaire will likely involve a combination of different types and may require separate sets of instructions to ensure respondent comprehension. Nevertheless, questions of different types must flow together seamlessly in order for you to collect first-rate data.

Strengths of Closed-Ended Questions

The strengths of using closed-ended questions are mostly on the back end, in the ease they bring to the compilation and analysis of data by the researcher. Strengths include the following:

- Responses are easy to quantify (e.g., 1 = Strongly Disagree; 2 = Disagree; 3 = Neutral; 4 = Agree; 5 = Strongly Agree).
- They are easier to enter into statistical analysis software and analyze.
- Data collection is usually quicker.
- Results are easier to summarize and present in tables, charts, and graphs.
- There is more reliability across responses—especially when only a few collapsed response categories are included.
- There is less interviewer and social desirability bias.
- There is a higher degree of anonymity.

Types of Closed-Ended Questions

Multiple Choice

Most readers will be familiar with the standard **multiple-choice** format so prevalent in the exams we encounter in our years of schooling. The only difference in survey questionnaires is that, ideally, less guesswork will be involved.

Which of the following is the mode of transportation you most frequently take to work?

1) Automobile (self-driven)

2) Automobile (carpool)

3) Bus

4) Train

5) Other (please specify) ______________.

As in all aspects of survey design, it is important to check that all response categories are clear and unambiguous, that they do not suggest different meanings to different (types of) respondents. For example, questions asking respondents about their occupations often list "education" among the options. However, "education" does not mean the same thing to everyone. "Education" includes students, teachers (at various levels), and administrators. These are all quite different but would be categorized as the same if the response options are ambiguous.

Dichotomous

When there are only two possible response options (e.g., agree/disagree, yes/no, true/false), the question is **dichotomous**. Technically, this is a type of multiple-choice question, but with only two options, which makes it simple to design. However, keep in mind that questions rarely have only two possible answers, and so responses to dichotomous questions are easy to misinterpret. They also make it even easier to respond incorrectly or thoughtlessly for ambivalent respondents already prone to random guessing. Consider whether the item below is well suited for a dichotomous type of response:

My neighbors are an important part of my life.

☐ Yes ☐ No

Checklist

A **checklist** is appropriate when you want to allow the respondent to select multiple responses. Note the use of check-boxes (rather than numbers or letters) to identify separate items, to remind respondents that choices are not mutually exclusive. For example:

In the past 30 days, which of the following have caused you a lot of stress? (Check all that apply).

- My friends
- My partner
- My job/finances
- My family
- My children
- None of the above

Scales

Scales provide a set of response options representing ordered points on a continuum of possible answers. There are several distinct types of scales suited to different types of applications, as outlined below.

Rating Scale. **Rating scale** questions are a type of multiple-choice option that uses ordered responses to represent a continuum from which respondents choose the single best answer choice. It is often helpful to include additional explication of the categories in parentheses to ensure all respondents (and researchers) interpret them in the same way. Consider this example:

How often are you late for work?

1) Very frequently (almost daily)
2) Frequently (twice a week)
3) Occasionally (once a week)
4) Seldom (twice a month)
5) Rarely (once every six months)
6) Never

Rank Order Scale. A **rank order scale** allows respondents to put answer choices in order themselves, according to some criteria expressed in the prompt. Note here that blanks or brackets should be used to differentiate the choices from a rating-type or checklist-type question. Here is an example:

If you had to choose an alternate mode of transportation to work, what would be your order of preference among the following? (1 is first choice, 2 is second choice, etc.)

☐ Walk/run
☐ Bicycle
☐ Skateboard
☐ Rollerblade
☐ Taxi cab

Likert Scale. In a **Likert scale**, participants are asked to indicate their agreement or disagreement with a statement (or number of statements) by scoring their response along a range. Responses typically range from "strongly agree" to "strongly disagree," with each response option on the scale associated with a numerical score. Likert scales are particularly helpful when measuring respondents' attitudes and opinions about particular topics, people, ideas, or experiences. Likert scales should not be used when the responses are not on a scale or when the items are not interrelated—these would, in effect, not even be called scales.

Typically, Likert scales will have a midpoint for a neutral response between agree and disagree (see below). However, researchers sometimes use an even number of possible responses, to the exclusion of a neutral/undecided option. This is called a **forced choice question,** because ambivalent respondents are forced to form an opinion in one direction or the other. The issue of whether or not to include a midpoint is addressed on page 62.

Overall, I feel that the current U.S. president is . . . :

		Strongly Agree	*Agree*	*Neither*	*Disagree*	*Strongly Disagree*
1	Trustworthy	[1]	[2]	[3]	[4]	[5]
2	Strong	[1]	[2]	[3]	[4]	[5]
3	Capable	[1]	[2]	[3]	[4]	[5]
4	Intelligent	[1]	[2]	[3]	[4]	[5]

Semantic Differential. **Semantic differential scales** provide contradictory adjectives as endpoints on a Likert-type scale where the respondent can assess a person, idea, or object according to a dimension of special interest to the researcher (Osgood, Suci, and Tannenbaum 1957):

Indicate your attitudes regarding the current president of the United States on the scale below:

Trustworthy	[1]	[2]	[3]	[4]	[5]	[6]	[7]	Untrustworthy
Strong	[1]	[2]	[3]	[4]	[5]	[6]	[7]	Weak
Capable	[1]	[2]	[3]	[4]	[5]	[6]	[7]	Incapable
Intelligent	[1]	[2]	[3]	[4]	[5]	[6]	[7]	Unintelligent
Respectful	[1]	[2]	[3]	[4]	[5]	[6]	[7]	Disrespectful

Important Guidelines for Categorization Scheme Development

When developing response categories for closed-ended/fixed-choice questions, there are three important things to keep in mind: relevance, comprehensiveness, and mutual exclusivity.

Relevant

Just as appropriate *questions* need to be designed with the population and topic in mind, *response* scales and categories must be designed with the same considerations. Researchers need to be familiar with the most **relevant** or common types of answers given in order to choose relevant response options. Response options can be based on common knowledge or can be identified through research or by asking individuals involved with or particularly knowledgeable about a specific topic. Appropriate response categories vary depending on culture, time, and even geographic region of the country. The goal is to make sure that all of the most important (and expected) possible response categories are listed, so respondents will not need to struggle to align their own ideas with the options available to them.

Comprehensive

On a distinct but related note, response options must reflect a **comprehensive** list of the possible options, exhausting all categories a respondent may wish to select. The best way to ensure a comprehensive category set is to include an "other" category at the end of a list, followed by the instructions "please specify" and a blank line for respondents to write on. This is also useful for future survey designs: If a large number of similar open-ended responses are noted, a researcher can create a new category option for it. Unless the researcher is 100% confident that all categories are covered, then an "other" category is necessary. As sociologists, we know that gender is composed of more than the typical two categories (e.g. male/female); therefore including an "other" response option will improve participant responses. A lack of comprehensive options is both common and very frustrating for individuals excluded by the choices (especially with regard to overlooked racial and ethnic categories). The examples below illustrate the difference between a noncomprehensive list and a comprehensive one:

What is your marital status?

1) Single
2) Married

What is your marital status?

1) Single
2) Married
3) Divorced
4) Widowed
5) Separated
6) Never Married

Mutual Exclusivity

Having **mutually exclusive** categories means that the response options do not conflict or overlap with each other in any way. In other words, respondents must perceive that only one of the available responses fits the answer they imagine (unless, of course, the item includes a checklist of responses). If not, respondents have the burden of deciding which is closest or most appropriate—and how they choose to do so may vary from survey to survey, lowering the precision and overall quality of your data. Note that this is the opposite of the previously discussed problem, that of a lack of comprehensive categories: In this case, there are *too many* possible choices instead of *not enough*. For example, consider the following question:

How long have you been seeing your primary care physician?

1) 1–2 Years

2) 3–5 Years

3) 6–10 Years

4) 11 or more years

How would an individual respond who has been seeing a primary care physician for 2.5 years? Do not assume everyone will round up—people who are rarely sick or do not frequently see a doctor may be inclined to round down. You also should not assume everyone will round down—people who like their doctor and frequent the doctor's office may round up. It is important to exercise caution when creating numerical categories where an individual might land in between two possibilities. Sometimes this requires instruction to round up or round down. Other times, it may be a better idea to simply add specificity to your presented options.

In recent years, it has become common to use an "infinite cap" on response options based on the last category listed. In order to avoid confusion, do not list categories using a plus sign (e.g., 1–2 times, 3–5 times, 6–10 times, 10+ times). An individual may not realize that "10+" implies "anything more than 10" and may interpret "10 times" as being included in this categorization. A better response option will spell out "11 or more" to avoid this confusion.

The Problem of the Neutral Point

As noted at the beginning of this chapter, the testing of a hypothesis or answering of a research question requires survey researchers to measure concepts as precisely as possible. Therefore, it is necessary to decide whether or not a midpoint or neutral point in a scale is helpful for your specific research purposes. There is no definitive evidence whether or not the midpoint is valuable—the best answer is that it depends on the respondent and the type of question being asked (Kulas and Stachowski 2013; Krosnick 2002).

When researchers argue that we should not include a midpoint, they are basically claiming that respondents should always be forced to take a stance on a given topic.

They also suggest that neutral points are potentially meaningless and offer no insight on an individual's real opinions or attitudes. However, the unavoidable reality is that people sometimes have neutral feelings. There are several scenarios when this is conceivable, such as when a respondent

- Lacks interest in a topic.
- Has limited recall regarding the event(s) in question.
- Is legitimately undecided on an issue.
- Lacks knowledge about a topic.
- Lacks experience relating to a topic.
- Finds the question too personal to answer.

In such cases, respondents may randomly guess, skip the question entirely, or abandon the survey altogether. (Recall from the previous section on sensitive questions that respondents may be hesitant to complete a survey when they feel forced to answer a question.) Therefore, given the topic, question, and types of respondents participating, a researcher should choose carefully whether or not a neutral point is advantageous for the study, whether the value of "forcing their hand" outweighs the risks of introducing error or additional respondent burden to the survey experience.

In addition to these general concerns, there are some common, more specific sources of error, as detailed in the next section.

Additional Guidelines for Response Options

- Use an equal number of positive and negative responses for scale questions. To understand why this is important, consider the question below, where 75% of the answers indicate some form of close relationship, and there is only one possible option for something other than close:

Incorrect: How emotionally close would you say you are to your mother?

1) Extremely close

2) Somewhat close

3) Close enough

4) Not close at all

Correct: How emotionally close would you say you are to your mother?

1) Very close

2) Somewhat close

3) Somewhat withdrawn

4) Very withdrawn

- Use a consistent rating scale throughout the entire survey. Do not mix questions with a scale where 1 = strongly *agree* with other questions with a scale where 1 = strongly *disagree*.
- Similarly, do not mix scale ratings within the same survey. Choose the standard number of points in your Likert scales (e.g., three, five, seven) and be consistent to avoid confusion.
- Limit the number of points on scales. Any more than nine points will hinder the respondent's ability to discriminate between points. Scales with five or seven points are common and reliable.
- Neutral is not the same as "no opinion." "Neutral" might actually be an opinion. Individuals may feel "neutral" about the hours they work per week, but this is not the same as having no opinion on the matter.

The above guidelines should sensitize you to some of the advantages, drawbacks, and special considerations surrounding the various types of closed-ended questions. In the next section, we turn to a very different type of survey item, the open-ended question, and elaborate a similar discussion of strengths, weaknesses, and other issues.

LEVEL OF MEASUREMENT

The end result of collecting survey data is to quantify our concepts into variables and then analyze them statistically to test our hypotheses (Nunnally and Bernstein 1994). The types of statistical analyses that are possible depend entirely on the levels at which variables are measured. To allow for our chosen type of statistical analysis, we must know, and even plan ahead for, the level of measurement of our variables. **Level of measurement** can be defined as the mathematical property of variables. As the precision of measurement increases, more mathematical options or tools become available with which to analyze the variables statistically. This ultimately suggests that the process of measurement is an ongoing iterative process that needs to consider both theoretical and empirical needs of the research (Carmines and Zeller 1979).

An important reason for choosing a particular set of response options for each survey question is that the response options dictate the level of measurement of the variables we will use to answer our research question. We are literally assigning numbers to attributes of the variables. Note that in the examples of survey questions presented above, all the response categories were tied to a number. This is measurement in a nutshell and the end product of all our hard work developing questions and assessing validity and reliability.

We classify variables with four levels of measurement that we will present in order from the lowest level of precision to the highest level of precision: nominal, ordinal, interval, and ratio. Again, precision is the degree of specificity of the numbers assigned to specific response options. Nunnally and Bernstein argue that measurement is really about "how much of the attribute is present in an object" (1994: 3). Therefore, as precision increases, we are better able to gauge how much of the attribute we have observed. Another way of thinking about it is that lower levels of precision mean there are fewer mathematical operations we can use with the variables because it's harder to estimate the quantity we have, while greater precision increases the mathematical options we have.

Nominal measures have the least precision. Nominally measured variables are actually qualitatively measured variables rather than numerically measured variables. That is, we cannot evaluate *how much* of an attribute is present; rather, we can only know whether the attribute *is or is not* present. Nominal variables can be distinguished only by their names. Favorite type of fruit is an example of a nominal variable. Response options include apples, oranges, grapes, bananas, et cetera. We can assign a number to apples (1), oranges (2), and bananas (3), but the number is essentially arbitrary. We cannot say, for example, that there is more favorableness associated with bananas than is associated with apples based on the number assigned. Any number used with a nominal variable is used as a label only (Nunnally 1967). Apples, oranges, and bananas are qualitatively distinct, and all we can do is examine whether or not participants chose apples (in the set of apples) or did not choose apples. A few other examples of nominal variables are gender (male, female, other), race/ethnicity (white, African American, Asian, Native American, Hispanic, multiracial), and participation in food stamp programs (yes, no).

It is possible to measure nonnominal variables nominally. For instance, let's say a research team is interested in the food security of Americans who are living below the poverty line. They use income as their primary variable of interest, because it defines the US poverty line. However, the researchers may decide to measure income—a variable that is easily and precisely quantifiable, simply as "yes" for below the poverty line or "no" for not below the poverty line. This limits what the researchers can do with income. They cannot tease out how variations in income levels among those below the poverty line may affect food security, because that information was not gathered; the nominal variable used lacks the precision necessary to conduct that analysis.

Ordinal measurement quantifies variables by ordering the response categories from least to most or most to least (Nunnally and Bernstein 1994). The following question is measured ordinally, because the three response categories are rank ordered from least problematic to most problematic.

Upon moving to your new home, please tell me to what extent your commute to work may be a problem.

Not a problem
Somewhat of a problem
A big problem

The numbers assigned to the response categories are rank ordered, with 1 being one unit less than 2, which is one unit less than 3. There is the same distance numerically between each category. Yet, the difference or distance between "not a problem" and "somewhat of a problem" may be bigger or smaller than the distance between "somewhat of a problem" and "a big problem." In terms of mathematical computation, this is limiting. All we really know is that 1 is less than 2, but we cannot calculate the actual distance between the ordered categories. This means we cannot add or subtract across the scores, nor can we multiply or divide the values of this variable. Most Likert scale variables, such as opinion or attitude scales with five category response options, are ordinal—going from least amount of agreement to most amount of agreement without meaningful numbers to determine the distance between the categories.

An **interval** level of measurement is one that rank orders response categories and, additionally, provides known distances between each response category without providing information about the absolute magnitude of the trait or characteristic (Nunnally and Bernstein 1994). Conceptually, this is very difficult to understand without an example. Temperature is an interval level of measurement. In the United States, temperature is measured on the Fahrenheit scale. On this scale, 32 degrees is considered freezing. In other parts of the world, temperature is measured on the Celsius scale where 0 degrees is considered freezing. Therefore, 32 degrees Fahrenheit and 0 degrees Celsius are the same value on different scales. The zero in Celsius is meaningless, though the "freezing" designation is meaningful. The difference between 0 degrees and 1 degree Celsius is clearly understood as a 1-degree change, as is the difference between 32 degrees and 33 degrees Fahrenheit. But, 33 degrees Fahrenheit is not equivalent to 1 degree Celsius. When the absolute magnitude of the trait is not specified, we do not have a zero score that is consistently anchored to a meaning. Mathematically, then, we can add and subtract values with interval measured variables, but we cannot multiply or divide them. Another example of an interval measured variable is intelligence quotient (IQ), which is measured on a scale created from many questions and is standardized to have a mean of zero. Thus, the zero has no true meaning, and we cannot say that someone with an IQ of 100 is twice as smart as someone with an IQ of 50.

Ratio measurement is the most mathematically precise of the levels of measurement. Variables that are measures on the ratio scale have response categories that can be rank ordered, the distances between the response categories are known, and there is a true zero value that is meaningfully anchored (Nunnally and Bernstein 1994). Income is an excellent example of a ratio measured variable. The question "How much did you earn in wages and salary in the previous year?" followed by a line for participants to write in a value will create a ratio measured version of income. A participant who earns $30,000 per year makes half as much as someone who earns $60,000 per year. If a person reports $0, than that person had no earnings or wages in the previous year. The absolute magnitude of the trait is known. Thus, we can add and subtract, multiply and divide, rank order, or create nominal variables out of income if it is measured on a ratio scale. Other examples of ratio measures are age, height, weight, and years of education.

When devising questions for a survey, think carefully about the best configuration of response categories. Measure them as precisely as possible to allow for more statistical analysis options later in the research process. Look to previous published literature to determine how the field is measuring the variable to see if there are known issues with measurement. For example, how well can people articulate their previous year's earnings and wages? If this is too hard, participants might guess, estimate, or skip the question entirely. If this is what the literature says, use a less precise level of measurement.

OPEN-ENDED QUESTIONS

Open-ended questions are survey items formatted to allow respondents to answer questions or provide feedback in their own words. In contrast to closed-ended questions, there are no limitations to the response possibilities, and respondents are encouraged to provide in-depth answers. A quick caveat might be raised before proceeding: Open-ended questions are not necessarily always questions per se; they may include any type of prompt—question or not—to elicit an original and self-guided response from the respondent. Consider the following example:

Closed-Ended Question: How emotionally close do you feel to your mother? (Add response options.)

Open-Ended Question: Tell me how you feel about your mother.

Open-ended questions are sometimes useful when they follow a closed-ended question. This configuration ensures that researchers can learn about some specific aspect of the issue they find relevant, but it also opens the floor to detailed elaboration, or even novel issues, that the respondent finds interesting or important as well. Consider the following question posed by a researcher studying public opinion of the US Supreme Court:

1. Please rank your support for the current US Supreme Court:

    1) Strongly support

    2) Somewhat support

    3) Somewhat oppose

    4) Strongly oppose

If researchers are studying public opinion of the US Supreme Court, they are probably not going to get the information they need from this single closed-ended question—even several more questions might not elicit the fine-grained information necessary. Assuming the researchers find that most people strongly oppose the current Supreme Court, they are faced with a new problem: They are unable to determine *why* there is such strong opposition. Thus, open-ended questions are sometimes necessary in order to produce more nuanced ideas about the topic in question.

Strengths of Open-Ended Questions

- Respondents are not limited in their responses. They are able to explain, qualify, and clarify their answers, especially when "other (please specify)" is an option.
- Open-ended questions are frequently easier to craft, because they do not require response options (which require a detailed design process).
- Open-ended responses do not force potentially invalid responses.
- Open-ended responses have more nuance, depth, and substance than closed-ended responses.
- Open-ended questions are fairly straightforward (unlike the many types of closed-ended questions and scales).

Guidelines for Open-Ended Questions

While open-ended questions are by definition less constrained than closed-ended ones, there are still some important guidelines to keep in mind to elicit the highest quality responses in the most efficient manner.

- Avoid dichotomous questions and other questions that elicit one-word replies (agree/disagree, yes/no, true/false).
- Do not supply response options in the question:
  - **Incorrect**: Did you feel happy or sad about having another baby?
  - **Correct**: How did you feel about having another baby?
- Try not to use phrases such as "To what extent were you happy?" or "How happy were you?"
- Be aware that the rich detail and varied responses you may receive can be of great value for some subsequent analyses, but will be ill-suited for others. For example, it can be very difficult to quantify such responses for use in statistical analysis.
- Too many open-ended questions can add to respondent burden and fatigue and therefore should be used sparingly.

COMPARATIVE CONCEPTS (VIGNETTES)

The next type of question can be either open- or closed-ended, or a combination of both. **Vignettes** are systematic descriptions of hypothetical situations; they are included in a survey to elicit respondents' thoughts and emotions about specific topics that cannot be encapsulated in the standard, concise question format (Finch 1987). They are often intended to elicit opinions, values, and attitudes arising from unique situations and/or social norms that are difficult to define or articulate. In a vignette item, respondents are presented with a hypothetical story and are asked to react to the events it describes. While stories have traditionally been presented as blocks of text, technology-based survey development (e.g., Qualtrics and Survey Monkey) has recently introduced the exciting possibility of including video vignettes in online surveys.

Vignettes can provide an opportunity for discussing more sensitive topics (for example, abortion, bullying, or racial prejudice) in a format that is potentially less aggressive and/or imposing than that of an outright question. The specific contexts vignettes provide can help respondents to feel less put on the spot to issue definitive, universal proclamations, reducing the pressure often associated with the discussion of sensitive issues. Hypothetical stories also offer the respondent specific illustrations for reference that can help them clarify some of their own otherwise ambiguous ideas or feelings. For example, rather than simply answering a question about abortion in specific circumstances (e.g., young and unprepared mother), a vignette allows respondents to read (or see) the context surrounding this situation, perhaps providing them with the cues they need to feel more invested in and committed to their subsequent responses.

Important Guidelines for Vignettes

- If you are using a written vignette, keep it practical and realistic so that it can be recreated on video at a later time if necessary or desired.
- Try to keep the story interesting. You do not want the respondent to get bored or lose motivation.
- Be realistic and avoid sensationalism.
- Try to keep it brief enough to maintain respondents' attention, while at the same time detailed enough to include all of the points you consider relevant for the study.
- Keep in mind that bias is especially problematic here, as the many details of a narrative—such as the race, age, marital status, et cetera of a woman in a video about abortion—can all introduce sources of bias (from both researcher and

respondent) that may be subtle and largely undetectable. Even seemingly extraneous or inconsequential elements of the narrative may color the general perceptions of respondents in significant ways.

- Depending on the length of the vignette, the number of questions that follow it will vary, but five to seven questions is suitable.

Sample Vignette

The following is an example of a vignette used to assess individuals' perceptions of later-life decision making. It incorporates both closed-ended and open-ended prompts.

Mr. and Mrs. Market are an elderly couple that were married directly out of high school and have lived in the same home for 40 years. Mr. Market has recently been diagnosed with terminal cancer, and his symptoms have become quite severe. He is unable to perform everyday tasks, can walk only very short distances, and reports that he is in constant pain. Mrs. Market is unable to attend to Mr. Market's many medical needs and is finding it increasingly difficult to mind her own health. Mr. and Mrs. Market do not have any children and cannot afford to move to a retirement home or later-life facility.

1. Of the following situations, which do you think would be best for the Markets?

    (1) Mr. and Mrs. Market should remain in their home and apply for welfare services.

    (2) Mr. and Mrs. Market should sell their home and relocate.

    (3) Mr. and Mrs. Market should appeal to friends for financial assistance.

    (4) Mr. Market should be hospitalized and Mrs. Market should remain in their home to care for herself.

2. Why do you believe this choice is the best decision for the Markets?

This concludes our discussion of the general classes and specific types of survey items you may find useful in the pursuit of your research goals. In the remainder of the chapter, we turn to data collection issues that can apply to all types of survey items. Attention to these should be part of every researcher's efforts to reduce error in the collection of survey data.

RETROSPECTIVE AND PROSPECTIVE QUESTIONS

Researchers will sometimes expect a respondent to recall events that happened in the past or to count the number of times some event has occurred. They also often ask about opinions formed, beliefs adopted, and behaviors displayed in the past. These are

retrospective questions. These are often necessary in cross-sectional surveys because we only talk to participants once. Because human memory is limited and fallible, it is important for researchers to try to obtain the most accurate retrospective results possible, and they should do their best to improve respondent recall. There are two ways to improve recall:

(1) Use *very* specific time and object references:

Unclear: How many times in the last year have you been to the library?

In this question, a respondent may not know how to answer, as "a year" can be interpreted differently by many people. Many things could be "about a year ago" and rounded into or out of the year timeline. People may also refer to a year as an *annual* year (e.g., an individual in September 2014 may refer back only as far as January 2014—and so they are only considering nine months). Students might interpret a year as being an *academic* year and go back as far as the prior August. Using very specific and standardized time references helps respondents frame the period in their minds to assist recall.

Clear: In the last twelve months, how many times have you been to the public library?

Being as specific as possible about reference dates is also important to reduce telescoping error and recall loss. **Telescoping error** is the tendency for respondents to remember things as happening more recently than they actually happened (Bradburn, Huttenlocher, and Hedges 1993). This occurs most often with recent events. **Recall loss** occurs when respondents forget that an event occurred. Recall loss occurs most often with events that occurred in the distant past (Sudman and Bradburn 1973).

(2) Limit retrospective questions and "time frame overload":

Questions that require recall may demand a great amount of mental energy from the respondent—and this energy is of finite supply. Therefore, it is important not to include too many retrospective items. When recall items are necessary, avoid alternating the length of time referenced ("How many times in the last week . . . ?" followed by "How many times in the last month . . . ?" followed by "How many times in the last week . . . ?" followed by "How many times in the last year?"). The mental gymnastics required to follow such questioning can easily lead to respondent burden and fatigue.

Another type of time-based question asks respondents to look forward and anticipate something happening, for instance, "At what age do you expect to be married?" "When do you plan on moving next?" and "How much more money will you be earning when you get your next raise?" When asking these types of questions, it is important to keep in mind that responses are often unreliable and inaccurate (because respondents cannot tell the future).

In a longitudinal study we can ask **prospective questions,** meaning questions about current time events, behaviors, and attitudes. If we ask these same questions multiple times, we can assess how past events affect current events or attitudes and know that recall bias has been minimized. Furthermore, we can follow up on the accuracy of future expectations or aspirations with prospective questions in a later round of data collection.

UPDATING TIME-SPECIFIC SURVEYS AND MULTILANGUAGE SURVEYS

Often, a researcher will use measures that have been used in past research ("tried and true" measures)—this is perfectly acceptable (and even recommended). When using or building on existing instruments, it is important to retain the essence of the question but also to appropriate it according to the specifics of your own, unique study. For instance, elements may need to be changed to reflect important societal changes that have occurred since the previous study, so your survey can maintain the impression of being timely and relevant to the outside world. By the same token, some words or entire topics may need to be updated or dropped to avoid referencing a past event that has since lost its meaning for your current respondents, who may no longer remember or care much about it. For example, it would not be very helpful to include a vignette about children's reactions to Cold War tensions that was developed in 1984, or to recycle a question about Mad Cow Disease for a questionnaire administered in 2014.

Adopting an existing measure as is does allow for valuable comparisons of newer results with those obtained by the past research. However, just because a survey or a scale or a single question has worked in the past, there is no assurance that it will work today, or that it will work with your particular types of respondents (based on cultural differences, etc.).

In addition to updating the content, it is important to update the format of your survey according to up-to-date technological advancements. For instance, a text vignette may work better as a video, now that video vignettes can be introduced into web-based survey instruments like Qualtrics and Survey Monkey. Even certain questions that were once posed on pen-and-paper surveys may need to be updated for online survey administration.

MULTILINGUAL AND CROSS-COMPARATIVE SURVEY PROJECTS

Given the diversity of most research in the social sciences, multilingual survey projects have become more common. The most important part of conducting multilingual studies is to plan survey translation as part of the study, rather than addressing it merely as an afterthought. When multilingual issues are taken into consideration at the outset, researchers can reduce the time and money associated with translation later (McKay et al. 1996). Furthermore, when considered early, researchers can develop survey instruments in two or more languages simultaneously to avoid a potential translation bias toward one language.

There is a reason that translation is a profession that requires rigorous understanding of different words, phrases, and meanings. A common mistake is to use web-based translation services to translate words, phrases, and entire survey instruments. For example, in the Spanish language, double negatives are often used to produce a negative, whereas in English, double negatives are confusing and usually imply a positive response. Using translation services that are anything less than professional invites more risk than is justified by whatever cost savings it generates..

It is advisable to seek the assistance of a pair of bilingual translators who are familiar with the study content and colloquialisms in both languages to **back translate** the survey. Back translation occurs when one person translates the survey into another language, and a second person (without seeing the original survey) translates this version back into the original language (Bernard 1988). The researcher is then able to check for inconsistencies in translation based on awkward and complex language in the back translation.

It is also important to account for cultural differences in cross-comparative research, especially when translating instruments from one language to another (as opposed to developing them simultaneously) (Bernard 1988). Even simple differences between "disagree" and "somewhat disagree" may bias the results of one survey. Examples provided with certain questions may differ based on culture. Even when translating US English to British English, there are culturally different terms. For example, a question about "football" will be interpreted differently depending on where and to whom the survey is administered.

Thus, cross-comparative survey conversion requires skilled translation and separate pretesting (see Chapter 6) to achieve linguistic, cultural, and conceptual equivalence—meaning that words and phrases as well as constructs and concepts are to be culturally and linguistically similar. It is also very important to document the translation process and to include the translation methods (and concerns about any potential problems with the translation) in the study report.

MEASUREMENT ERROR

Before closing our discussion of question construction, it is worth noting that throughout this chapter, the word *error* has been mentioned several times. This is because error is an inescapable aspect of all surveys and indeed all research in general. In the social sciences, we strive to find the best way to estimate a given concept, but we also acknowledge that to some degree, our research will always be prone to measurement error. **Measurement error** occurs when the question chosen to gather data on a particular concept does not reflect that concept accurately. It is not a valid or reliable question to some degree, and this is the topic of Chapter 5. This does not mean we ignore this propensity, however. Rather, we constantly work to reduce error by studying and defining it. To this end, social scientists have defined distinct types of error; these include nonresponse bias, selection bias, poorly designed survey questions, and data-processing errors. Delineating and addressing each of these types in its own terms allows us to make headway in the constant struggle to reduce error.

Not all measurement error is the same, and the different types of error are dealt with in different ways. The two main causes of error in survey research are *systematic error* and *random error*. **Systematic error**, also known as bias, occurs when the instrument is skewed toward a certain type of measurement or a specific (incomplete) representation of the population under study. Such bias is "systematic" because it affects all of the data collected by the skewed instrument equally.

For example, if the US Census were conducted only in metropolitan areas, there would be a systematic bias in the sampling frame. Any results would be biased in favor of urban residents and against residents of suburban and rural areas. No matter what section of the census you looked at, from population to employment, the error would be present. In another example, if students taking an exam were interrupted by a fire alarm, there would be a systematic downward bias across all of their scores that would make the entire population appear to have been less prepared for the exam than they actually were.

In contrast, **random error** is error that affects results for any single individual (in any direction), but it is expected to balance itself out in large samples. With large sample sizes, random errors average to zero, because some respondents are randomly overestimating and some are randomly underestimating.

Primary Types of Systematic Survey Error

Nonresponse bias occurs when individuals who do not respond, refuse to answer, or are unable to answer specific survey items differ from respondents who *are* able or willing to answer—especially with regard to the attributes being measured. When measuring religiosity, it may be that individuals who refuse to answer certain questions are similar in certain characteristics (less religious, perhaps)—and different from those who do answer (perhaps those who are more religious). The resulting data would underrepresent this important group, and thus would not truly speak to the population it claimed to reflect. In other, more severe instances, entire surveys may go uncompleted and unreturned by members of some significant group, whose data are then never collected. To expand on the previous example, if highly religious individuals were less inclined to return the survey, complete the survey, or answer certain questions, then the data and results would be biased, because the responses of highly religious people would be less likely to be included, and again the results would claim to speak for a group that was not fairly represented in reality.

Questionnaire bias is error created by the questionnaire design. This is usually associated with a confusing layout of the survey and question order, poor wording, or survey content that otherwise confuses or misleads respondents. Questionnaire bias is more likely when the questionnaire is too long or cluttered, but it can occur in any project in which researchers do not take the time to plan, assess, and test their instrument in the various manners described in this text.

Interviewer bias occurs when characteristics of the interviewer (or just the interviewer's presence) can influence the way a respondent answers questions. This bias is also related to poorly trained interviewers (and their ability to conduct an interview, prompt for answers, and record open-ended responses).

Strategies to Minimize Error

Improving Nonresponse Bias: Minimization of this type of error is based on assurance of confidentiality, compensation for participation, calling back or mailing reminders, properly training surveyors and interviewers, and having clearly defined and simple concepts in the survey.

Questionnaire Design Bias: Survey questions should be unambiguous, clear, and free of unnecessary technical language and jargon. They should also be short to avoid respondent fatigue.

Interviewer Bias: The researcher should ensure that interviewers are properly trained and not overworked, to avoid interviewer fatigue. In many cases, it is important to conduct field testing; to train interviewers in proper interviewing techniques, the topic of the survey, the research procedure and scope, and to manage the workload of interviewers carefully.

Environmental Bias: It is important to keep in mind the context in which the survey is administered. Asking respondents to remark on their current health during flu season might lead to a downward bias in responses, since more people are ill during this time.

All in all, measurement error is often difficult to recognize (and measure), but it can be minimized with proper sampling, up-to-date and precise measurement, properly trained interviewers, carefully scheduled survey times and intervals between surveys, and carefully and meticulously planned research design. Refer to the checklist below, which summarizes all of the guidelines presented in this chapter, to help reduce error in your own research projects.

CHECKLIST: SURVEY QUESTION CONSTRUCTION

Early Stages

- ☐ Set concrete research goals.
- ☐ Clearly define your population.
- ☐ Address your own biases and limitations.
- ☐ Review existing survey instruments to inform the questionnaire.
- ☐ Decide on survey length.
- ☐ Construct simply written and well-structured questions.

Development Stages

Questions

- ☐ Are the questions short and worded simply?
- ☐ Are the questions specific and direct?
- ☐ Is only one question posed at a time?
- ☐ Is there any way to rephrase sensitive or private questions?
- ☐ Are specific time references included for questions that require recall?
    - ☐ Longer time periods are fine for important milestones.
    - ☐ Shorter time periods are preferred for items of low importance.

Response Options

- ☐ Given the social context, are these response options relevant?
- ☐ Is an "other" category necessary in order to have comprehensive categories?
- ☐ Are response options mutually exclusive?
- ☐ Are response options weighted appropriately with equal numbers of positive and negative responses?

Overall Survey Design

- ☐ Are sensitive questions in the middle?
- ☐ Are demographic questions at the end?
- ☐ Are all questions and response options absolutely necessary?

KEY TERMS

Variable 44
Single construct 45
Unidimensional concept 45
Simple concept 45
Multidimensional concept 46
Double-barreled question 49

Leading question 51
Item nonresponse 53
Bracketed categories 54
Closed-ended question 56
Multiple-choice question 57
Fixed-choice question 56
Dichotomous question 58
Checklist 58
Rating scale 58
Rank order scale 59
Likert scale 59
Forced-choice question 59
Semantic differential scales 60
Relevant 60
Comprehensive 61
Mutually exclusive 61
Open-ended question 67
Vignette 69
Telescoping error 71
Recall loss 71
Prospective question 72
Retrospective question 71
Back translation 73
Measurement error 74
Systematic error 74
Random error 74
Nonresponse bias 74
Questionnaire bias 75
Interviewer bias 75
Level of measurement 64
Nominal 65
Ordinal 65
Interval 66
Ratio 66

CRITICAL THINKING QUESTIONS

Below you will find three questions that ask you to think critically about core concepts addressed in this chapter. Be sure you understand each one; if you don't, this is a good time to review the relevant sections of this chapter.

1. In addition to religiosity, what is another multidimensional concept used in the social sciences? Identify the different dimensions of this concept and how you might measure them in a survey.

2. How might a double-barreled question influence the measurement error of a survey?

3. Identify the rationale for and steps involved in back translation. How might this be an effective safeguard against measurement error in multilingual survey designs?

4. Discuss the ways you might measure (a) family size, (b) age, and (c) income at the nominal, ordinal, and interval/ratio level.

5

The Quality of Measurement

Reliability and Validity

INTRODUCTION

Once the outline of a survey instrument has been developed and specific questions are in place, the next step is to validate the instrument and its measurements. This is arguably a more complex task in the social and behavioral sciences than in many of the biological and physical sciences, as social science concepts are often abstract, intangible, or otherwise not easily observed.

Nevertheless, in order for survey research measurements to be accurate, they must be precise and stable. Validity and reliability are closely related research concepts. **Validity** asks, "Is this measurement truly representative of the concept under study?" **Reliability** asks "If we repeat this measurement multiple times, will we obtain consistent results?" Both are necessary in order to classify a measurement as being sound, accurate, relevant, and free of bias. However, they are not all-or-nothing concepts; rather, they comprise a spectrum from low to high, and it is in fact rare that any item on a survey is 100% valid and reliable. We still strive to approach this goal, though, and it is to this end we offer the guidelines in the following pages. This chapter discusses first the concept of reliability, types and assessments of reliability, and threats to reliability from various sources of error. We then move on to a similarly organized discussion of validity, including concepts, types, and threats. As in previous chapters, there are several examples and checklists included to help illustrate concepts and prepare you for your own research projects.

Concerns over reliability and validity are really concerns about **error:** Any strategy that decreases measurement error will improve both the reliability and validity of the measure. As discussed in Chapter 4, the two main causes of measurement error in survey research are systematic error and random error. To review, systematic error occurs when *all* of the data from a question are biased in a "systematic" or pervasive fashion, typically due to some underlying flaw in the research design that colors all of the data collected. Systematic errors thus affect the validity of a measurement, because they cast doubt on whether the data collected are a true reflection of the phenomenon you wish to describe. Random error is error that affects the results for any *single* individual from whom you collect data, but which is expected to "balance out" in large samples when all individual variations are aggregated together. Random errors affect the reliability of a measurement, because they cast doubt on whether the instrument performs consistently when measuring different individuals or measuring across time. Careful examination of survey measurements' validity and reliability thus helps considerably to reduce these types of measurement error.

RELIABILITY

In order to be reliable, a measurement must be dependable, replicable, and consistent. In other words, the measurement must minimize random error. Random error occurs in two ways: (1) when an individual randomly guesses a response, perhaps because the question is poorly worded or has misleading directions, and (2) when an individual accidentally chooses a response unintentionally. In both cases, the response given is not reflective of a "true" value; it is not an accurate response, and the response might change from measure to measure. This often occurs with survey items that respondents know very little about. For example, if researchers are trying to determine how an individual feels about age discrimination in the workplace, they might ask this question:

1a. How much do you agree or disagree with the U.S. Supreme Court's 2013 ruling on Madigan v. Levin?

1) Strongly agree

2) Somewhat agree

3) Somewhat disagree

4) Strongly disagree

This question will probably suffer low reliability, since very few people will know much about Madigan v. Levin. Therefore, a question of this nature may be prone to a guessed response (which means it is not a very reliable measure). One solution would be to include a "don't know" response. This might improve reliability, but the researchers would still not know what the population under study feels about age discrimination in the workplace. This is a similar question that may result in less random error (and higher reliability):

1b. Please tell us how much you agree or disagree with the statement: An employer has the right to terminate employment based on an individual's age?

1) Strongly agree

2) Somewhat agree

3) Somewhat disagree

4) Strongly disagree

This question is likely to be a more reliable question, because it does not assume that an individual has knowledge about a specific legal case, and many people have opinions on workplace discrimination. Individuals will thus be less likely to randomly guess, so we may count on a more consistent response to this question. Furthermore, improving reliability might also improve validity—again, these are closely related concepts. When a measurement is unreliable, it is also invalid, since a measurement cannot be precise if the responses are inconsistent. The presence of reliability thus does not ensure measurement validity, but a lack of reliability certainly does decrease the validity of a measure.

Correlation

Before discussing the different types of reliability, it is important to cover the concept of a correlation coefficient. A **correlation coefficient** is a quantified summary of the linear relationship between two continuous variables—that is, how closely changes in one variable are mirrored by changes in another (Warner 2009). This figure is the most common way of measuring the strength and direction of a correlation between two variables, two testing instruments, or two data coders. Correlation coefficients range between -1 and 1, with -1 reflecting a perfect negative correlation between two variables (as one increases, the other always decreases, and vice versa), and 1 reflecting a perfect positive correlation (as one increases or decreases, so the other increases or decreases too), and 0 reflecting no correlation whatsoever (or no pattern linking changes in variables). Various statistical software packages will help produce correlation coefficients once your data (or pilot test results) have been collected. Although there are no general conventions regarding what constitutes an acceptably small, medium, or large correlation, the values in Box 5.1 should be a rule of thumb.

BOX 5.1

Suggested Correlation Coefficient Interpretation

	XY		XY
+1.0 → perfect positive linear relationship:	↑↑	or	↓↓
0.8 to 1.0 → strong positive linear relationship:	↑↑	or	↓↓
0.4 to 0.7 → moderate positive linear relationship:	↑↑	or	↓↓
0.1 to 0.3 → weak positive linear relationship:	↑↑	or	↓↓
0 → no linear relationship	↑-	or	↓-
–0.1 to -0.3 → weak negative linear relationship:	↑↓	or	↓↑
–0.4 to -0.7 → moderate negative linear relationship:	↑↓	or	↓↑
–0.8 to -1.0 → strong positive linear relationship:	↑↓	or	↓↑
–1.0 → perfect negative linear relationship:	↑↓	or	↓↑

Most assessments of the reliability of measures utilize this correlation coefficient. We turn now to these different types of assessments in the space below.

Types of Reliability and Estimation

Test–Retest Reliability

Test–retest reliability is an estimation of a measurement's reliability based on the consistency of results after repeated administration (Rousson, Gasser, and Seifert 2002). The responses from Measures 1 and 2 are correlated to estimate the stability of the measure over the two time points. A well-crafted, reliable question should elicit a similar response from one asking to the next, and thus the answers given should be highly correlated.

For example, assume a respondent is asked, "How many individuals live in your household?" at two different time points (with the second point coming a week or so after the first). The coefficient measuring the correlation between the two answers (Measure 1 and Measure 2) will indicate the level of consistency between the scores. Thus, a high correlation between the two items indicates that they are consistent over repeated administrations. Consider the example below, which compares two ways of measuring a similar concept that have varying prospects for reliability.

Test–Retest Option 1:

1. How many times have you attended religious services in your entire life? ______ (T1/T2)

Using this measurement for religiosity at two points in time will likely produce low reliability, given that the question is assessing religious service attendance over the course of an individual's entire life—a very long and difficult time span to consider. This may lead to loose estimation based on recall, which may well vary from one asking to the next, not to mention that as time passes the true answer will change for religious individuals. A better question might be this:

Test–Retest Option 2:

1. In the previous month, how many times have you attended religious services? (T1/T2)

   1) 0

   2) 1–2

   3) 3–4

   4) 5 or more

By recasting the question to cover a much shorter, more finite, and more recent time period, this question makes a much more reasonable demand on respondents' recall. This will likely elicit a very similar answer from test to retest, which means that responses will achieve a higher correlation coefficient, and that the question is thus higher in reliability than the previous example.

The examples above raise another issue worth noting: It is important to measure test–retest reliability over a short period of time when those measurements are unlikely to change between the time of the initial test and the time of the retest. (In contrast, measures of happiness, financial stability, or self-report of physical health all may fluctuate over time.) In the above example, an individual might attend a religious service or two between the initial test and the retest. In this case, the respondent's retest response would be justifiably different, reflecting a true change in attendance; but the reliability coefficient would suffer, exhibiting a downward bias.

Alternate Form Reliability

Alternate form reliability refers to consistency between two different versions of a measure that is probing the same construct—often with just slightly different wording (DeVellis 2011). Consider this example:

1a. In the previous month, how many times have you attended religious services?

1) 0

2) 1–2

3) 3–4

4) 5 or more

1b. How many times in the last four weeks have you attended religious services?

1) More than once per week

2) Once per week

3) Every two to three weeks

4) Never

The above items are not identical, but they are similar enough that responses should achieve a high correlation coefficient (and thus high reliability). Note that while the question must vary somewhat across versions, it is important that you are measuring the same behaviors and referencing the same concepts, and that the level of difficulty is the same from question to question. (Think of the difficulty of recalling a lifetime versus a month, as in the earlier example.) All that changes from a question to its next version should be the order of words and response options, or inconsequential terminology—words that are truly synonymous. If there is only one word or phrase to describe a concept, then you cannot vary this word or phrase in the next version without changing the meaning of the question. For example, it would not make sense to have an alternate form of the above question ask, "In the last month, how many times have you attended *church?*" because church is only one type of religious service. This question is conceptually different from the alternate, and thus we should not expect correlated, reliable responses.

Internal Consistency Reliability

Internal consistency is a measure of reliability used to estimate the degree to which different items probing the same construct produce similar results. The responses to both versions can be compared and correlated to assess the consistency between the alternate versions. While similar to the alternate form reliability detailed above, internal consistency measures take more complex forms, primarily these two:

Split-Test (Split-Half) Reliability. In assessing **split-test** or **split-half** reliability (DeVellis 2011), all items in a survey that probe the same construct are grouped and then split into two sets of equivalent items. The entire test is then administered to a group of respondents, and an aggregate score for each "half" group of questions is calculated. The scores from each set of "halves" are then compared to assess the correlation between them, which should be high among questions reliably measuring the same concept.

Average Internal Consistency Correlation (Interitem Correlation). With **interitem** correlation, a researcher arranges all of the items on a test that measure the same construct (e.g., all questions measuring "religiosity") into pairs, and then determines the correlation coefficient for each of the item-pairs in the test. These correlations are then averaged to produce the **average internal consistency** of the instrument.

For example, the items below would be good candidates for a test of interitem correlation, as they all measure the religiosity of the respondent:

1. I consider myself to be
   1) Not very religious
   2) Somewhat religious
   3) Very religious
2. I attend religious services
   1) Not very often
   2) Somewhat often
   3) Very often
3. I read religious texts
   1) Not very often
   2) Somewhat often
   3) Very often
4. I pray
   1) Frequently
   2) Somewhat frequently
   3) Infrequently

Internal consistency correlation asks, "How well do all of the items on a religiosity scale correspond with each other?" The measure is thus not related to a single item but rather assesses how a whole group of conceptually similar questions hang together. This is done through calculation of **Cronbach's alpha** coefficient—a statistical summary measure of the consistency of the data collected across multiple items that form a complementary scale (Cronbach 1951). Much like the correlation coefficient, Cronbach's alpha can be effortlessly computed using statistical software. If reliability across the measurements is low, it is then possible to add or remove items and recalculate the coefficient in order to increase internal consistency across items. While there are no hard and fast rules regarding interpretation of Cronbach's alpha, it is generally agreed that an interpretation similar to that of the correlation coefficient (as previously described; see page 80). As can be seen in Table 5.1, Cronbach's alpha is .76 and can be interpreted as 76% of the variation among the 6 items is shared or consistent across the items. It is conventional to report these values when discussing research methods and design so that readers and other researchers can feel comfortable about your claim to have measured a complex and potentially abstract concept.

Table 5.1 Correlation Matrix and Cronbach's Alpha

	Item 1	**Item 2**	**Item 3**	**Item 4**	**Item 5**	**Item 6**
Item 1	1.00					
Item 2	.75	1.00				
Item 3	.88	.76	1.00			
Item 4	.73	.88	.45	1.00		
Item 5	.89	.93	.29	.88	1.00	
Item 6	.34	.91	.88	.98	.87	1.00
	Average Correlation = .76					

Interrater Reliability

Interrater reliability is the degree of consistency with which two researchers interpret the same data (DeVellis 2005). For survey research, interrater reliability is important when considering and coding (assigning numerical values to) qualitative responses to open-ended questions, because raters may not interpret the same response the same way. To assess this form of reliability, you would look not at two or more different *items* on the survey or surveys, but rather at the same item as coded by two or more *different researchers*. A high correlation between researchers' codes would thus evidence a reliable question—that is, one that may be reliably coded without subjective (mis)interpretations by different researchers.

For example, researchers probing respondents' level of religiosity might ask them to "discuss how religious you are" and then convert the response to a score or category along a scale, such as one that ranged from "very religious" to "not religious." This question is a poor measure of religiosity, as it is rather vague and is likely to elicit a wide range of responses based on respondents' varying interpretations of the concept "religious." A respondent might write, "Religion is important to me"—an imprecise answer to an imprecise question. One researcher might code this sentiment as being "very religious," while another codes it as "somewhat religious." The value of the data is effectively "lost in translation." But if interrater reliability is subsequently assessed and found lacking, steps could be taken to improve it, either by rephrasing the question to elicit greater precision in responses or by training the coders to use a more consistent, standardized rubric for interpreting answers.

A similar assessment known as **intrarater reliability** refers to the consistency of a single researcher's coding of the same item or subject across different occasions but under identical conditions. Similar to test–retest reliability, this method assesses the degree to which a researcher can apply the same coding strategy multiple times, interpreting the same data the same way from one test to the next. As in the example above, reliability here can be improved both by rephrasing questions to elicit greater precision and also by training coders to improve their consistency or by improving the coding rubric to provide better guidance and less room for interpretation and error.

Improving Reliability

In order to have a reliable measurement, surveys should have similar standards of judgment, unbiased measurements, and assess relevant (and when possible, recent) phenomena. Clearly written surveys that avoid ambiguous language in questions and response options are much more reliable sources of data than less carefully constructed instruments, so take great care to craft items that will be easy to understand for all of your potential respondents.

In addition to clarity, brevity (once again!) is a great virtue. Not only the language, but the mere number of possible response options can strongly influence how an individual is going to respond at a given time—and whether or not the response will differ the next time. Meaningful response options are important, because the presence of unnecessary possibilities invites unnecessary flexibility and minimizes consistency. Consider the following example, which compares a question with few response options to another version with many response options and to a third version with open-ended questions with unlimited response options. The question with the fewest response options will have the more reliability, given it requires less concentration and memory.

1a. How many times have you attended religious services in the past year? _______

1b. How many times have you attended religious services in the past year?

1) 0
2) 1–3
3) 4–6
4) 7–10
5) 10–12
6) 13 or more

1c. How many times have you attended religious services in the past year?

1) 0
2) 1–3
3) 4–5
4) 6 or more

Version 1c is clearly the best one. By sacrificing a modicum of precision, you have saved the respondent a great deal of burden, requiring much less concentration and memory to complete this item and move on quickly to the next. However, it should be noted that on attitudinal questions, providing more response options has been found to result in more reliable responses (Alwin and Krosnick 1991). In addition, Alwin and Krosnick found that a greater verbal labeling of response options was also associated with higher reliability. That is, increasing the amount of description tied to each response improves reliability.

As noted above, improving inter- and intrarater reliability can likewise involve the rephrasing of a question in a more clear and brief format; however, the problem here may not lie between the respondent and the question, but between the response and the rater. Taking the time to produce a detailed and comprehensive codebook and coding rubric, as well as training coders to use it properly, are essential steps to ensure reliable data interpretation across open-ended responses. It is a mistake to assume that subjective misinterpretation and error can occur only among respondents; researchers can introduce sources of error as well.

Establishing the reliability of a survey instrument is an essential part of survey research. Just as you would not trust the reading from a scale that says you weigh 200 pounds at first try, then 160 pounds a moment later, you likewise will have little use for the dubious data collected by an unreliable survey questionnaire.

Of course, there is more to quality measurement than merely getting the same data on a consistent basis: We also want this consistent data to be the *right* data—that which truly reflects the concepts and phenomena we set out to study. This concern is what we mean when we talk about validity in social science research, the topic to which we turn now.

VALIDITY

Valid research is that which accurately reflects the real world phenomena it is intended to describe (and sometimes, to explain) (deVellis 2011). If we think carefully about this, there are actually several dimensions behind this ostensibly simple concept. First, perhaps most obviously, we must be sure we are measuring what we think we are—those characteristics, attitudes, opinions, and beliefs we intend to summarize and discuss later on. But we also need to make sure that those items we have measured are the ones that are truly important for our research goals—that the specifics we have measured really do fit the bigger picture we are describing. And finally, even if we have good measurements on all the right topics, we must be sure we have measured the right people—that our small group of respondents really does represent the larger world we want to know about. Each of these tasks carries its own distinct challenges.

Accordingly, there are three different types of validity we may talk about in survey research design: measurement validity, internal validity, and external validity. **Measurement validity** describes researchers' confidence that a measure operates the way they expect. **Internal validity** refers to researchers' claims that the data they have measured reveal a causal process at work. **External validity** refers to the representativeness, or generalizability of research findings, linking the patterns and relationships found in a limited sample to a larger social world. All three types are absolutely essential in survey research, because they assure researchers that they are, in fact, studying what they claim to be studying.

Measurement Validity

Measurement validity refers to the extent that a survey item (or group of items) elicits an accurate description of its target concept (DeVellis 2011). This requires first a clear definition of the target concept, one that suggests some appropriate dimensions that we can measure with our survey questions.

For example, if a survey of students at a university claims to measure "school spirit," the survey should be based on a clear definition of this concept, something like, "the extent to which students exhibit a positive emotional connection with their university." Such a definition would lead researchers to think about how students display positive feelings of attachment, so researchers might ask students whether they participate in school activities, wear university apparel, and attend sporting events. On the other hand, researchers would *not* ask about how many classes students are taking—one's course schedule has little to do with school spirit as positive emotional connection. (Part-time students exhibit spirit, too, and not all full-timers are emotionally invested.)

Naturally, assessing the validity of some measures is easier than others. For example, when you ask someone's age, the response is usually quite accurate. It is unlikely that individuals will forget their age or need to guess their own age, or that multiple measures will be needed to assess it. Questions about age are usually answered in a way that really does tell you about someone's age—these questions are thus high in validity.

On the other hand, measuring complex concepts like "social class" entails much greater risks for validity. Class is not something directly observable, and for this reason many people might not even be aware of their true class position. Because class is a concept that includes a number of different characteristics (e.g., income, occupational prestige, education), a measure of social class risks lower validity if it cannot incorporate all of these relevant dimensions. This is why researchers are concerned about *what is* and *what is not* being measured and *how accurately* a measurement is made. If measurements are not valid, researchers may not be studying what they actually set out to study and may instead be measuring some other concept altogether.

Types of Measurement Validity

There are multiple ways to assess measurement validity. In survey research, four principal types of measurement validity are sought: face validity, content validity, criterion-based validity, and construct validity (Babbie 2013).

Face Validity

Face validity means simply that the measure appears to be a reasonable way to estimate the targeted construct—that it looks good at face value (Nunnally and Bernstein 1994). Of course, this is far from proof positive of a measure's validity, and for this reason face validity is regarded as a rather weak, superficial, and subjective assessment of a measure's accuracy, little more than a first step in assessing measurement validity.

However, attention to face validity does sometimes have its uses. For example, when a given measure is subject to interviewer bias and social desirability, a question purposely selected for its *low* face value may actually *increase* the overall measurement validity of the item. That is, in situations where respondents are likely to tailor their responses about a sensitive or controversial topic, this tendency may be minimized if the question does not appear to be about such topics at face value.

For example, consider a survey designed to measure "acceptance of homosexuality." The following measure of attitudes toward homosexuality has face validity, as the measure *appears* to tap into an individual's feelings about homosexuals:

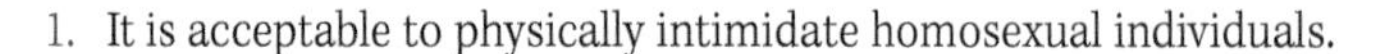

1. It is acceptable to physically intimidate homosexual individuals.

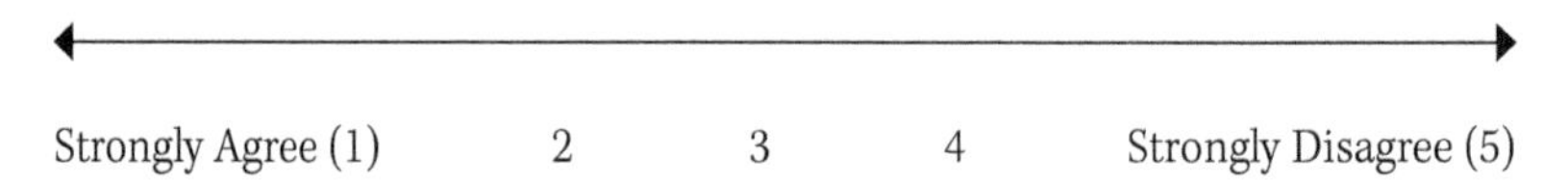

Even respondents who have negative attitudes toward homosexuals would be unlikely to voice the unpopular opinion that physically threatening them is okay (especially in a face-to-face interview). For this reason, while we would agree that this question is high in face validity, it may not be the best measure of attitudes toward homosexuality. A question *lower* in face validity might elicit a more honest and valid response, even though at face value it is less obvious:

1. I would disown a member of my immediate family if she or he identified as a homosexual.

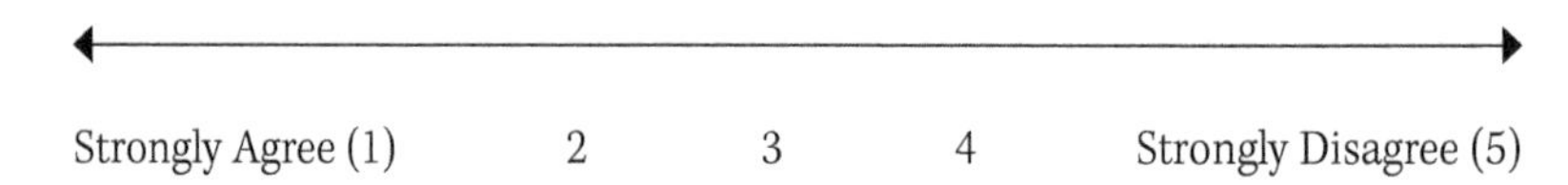

On the other hand, certain measures that have low face validity may simply be inadequate measures of a construct:

1. I think that a person chooses to be homosexual.

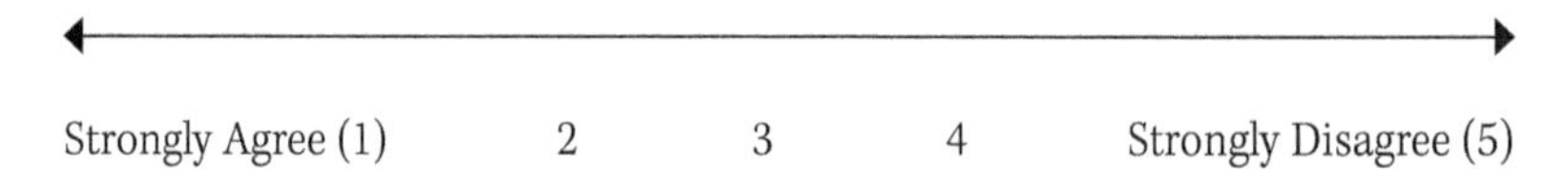

In reality, agreement or disagreement that homosexuality is a choice has little to do with one's *acceptance of homosexuality*, which after all was the point of the survey. An individual who believes that a person chooses to be homosexual may be more or less accepting of homosexuals. This question does not pass the face validity "litmus test" and would be considered a poorly calibrated measure of attitudes toward homosexuality.

Content Validity

Content validity refers to the comprehensiveness, relevance, and representativeness of the measurement. This consideration is especially salient when dealing with complex, multidimensional concepts (such as social class, referenced earlier in this chapter), which by definition encapsulate a wide breadth of particular items, all of which must be included in a valid measure. Survey researchers often engage panels of experts on a given topic to assess the content validity of their measures of complex constructs.

For example, a survey researcher might refer to sociologists to list the conditions necessary to measure social class, and then include each of these as (partial) indicators of social class in the survey. This is because sociologists are expert in the field and are able to comprehensively define the concept, which is needed to ensure content validity (DeVellis 2011). In order to be high in content validity, the survey must contain items assessing all the known specifications of social class—the *content* of the measure must be associated with the *content* being studied.

For a further example, consider the following questions aimed at assessing "religiosity," a multidimensional concept (previously referenced in Chapter 4) incorporating several elements related to religious beliefs and practice. A researcher might be tempted to approach this concept from one single, easily-observed dimension, such as the following:

1. How many times per month do you attend religious services?

    1) 0

    2) 1–3

    3) 4–5

    4) 6 or more

While this measure is high in face validity (it appears to be measuring how religious an individual is), it is low in content validity, because it is tapping into only one dimension of religiosity (the *behavioral* dimension). An individual might be very religious while not necessarily engaging in the behavioral aspects of organized religion (e.g., attending services). An expert would be quick to declare that this measure of religiosity is missing an attitudinal measure (e.g., feeling that religion is important in life). Figure 5.1 lists some of the measures that can get at several of the dimensions of the concept religiosity.

Face and content validity are the most common assessments of validity in survey research methods, in part because they are the easiest to establish. However, these tests are really only the first steps in assessing a measurement's precision; they examine whether the item is an adequate reflection of a concept but stop short of describing the actual mechanics of measurement. Building on these, the more complex concepts of criterion-based validity and construct validity focus on whether the measurement operates the way it is expected to, as informed by theory and by other established measures.

Criterion-Based Validity

Criterion-based validity refers to a measurement's agreement with or empirical association with some criterion that is considered the "gold standard" for measuring that particular concept (DeVellis 2011). For example, if we are interested in

Figure 5.1 Multiple Items that Cover the Content of Religiosity

	Strongly Agree	*Agree*	*Neutral*	*Disagree*	*Strongly Disagree*
Religion is important in my life... *(attitudinal)*	1	2	3	4	5
I regularly attend religious services... *(behavioral)*	1	2	3	4	5
I feel connected to a higher power *(spiritual)*	1	2	3	4	5
Religion is the one true path to eternal live... *(attitudinal)*	1	2	3	4	5
I frequently read religious literature... *(behavioral)*	1	2	3	4	5
I believe that religion is sacred... *(spiritual)*	1	2	3	4	5

validating a self-report of whether or not participants use condoms regularly, what might be a gold standard criterion that could predict the self-reports of participants? Perhaps we could ask participants to show us condoms that they may be carrying in their pockets, purses, or backpacks. This may not validate the self-reports of monogamous participants who use condoms regularly but keep their condoms at home. This type of criterion validity is known as concurrent validity, because the criterion and self-reports take place at the same time. Another form of criterion validity is called predictive validity; in this form, the new measure and the criterion take place at different times.

Concurrent Validity. A measure is said to have **concurrent validity** when its resulting data correlate with results from other theoretically relevant measures that are also in the survey. The researcher thus assesses the extent to which a given measurement accurately estimates some other concurrently measured criterion. For example, researchers studying school-related behaviors might have reason to believe that participation in school activities is related to school spirit. They would then compare their measurement of school spirit to a measure of participation in school activities at the same point in time. If the two are, in fact, correlated, they will have established the concurrent validity of their measures.

Predictive Validity. **Predictive validity** is based on whether or not a measure predicts future values of some theoretically relevant preestablished criterion. Predictive validity differs from concurrent validity because it is not established by comparing measures developed in the same survey instrument. Instead, the criterion for comparison in predictive validity is a similar construct (e.g., behavior, attitude, performance) measured at some point in the future (relative to the original study). For instance, if researchers have reason to believe that school spirit is closely associated with GPA at graduation, they will measure school spirit (and its various dimensions) at one point in time, and then correlate the measure with student GPA at the time the participants graduate. In this case, GPA is the criterion, and school spirit is the predictor; if the two are related, the researchers have empirically established predictive validity for their measure of school spirit.

One common example of predictive validity is the SAT. The reason most colleges require applicants to report their SAT scores is that the SAT has established its predictive validity relative to later measures of students' grade point averages in their first year of college (Kobrin et al. 2008). Because the SAT has such predictive validity, universities require SAT scores so that they can estimate a potential student's future performance (and base their admissions decision partly on this score).

Construct Validity. Construct validity is the soundest but also the most rigorous measure of validity. The term *construct* may seem misleading, since it has little to do with how a measure is *constructed,* per se. Rather, **construct validity** is demonstrated when the instrument is truly measuring the *construct* it was designed to measure, and not some other construct. In order to assess whether the measure has construct validity, we turn to theory and use it to hypothesize the varied ways our new measure should be associated with other variables (DeVellis 2011). If the new measure is associated with these other variables as theory suggests, then our measure has construct validity. In order to establish construct validity, a measurement must have convergent validity and discriminant validity.

Convergent Validity. **Convergent validity** is established when two or more measures in the same study that are designed to describe the same complex construct are in fact correlated with each other. This is similar to the aforementioned concept of concurrent validity, as both types are established by correlating different measures within the same survey instrument. However, convergent validity differs in that the correlated variables are not thought to have a causal relationship with each other (as they do in concurrent validity), but rather are assumed to be correlated because they are attempting to measure the same underlying construct, albeit from distinct, but *converging,* angles (DeVellis 2011). Recall that this is necessary because the construct targeted by these measures is something that exists only in the abstract and thus cannot be directly observed or measured.

Let us return to our earlier example in which researchers wanted to measure "school spirit." This is an abstract concept with no established metric, so questions must approach it indirectly, focusing on attending events, wearing branded clothing, et cetera.

The measurement is not precisely measuring school spirit, per se, because all of these indicators exist outside of it, but are all assumed to approach it from their respective various angles. If this assumption is true, then they should all be highly correlated, as they will all vary according to the underlying abstract construct of school spirit. Furthermore, convergent validation requires evidence that the instrument is measuring school spirit as opposed to "overall happiness" or some other related concept (despite the positive association between these concepts). This is often done by comparing correlations between "school spirit" measures and other potentially confounding variables.

Discriminant Validity. In contrast to convergent validity, **discriminant validity** is established when a measurement is *not* correlated with constructs to which it is assumed to be dissimilar—also known as divergent validity (DeVellis 2011). For example, "school spirit" is theoretically antithetical to "school apathy," so a measure of school spirit should be negatively correlated with measures of school indifference. By the same token, school spirit should have little or no correlation with theoretically irrelevant measures, such as number of classes being taken.

Convergent and discriminant validity thus establish that measures fit the appropriate and expected patterns of relationships with other constructs. Construct validity thus provides important evidence that a measure will be successful in the real world, which is the basis of all validity in the social sciences.

Improving Measurement Validity

Assessment of a measure's validity is not an all-or-nothing test. Because social science deals with very many unobservable and abstract concepts, some measures are bound to have more validity than others. Although validating research instruments is challenging, it is an absolutely necessary endeavor in the production of trustworthy social science research.

Researchers never attempt to "prove" that a measurement is valid in a philosophical, universalistic sense. Rather, they strive to demonstrate the *effectiveness* of each of the measures in the study. Toward this end, it is important to note any measurement limitations after data collection, and to discuss how they may influence the research results. Keep the following points in mind when assessing measurement validity:

Face Validity:

- ☐ Does the measurement appear to intuitively measure the construct?
- ☐ Are there any obvious errors in the measurement?
- ☐ Would the question be better posed with less face validity (e.g., in order to avoid interviewer bias or social desirability)?

Content Validity:

- ☐ Are all components of the construct being measured?
- ☐ Is each component necessary, relevant, and representative of the concept?
- ☐ Do the components together compose the comprehensive range for the concept?
- ☐ Have experts agreed that this is an adequate and precise measurement?

Criterion-Based Validity:

- ☐ Is the measurement correlated with similar constructs in the survey?
- ☐ Can the measure accurately predict future attitudes or behaviors?

Construct Validity:

- ☐ Is the measurement positively related to similar constructs?
- ☐ Is the measurement negatively related to different constructs?
- ☐ Is the measurement only minimally (or not at all) correlated with unrelated constructs?

Internal Validity

Internal validity refers to how well a researcher's survey design is testing the true relationship between the independent variable and dependent variable (Chambliss and Schutt 2013). Often, survey researchers are looking to establish a causal relationship between the two (i.e., the independent variable causes a change in the dependent variable or X → Y). Internal validity is established when a researcher has provided sound arguments, adequate statistical controls, and rigorous research design to establish a causal relationship between two correlated variables.

External Validity

External validity is the extent to which research findings can be generalized to other populations, environments, times, and settings (Flick 2011). In practical terms, external validity is associated with where else the results of a study can be applied. Do the findings of the research also hold *outside* the study (i.e., external to it)? There are three potential threats to a survey's external validity; these are based on the nongeneralizability of the population, the situation, or the time frame under study. These threats are each elaborated in the illustrative examples that follow.

Nongeneralizable Population

Research on close adult friendships conducted among college students may not necessarily be generalizable to a more general population of adults. When asking college students about their close friendships, a researcher must note that they are mostly a given age, are mostly unmarried, and may have more liberal ideas about cross-gender friendships than members of a wider population. Data collected on this sample population are not representative of the rest of the United States, which has a significantly larger dispersion of ages and marital statuses. Even when asking about something very specific to college students, such as student loan debt, establishing external validity is problematic, because results may differ depending on the type of college students being studied. (For example, a private university known to charge significantly higher tuition may have students with higher student loan debt.) This study will have limited external validity based on the population under study.

Nongeneralizable Situation

Imagine a study that examines how parents discipline their children. If a survey incorporates a vignette about disciplining a hyperactive child and then probes the responses of 40 suburban mothers, it will have limited external validity based on a nongeneralizable situation. This is because these researchers are studying only how parents discipline their children if the children are hyperactive; they are not studying child discipline in any other, more general context. In addition, as only *suburban mothers* are studied (to the exclusion of urban mothers and urban and suburban fathers), the researchers have targeted a nongeneralizable population, and so the results of the study cannot be presented as a reflection of all attitudes toward parental discipline.

Nongeneralizable Time

A study can be representative of a wide population and broad range of situations but still have limited external validity with regard to time. If research was conducted on perceptions of homosexuality using data from the 1980s, there would be limited generalizability to populations in the 2010s, given how much social change has occurred over the past 30 years, especially related to this topic. For another example, research conducted on job satisfaction during the recent Great Recession may not yield results generalizable to the US population even a few years later, once economic circumstances improved. Researchers must thus always think about the broader historical contexts that bracket, and potentially color, their results.

It is thus important to assess external validity across groups of people, varying situations, and significant periods of time. Be cautious about sampling from a larger population and about framing your research and findings properly to ensure that the claims being made are generalizable to the real world external to the study.

Remember also that assessments of validity are not necessarily correlated—research findings (and research generally) may have sound measurement validity but enjoy only limited external validity. In other words, a measurement may be adequate to measure a certain, specific social reality, but the conclusions drawn may not be generalizable to other groups. However, if the concepts are not being adequately measured (i.e., if the survey has poor measurement validity), then findings cannot possibly be generalized to a larger population.

Of course, no study enjoys complete external validity—beyond some boundary, all findings become obsolete. But identifying the precise limits of external validity is important to know that the results obtained are at least more-or-less representative of some larger population. In this sense, external validity depends largely upon sampling procedures, which will be discussed in greater detail later, in Chapter 7.

Other Validity Issues

Cross-Comparative Research

Problems with measurement validity arise when researchers try to compare the results of two samples that were not measured with similar instruments. Therefore, when conducting cross-comparative research, it is important to cross-validate the multilingual and multicultural survey instruments (Bernard 1988). As mentioned in the previous chapter, translation is a complex process that requires skilled professionals and entirely separate pretesting. (For more on pretesting, see Chapter 6.) In order to be high in validity and reliability, cross-comparative surveys must have semantic, cultural, and conceptual equivalence. This means that the words and concepts in each survey need to be culturally and linguistically comparable. Otherwise, every respondent will not be interpreting the concepts *in the exact same way*, and results will lose precision and validity. Methods for developing comparable cross-comparative surveys are discussed in Chapter 4.

Validity and Measurement Type

Question format (open-ended vs. closed-ended) also has consequences for the validity and reliability of a measurement (Reja, et al. 2003). In short, there is greater reliability when using closed-ended questions (as respondents must align their thoughts with a predefined answer choice) and greater validity when asking open-ended questions (as respondents are free to express exactly the response they have in mind).

Because closed-ended questions suggest responses to individuals, they tend to have greater consistency over time. Of course, the reliability and validity of closed-ended questions ultimately depends on the comprehensiveness of the response categories provided (see Chapter 4). On the other hand, open-ended questions allow the respondent to express opinions, thoughts, and behaviors in their own words, often providing more detail than is garnered from closed-ended questions; therefore, open-ended questions have higher validity because they are usually more accurately measuring a concept. Ultimately, the reliability and validity of open-ended questions depends on whether or not the questions are interpreted in the way the researcher intends.

CONCLUSION

Validity and reliability must be considered in tandem but also as distinct elements in research design. Both are crucial elements guiding the production of accurate and meaningful research. But a test that is reliable is not necessarily a valid one. Researchers might reliably obtain a similar answer each time they ask a respondent about the number of drinks the respondent has had in a week, but said reliable data would not achieve much validity in measuring, say, the respondent's overall degree of religiosity. And even results with apparent validity on some levels might belie an unreliable instrument, as illustrated in the Figure 5.2

Figure 5.2 Target Diagram for Validity and Reliability

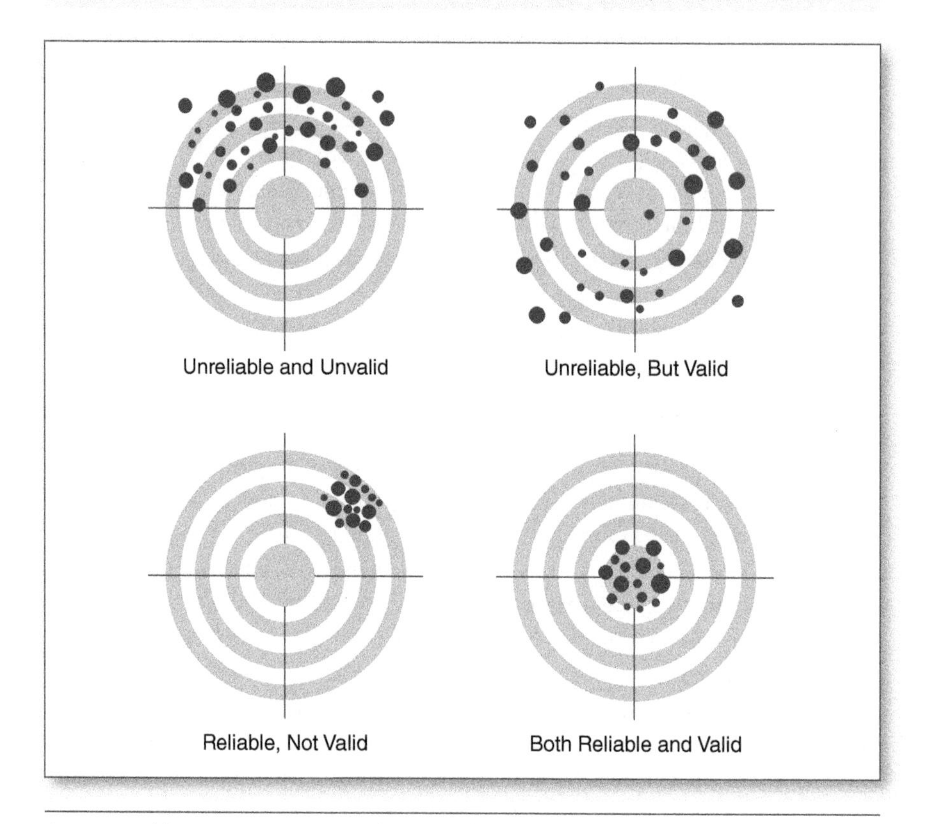

Source: Babbie 2014; © Nevit Dilmen, Wikimedia Commons.

Meaningful research is thus high in both measurement validity and reliability. Without measurement validity, the findings have no real meaning, and without reliability, the answers are inconsistent and undependable.

The guidelines laid out in this chapter should help you to address the many issues in reliability and validity that quality research must take into consideration. But in actuality, every chapter of this book has advice that will further this goal, because the pursuit of precision pervades every aspect of research design. From the very outset of the process, outline your research goals and expectations, clearly defining the constructs you seek to describe and carefully weighing all of your options to measure them. Use scales to combine related items into scores that can help strengthen your measurement of complex concepts. Looking back to Chapter 4, triangulating results across the multiple types of measurement we have discussed helps to overcome the biases inherent in each individual research strategy. Looking ahead to Chapter 6, pretesting and pilot testing a survey is one of the most important ways to establish and increase reliability and validity. All of these elements and more make a distinct contribution to the quality of your research, together producing more scientifically accurate, sound, and cross-validated research findings that make a meaningful contribution to the social-scientific study of our world.

KEY TERMS

CRITICAL THINKING QUESTIONS

Below you will find three questions that ask you to think critically about core concepts addressed in this chapter. Be sure you understand each one; if you do not, this is a good time to review the relevant sections of this chapter.

1. How might open-ended and closed-ended survey questions differ in the reliability and validity in the data they yield?

2. What are the primary differences between internal validity and external validity? Can a measurement have both types of validity?

3. Provide an example of a social science survey measurement that is

   a. High in reliability but low in validity.

   b. High in validity but low in reliability.

6

Pretesting and Pilot Testing

INTRODUCTION

In this chapter, we detail the possibilities and pitfalls presented by **pretesting**, the methods of validating the survey instrument and its measurements, and **pilot testing**, the "dress rehearsal" of survey administration and procedures (Rothgeb 2008, 584). Pretesting and pilot testing are invaluable components of survey research, affording researchers a valuable opportunity for reflection and revision of their project before the costs of errors begin to multiply later on. We begin this chapter with a discussion of the goals of and guidelines for pretesting followed by a summary checklist to help you make the most of this procedure. Then we provide an elaboration of the broader process of pilot testing the entire project from start to finish. If you pay close attention to the issues outlined in this chapter, pretesting and pilot testing could lead you to that early "stitch in time" that saves countless dollars and hours later on down the road.

PRETESTING

Once you have a complete draft of your survey, a pretest is a necessary next component of the research process. Pretesting your survey is an important way to pinpoint problem areas, reduce measurement error, reduce respondent burden, determine whether or not respondents are interpreting questions correctly, and ensure that the order of questions is not influencing the way a respondent answers. In other words, a pretest is a critical examination of your survey instrument that will help determine if your survey will function properly as a valid and reliable social science research tool (Converse and Presser 1986).

Using a pretest of the survey, researchers are able to ensure that the questions are clearly articulated and that the response options are relevant, comprehensive, and mutually exclusive—and not just in their own estimation, but from the point of view of the respondents as well. Making sure that researchers and respondents interpret the survey in the same way is of the very highest concern in survey design, and pretesting is one of the best ways to do this (Converse and Presser 1986). Pretesting can bring to light those inevitable instances of obscure terminology, unfamiliar references, and ambiguous words and phrases that the developer did not initially see as problematic, but that could confound and frustrate the respondent and hurt data quality and response rates. Furthermore, the pretest also allows the researcher to assess **response latency**, the amount of time it takes to complete individual items in the survey as well as the full survey, which can then be reported in the introduction of the full-scale survey (for reasons discussed in Chapter 3; Bassili and Scott 1996; Draisma and Dijkstra 2004).

Another important feature of pretesting a survey is the technical report (paper trail) left for future research endeavors. When a survey researcher has conducted similar research in the past, and has pretested and sufficiently documented survey materials, these tried and true measures help design a valid survey instrument. Thus, a meticulous record of the pretest process helps avoid future problems encountered at the various stages of study design.

When considering research funding sources, pretesting your survey instrument prior to full-scale administration lends credibility to your proposed work and accountability to you as a researcher, which could also potentially increase the probability of obtaining research funding.

Pretesting also serves as practice administration and a way to evaluate respondents' understanding of the concepts under study as well as the quality of their interviews (Converse and Presser 1986). All respondents should understand the concepts and ideas *in the same exact way*. In the following example, *housework* may be interpreted differently by men and women and by individuals with and without children. Some might argue that childcare is included in housework, while others might argue that it is not:

1. Considering your work and commute schedules, would you say the division of your housework is fair?

    1) No, I do way too much of the work.

    2) No, I do somewhat more than I should.

    3) No, my partner does way too much of the work.

    4) No, my partner does somewhat more than she/he should.

    5) Yes, it is fair enough.

Choosing not to pretest a questionnaire poses a potentially serious threat to the accuracy of the survey questions and resulting data. It is better to pretest a questionnaire on even just one person rather than field the survey without pretesting. The rule of thumb is to test the survey on at least 12 to 50 people prior to pilot testing or full-scale administration (Sheatsley 1983; Sudman 1983). This is a cost-, energy-, and time-efficient number of people—a large enough number that many will note the same problems with the survey questions. Inclusion of more than 50 "test respondents" *may* lead to the identification of more problems, but there comes a point of diminishing return, as the financial and time costs of further pretesting outweigh the benefits of discovering more relatively small issues and inconsistencies in the instrument.

The time involved in pretesting a survey (and the posttest assessment) depends largely on the length of the survey. The following section discusses who should participate in a survey pretest (i.e., the sample of testing participants), how the pretest should be carried out, how to collect pretest data, and what to do with feedback from the survey pretest.

Expert-Driven Pretests

Researchers sometimes call upon experts in a given field to identify problems with questions or response options in a survey (Presser and Blair 1994). For instance, a child behavior specialist may help pinpoint measurement issues in a newly developed child behavior checklist. As noted in Chapter 5, expert-driven pretests are crucial when assessing the face validity and construct validity of a measurement.

You might ask experts to pretest your survey items by going through the entire survey themselves, and, rather than asking them to provide an individual assessment of each item, ask them to rate the items on a Likert scale such as that outlined below. The idea is not to collect the experts' opinions and beliefs but to get their judgment of how well each questionnaire item truly reflects the construct you intend it to measure (Jansen and Hak 2005). Soliciting such expert appraisals of each and every survey question, using Likert-type scale items such as those below, can be an extremely valuable strategy for identifying problems and fine tuning items to collect optimal measurements:

1) Very strongly represents the construct
2) Somewhat strongly represents the construct
3) Unsure
4) Somewhat weakly represents the construct
5) Very weakly represents the construct

Experts are important not only for cross-checking the substantive aspects of the survey but for improving the overall style of the instrument as well. With their finer knowledge of the breadth of the given field, experts can tell you if all questions in the survey are relevant and necessary, or if some may be cut to shorten the questionnaire length and reduce respondent burden. They can also help decide if the survey flows seamlessly from one question to the next, thus following a logical and intuitive layout that again reduces respondent burden and improves the quality of your data (Olson 2010).

Finally, whether you have access to experts in the relevant field(s) or not, you can familiarize yourself with some of the extant expert research in the field, as well as with previous surveys on the same topic, to compare your newly designed measures to those in the established literature.

Respondent-Driven Pretests

Administration of the pretest survey to friends and colleagues is encouraged. However, the most useful pretesting is often done on a small subsample of the sample population, so that your pretesters fit the cultural and demographic profile of the larger sample to be surveyed later (Ferketich, Phillips, and Verran 1993). At the same time, you want your pretest group to encompass some variation within the broader profile, to ensure enough variety to notice any potential issues across the entire range of your questionnaire.

For example, if you plan to survey fundamentalist Christians, make sure to test individuals within different subgroups of that population. Fundamentalist Christians belong to different social classes and have varying ages and levels of education. If the terminology used in the questionnaire is widely understood only to younger populations, this oversight will be salient in the pretest of older individuals. Thus, a researcher will know to edit this terminology in the full-scale survey. If possible, pretest the study on multiple people within the various important subgroups of your sample too, so that their views can be confirmed by others in their subgroup.

Finally, when you administer the pretest, include an additional introduction to the questionnaire that once again thanks your participants and highlights the special importance of the pretesting process. For example, an introduction might read as follows:

> *In an effort to collect high-quality data on residential mobility patterns in the United States, we are developing a questionnaire to assess rates of and experiences with residential relocation. We greatly appreciate your willingness to participate in a preliminary assessment of this survey. After you have finished filling out the questionnaire, we will ask you to provide feedback on your understanding of the individual items in the survey. We would like to thank you in advance for this assistance.*

Collecting Pretest Data

When collecting the pretest data, it is important to use the same administration technique that will be used in the full-scale survey. If the full survey is to be conducted via phone interviews, for example, then you would not want to employ face-to-face interviews for the pretest—this would change the entire dynamic of data collection and cause you to overlook salient issues, and it could introduce extraneous issues that would not come up in the full survey. In general, when analyzing pretest results, you should pay particular attention to those more complex questions and items that were difficult for you to develop (such as, perhaps, multidimensional questions), as these items by definition contain more "moving parts" that could introduce problems. In addition to this, there are four more-specific strategies to follow to conduct a valid and reliable pretest assessment of your survey: behavior coding, cognitive interviews, individual debriefing, and group debriefing. We turn to each of these strategies in the sections below.

Behavior Coding

In **behavior coding** pretest assessment, researchers themselves administer the survey and ask respondents to take it in their presence (DeMaio, Rothgeb, and Hess 1998). Researchers watch as the respondent progresses through the questionnaire, noting behaviors of the respondent that may indicate problems with the survey, such as hesitation, confusion, and frustration. When the respondent has finished taking the survey, researchers also note which items were skipped, if and where any responses were erased or crossed out, and if there are any mistakes or other physical traces of confusion or miscommunication on the instrument itself. For example, on the item in Table 6.1, answers appear to have been provided backwards (reversing the poles of the scale) and then corrected. This could indicate a problematic scale, whose logic or specific points are not as clear as they could be:

Table 6.1 Religiosity Scale

	Agree		→		*Disagree*
Religion is important in my life...	1	⊗2 (crossed out)	3	(4)	5
I regularly attend religious services...	1	2	**3**	4	5
I feel connected to a higher power...	⊗1 (crossed out)	2	3	4	(5)

The respondent in the example above may have initially thought she was rating the "correctness" of the statements, rewarding more or fewer points for more or less correct statements. Should such an intuition prove common among pretesters, the researcher may want to reverse the scale as it appears on the instrument, or, at the least, add or clarify item instructions.

Cognitive Interview

In a **cognitive interview,** the researcher encourages pretest respondents to think out loud and voice their ongoing mental reactions, essentially narrating their thought processes while they take the survey (DeMaio, Rothgeb, and Hess 1998). For instance, thinking aloud, a respondent may respond to a question about how many times he has relocated in the last year by stating "Well, we moved from our primary house to our summer home in Sarasota at the end of June, and then back to our primary house in September. I guess that means we moved twice if we count the times we moved to our summer home. It would be zero if that doesn't count." This is a valuable revelation for the attentive researcher. The confusion highlighted in this answer is an indication that the question is not clearly worded, and should be changed or made more specific to more clearly measure residential relocation, so that it can be understood by everyone the same way.

Individual Debriefing

In an **individual debriefing assessment**, researchers debrief respondents after they have completed the survey, explicitly to gather feedback and reactions to specific questions (not just those eliciting respondent comments, as in the example above), the survey design, and the survey process (DeMaio, Rothgeb, and Hess 1998). Each question is reviewed and discussed individually with the respondents, and particular attention is paid to elements such as these:

- Question wording and language
- Comprehensive measurement
- Mutually exclusive measurement
- Additional comments

Once respondents have completed the survey, the researcher reviews each survey question with each respondent individually, asking them to remark about what they *believe* they are being asked and if they found anything confusing or misleading about the survey question. For example, with respect to the question, "How many times have you relocated in the past 12 months?" a respondent might respond, "I said twice because my family moves to Florida in the summer and then back to New York in the fall. I wasn't sure if that counts since we still maintain the same primary residence." Again, this might prompt researchers to reconsider their question, perhaps even with help from the respondent, to accurately measure the concept intended. This might lead to a clearer question: "In the last 12 months, how many times have you and your immediate family undergone a permanent change of residence?"

Such individual-item debriefing may evoke a greater range of feedback or detail than a cognitive interview. However, there is also a danger in overusing this technique, as it may encourage respondents to retrospectively over-think items that were actually properly answered and unproblematic during the actual completion of the survey.

Group Debriefing

In **group debriefing assessment**, researchers bring test respondents together after the survey for a focus group discussion of the instrument (Vogt, King, and King 2004). They can then read the individual questions aloud and assess the test participants' reactions. Often, group debriefing will help researchers assess the magnitude of confusion for certain items, so that they do not over- or underreact to issues raised by any one individual respondent. For example, even though only one pretester might mention a specific item or scale in an individual interview, sharing this issue in a group debriefing might remind others that they too found it problematic. It could also encourage them to be more confident and forthcoming about an issue they were not sure they should raise or could not clearly articulate themselves. And even if one respondent's issue is not echoed by the group, this process confirms it as mere idiosyncrasy, making it easier for researchers to simply note and then move on.

Important Issues to Identify in Pretests

When analyzing pretester responses, researchers are likely to find issues converging on some common themes. Be attuned to the possibility of each of the general problems below, and pay special attention should one or two prove much more common than the others, as these may lead you to rethink the organization or design of the instrument.

Unclear Directions

Are all directions clearly articulated? Are ambiguities centered on a single item that needs reworking, a counterintuitive scale, a larger group of questions, or on all of the instructions in general? In the following example, there are no directions for respondents to mark all that apply. Respondents might therefore mark only the most important option:

2. Which of the following causes you a lot of stress?
   - ☐ My friends
   - ☐ My partner
   - ☐ My job/finances
   - ☐ My family
   - ☐ My children

Skipped Items

Are there multiple items in the survey (not part of a skip pattern) that were missed or avoided? Look for patterns among skipped items—do they relate to similar, difficult content? Personal information? Complex instructions? Or are they perhaps clustered toward the beginning, middle, or the end of a survey, indicating patterns in respondents' attentiveness at various points?

Refusal or Inability to Answer

"I don't know" and "N/A" are response options that should ideally be selected for only a very few items. These options often indicate an inability or refusal to answer a question. Thus, an inordinate number of "I don't know" or "N/A" responses implies there may be a problem with a question. Consider the example below:

3. How do you feel about the systemic reform of immigration policies that will assist lawmakers with adequately addressing delays in visa processing and the enforcement of contemporary immigration laws?
   1) Strongly agree
   2) Agree
   3) Neutral
   4) Disagree
   5) Strongly disagree
   6) Not applicable

When asking a long or difficult question, many individuals may skim the question and select "not applicable" if the question is too complex, takes too much time, requires too much thought, or must be read multiple times. The question above may need to be simplified or completely redesigned with introductory information for inclusion in the final survey.

"Other" Responses

Did respondents mark "other" on a frequent basis? If so, this may indicate that there are additional response options that may have been overlooked and need consideration. For example, a question asking about an individual's political party affiliation that lists only Democrat, Republican, and other as the options may lead to too many "other" responses, given that there are other common political party possibilities (Libertarians, independents, Greens, etc.).

Assuming that party affiliation is a major variable in the study, a researcher could, for example, be overlooking a potentially large group of Libertarians who have repeatedly marked "other." It could be problematic to merge their responses with the responses of other survey takers who mark "other"—such as independents, respondents who are undecided, and members of other political denominations like the Green Party, as these groups may have little in common other than not being members of one of the major parties. Including an open-ended response line for "other" to "please specify" in the pretest survey allows respondents to indicate precisely what they meant with their "other" responses. When analyzing the pretest results, if a given answer seems common among respondents, it might warrant inclusion as a separate, additional categorical response option.

Little or No Response Variation

How much variation is there across test respondents? Assuming that you have a heterogeneous test sample, the responses should differ across surveys, for the most part. If they don't, there may be a problem with the question itself, or, if the attribute measured really is universally shared, then the question may not be a necessary component of the survey at all. For example, in a study of adolescent risk behavior, the following question would likely have very little variation:

4. Before age five, how many times did you consume alcohol?

    1) Never

    2) 1–3 times

    3) 4–5 times

    4) 6 or more times

Since we know that an overwhelming majority of individuals did not consume alcohol before the age of five, most respondents will be inclined to select "never." When analyzing pretest data, a researcher should be mindful of questions with very little variation in responses. A lack of variation in responses can be an indication that a question is not relevant enough to warrant inclusion in the final survey.

Easily Misinterpreted Questions

Are there double-barreled questions in the survey or other questions that could possibly be misinterpreted? The following question is an example of a double-barreled question that was identified in the pretest of an open-ended survey:

5. Who do you feel closer to, your friends or your partner? Who's more fun? Tell us who and why.

The pretest of this open-ended question would allow researchers to note the double-barreled nature of the question. For instance, when respondents replied with "my partner," researchers would be unable to determine if the response indicated that an individual was closer to the partner, if the partner was more fun, or both.

Other misleading and confusing types of questions are those that are posed with negative wording. If a negative clause is necessary, try to avoid adding additional ones. For example, the double negative in the following question would be very likely to confuse a respondent:

6. Is it true that *not* ending the war will lead to *negative* economic outcomes?

Perhaps even more confusing are complex questions posed with double and triple negatives in the wording that would take multiple attempts to interpret: "Would you *disagree* that *not* ending the war would have a *negative* influence on the economy?" See Chapter 4 for more examples of confusing items and ways to improve them.

Sensitive Questions

Pretesting helps researchers determine whether or not respondents will be overly sensitive to specific questions, causing respondents to hesitate, hold back, or skip survey items. A pretest design can also help determine where sensitive and private questions work best within the overall layout of the survey.

Inconsistent Scales

The pretest allows researchers to verify that all scales are standardized to include the same number of points. For instance, if a question asks individuals to rate their concern with current environmental issues on a 1–7 scale where 1 = "very concerned," it is unwise to follow this up with a scale where 5 = "very concerned." In this case, respondents may condition their response to the scale from the first question and unintentionally report the opposite answer in the second question.

A pretest also helps researchers ensure that respondents are able to differentiate the points on a scale clearly. If a 9-point scale has too many options and does not allow the respondent to differentiate between them, a smaller 5- or 7-point scale may be warranted.

Order of Response Options

Are responses influenced by the order of questions or response options? The order of possible responses in the following question presents this issue:

7. Which of the following cause you a lot of stress these days? (Please check all that apply.)

   ☐ Job

   ☐ Pets

   ☐ Financial situation

   ☐ Household chores

   ☐ My health

   ☐ Relationships with friends

   ☐ Relationships with family members

   ☐ Relationship with my partner

   ☐ Not enough time to spend with people I care about

   ☐ Not able to exercise enough

   ☐ Too little personal time to myself

   ☐ Day-to-day responsibilities that come with raising kids

   ☐ Other

   ☐ None of the above

Let us assume that "job" is really the item causing our respondent the most stress. If this option is presented at the top of the list, the respondent will likely have no trouble finding and checking the appropriate box. However, if the response is listed closer to the end of the list, the individual may be influenced to choose other preceding list items first, identifying health, friends, and household chores as sources of stress. By the time he reaches the "job" option, he has been distracted by other thoughts and may no longer consider this to be a significant cause of stress. This bias toward marking early response options to the exclusion of later ones is a common phenomenon. A possible safeguard against this is to randomize the list so that the order is different across each survey. (Of course, this is a much more practical approach in computer assisted surveys, which can be randomized much more efficiently than can pen-and-paper surveys.) Or, it may be more effective to shorten or collapse the list or redesign the question altogether.

Computer-Based and Technical Problems

Are skip patterns correctly designed and implemented? If you used a progress bar on a computer-based survey, is it functioning properly throughout the instrument? Are survey filters working correctly? Difficulties here may require simple reprogramming of the instrument, or they may encourage an alternative method of administration.

Other Pretesting Issues

Even if pretest survey items are not skipped, answered incorrectly, or identified as problematic in follow-up interviews, researchers should be attuned to a few more issues and opportunities this valuable tool presents.

Check and Improve Respondent Recall

Pretests are a good way to determine whether or not recall is too strenuous for retrospective questions. Questions may need to be more clearly defined, and respondents may need to be given specific time references to help them recall events that occurred in the past.

Clarify Complex Concepts

Researchers can ask pretest respondents to define specific concepts in order to help design questions for those concepts in the full-scale survey. For example, a researcher might ask test respondents to "define what the term *family values* means to you." Since "family values" means a number of different things to different people, a researcher can assess the different meanings individuals associate with this term.

Track Question Response Timing

Web-based surveys allow for the assessment of response latency, the timing of respondents' completion of individual questions, which is helpful to determine if certain questions can be streamlined for quicker response. Some survey software may have additional features to track the number of clicks a respondent makes on a given page (Heerwegh 2003).

Assess Adequacy of Space for Reponses to Open-Ended Questions

The pretest allows researchers to assess whether or not more room is needed for open-ended responses. This is important for pen-and-paper surveys, where physical space is important. However, this also allows for assessment of the space needed in certain web-based surveys that allow only a certain number of characters in an open-ended response field.

Assess Survey Appearance on Varying Media

Researchers should pretest each medium used to collect data. For example, can web-based surveys be taken on a smartphone without zooming in and out to view questions?

Updating Time-Specific Surveys and Multilanguage Surveys

When using or building on existing instruments, pretesting the instrument is important to assess whether the questions have stood the test of time. Respondents may draw attention to questions with outdated wording or poorly designed content. After the pretest, researchers can compare these preliminary results with those from existing studies using the results from the pretest as a cross-validation of the measure's accuracy.

Pretesting is also necessary when using surveys developed in multiple languages (McKay et al. 1996). Translation requires rigorous understanding of different words, phrases, and colloquial meanings. In addition to arranging for professional translation, researchers can use a pretesting audience to help identify inconsistencies or irregularities in language and/or cultural accessibility issues within the survey instrument (Ferketich, Phillips, and Verran 1993).

After pretesting, the major issues with questions, measurement, and design should become apparent. Researchers should then prepare a memo summarizing all of the concerns about the survey for their research team and, using data gathered from the survey assessment(s), make revisions to the survey design to improve the quality of the questionnaire and its resultant data. Usually, this produces a more complete survey instrument that is ready for fielding or pilot testing. However, depending on the amount of content revised, another round of pretesting might be in order.

Pretesting Checklist

Refer to the following checklist as a summary of the above issues and guidelines. Careful consideration of each of the elements will help you make the most of your pretest and produce the most effective survey instrument possible.

ADMINISTRATION

- ☐ How long does the survey take to complete?
- ☐ Did the time to complete the survey vary widely among the test participants?

- ☐ Are the instructions for each section clear and unambiguous?
- ☐ Did you thank the respondents for their time?

ORGANIZATION

- ☐ Do the different sections flow reasonably from one to the next?
- ☐ Are all questions necessary in order to collect information on your topic?
- ☐ Are the questions within each section logically ordered?

CONTENT

- ☐ Are the questions direct and concise?
- ☐ Are the questions measuring what they are intended to measure?
- ☐ Are the questions free of unnecessary technical language and jargon?
- ☐ Are examples and analogies relevant for individuals of other cultures?
- ☐ Are questions unbiased?
- ☐ Are there questions that make respondents feel uncomfortable, embarrassed, annoyed, or confused? If so, can these be worded differently to avoid doing so?
- ☐ Are the response choices mutually exclusive and exhaustive?
- ☐ Are all response options necessary for inclusion?

When pretesting is complete, be sure to include your use of this procedure in the methods section of your research paper, as it increases the credibility of your research.

PILOT TESTING

In a **pilot test** (also known as a *feasibility study*), the interviewers, final survey, and some stages of coding and analysis are rehearsed prior to the actual survey administration. In other words, a pilot study is a trial run of the entire study from start to finish that increases the likelihood of success for the main study. Pilot studies are conducted to test the entire research process—usually from a methodological standpoint (e.g., sampling and recruitment strategies, administration, data collection and analysis) in actual field conditions.

Unlike survey pretests, which are usually done on a small scale, pilot studies have no cognitive interviews or focus groups to determine which measure and concepts are appropriate in the survey questionnaire. Rather, a pilot test is systematically administered to a diverse cross-section of the sample to ensure that the entire survey schedule runs smoothly and that coding and analysis can be done properly and efficiently. A general rule of thumb is to pilot test the survey on 30 to 100 pilot participants (this number will vary, of course, depending on the number of respondents in your entire sample; Courtenay 1978). Once pilot testing is complete, final revisions to the survey process can be made, and the survey is ready for full-scale administration.

There are several reasons for undertaking a pilot study. They help identify potential problems throughout the entire survey procedure and assess whether the project is feasible, realistic, and rational from start to finish. Prior to administering the full-scale study, pilot research helps researchers address several issues that will affect the success of the study, as outlined below.

Necessary Resources

The pilot study helps the researcher determine what resources are necessary for the full study. The researcher is able to gauge the number of interviewers, staff, data coders, and analysts that will be necessary for the full-scale study and to identify what software will be necessary for the analysis. Researchers are also able to assess whether or not any incentives provided to respondents are commensurate with the time and energy necessary to complete the survey.

Trained Surveyors/Interviewers

The pilot test serves as a means to validate the field-testing process (i.e., interviewer training). The researcher is able to observe whether or not the interviewers are knowledgeable about the survey items, able to answer questions, and competent in clarifying points about the survey and research topic. The researcher is also able to assess whether the interviewers are objective and unbiased during the interview.

Administration Procedures

Pilot testing also allows a researcher to test for possible flaws with the sampling and administration of the survey. For example, in a study asking about fairness in housework, surveying both individuals in a couple together might lead to a bias in responses, because respondents would be more inclined to respond favorably about fairness in housework when their spouses were present. A pilot study would allow for comparison of responses where individuals in a couple were surveyed individually with those where both individuals were surveyed together. In preliminary analysis, researchers might find that the answers of simultaneously surveyed individuals in a couple are biased, and they might also determine that individual surveys lead to less biased responses; thus they could choose to conduct only individual surveys in the full-scale study.

Recruitment Approaches

Pilot studies are also important for uncovering problematic features of the sample. As an illustration, a pilot study conducted by one of the authors of this text explored the use of public spaces (e.g., parks and recreation centers) among homeless individuals. The study was conducted on a small sample of homeless individuals in a public park. Inadvertently, in the process of conducting the pilot study, the researchers brought unwanted public attention to homeless individuals. This attention led to the removal of the homeless from the park due to restrictions against loitering. This unforeseen issue brought an untimely end to the pilot test and also made a segment of the research population less likely to participate in future studies for fear of legal reprimand. As a result, the researchers had to develop alternate strategies for recruitment for the full-scale study. Ultimately, they learned that a completely different research design may have been more successful than the survey they administered.

Data Analysis

The pilot test also provides raw data to test data entry and data processing procedures. Preliminary coding and analysis should be completed to test the accuracy and capability of data analysis programs, allowing for correction of critical issues at even the latest stages of data collection. In addition, researchers should be able to identify whether initial data input, management, and coding are properly, effectively, and precisely executed in a timely fashion. Even if the results of the pilot study are ultimately not meaningful, preliminary analyses and tables should be produced from these results, simply to test the viability and efficacy of the survey *process* through to the final stages.

Similar to pretesting, pilot testing has practical importance for funding and support, because it lends credibility to the research project design. Thus, like pretests, pilot tests are an important way to convince stakeholders and funding sources that the study is workable and merits financial support.

PRETEST AND PILOT TEST LIMITATIONS

Successfully pretesting and pilot testing a survey does not necessarily ensure the success of the full study. There are a number of concerns that are not addressed in the pretesting or pilot stages of survey administration, and some issues may not arise until the full-scale study is conducted. It is important to be aware of these problems before they arise.

Firstly, given the smaller number of surveys administered in a pilot study, it cannot predict, or even estimate, a response rate for the full-scale study. Even if a study has been vetted by a well-designed and successfully executed pilot study, the full-scale study may still suffer from extremely low response rates.

Another important problem that confronts researchers is contamination of the data as a result of including pretest and pilot test survey results in the final, full-scale study. Because modifications to the survey instrument may have taken place, the data collected in the pretest and pilot test of the surveys could be inaccurate or biased compared to the results of the full-scale study. For example, in the pretest, the ambiguous question, "How many times have you relocated in the last year?" might elicit a response of "twice" that was based on temporary moves. If the question were subsequently reworded to "How many times did you permanently change your residence in the last twelve months?" for the full-scale study, then including the pretest data (based on different wording) would add an incorrect response to the dataset and lower the overall quality of the survey. To avoid this, some researchers have chosen to redesign the questionnaire and readminister the revised survey to respondents who participated in the pretest or pilot study. However, this comes with its own set of complications and poses threats to the internal validity of the study. These respondents may respond differently than they would have otherwise responded had they not been conditioned by the pretesting experience; in experimental psychology, this is known as a "pretesting effect" (Richland, Kornell, and Kao 2009). For example, achievement scales may be positively influenced with a pretest: An individual completing a math problem would likely be more successful when the question is presented a second time, in the full-scale survey, after having first responded to it on the pretest. In other words, individuals who were involved in the pretest study will have experienced these questions, may have thought about them, and may be better equipped to answer when they respond to the survey in the full-scale study.

Of course, it may be unreasonable to exclude these participants from the entire study, especially in small-scale studies or with difficult-to-locate samples. In this case, comparison and discussion of the differences between the pretested groups and the full-scale group is necessary. It is also important to exercise caution when interpreting these results, and it is important to note this potential data contamination as a possible limitation of the research.

Finally, it is highly recommended to organize the timing of pretests and pilot studies to allow for analysis and revision before conducting the full-scale study. It is important to have enough time between administration of the pretest, the pilot test, and the full-scale survey so that edits to the survey can be implemented—and this can often be problematic when a pilot test does not go according to plan and major changes to the study design are necessary. The effort put into conducting a pretest and pilot study are wasted if the results are not made available in time for efficient planning of the full-scale survey.

Despite the time, financial cost, and energy invested in pretesting and pilot testing a survey, these procedures rarely warrant more than a single line in the methods section of a research paper, if any mention at all (Presser et al. 2007). Given the strict word and space limitations required for publication, the presentation of the final research product typically receives more attention than descriptions of behind-the-scenes research. But these procedures are no less important for this fact; they allow you to learn from your methodological mistakes and to leave a detailed record of your efforts, so that you and others can avoid the pitfalls of survey development and administration in future research. For this reason, there are meta-analytic research reports (research undertaken on the process of research) that help us acknowledge these issues and bring them to the attention of the larger research community.

CONCLUSION

While it may require much time and energy for careful planning and high precision, testing the entire survey process from beginning to end is an essential process for good survey research. The sole purpose of pretesting and pilot testing early on is to reduce measurement error on a larger scale later. When the full-scale study begins, all research procedures should already be carefully checked and tested for errors and potential issues; when discovered during full-scale data collection, these glitches are much more difficult to remedy. Thus, it is important to acknowledge these problems early in the research process by conducting pretests and pilot studies. Well-organized and well-documented pretests and pilot surveys help improve the validity, reliability, accuracy, and efficiency of the full-scale study. It is better to spend a relatively modest amount of time and money uncovering potentially serious flaws in a survey instrument than to spend a serious amount of time and money engaging in potentially flawed research.

KEY TERMS

Pretest 101
Behavior coding 105
Cognitive interview 106
Individual debriefing assessment 106
Group debriefing assessment 107
Pilot test 101
Response latency 102

CRITICAL THINKING QUESTIONS

Below you will find four questions that ask you to think critically about core concepts addressed in this chapter. Be sure you understand each one; if you don't, this is a good time to review the relevant sections of this chapter.

1. What are two ways that pretesting a survey prior to administration might increase the instrument's *validity*?
2. What are two ways a pretest might improve the instrument's *reliability*?
3. What are some of the problems researchers might encounter if they *pretest* their survey but do not *pilot test* it?
4. What are some problems researchers might encounter if they *pilot test* their survey but do not *pretest* it?

SECTION III

Implementing a Survey

In the previous section, making decisions on the administration of a given survey, developing the questionnaire, and assessing the validity and reliability of the questionnaire were presented. This section will focus on creating the sample and conducting the survey.

Chapter 7, "Selecting a Sample: Probability Sampling," will focus on traditional probability sampling techniques. The chapter will start by introducing the reader to basic sampling terminology and proceed to a brief discussion of sampling theory. Next, it will introduce four probability sampling techniques: simple random sampling, stratified sampling, cluster sampling, and multistage stratified sampling. Variations such as systematic random sampling and proportional versus disproportionate stratified sampling will be discussed. In addition, the chapter will address issues such as choosing a sample size, oversampling some subpopulations, and weighting. It will introduce the errors that can result from incomplete coverage of the population, nonresponse, and attrition.

Chapter 8, "Nonprobability Sampling and Sampling Hard-to-Find Populations," continues to examine sampling. However in this chapter, nonprobability sampling will be discussed. Additionally, methods for sampling nontraditional populations and hard-to-find populations will be introduced, including respondent-driven sampling techniques, and snowball sampling.

Chapter 9, "Improving Response Rates and Retention," addresses two primary types of error associated with sampling: nonresponse and attrition. The chapter will discuss some of the reasons for attrition and provide strategies to improve responses for all types of survey administration. This information is useful for good decision making regarding improving sample response rates and retention of the sample.

Chapter 10, "Technologies to Develop and Implement Surveys," discusses several software programs used in survey research, with an emphasis on newer software for web-based surveys. Also discussed are two types of computer assisted software (CAPI and CATI) for telephone or face-to-face administration methods.

Chapter 11, "Data Collection," discusses the data collection process. It discusses types of survey administration, working with staff, and auditing the data collection process. It addresses decision making with respect to the number of contacts to make, and how to handle refusals, ineligibles, deaths, and final response rates. Next it addresses data entry issues and the strengths and weakness of data entry for each administration type. It ends with a discussion of data storage and back-up needs.

7

Selecting a Sample

Probability Sampling

INTRODUCTION

The major goals in conducting survey research are to test a theory, expand upon a theory, or predict an outcome for a population or subpopulation. Often the population is far too large to survey all of its members. We can select a sample of individuals to survey, primarily because it is not feasible to conduct the survey on the entire population. Unless it is a very small population, most researchers have neither the time nor the money to collect data from a large population. Furthermore, the quality of the data using a sample may be of higher quality than data from the entire population, because resources are not spread thin trying to collect data from too many elements (Kalton 1983). Without a high-quality sample, it is impossible to answer research questions with any certainty.

There are two overarching types of sampling techniques: probability sampling and nonprobability sampling. This chapter focuses on probability sampling, while chapter 8 will discuss nonprobability sampling methods. Probability sampling methods are those that use random chance to select members of the population to be included in the sample. The word *random* is not used here in the colloquial sense that the Valley Girl uses it when she exclaims, "Oh my God, that is so random!" A behavior that is simply weird cannot be considered to be mathematically random. Rather, *random* means that chance, and chance alone, dictates or predicts which population members are selected into the sample.

As the reader will see when sampling theory is introduced, random selection is a very powerful tool. It is the aspect of the survey process that allows researchers to generalize findings from the sample back to the population from which it was drawn; thus, random sampling is a very important part of the survey process. But, this is only true if the sample is representative of the population from which it is drawn. Technically, only probability based samples are representative, thus, when conducting a survey, the best results, meaning generalizable results, will occur with a probability sample. In this chapter we present three major forms of probability sampling: simple random sampling, stratified sampling, and cluster sampling. In addition, we will discuss modifications of each (e.g., systematic random sampling) as well as combinations of them (e.g., multistage stratified sampling). Before we can do that, we need to define the terminology of sampling and introduce the statistical theories that demonstrate the usefulness of probability sampling techniques. Then the actual process of selecting a probability sample will be presented.

SAMPLING TERMINOLOGY

Let's spend some time defining terms to help make sampling more understandable. First, the **population** is defined as the total set of all elements that we are interested in studying. It is often denoted by the symbol N. Because findings will be based on the population used, the population should be carefully, explicitly, and fully defined in relation to the research being conducted. Defining the population is not as straightforward as it may seem. Not even with national studies of the United States is the population defined as all US citizens. Citizens living abroad generally are not included. Citizens living in institutions are often excluded. And, given the expenses of interviewing in Alaska and Hawaii, most national samples focus only on the contiguous 48 states. This means that while we may want to generalize to the entire population, feasibility dictates that we often create a **target population**; that is, a reduced population that fits feasibility constraints, but consists of the entire population to which the researcher will generalize results.

A **sample** is a subset of the defined population often denoted by the symbol n. The sample **elements** are the people, things, places, or events in which social scientists are interested; in other words, the people, things, places, or events are the **units of analysis**. Usually, the population consists of people and, therefore, so does the sample. An element in the population then would refer to a single person, and the unit of analysis would be people. There are times, however, when we survey people as representatives of some other entity, such as a corporation, or government body. In this case, the units of analysis would be corporations or government bodies. For example if we are interested in racial hiring disparities, we could be interested in hiring practices of corporations, which means the unit of analysis is at the corporation level, and anyone we interview will be representing the corporation. However, if we are interested in whether or not individuals get hired, we may wish to speak to individuals of various races who have attempted to find work. This alternative study would have people as the unit of analysis.

While our analyses will be conducted on the elements of the sample, we want to be able to say something about the population. In other words, we want to ensure that our sample is **representative** of the population from which it was drawn. When the sample does represent the population, we say the sample is **generalizable**. Under this condition, any statistically significant findings about the sample can be inferred to the population from which it was drawn. Only a **random sample** or **probability sample** allows us to do this. A random or probability sample is one where chance and chance alone dictates which elements are selected into the sample, and in which each element has a known and nonzero probability of being selected into the sample.

In order to select a probability sample, researchers must be able to create a list of all population members. We call this list a **sampling frame**. For example, if researchers are interested in understanding the range of county public health policies in the state of Georgia, they need to find a way to access the population of Georgia counties. Figure 7.1 provides a map of all the counties in Georgia, followed by an alphabetic listing of all the counties in the state of Georgia; this list is a sampling frame. The counties are organized alphabetically and numbered from 1 to 159. The numbers are extremely important in a probability sample, because that is often what we are actually going to use to generate the sample: the number associated with a county. Thus, if number 56 is selected into the sample, that means the county associated with number 56, Fayette, will be included in the sample.

One common error in creating sampling frames is called **coverage error**. Coverage error occurs when not all population members are included in the sampling frame (Dillman, Smyth, and Christian 2009). It is quite easy to include all the counties of a single state. However, if we were interested in all the stores that sell food in Georgia, including supermarkets, grocery stores, convenience stores, and gas station stores, we would have more trouble. There is no comprehensive list of stores.

The yellow pages will have a decent list, and it is possible to buy a list of stores by SIC (standard industry code). Smaller stores, however, come and go quickly. A store may exist but may not yet be in the yellow pages. Alternatively, a store may be in the yellow pages and have already gone out of business. Given that the size and type of store is related to our ability to capture the store for the sampling frame, coverage error can produce bias in the sample. **Bias** can be thought of as the systematic difference between the true value of some given characteristic in a population and what is claimed about that value, based on analysis of the sample (Kish 1995). Therefore, it is expedient to carefully construct the sampling frame using as many sources as possible and eliminating the duplicate elements that this method will create. This will minimize bias in the sample. So, for the example of stores, we might buy a list of stores based on SIC codes *and* use this year's yellow pages. We may not capture the newest stores, but using both lists to construct the sampling frame will minimize coverage error.

Figure 7.1 County Map and Alphabetically Ordered Sampling Frame of Georgia Counties

Source: U.S. Census Bureau, 2010. Census of Population and Housing, *Population and Housing Unit Counts,* CPH-2-12, Georgia. U.S. Government Printing Office, Washington, DC, 2012.

Count	*Counties*	*Pop. Density*
1	Appling	36.0
2	Atkinson	24.7
3	Bacon	42.9
4	Baker	10.1
5	Baldwin	177.3
6	Banks	79.3

Count	*Counties*	*Pop. Density*
7	Barrow	432.7
8	Bartow	218.0
9	Ben Hill	70.5
10	Berrien	42.7
11	Bibb	622.8
12	Bleckley	60.5

Count	Counties	Pop. Density
13	Brantley	41.6
14	Brooks	32.9
15	Bryan	69.3
16	Bulloch	104.4
17	Burke	28.2
18	Butts	128.3
19	Calhoun	23.9
20	Camden	82.4
21	Candler	45.3
22	Carroll	221.5
23	Catoosa	394.3
24	Charlton	15.7
25	Chatham	621.7
26	Chattahoochee	45.3
27	Chattooga	83.0
28	Cherokee	508.3
29	Clarke	979.1
30	Clay	16.3
31	Clayton	1832.5
32	Clinch	8.5
33	Cobb	2026.4
34	Coffee	73.6
35	Colquit	83.6
36	Columbia	427.6
37	Cook	75.8
38	Coweta	288.8
39	Crawford	38.9
40	Crisp	86.0
41	Dade	95.6
42	Dawson	105.9
43	Decatur	46.6
44	Dekalb	2585.7
45	Dodge	44.0
46	Dooly	38.1
47	Dougherty	287.7
48	Douglas	661.8
49	Early	21.5
50	Echols	9.7
51	Effingham	109.4
52	Elbert	57.4

Count	Counties	Pop. Density
53	Emanuel	33.2
54	Evans	60.2
55	Fannin	61.2
56	Fayette	548.4
57	Floyd	188.9
58	Forsyth	783.5
59	Franklin	84.5
60	Fulton	1748.1
61	Gilmer	66.3
62	Glascock	21.4
63	Glynn	189.7
64	Gordon	155.1
65	Grady	55.0
66	Greene	41.3
67	Gwinnett	1871.2
68	Habersham	155.5
69	Hall	457.5
70	Hancock	20.0
71	Haralson	102.0
72	Harris	69.0
73	Hart	108.5
74	Heard	40.0
75	Henry	633.0
76	Houston	372.5
77	Irwin	26.9
78	Jackson	178.1
79	Jasper	37.8
80	Jeff Davis	45.6
81	Jefferson	32.2
82	Jenkins	24.0
83	Johnson	32.9
84	Jones	72.8
85	Lamar	99.8
86	Lanier	54.4
87	Laurens	60.0
88	Lee	79.5
89	Liberty	129.5
90	Lincoln	38.0
91	Long	36.1
92	Lowndes	220.2

(Continued)

(Continued)

Count	Counties	Pop. Density
93	Lumpkin	105.9
94	Macon	85.0
95	Madison	33.8
96	Marion	36.8
97	McDuffie	99.6
98	McIntosh	23.9
99	Meriwether	43.9
100	Miller	21.7
101	Mitchell	45.9
102	Monroe	66.8
103	Montgomery	38.1
104	Morgan	51.4
105	Murray	115.0
106	Muscogee	877.5
107	Newton	367.3
108	Oconee	178.0
109	Oglethorpe	33.9
110	Pauding	455.8
111	Peach	184.3
112	Pickens	126.8
113	Pierce	59.3
114	Pike	82.7
115	Polk	133.6
116	Pulaski	48.2
117	Putnum	61.6
118	Quitman	16.6
119	Rabun	44.0
120	Randolph	18.0
121	Richmond	618.3
122	Rockdale	656.6
123	Schley	30.0
124	Screven	22.6
125	Seminole	37.1
126	Spalding	326.1

Count	Counties	Pop. Density
127	Stephens	146.1
128	Stewart	13.2
129	Sumter	68.0
130	Talbot	17.5
131	Taliaferro	8.8
132	Tattnall	53.2
133	Taylor	23.6
134	Telfair	37.7
135	Terrell	27.8
136	Thomas	82.1
137	Tift	154.9
138	Toombs	74.8
139	Towns	62.9
140	Treutlen	34.5
141	Troup	161.9
142	Turner	31.3
143	Twiggs	25.2
144	Union	66.3
145	Upson	84.0
146	Walker	154.0
147	Walton	257.2
148	Ware	40.7
149	Warren	20.5
150	Washington	31.2
151	Wayne	46.9
152	Webster	13.4
153	Wheeler	25.1
154	White	112.8
155	Whitfield	353.2
156	Wikes	24.5
157	Wilcox	22.6
158	Wilkinson	21.4
159	Worth	38.0

Source: US Census Bureau 2010.

SAMPLING THEORY

Our goal is to produce sample estimators of given characteristics that are reflective of the population. Rarely do we know the population value of a given characteristic. If we did, the research might not be necessary. However, for the sake of an example, we will use playing cards. There are 52 cards in a deck with four suits of 13 cards: diamonds, hearts, clubs, and spades. Twenty-five percent of the deck is made up of each suit—therefore, we know the population parameters. Thus, if we put the cards in a hat, mix them up, and then choose a sample of 12 without looking at them and without immediately replacing them, what is the probability that the distribution of the sample will look like the population? That is, what is the likelihood that 25% of the sample will be diamonds, 25% hearts, 25% clubs, and 25% spades?

Table 7.1 Drawing Random Samples

	Clubs	*Diamonds*	*Hearts*	*Spades*
Population	25%	25%	25%	25%
Sample 1	33%	16%	25%	25%
Sample 2	16%	42%	25%	16%
Sample 3	25%	16%	50%	6%
Sample 4	16%	33%	16%	33%
Sample 5	16%	42%	16%	25%
Sample 6	33%	25%	16%	25%
Mean of 6 samples	23%	29%	25%	22%

Sample size $n = 12$

Note: All numbers rounded up; each row may not add up to 100% due to rounding.

Table 7.1 shows the results of drawing six random samples. Not a single sample exactly represented the population. In fact, it is rare for a single sample to exactly represent the population. However, if we take the mean of a sampling distribution of an infinite number of samples, we will approximate the population. So, if we take the mean of the distribution of clubs in all the samples an infinite number of times, we will get the population mean of 25%. Let's do that over the six samples and see what happens. The formula for the sample mean, which is a measure of the average or central tendency, is this:

$$\bar{y} = \sum_{i=1}^{n} \frac{y_i}{n}$$

Here $\bar{y}$ is the mean of the clubs distributions. The sigma, Σ, tells us to sum the sample distributions of clubs across all samples y_i (the observed sample means for each draw i = 1 to i = *n*, or in this case, 6) and then divide the sum by the total number of samples drawn.

If we were calculating the population mean, the formula would be the same, but we would use different symbols (capital letters) for the population:

$$\bar{Y} = \sum_{i=1}^{N} \frac{Y_i}{N}$$

To calculate for the deck of cards example, we solve the equation as follows:

$$(33 + 16 + 25 + 16 + 16 + 33)/6 = 139/6 = 23.16 \text{ for clubs}$$

The last row in Table 7.1 provides the means for each suit in the deck of cards. The theory holds that over an *infinite* number of samples, the mean of the distribution will be the population mean. Look how close we came to the population distribution with only six samples.

Unfortunately, if it is not feasible to collect data on the population, it certainly is not going to be feasible to collect an infinite number of samples. Therefore, we are limited to collecting only one sample, which will most likely represent the population to some degree. Using chance and chance alone means that nothing else is dictating how the sample is being chosen. Because we could not see the cards, a preference for spades, for example, did not influence the choosing of the sample.

There are some things we can do to help ensure our sample represents the population well. As we've already stated, the mean of the infinite sampling distribution is the population mean ($\bar{Y}$). Statistical theory further tells us that if this is the case, then the mean of the sampling distribution is an *unbiased estimator* of the population mean. Bias takes place when there is some sort of systematic error in the sampling process. Having a preference for spades would lead to systematic error. Therefore, in any single randomly selected sample, the difference between the population mean and the sample mean is **random sampling error** ($\bar{Y} - \bar{y} = \varepsilon$).

While random error is not as problematic as systematic error, we would definitely like as little random error as possible. One way to minimize random sampling error is to take a large sample. The central limit theorem states, in fact, that as *n* approaches infinity, the mean of the sampling distribution converges to the normal distribution. Thus, sample size is extremely important. The larger the sample size—not as a proportion of the population, but in terms of gross numbers—the more normally distributed the sampling distribution of the mean will be and the smaller the random error will be (Kish 1995). Provided our sample size n is large enough, at least 200 cases, based on statistical theory, we have approximated the normal distribution, which has wonderful properties. Figure 7.2 provides an example of a normal distribution.

Figure 7.2 Sampling Distribution of the Mean or Normal distribution

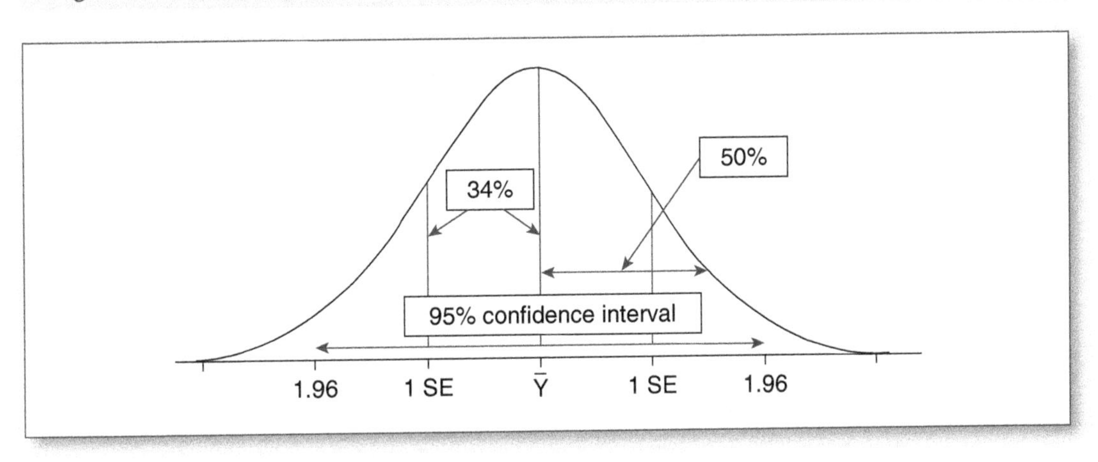

The normal distribution is a bell shaped curve that is bisected by the population mean—the measure of central tendency. Fifty percent of the infinite number of samples will fit under the normal distribution curve to the right of the mean and to the left of the mean. Samples that provide very unusual distributions of the suits of cards will appear in the tails of the distribution at either end. The bell curve tells us that this happens very rarely. More common are samples that provide estimates that are very close to the population mean—close to the center of the distribution.

In fact, 34% of all samples will have a mean within 1 standard deviation to the left of the population mean, and 95% of all samples will be within about 2 standard deviations of the population mean. (The value on the horizontal axis at the bottom of the bell curve is actually 1.96 standard deviations.) Thus, we learn that the variation about the mean is extremely important. We measure variation about the mean of some characteristic by calculating the standard deviation. The formula for the standard deviation of some characteristic in the sample is as follows:

$$s = \sqrt{s^2} = \sqrt{\sum_{i=1}^{n} \frac{(y_i - \bar{y})^2}{(n-1)}}$$

Here s represents the standard deviation, and it is calculated as the square root of the variance (s^2), which can be calculated by subtracting the mean of the sample distribution from the mean of each sample, summing the resulting differences over the total number of samples, and dividing by n the total number of samples drawn minus one. Likewise, the formula for the standard deviation of a variable in the population is this:

$$S = \sqrt{S^2} = \sqrt{\sum_{i=1}^{N} \frac{(Y_i - \bar{Y})^2}{(N-1)}}$$

Here all terms are defined as they were for the sample, except capital letters are used.

While the population standard deviation is not known, the standard deviation of the sampling distribution of the mean is an unbiased estimator of it. Thus, we can use the sampling distribution of the mean's standard deviation—usually known as the **standard error**, to estimate it. We can denote the mean and standard error of the sampling distribution by $\bar{y}_0$ and s_{se}. The formula for the standard error is as follows:

$$S_{se} = S_y / \sqrt{N}$$

Here s_{se} is the standard error of the sampling distribution, S_y is the sample standard deviation, and N is the population size.

Recall that any single sample that we draw will include random sampling error. Random sampling error can be defined as the difference between the population mean and the sample mean on whatever characteristic is of importance. Random error, unlike bias, is not a systematic error. Over a large sampling distribution, random error will sum to zero. However, in the case of everyday survey research, we have a single sample, and it will include sampling error. Thus, our sample mean will not exactly represent our population mean. We can use the standard error however, to create an interval around the sample mean within which we are confident the population mean resides. We call this a **confidence interval** (CI)

The bottom arrow in Figure 7.2 presents the 95% confidence interval that is typically used. It is associated with 1.96 standard deviations from the mean of the sampling distribution of the mean. The formula for a confidence interval is this:

$$\bar{y} \pm 1.96 * s_{se}$$

Here $\bar{y}$ is the sample mean to which we add and subtract 1.96 standard deviations times the standard error to obtain the confidence interval. For example, in the first sample of cards we chose, clubs had a mean of 33% based on a sample of size $n = 12$ from a population of size 52. We did not calculate the standard deviation, but let's say it is 5%. Based on this information we can calculate a (CI) around the sample mean:

$$CI = .33 \pm 1.96 * \sqrt{(1-12/52) * \frac{.70}{12}}$$

$$CI = .33 \pm 1.96 * \sqrt{(.769) * .058}$$

$$CI = .33 \pm 1.96 * .211$$

$$CI = -.085 - .745$$

We are 95% confident that the population mean is between -.085% and .745%. Given that we know the population mean is .25 (25%), it is, in fact, within the confidence interval despite the artificiality of the example.

Now that sampling theory has been elaborated upon, we will next turn to examining several probability sampling techniques.

PROBABILITY SAMPLING TECHNIQUES

Random sampling provides an appropriate sample suitable for statistical analysis, since the probability of selecting any member of the population for the sample is known in advance. Of course, it is not necessary that every member of the population has the *same* probability of selection, just that each individual's probability of selection is *known*. A sample can truly be deemed representative only if the way in which the sample has been chosen was through some sort of random method, since random sampling minimizes the likelihood of bias.

It is important to note that the mechanism for selection must be truly random. This can be done the old-fashioned way, by dumping all elements from the sampling frame into a bag, mixing them up thoroughly, and then blindly choosing elements from the bag until the sample is complete. Or, in today's high-technology world, you can choose a random sample using a calculator's random number function, a table of random numbers (though this can be cumbersome), a computer and statistical software program, or even an application for a tablet or smartphone.

What are random number tables or random number generators? These are carefully constructed tables or methods that ensure over the long run that each number, pair of numbers, or set of numbers appears with the same frequency (Kalton 1983). This means that each number generated is completely independent of every other number that is generated, and that randomness, or chance, and chance alone, predicts which numbered elements are chosen to be included in the sample.

When choosing a sample, researchers need to decide whether they will sample with or without replacement. Sampling with replacement means the same element can be included in the sample more than one time. Sampling without replacement means an element can be selected into the sample only once. Most survey research is conducted using sampling without replacement, because this method gives more precise estimators despite the restrictions on sampling (Kish 1995).

Simple Random Sampling

Simple random sampling is the most basic type of random sampling, where all members of the population have the same likelihood of selection for the sample. This is also known as an *equal probability sample.* All members of the sample must be chosen using the same random mechanism. All samples of the same size will have the exact same probability of being selected. The probability can be calculated by dividing the sample size by the population size. Thus, if we were to take a sample of 12 counties from the population of Georgia counties, the probability of selection would be 12/159 = .075472. Each randomly selected sample of size 12 (assuming nonreplacement) would have the same probability of selection, though the combination of counties in each sample would be different. These days it is quite easy to find a free online sampling program. For the examples found in Table 7.1, we used the random number generator on the website stattrek (http://stattrek.com/statistics/random-number-generator.aspx).

Table 7.2 provides two samples of size 12 drawn using the simple random sampling technique. There is some overlap between the samples, but each was drawn independently of the other. The probability of selection for each sample is identical. We have included the population density of each county selected into the sample. The last row provides the average or mean population density for each sample. The average population density differs for each sample. In fact, the average population density for the entire population is 193.6. Any sample chosen will have a different average population density. This sampling variability is not bias, because chance and only chance determined which counties were included in the sample. Recall that this is called random sampling error. For Sample 1, the sampling error for population density is 193.6 – 151.8 = 41.8, and for Sample 2, sampling error is 193.6 – 165.4 = 28.2. Sampling error will exist in all samples. The central limit theorem reminds us that sampling error will decrease as the sample size increases.

Simple random sampling is the best method for selecting a sample, because chance and chance alone determines who or what gets into the sample. Each element has the same, known, nonzero probability of selection. It is not always feasible, however, to use this technique; it works best with smaller populations or findable populations that can be placed on a sampling frame. The next three techniques are variations that improve either the efficiency of selecting the sample (systematic sampling) or handle complicated sampling issues (stratified or cluster sampling).

Table 7.2 Simple Random Samples

Sample 1			*Sample 2*		
Random Number	*County*	*Population Density*	*Random Number*	*County*	*Population Density*
158	Wilkinson	21.4	12	Bleckley	60.5
48	Douglas	661.8	48	Douglas	661.8
97	McDuffie	99.6	134	Telfair	37.7
146	Walker	154.0	73	Hart	108.5
35	Colquit	83.6	11	Bibb	622.8
84	Jones	72.8	109	Oglethorpe	33.15
133	Taylor	23.6	146	Walker	154.0
102	Monroe	66.8	13	Brantley	41.6
47	Dougherty	287.7	62	Glascock	21.4
151	Wayne	46.9	111	Peach	184.3
96	Marion	36.8	159	Worth	38.0
41	Dade	95.6	49	Early	21.5
Mean		151.8			165.4

Systematic Random Sampling

Systematic random sampling is done by first selecting a member of the population at random. Next every *k*th element where k = population size/sample size is chosen until the predetermined sample size is reached. In this case, the researcher must view the sampling frame as a circle with the last element coming before the first element on the frame. This method is similar to simple random sampling, yet is more efficient in terms of time spent in sampling. If done properly, systematic sampling will produce a sample for which all members of the population do not have an equal likelihood of selection.

Unlike simple random sampling, the probability that any given set of elements or samples will be gathered is not equal for all sets of elements or samples. For example, samples with connected elements on the sampling frame, such as a sample that includes elements 5 and 6, have a probability of zero (Kalton 1983; Kish 1995). In addition, the probability of selecting a sample that includes the first randomly chosen element plus the first element at a distance of *k* down the sampling frame is quite high—much higher than in simple random sampling, since every *k*th element will be selected. Thus, researchers must be very careful to choose a sample size, interval, and sample frame organization that are unrelated to each other.

Caveat: Pay careful attention to the structure of the population from which the sample is drawn to make sure the interval, *k*, does not coincide with some naturally occurring structure therein. If there exists a convergence of *k* and such a structure in the population, the result is termed **periodicity**. Periodicity is an indicator of a biased sample and must be avoided.

An instance of periodicity would emerge if you were to sample 10 students from a population of 100 students ($k = 100/10 = 10$) from an introductory sociology class. Assume that all students are present and that there are 10 rows of 10 desks. Regardless of which student gets chosen from the first row, all students in that same position would be chosen from each successive row (each *k*th, or 10th, student). As can be seen in Figure 7.3, if the first randomly chosen element is the student seated at desk 10, then the sample would be all the students in the first row. Students who sit in the first row

Figure 7.3 Example of Periodicity

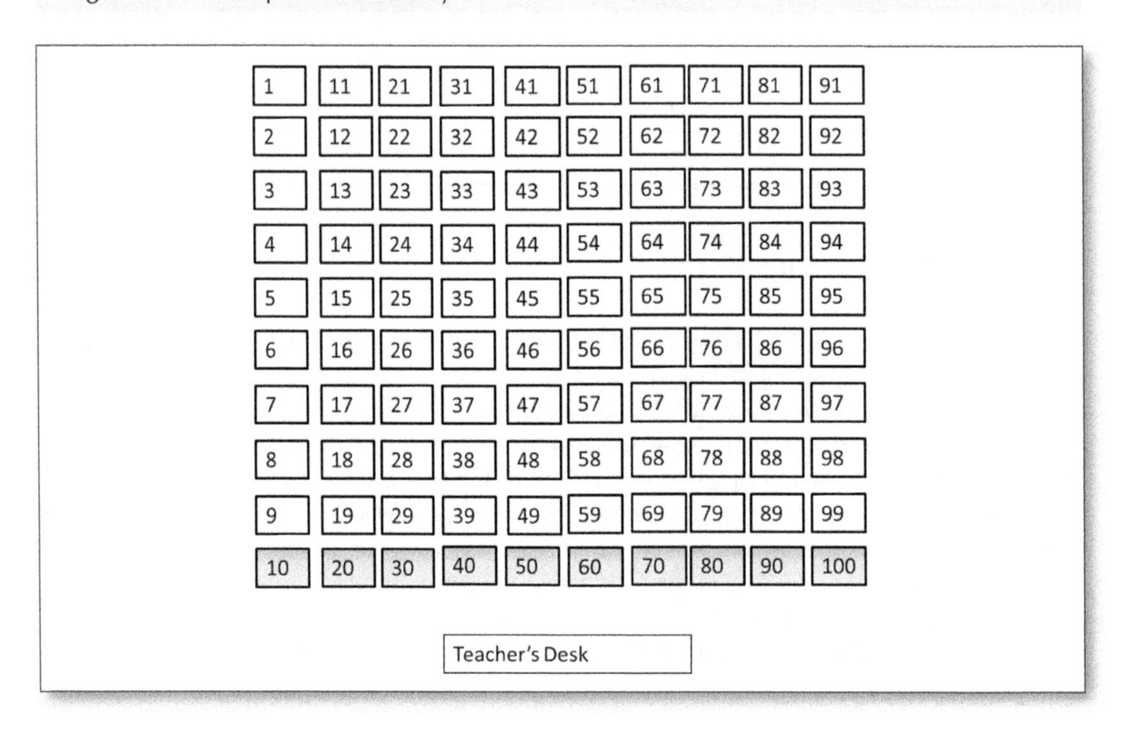

tend to be qualitatively different from students who sit in the rear. Thus, this sample suffers from periodicity and is biased rather than representative.

Stratified Random Sampling

Utilizing stratified random sampling allows a researcher to guarantee a distribution of members of the population across the sample. It can be done so that the proportion of a particular variable (say, gender or race) in the sample mirrors the proportion of that variable in the population. This is called **proportionate stratified sampling**. Alternatively, if one subgroup of a population is particularly small, **disproportionate stratified sampling** allows for a greater proportion of that subgroup to be included so that there is a sufficient number of that group in the sample to allow for statistical analysis.

A stratified sampling technique may be useful when there are large differences between the strata and few differences within each stratum. It may also reduce costs, because general sampling frames will be needed only for the randomly selected strata rather than the entire population. The stratification variables should be correlated with the outcome variable. The benefits of conducting stratified sampling are that it improves on the accuracy of estimation—at least on the selected variables—and it also focuses on important subpopulations and improves the balance of statistical tests between strata (Kalton 1983; Kish 1995). Disadvantages are that the precision gained through stratifying on one variable may not improve precision on all the variables to be collected. Stratifying the population will also increase sampling costs over those for a simple random sample.

When employing stratified sampling, a researcher simply categorizes the population and then creates a separate sampling frame for each stratum. The researcher can then conduct simple random sampling or systematic sampling separately on each stratum.

Let's start with an example of a proportionate stratified sample. In the simple random samples drawn in Table 7.1, it turned out that counties located in the eastern region were overrepresented, and counties from the northern region were underrepresented. Figure 7.4 presents a new sampling frame of Georgia counties organized by region rather than alphabetically. Population density is correlated with region, as the southern region is rural, and northern and eastern regions are more urban. Again, we want to draw a sample of 12 counties. We want the sample to proportionately reflect the regional distribution of counties in the state. In order to obtain a proportionate stratified sample, we first need to determine the proportion of all counties in the state that are located in each region.

Table 7.3 provides the calculations. Column 1 provides the count of counties within each region. Column two provides the regional proportion of counties. To get this number, simply divide the number of counties in each region by the total number of counties. There are 40 counties in the eastern region, which gives us the eastern proportion of .25 or a quarter of all counties, 34 counties in the northern region or .21 proportion of all counties, 56 counties in the southern region or .36 proportion of all counties, and 29 counties in the western region or .18 proportion of all counties. Once we have the proportions, we can calculate the number of counties needed from each region to obtain our proportionate sample size of 12. This calculation is located in Column 3 of Table 7.3. We do this by multiplying the regional proportion (from the above calculations) by the total sample size for each region. To determine whether the sample will be proportionate, we can now determine the probability of a county in each region being selected into the sample (see Column 4). Essentially the probability of selection—minus some rounding error—is the same for each region. Since we cannot sample a fraction of a county, we need to round to the nearest whole digit. Anything .5 or higher is rounded up, and anything less than .5 is rounded down. Thus, we need to select three counties from the east, three from the north, four from the south, and two from the west. At this point we can collect four simple random samples—one from each region—to create our proportionate stratified sample.

Given that the population densities of the counties are related to the regions of the state, a disproportionate stratified sample may be desired. Table 7.4 presents the average population density within each region. It seems the south and west have the lowest population densities on average. If our study is policy driven and designed for locales with higher population densities, we may decide to oversample the regions with higher population densities. This would give us a disproportionate stratified sample. We decide how many counties from each region we want to include rather than calculating this number as we did for the proportionate stratified sample. In this example, we have decided on four counties each from the east and north and two counties each from the south and west. To collect the sample, we simply collect four simple random samples, one of the designated size from each region.

Next, we can calculate the probability of selection in Column 4 of Table 7.4. In the case of a disproportionate sample, the probability of selection will differ for each region. Thus, each county has a known and nonzero probability of selection, but the probabilities are not equal for all counties. This introduces something beyond chance dictating which counties are included in the sample. The sample is not quite representative. The last column in Table 7.4 has the heading "Weights." The **weight** is the inverse of the probability of selection. In this case it tells us that each county selected from the east is representing 10 eastern counties. Each western county selected for the sample is representing 28 counties. Thus, eastern counties are overrepresented in the sample, and western counties are underrepresented. We can use the weights in our statistical analyses to bring the sample back to representativeness.

Stratified sampling is an important technique, as it allows us to sample large areas more effectively or to precisely represent some characteristic of our population. This does not mean that every population characteristic will be precisely represented in our

Figure 7.4 Regionally Organized Sampling Frame of Georgia Counties

Count	Counties	Pop Density	Region
1	Dekalb	2585.7	East
2	Clayton	1832.5	East
3	Fulton	1748.1	East
4	Muscogee	877.5	East
5	Douglas	661.8	East
6	Rockdale	656.6	East
7	Henry	633.0	East
8	Bibb	622.8	East
9	Fayette	548.4	East
10	Houston	372.5	East
11	Newton	367.3	East
12	Spalding	326.1	East
13	Coweta	288.8	East
14	Walton	257.2	East
15	Carroll	221.5	East
16	Peach	184.3	East
17	Troup	161.9	East
18	Butts	128.3	East
19	Haralson	102.0	East
20	Lamar	99.8	East
21	Macon	85.0	East
22	Upson	84.0	East
23	Pike	82.7	East
24	Jones	72.8	East
25	Harris	69.0	East

Count	Counties	Pop Density	Region
26	Monroe	66.8	East
27	Bleckley	60.5	East
28	Pulaski	48.2	East
29	Chattahoochee	45.3	East
30	Dodge	44.0	East
31	Meriwether	43.9	East
32	Heard	40.0	East
33	Crawford	38.9	East
34	Dooly	38.1	East
35	Jasper	37.8	East
36	Marion	36.8	East
37	Schley	30.0	East
38	Twiggs	25.2	East
39	Taylor	23.6	East
40	Talbot	17.5	East
41	Cobb	2026.4	North
42	Gwinnett	1871.2	North
43	Forsyth	783.5	North
44	Cherokee	508.3	North
45	Hall	457.5	North
46	Pauding	455.8	North
47	Barrow	432.7	North
48	Catoosa	394.3	North
49	Whitfield	353.2	North
50	Bartow	218.0	North

(Continued)

Figure 7.4 (Continued)

Count	*Counties*	*Pop Density*	*Region*
51	Floyd	188.9	North
52	Jackson	178.1	North
53	Habersham	155.5	North
54	Gordon	155.1	North
55	Walker	154.0	North
56	Stephens	146.1	North
57	Polk	133.6	North
58	Pickens	126.8	North
59	Murray	115.0	North
60	White	112.8	North
61	Hart	108.5	North
62	Dawson	105.9	North
63	Lumpkin	105.9	North
64	Dade	95.6	North
65	Franklin	84.5	North
66	Chattooga	83.0	North
67	Banks	79.3	North
68	Gilmer	66.3	North
69	Union	66.3	North
70	Towns	62.9	North
71	Fannin	61.2	North
72	Elbert	57.4	North
73	Rabun	44.0	North
74	Madison	33.8	North
75	Chatham	621.7	South
76	Dougherty	287.7	South
77	Lowndes	220.2	South

Count	*Counties*	*Pop Density*	*Region*
78	Glynn	189.7	South
79	Tift	154.9	South
80	Liberty	129.5	South
81	Crisp	86.0	South
82	Colquit	83.6	South
83	Camden	82.4	South
84	Thomas	82.1	South
85	Lee	79.5	South
86	Cook	75.8	South
87	Toombs	74.8	South
88	Coffee	73.6	South
89	Ben Hill	70.5	South
90	Bryan	69.3	South
91	Sumter	68.0	South
92	Evans	60.2	South
93	Pierce	59.3	South
94	Grady	55.0	South
95	Lanier	54.4	South
96	Tattnall	53.2	South
97	Wayne	46.9	South
98	Decatur	46.6	South
99	Mitchell	45.9	South
100	Jeff Davis	45.6	South
101	Bacon	42.9	South
102	Berrien	42.7	South
103	Brantley	41.6	South
104	Ware	40.7	South

Count	Counties	Pop Density	Region
105	Montgomery	38.1	South
106	Worth	38.0	South
107	Telfair	37.7	South
108	Seminole	37.1	South
109	Long	36.1	South
110	Appling	36.0	South
111	Brooks	32.9	South
112	Turner	31.3	South
113	Terrell	27.8	South
114	Irwin	26.9	South
115	Wheeler	25.1	South
116	Atkinson	24.7	South
117	Calhoun	23.9	South
118	McIntosh	23.9	South
119	Wilcox	22.6	South
120	Miller	21.7	South
121	Early	21.5	South
122	Randolph	18.0	South
123	Quitman	16.6	South
124	Clay	16.3	South
125	Charlton	15.7	South
126	Webster	13.4	South
127	Stewart	13.2	South
128	Baker	10.1	South
129	Echols	9.7	South
130	Clinch	8.5	South
131	Clarke	979.1	West
132	Richmond	618.3	West

Count	Counties	Pop Density	Region
133	Columbia	427.6	West
134	Oconee	178.0	West
135	Baldwin	177.3	West
136	Effingham	109.4	West
137	Bulloch	104.4	West
138	McDuffie	99.6	West
139	Putnum	61.6	West
140	Laurens	60.0	West
141	Morgan	51.4	West
142	Candler	45.3	West
143	Greene	41.3	West
144	Lincoln	38.0	West
145	Treutlen	34.5	West
146	Oglethorpe	33.9	West
147	Emanuel	33.2	West
148	Johnson	32.9	West
149	Jefferson	32.2	West
150	Washington	31.2	West
151	Burke	28.2	West
152	Wikes	24.5	West
153	Jenkins	24.0	West
154	Screven	22.6	West
155	Glascock	21.4	West
156	Wilkinson	21.4	West
157	Warren	20.5	West
158	Hancock	20.0	West
159	Taliaferro	8.8	West

Source: U.S. Census Bureau, 2010. Census of Population and Housing, *Population and Housing Unit Counts,* CPH-2-12, Georgia. U.S. Government Printing Office, Washington, DC, 2012.

Table 7.3 Proportionate Stratified Sampling

	Number of Counties	*Proportion of all Counties*	*Sample Size*	*Probability of Selection*	*Rounding*
East	40	.25 (40/159)	3 (.25*12)	.075 (3/40)	3
North	34	.21	2.5	.074	3
South	56	.36	4.3	.076	4
West	29	.18	2.2	.076	2
Total	159	1.0	12		12

Table 7.4 Disproportionate Stratified Sampling

	Number of Counties	*Mean Population Density*	*Sample Size*	*Probability of Selection*	*Weights*
East	40	341.7	4	.10 (4/40)	10 (1/.10)
North	34	294.7	4	.12	8.3
South	56	66.3	2	.036	28
West	29	116.6	2	.069	14.5
Total	159		12		

sample. In fact, this technique has the potential to introduce bias into the sample due to our manipulation of one variable. Even in a case where a given element has a probability of selection into a proportionate stratified sample that is similar to its probability of selection into a simple random sample, our manipulation of the strata may introduce systematic error above and beyond sampling error.

Cluster Sampling

Cluster sampling allows for random sampling from within naturally occurring structures, or *clusters*, within a population. First, a prescribed number of clusters are randomly chosen; then, every member of each of those clusters is chosen (Kalton 1983; Kish 1995). A variation on this could be to first randomly select clusters, then create new sampling frames of all the elements within each selected cluster, and then randomly select *n* elements from within each cluster.

Schools are an obvious structure to use for engaging in cluster sampling, primarily because there are no sampling frames of school-aged children easily available. But, it is quite easy to create a sampling frame of schools. In addition, cluster sampling reduces expenses, as many elements are collected within a single structure.

While each member of a cluster may have the same likelihood of being selected for the sample, members of different clusters will not have the same likelihood of selection if the sizes of the clusters are not equal. In addition, if there is great between-cluster variation and little within-cluster variation, then a sample of many elements from a few clusters will not adequately represent the population. In general, this method increases the variability of the sample estimates more than does simple random sampling. Therefore, a larger sample will be necessary to achieve the same results that simple random sampling would provide (Kalton 1983). In addition, researchers should think about ways to increase the number of clusters and minimize the number of elements per cluster. While this will increase costs, it will decrease the variability problem.

Multistage Cluster Sampling

Multistage cluster sampling, also known as *multilevel cluster sampling*, randomly samples from clusters within clusters to acquire a random sample of a population. This method is particularly useful when there exists no list of members of a target population. For instance, suppose you want to sample the population of all fifth graders in the United States. There is no complete list (unless the NSA is keeping one, which they won't share with you anyway.) However, each school certainly has a list. So, one way to use cluster sampling in this case is as follows:

Step 1: Take a random sample of states from among all 50 US states plus the District of Columbia.

Step 2: Take a random sample of school districts that include Grade 5 from within each state cluster selected in Step 1.

Step 3: Take a random sample of schools from within each of those school districts.

Step 4: Select a random sample of fifth graders from each of those schools.

This is a powerful sampling technique that allows us to sample from large dispersed groups for whom we cannot create a sampling frame. Again, variability will be greater than with simple random sampling, and thus to achieve comparable results, we would need to gather a larger sample.

POWER ANALYSIS FOR SELECTING SAMPLE SIZES

We are using survey methodologies to answer a particular research question whereby one variable has an effect (or association) on another variable. One often neglected part of the study is to determine what sample size is needed in order for that effect to be statistically significant in the analysis. Given our limited resources, we want to limit the sample size as much as possible. On the other hand, if there is a true effect of variable *X* on variable *Y* in the population, but we collect a sample that is too small to detect that effect, we have wasted our time and money. Alternatively if the effect of *X* on *Y* is very small and substantively uninteresting, we do not want a sample size that is so large it will detect any effect. In order to set the appropriate sample size, we need to meet three criteria as our starting point: the alpha, the power level, and the effect size.

The alpha criterion represents the maximum risk one is prepared to take of making a Type I error (Warner 2009). Thinking back to basic statistic courses, recall the important Type I and Type II errors of inferential statistics. A Type I error occurs when researchers reject the null hypothesis as false, when in fact, it is true. The rate of a Type I error is predetermined by setting the alpha (α) to some error rate, usually to .05. A Type II error occurs when we fail to reject the null hypothesis as true, when in fact, it is false. The probability of a Type II error is denoted by the symbol β. The power level is defined as $1-\beta$, or the probability of successfully rejecting the null hypothesis when it is false (Cohen 1992).

Given the relationship between Type I and Type II errors, the test outcome depends not only on power, but on the alpha level set. The smaller the alpha, the more power that is needed to detect the effect; this would result in needing a much larger sample. Additionally, a two-sided test is more stringent then a one-sided test, and therefore a larger sample size would be needed to have enough power to detect an effect. A two-sided test is one in which we do not hypothesize the direction of the effect—we simply state that the effect exists ($x \rightarrow y \neq 0$). If we have information on the direction of the effect, we can use a one sided test ($x \rightarrow y > 0$). Because power analysis is so difficult, Cohen recommends using an alpha of .05 and a power of .80, because making a Type I error is more serious than making a Type II error, and this setup means a researcher is four times more likely to make a Type II error than a Type I error (Cohen 1992).

Effect sizes are more difficult to determine. We can look to the literature to discover the size and direction of the effect, or perhaps conduct a pilot study to ascertain the probable effect size. Because effect sizes are very difficult to determine, Cohen (1992) has developed some standards for researchers to use as comparisons and placed them in a sample size table. Cohen created small, medium, and large effect sizes (based on correlations, so they are standardized, which means not in any particular units). Small effect sizes include a correlation of .10 for a population point estimate and .20 for a group mean difference test. Medium and large effect sizes for a point estimate or group differences would be .30 and .50, and .50 and .80, respectively.

Table 7.5 provides an example of a sample size table. These tables provide sample size ranges that can help to determine the best sample size to detect the effect of interest. Power (1− β) ranges from .25, or low power, to .99, or very high power. The effect sizes across the columns range from .2, or a small effect, to .8 which is a large effect. When power is low (.25) and the effect size is small (.2), a sample of $n = 84$ is needed to detect the effect, whereas, when power is higher at .80 and the effect size is small, a

Table 7.5 Cohen's Sample Size Table*

Power	*Cohen's d (Effect Size)*		
	.2	.5	.8
	n	*n*	*n*
.25	84	14	6
.5	193	32	13
.6	246	40	16
.7	310	50	20
.8	393	64	26
.9	526	85	34
.95	651	105	42
.99	920	148	58

*This table assumes an alpha of .05.

Source: Cohen 1992, 100.

sample of $n = 393$ is needed to detect the effect. If the effect size is large, a sample of only $n = 26$ is sufficient to detect the effect.

Let's say we have a medium effect size and want to follow Cohen's suggestions. Then we would choose a power level of .80. This would suggest that we need a sample size of $n = 64$ to detect a medium effect size. If we have a small effect, then we would need a sample of $n = 393$. This is a guide only, and a researcher should not stop here. This gives a ballpark figure only and provides a range of potential sample sizes and range of resources researchers may need.

Nonresponse, or the effect of individuals in the sample refusing to take the survey, is pretty typical in surveys these days, and we need to make sure to account for nonresponse in our sample size as well. If we really need a sample of $n = 64$ after nonresponse has been accounted for, we will need to increase the sample size we initially select. If we estimate that nonresponse will be at a rate of 25% (based on other surveys of same administration type, same population, and similar topic area), then this means we need to increase our sample size by that amount. With a medium effect size, alpha = .05 and power = .80, we would need a sample of size $n = 64/(1 - .25) = 64/.75 = 85.3$ or 85 individuals in the sample.

Much of this discussion of power analysis and choosing a sample size assumes a simple random sampling technique and a cross-sectional survey using OLS (ordinary least squares) regression. As the sampling technique and statistical analysis becomes more complicated, the power analysis increases in complexity as well. Some techniques will reduce the needed sample size, while others will increase the sample size needs. Alongside the revolution in computer technology, the field of power analysis has also grown. There are now several excellent power or sample size programs available, such as unifypow, a SAS macro created by Ralph O'Brien (http://www.bio.ri.ccf.org/power.html) and nquery advisor (http://www.statsols.com/products/nquery-advisor-nterim/), as well as any number of online sample size calculators. A problem with many of these online calculators is that they are generic, meaning that they provide a sample size that does not depend on the effect size researchers may expect.

Given that the sample size needed depends on (1) the effect size, (2) the instruments used to measure the effect (Lenth 2001), (3) the method of analysis, and (4) the sample design, expending some resources on hiring a sampling specialist or consultant to assist with the sample design and sample size is well worth the expense.

CONCLUSION

In this chapter we introduced the language and techniques of survey sampling. We start by identifying the population of interest and choosing a probability sampling method based on our ability to numerate the population into a sampling frame. For smaller local samples, this might be simple, and thus we might decide to use a simple random sample. This is a nice sampling technique, because each element has an equal probability of being selected into the sample. It also has the nice property of not being subjected to bias. The only error will be random sampling error. Other methods discussed open the door to the potential of adding bias into the sample alongside random sampling error.

For more heterogeneous populations, we may want to stratify first and risk the potential bias that may arise if we are not careful. This improves the precision of our estimator but possibly at the expense of estimating other variables. If the population is larger and more dispersed, a sampling frame might not be conceivable, and thus moving on to a cluster or multistage cluster sampling technique may make more sense and be more feasible. These methods allow for creating sampling frames at a higher unit of analysis first, and creating sampling frames of each selected cluster or stratum only after the initial set is randomly chosen. Variability is greater with this method, and thus a larger sample size is recommended.

All the sampling techniques are based on probability sampling, and all the methods give each population element a known, nonzero probability of being selected into the sample. This allows us to calculate the amount of random sampling error that exists for each of our variables. Ultimately, this allows us to infer from the sample back to the population from which it was drawn. If we find that our sample is not a good representation of our population, we can use weights, which are simply the inverse of the probability of selection, to make the sample we have chosen be representative again.

Finally, we presented a brief introduction into choosing a sample size. This is a complicated topic, and we encourage readers to seek out more information on this topic, as it is too complicated for a single chapter of a survey text.

KEY TERMS

CRITICAL THINKING QUESTIONS

Below you will find three questions that ask you to think critically about core concepts addressed in this chapter. Be sure you understand each one; if you don't, this is a good time to review the relevant sections of this chapter.

1. How can researchers reduce the potential for coverage error?
2. What are the differences between simple random sampling, stratified sampling, and cluster sampling?
3. What are the criteria we use to decide on the sampling technique we will use to gather our sample?

8

Nonprobability Sampling and Sampling Hard-to-Find Populations

INTRODUCTION

While it is true that only a randomly drawn sample can be truly representative, there are times when a mathematically random sample cannot be obtained for one reason or another. Given the very real possibility that a random sample is not feasible or possible at all, consider an appropriate **nonrandom sampling** method. While researchers using many of these methods make efforts to represent the population well, nonrandom sampling methods do not use randomness or chance to ensure representation in a sample. This means that a whole host of things other than chance may be affecting who is in the sample, and these things may keep the sample from being representative. Additionally, because we do not know the probability of selection into the sample when we are not using randomness to select it, we cannot estimate sampling error or bias. Thus, despite efforts to represent the population, we can never know with any certainty if the sample does or does not, in fact, represent the population.

In this chapter we briefly introduce five nonprobability sampling techniques that researchers can use when they are not able to collect a probability sample by using a sampling frame: convenience sampling, quota sampling, purposive sampling, snowball sampling, and respondent driven sampling.

CONVENIENCE SAMPLING

Convenience sampling is the crudest form of nonrandom sampling. It is also referred to as *availability sampling* or *haphazard sampling* (Kalton 1983). With convenience sampling, elements are selected into the sample because it is easy to include them or they are easily available. This might include a sample of the closest respondents to those administering the survey, such as family, friends, colleagues, et cetera. These samples are known to be subject to several types of bias, including **subjectivity**—researchers tend to ask people to be part of the survey who they are most comfortable asking or who happen to be around. In addition, the respondents will have shared characteristics, because they are part of the researcher's network. As you can gather from the names applied to it, this method of sampling is not to be trusted to produce a representative sample of the target population.

One example of a convenience sample that many will recognize is the mall survey. An interviewer stands in wait with a clipboard (or nowadays more often with an iPad) in the mall and asks individuals to participate in a quick survey. The types of people who go to that particular mall may be very similar. For example, an exclusive mall filled with designer shops will attract a wealthy clientele. Those from less wealthy groups will be more likely to go to a more affordable mall that is centered on a Walmart or Target type of store. Some people simply prefer to not shop at malls, and they purchase items online or at stores not connected to a mall. This sampling method leads to a form of error called *selection bias.* The characteristics of the people who attend different malls are associated with the malls themselves. The place and clientele are not independent of one another. Other convenience samples that are subject to selection bias include readers of a specific magazine, a local clinic's patients, a church's members, and voters for American Idol.

Extreme caution should be exercised with convenience sampling, since there is absolutely no basis upon which to conclude that the sample would in any way be representative of a larger population. Generalizations from the survey findings cannot be supported with this sampling method. In short, do not use this method to draw a sample for survey research if you can at all help it. If you do, you will need to disclose that results are largely for discussion purposes only.

QUOTA SAMPLING

One of the most obvious drawbacks to convenience sampling is that there is no guarantee that different types of people (e.g., persons of different genders, races, and ages) would be included in the sample at all. **Quota sampling** is convenience sampling with the addition of quotas, or limits on the number of people of a particular socioeconomic group, race, gender, or age who can be included in the sample. Often the quotas are used to reflect known properties of the population. Thus, quotas might be set to ensure that 50% of the sample is female and 50% male. This method does at least guarantee that the sample will reflect variation in the population with respect to the variables used to create the quota. We use the word *reflect* here, rather than *represent*, because we have no idea whether the sample represents the population.

The mall researcher from the previous example may be aware of the **selection effect** bias found in the convenience sampling method and decide that a quota sample would be better. Therefore, the mall researcher will choose to conduct surveys in three different malls: the high-end mall, a mall located in a middle class suburb, and a low-end mall in a poor part of town. Thus, the researcher will have three convenience samples that better reflect the socioeconomic conditions of the area. In addition to creating a sample that has socioeconomic quotas, the investigator may decide to add gender and race quotas. Thus, half of each mall sample will be male and half will be female. In terms of race, the investigator will have to determine the racial distribution across the locale and make sure the sample from each mall, or across all three malls, matches the locale's racial distribution. For example, if the distribution is 15% African American, 14% Hispanic, 5% Asian, and 66% white, the investigator will create quotas that will result in the same racial distribution in the sample.

This may sound very similar to a proportionate stratified sampling method (see Chapter 7). But it is not. It is still a convenience sample that improves variation within the sample to reflect some aspects of the population. However, it is still subject to both selection bias and subjectivity. This is especially so when we consider that if someone does not agree to participate, there is no record of that. We simply replace that person with someone who is willing to participate. The characteristics of willing participants may be significantly different from the characteristics of those who refuse to participate (unwilling nonparticipants). This will be hidden in the research process and adds to selection bias.

Again, we do not know the probability of selection. When the desired sample size is very small, a quota sample will be about as effective as a probability sample. This is because a small sample size produces a large variance about the sample estimator, and thus it is already not very precise (Kalton 1983). Only for medium to large sample sizes do we see the benefits of random sampling.

Like most things, quota sampling can be done well or it can be done poorly. It is important to select the critical variables, across which representation is key in order to be able to generalize at all (at least across those chosen variables). It is also critical for staff who may be administering a survey to be keenly aware of the quotas, how to implement them, and the rationale behind them. Beyond such awareness, a system should be in place to validate the quotas.

PURPOSIVE SAMPLING

Purposive sampling, also called *judgmental sampling*, is a special type of convenience sample in that the sample participants are chosen specifically based on their specialized knowledge of the subject area under investigation (Kalton 1983). Another term for this is a *key informant interview*, where the key informants are experts in the field being investigated. For example, a study called Impacteen was carried out by researchers at the University of Illinois at Chicago; it addressed youth drug and alcohol use (www.impacteen.org). One aspect of the study investigated how different cities' justice departments adjudicated first-time youth substance use offenses. Some cities handled this at the level of the police department. Other cities handled it at the prosecutor's office, while in other cities, the courts were involved. The study researchers cold-called various members of the justice system of each city and asked who the individuals most knowledgeable about adolescent and youth first-time arrests for drug and alcohol were in their city. It did not make sense for the Impacteen researchers to talk to just any police officer or prosecutor, because the researchers needed to talk to those with the knowledge or expertise needed for the study. Once the researchers located the correct persons in each city, those persons were contacted for participation in a survey interview.

Purposive sampling also is often used with marginalized populations. It is difficult to gather a sampling frame for a marginalized population, and marginalized populations are not always conveniently located. Suppose, for example, that a researcher is interested in permanently homeless individuals who avoid shelters. In order to understand how this group manages to survive, stay in contact with family, and use its social networks, researchers must find knowledgeable individuals to include in a sample. Not just any homeless individual will do, because that individual may not have the specialized knowledge the study needs.

Like the convenience and quota sampling techniques, purposive sampling is a nonprobability sampling technique. This means the sample drawn is not representative of the larger population, and we cannot estimate sampling error or bias. Given the specialized knowledge being sought, however, if a large sample is gathered, it is possible that a survey using such a sample could produce excellent data. We will never know, though, to what degree the data represent the knowledge of the population of experts.

SAMPLING HARD-TO-FIND POPULATIONS

The next two methods are designed to sample hard-to-find or hidden populations. Hard-to-find populations are defined as those for whom you cannot create a sampling frame or list of the population members, either because the size and locations of the members are not known, or because the population is marginalized and stigmatized. They may be homeless and therefore not likely to be found in the phone book or counted in the US census, and they might migrate regularly, making it difficult to find them. They may be members of a special identity group that you will not find or even know exists unless you have some insider knowledge about the group. For example, transgendered persons are difficult to find, persons with HIV are not readily visible, and illicit drug users do not have membership lists, for obvious reasons. These groups are most likely stigmatized in some way, which makes it difficult for the researcher to get close and be trusted. Thus, finding one member to start with may be the best way to get access to this type of population.

Snowball Sampling

The first method is called **snowball sampling**. Freezing temperatures are not required for snowball sampling. Snowball sampling, also known as *chain sampling* or *chain referral,* is a nonrandom sampling method where a member of the sample refers the researcher to others who fall within the target population, who then refer others still, and so on. This method is helpful in procuring a sample when the target population is not easily reached, is smaller than the general population, and may be dispersed geographically; and when it is likely that members of that target population may know or know of one another (Heckathorn 2011).

Snowball sampling begins when researchers find one or more members of the hard-to-find population through convenience methods. These are the first wave of sample members. Figure 8.1 provides a visual representation of what snowball sampling looks like. The subjects in Wave 1 will recruit those in Wave 2 either by themselves or by giving the researchers names of other members of the hard-to-find group. Wave 2 recruits will provide an additional list of individuals, who will become Wave 3 recruits (Heckathorn 2011). At each wave the sample gets larger and larger as would a snowball rolling down the side of a hill. This will continue until the researchers are satisfied with the sample they have collected.

The graphic in Figure 8.1 also demonstrates a serious problem found in snowball sampling; that is, snowball sampling has a particular weakness in that whoever is included as the Wave 1 recruit can have a strong influence on the rest of the sample. In this example, the person at Wave 1 is the only homeless person providing the next set of names. If the person at Wave 1 is unusual, we will obtain a rather unusual sample and may not have a clear picture of the permanently homeless. This is another example of selection bias. One way to solve this is to have more than one recruit at Wave 1 and to make sure the recruits at Wave 1 do not know each other.

The homeless are a heterogeneous group of individuals. Some are chronic homeless and may live on the streets and be difficult to find and interact with. Others may

Figure 8.1 Snowball Sampling

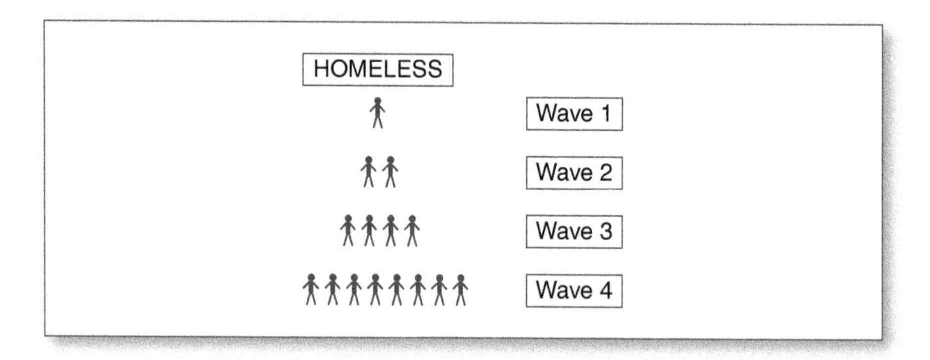

be long-term homeless who take advantage of shelters and other services and thus are easier to locate. Another group, which expanded during the great recession of 2008 with its high foreclosure rates, includes the temporary homeless who are living in family members' or friends' homes temporarily. Therefore, the sample drawn in Figure 8.1 may be limited in its ability to provide a good picture of the homeless condition.

One way to minimize this problem is to have several Wave 1 recruits from different homeless populations providing Wave 2 recruitment names. Drawing Wave 1 recruits randomly, if possible, is another good solution. Figure 8.2 provides an example of how snowball sampling might be improved to address some of these shortcomings. In Figure 8.2 there are three Wave 1 recruits, one for each type of homelessness situation discussed.

Figure 8.2 Snowball Sampling Revisited

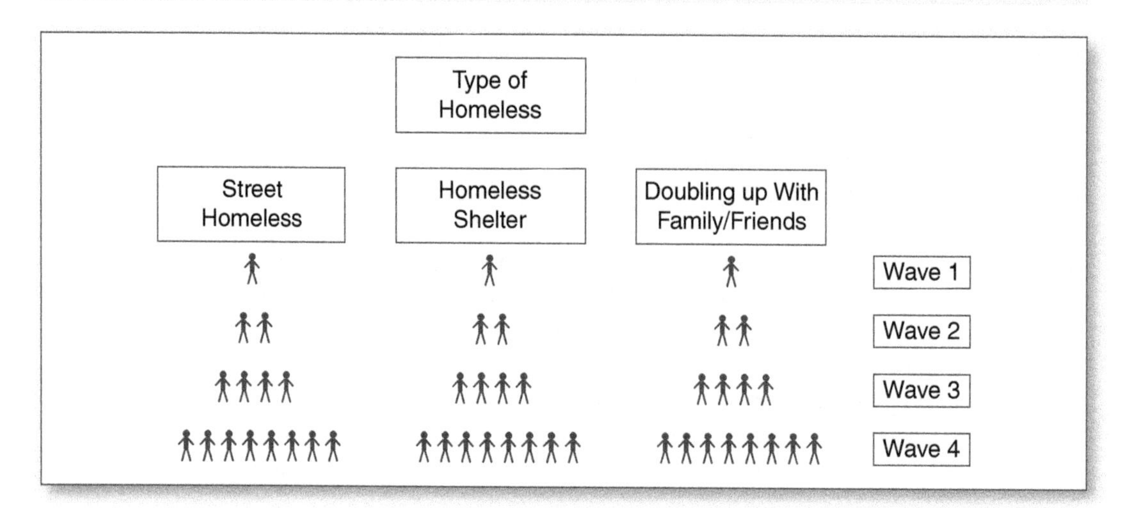

The third group, those doubling up with family or friends, may not be an easy group to obtain through snowball sampling given that they are still outside the system. The researcher in that case would want to create a multimethod sample, whereby the first two groups are gathered through snowball samples and the third might be gathered through a convenience sampling method. These methods can be combined to best effect. Recall that these are not representative samples. This means that as long as the methods are rigorously applied and systematically documented, they can be used as needed within a single project.

Respondent-Driven Sampling

Respondent-driven sampling (RDS) is a sophisticated variation of snowball or chain sampling that results in a better sample capable of greater generalizability. Heckathorn and colleagues developed RDS in order to conduct an HIV prevention program in Connecticut based on understanding and taking advantage of social network structures. It differs from snowball sampling in that the RDS sample is independent of the Wave 1 recruit selection bias, which means researchers do not have to draw their Wave 1 recruits randomly in order to generalize to the population. It also is able to control for differences in personal networks that can lead to biases such as size of network (Heckathorn 1997).

It works like snowball sampling, except that incentives are provided to sample members who refer others as well as to those who are referred. *Secondary incentives* encourage sample members to refer others for inclusion in the sample (see Chapter 9 for more on incentives). *Primary incentives* go to the individuals the sample members refer, to encourage them to participate. This engages a social or group peer influence as well as a monitoring influence, and is highly effective at convincing new recruits to participate (Heckathorn 1990). This dual incentive increases the likelihood of participation and helps mitigate the self-selecting nature of the participation of those who have been referred.

Another difference between snowball sampling and RDS is who is doing the recruiting. In snowball sampling, the investigator obtains names of potential sample members from the prior wave, tracks them down, and asks if they would like to participate. There may or may not be an incentive to participate. With RDS, the prior wave participant is tasked with accomplishing the recruitment of the subsequent wave. Given the stigmatized nature of hard-to-find populations, this may be more effective in getting a more diverse set of recruits. This would, in turn, reduce selection bias.

RDS begins similarly to snowball sampling with the researcher selecting a few recruits to act as "seeds" at Wave 1. (This section is based heavily on Heckathorn 1997.) Unlike snowball sampling, these seeds are given "recruitment coupons" to use to recruit additional sample members (Wave 2 recruits). For every Wave 2 recruit who comes to the research office with a coupon and participates, the Wave 1 referring sample member gets an additional incentive, say $10.00. Wave 2 recruits also get participation incentives just like the original Wave 1 seeds did, and they get a set of recruitment coupons to use to recruit new sample members (Wave 3).

If the incentives are sufficient, this sampling procedure will create an ever-expanding chain referral system. To keep some control over the recruitment process—that is, to keep some entrepreneurial sample members from doing professional recruitment, researchers limit the number of referrals they will accept from a single recruiter. This ensures a more varied group of recruiters and recruited members. Researchers can expect to recruit more waves of data with RDS than they would collect with snowball sampling.

Given that researchers are not doing the actual recruiting, how do they verify that the recruit coming to the research office with a referral coupon fits their eligibility requirements? Limiting the number of referrals reduces the problem of ineligibles trying to participate. But researchers will need to think of ways to verify eligibility. With a hidden population, there is probably some hidden knowledge that researchers can quiz recruits about. For example, Heckathorn and colleagues queried potential recruits for their HIV prevention study by asking detailed questions about drug preparation and injection techniques (Heckathorn 1997). Researchers will also want to make sure that earlier recruits do not attempt to return and participate a second or third time with a fake identification. Of course, with some marginalized populations, this is a problem regardless of sampling techniques.

Researchers can introduce some quotas for their recruitment by adding a targeting bonus. Heckathorn and colleagues increased the secondary incentive by $5.00 for recruiters who brought in female injection drug users (Heckathorn 1997).

Finally, sampling can be ended based on one of two criteria. First, it can be stopped when the community is saturated. Second, it can be stopped when the enrollment targets have been reached, and the composition of the sample reaches the desired state according to the research focus.

RDS sampling is limited to hard-to-find populations that share a network tie. To some extent they are also limited geographically, but given the increase in online social networks, this is not always the case. Using these networks is an excellent method if the goal is to survey hard-to-find online communities.

A strength of RDS is that, unlike other chain referral methods, the final recruitment pattern tends to be independent of the initial recruitment pattern. Heckathorn (1997) found that regardless of the race of the initial seed, after several waves of recruitment, an equilibrium pattern resulted that was essentially the same regardless of whether the initial seed was white or black. This is due to RDS following the Markov chain principle of large numbers, which states that over a large number of steps, the probability that some system will be in a particular state is independent of its starting state (Kemeny and Snell 1960: 73). The Markov chain is simply a mathematical term used to describe how a process of change over time occurs in some system. The principle is based on probability distributions and essentially states that the current state of the system is the most probable future state of the system, but that there are fixed probabilities of all possible future states.

Another difference between RDS and snowball sampling is that in RDS, methods have been generated to develop estimators of the population. Thus, while RDS is not a probability sampling method, if it is done properly, researchers can generalize from an RDS sample. Heckathorn's work (2002, 2011) introduced new RDS estimators and was also able to show that RDS provides both reliable and valid population estimates. Over the course of several years, additional refinements have been made to estimating population estimates, improving the efficiency and precision of estimates and confidence intervals (Heckathorn 2007). Over the years, Heckathorn and his colleagues have made improvements to the RDS method that provide a greater sense of confidence that we can generalize to the population. For example, in 2004, Salganik and Heckathorn introduced a population estimator and demonstrated that it was unbiased when model assumptions were met. It required, however, that each recruiter recruit only one new member to the sample. This eliminates a selection bias called **differential recruitment bias**. But, in a 2007 article, Heckathorn introduced a way to control for differential recruitment bias without limiting to a single recruit from each recruiter. Differential recruitment bias occurs because some recruiters are better at recruiting than others. In this population estimator method, different recruiters can recruit different numbers of new sample members, because the calculation can control for this difference, making RDS more flexible.

RDS is a newer sampling method and is still being refined. This is a nonprobability method that can be used to generalize to the population from which it was drawn. It tends to work only with hidden populations and is a time consuming and expensive method of sampling. Still this is a promising and exciting new sampling methodology.

ETHICS CORNER

Some of these sampling methods involve respondents (informers) providing contact information to the researchers (snowball sampling), or recruiting new respondents for an incentive (RDS). Both methods involve a loss of confidentiality to some extent. In the case of snowball sampling, the researchers contact the new potential recruits. Prior wave informers do not know the outcome of the attempts to recruit the new participants. They do know that there is a greater than zero probability that the individual is a study participant. The new recruit does not know the identity of the informer. Thus, in its strictest sense, confidentiality is not broken.

What about in the case of RDS? In RDS, the new recruit is recruited by a study participant. This means that confidentiality is violated. However, in a group interview situation, participants can see all the other study participants as well. So, confidentiality is broken in this sense with either method. Confidentiality is the promise by researchers to study participants that their identity and responses to the study will not be linked and made public. Thus, instances where participants know that other participants are involved in the study do not, in and of themselves, violate the confidentiality principle. However, when using participants to help gather the sample, researchers need to think carefully about what additional steps need to be taken to ensure that any findings do not identify individual participants. For example, researchers may choose to change the name of the settings, mix up characteristics of the participants, or avoid presenting individual information; they should also make sure that all data are presented in aggregate form.

CONCLUSION

In this chapter we introduced five nonprobability sampling techniques. These techniques should only be used when a sampling frame cannot be created and, therefore, a probability sample is not feasible. Using a convenience sample is simply not appropriate for use with a survey. If it is used, we should simply be aware that results cannot be generalized to the larger population. A quota sample is a convenience sample that adequately reflects the population on one or more characteristics, but we have no idea how well it represents the population in general. It does, however, improve upon the convenience sample. Like convenience and quota samples, a purposive sample is not generalizable. For purposive samples, participants are chosen specifically due to their specialized knowledge. If the sample is large and the population is small, we may end up with a sample that represents the population. Unfortunately, we cannot calculate whether that is the case. A snowball sample is a convenience sample that works well with hard-to-find populations. By restricting the number of new recruits each member of the sample provides, and by recruiting over many waves, it is possible to get a sample that represents the population reasonably well, but rarely are these samples created in such a way that they do so. Respondent-driven sampling (RDS) improves upon this strength of snowball sampling. Through dual incentives, sample member recruiting, and recruiting over a large number of waves, RDS can generate population estimators that are calculable, reliable, and valid. RDS samples, when applied appropriately to hard-to-reach populations, are representative, can be used with survey research, and generate findings that are generalizable.

KEY TERMS

Nonrandom sampling 149
Convenience sampling 150
Subjectivity 150
Quota sampling 150
Selection effect 151
Purposive sampling 152
Snowball sampling 153
Respondent-driven sampling (rds) 155
Differential recruitment bias 157

CRITICAL THINKING QUESTIONS

Below you will find three questions that ask you to think critically about core concepts addressed in this chapter. Be sure you understand each one; if you don't, this is a good time to review the relevant sections of this chapter.

1. In conducting a study on uses of feminist methodology research, the investigator collects a convenience sample of female researchers from the fields of sociology, political science, women's studies, and African American studies who are members of a campus group called Feminist Methods First. What might be the biases included in the sample?
2. How might we improve upon the sample in Question 1 by using a quota sample? What would you base the quota(s) on?
3. How would you design a respondent-driven sample to conduct surveys on the health and well-being of transgendered men and women?

9

Improving Response Rates and Retention

INTRODUCTION

In the previous two chapters, we discussed various methods for determining who will be included in the sample. The major sampling error or problem we discussed was coverage error. That is, has the researcher managed to include all members of the population on the sampling frame? If not, there is coverage error, and the probability that a given element will be selected into the sample will be inaccurate; that is, the sample may not well represent the population from which it was drawn. Believe it or not, that is the easy part. The researcher does have some control over the process. Once the sample is selected, however, the researcher must reach out to the sampled elements and lobby them to participate. In the case of a panel study, lobbying will need to continue over time to convince respondents to continue participating at later time intervals. If the researcher cannot convince respondents to participate or continue to participate, the study will face two serious errors, nonresponse and attrition. It is important to know and understand the effect nonresponse may have on the sample's ability to represent the population (Groves 2006).

How do researchers convince selected respondents to participate? What happens when the interviewer calls them or sends them an e-mail or letter letting them know they have been chosen? Will respondents be so flattered that they drop everything and immediately fill out the survey, buy a postage stamp, and send the survey back right away? Will they, out of a sense of obligation to science for the benefits they enjoy, agree to participate in the study? It's not very likely that they will even pick up the phone or open the cover letter. Today, most people have caller ID, and many have their phone numbers listed on the national "no call" list. People receive so many solicitation calls and telemarketing calls that many do not answer the phone if the caller's identification is unknown or blocked. In fact, many people have eliminated their home phone lines entirely and rely only a cell phone. Getting through to respondents with a cold call is not an easy task. Suppose the researcher sends them a letter or e-mail first? In this era of spam filters, junk e-mails, and computer viruses, most people will not open an e-mail from an unknown source. At home, people are inundated with junk mail, and most of it goes straight into the garbage or shredder. How do researchers ensure that their e-mails or letters will get through? Once contact has occurred, how do researchers convince respondents to participate? In this chapter, we first discuss nonresponse and retention errors, and we follow that with ways to approach members of the sample and convince them to participate.

RESPONSE RATES AND NONRESPONSE ERRORS

One way in which the quality of a survey may be assessed is by examining the **response rate**, or the percentage of the chosen sample that completes the survey. That is, a response is a completed survey. Response rates vary by type of survey administration. Face-to-face surveys receive the highest response rates; they are followed by phone surveys, although recently response rates have fallen off for phone surveys to a level similar to that of mail surveys (Dillman, Smyth, and Christian 2009; Curtin, Presser, and Singer 2005). Mail surveys have the lowest response rates (Hox and de Leeuw 1994). The response rate is calculated by dividing the actual number of completed surveys by the total number of surveys disseminated to eligible participants.

Calculating Response Rates

You choose a sample of 1,000 participants and distribute surveys to all of them. Nine hundred surveys are completed. What is the response rate? Assuming all are eligible—the simplest case— the formula is number of completed surveys divided by the sample size (n). So, in this case, 900/1,000 = .9 or a 90% response rate. If 10 participants died prior to responding to the survey, then you may consider them ineligible; thus the adjusted response rate would be: 900/(1,000 – 10) = 900/990= .91 or a 91% response rate.

In actuality there are several ways to calculate response rates. Here we have shown two ways. The first way assumes all uncontacted individuals are eligible, and the second is based on specific disposition codes that remove all ineligibles from the denominator prior to calculating the response rate (Smith 2009). The American Association of Public Opinion

Research has a wonderful webpage and guide to calculating response rates for those interested in learning more about this topic: http://www.aapor.org/AAPORKentico/Education-Resources/For-Researchers/Poll-Survey-FAQ/Do-Response-Rates-Matter.aspx.

It is impractical to expect all members of the sample to be able to complete the survey. Thus, researchers will rarely if ever obtain response rates of 100%. If a respondent refuses to participate or cannot be located, then the survey is not completed, and this failure is called a nonresponse. The **nonresponse rate** can be calculated directly as number of uncompleted surveys divided by the total expected sample size.

Calculating Nonresponse Rates

The nonresponse rate can be calculated directly as the number of uncompleted surveys divided by the total sample size. In the example of response rates above, of a total expected sample size of 1,000, 900 surveys are completed, and that leaves 100 (1,000 – 900) uncompleted. Thus the nonresponse rate = 100/1,000 = .1 or a 10% nonresponse rate. Alternatively, you can calculate the nonresponse rate directly from the response rate as 1.0 less the response rate, or 1.0 – (900/1,000) = 1.0 – .9 = .1.

The higher the response rate (the lower the nonresponse rate), potentially, the higher the quality of the data, meaning that we still assess the sample as representative of the population from which it was drawn. There is some consensus that a good response rate cutoff for maintaining representativeness is 70%. Singleton and Straits (2005), however, argue, "For interview surveys, a response rate of 85% is minimally adequate; below 70% there is a serious chance of bias" (p. 145). If a study has too high a nonresponse rate, then the representativeness of the sample is compromised, and the researcher must determine how problematic the low response rate is. Has it led to bias?

It is possible that the nonresponses are randomly distributed throughout the sample—meaning that there is no pattern to the types of people who did not complete a survey. Thus, the reduced-size sample still matches the population in terms of basic demographics. Unfortunately, we cannot be sure that the reduced-size sample matches the population in terms of unobserved variables. Additionally, a loss of power to detect an effect may become a problem, as there may not be a large enough sample size now to determine if X leads to Y. This may lead to a Type II statistical error, where the researcher mistakenly fails to detect the hypothesized effect between the dependent and independent variables when it is a true effect.

If nonresponse occurs randomly, meaning there is no pattern to the level of nonresponse and the response rate is greater than 70%, then the dataset is of good quality and can be considered to represent the population. In other words, nonresponse has not led to nonresponse bias. If there is a response rate greater than 70% but nonresponse does not occur randomly, then the sample may not be representative of the population despite the high response rate. This, in turn may lead to increases in **measurement error**. Table 9.1 presents each of these possible scenarios. The gender and age distributions of the population and of two possible samples are presented in columns 2–4. In each case, the researcher has drawn a sample of 1,000 and ultimately achieved a response rate of 80%. In the case of Sample 1, there is no clear pattern to the nonresponses. The gender and age distributions very closely match the gender and age distributions of the population. Thus, Sample 1 with its high response rate and lack of nonresponse pattern appears to be a representative sample. In the case of Sample 2, the gender distribution of the sample also appears to match well the gender distribution of the population. Unfortunately, this is not the case for the age distribution. In Sample 2, it is clear that younger members of the sample did not participate. Age group 18–30 is underrepresented in Sample 2, and age groups 31–45, 46–60, and 61 and older are overrepresented in the sample. So, even though the response rate is high, Sample 2 does not do a good job of representing the population from which it was drawn.

Table 9.1 Samples With and Without Nonresponse Patterns

	Population	*Sample 1*	*Sample 2*
Male	48%	47%	49%
Female	52%	53%	51%
Total	100%	100%	100%
Ages 18–30	21%	19%	4%
Ages 31–45	30%	31%	32%
Ages 46–60	32%	31%	39%
Ages 61 and over	17%	19%	25%
Total	100%	100%	100%

NONRESPONSE BIAS

Nonresponse bias is the difference that results when participants are significantly and qualitatively distinct from nonparticipants. If the variable of interest is highly correlated with the reason for nonresponse, then bias will be high. For example, if a study is interested in examining workplace discrimination, and persons who have experienced said discrimination are much more likely to refuse to participate, then a nonresponse bias will exist. However, if the study is also interested in job training, and job training is not associated with workplace discrimination, then nonresponse bias in mean levels of job training is likely to be low. This means that bias is not a constant within a survey, but can vary with the variable being measured. A further implication is that even with a high response rate, it is possible to have to contend with bias on some variables. Alternatively, there can be some surveys with low response rates that have little to no bias with respect to the variables of interest, and thus the samples may be representative of the population (Groves 2006).

Current survey research is asking and answering the question, Does convincing unwilling participants to complete the survey really improve the quality of the data? Best practices as expressed here suggest that we should do everything we can to achieve high response rates (Keeter et al. 2000). Several studies question these best practices. Recent studies show there is no significant correlation between nonresponse rates and nonresponse bias (Groves 2006; Keeter et al. 2000; Merkle and Edelman 2002). Therefore, we cannot assume bias exists simply because nonresponse exists. Other research suggests that reducing nonresponse by including reluctant participants will lead to higher measurement error or poor data quality (Biemer 2001; Groves and Couper 1998). Olson (2006), however, finds limited support for increases in measurement error, and in addition finds that including reluctant participants leads to decreases in total bias, despite any increase in measurement error. As a result, we conclude that the best practice of minimizing nonresponse holds.

However, that does not absolve us from assessing whether the nonresponse found in our study is biased or unbiased. One place to start assessing whether nonresponse leads to bias is to compare response rates across subgroups (see Table 9.1). You can also compare the demographic composition of your sample to a population-based study (e.g., census data or the American Community Survey). This is also a limited solution, since the variables we are interested in are rarely included in these other studies. If demographic information about the population is available and included in your sampling frame, it is possible to determine how different the sample is from the population.

Alternatively, comparing the sample to a **benchmark sample** is another way to ascertain if, in the sample, regardless of the response rate, there is bias in the variables of interest. Benchmarking is comparing a statistic from a sample to the same publicly known statistic for the same population found in population data (e.g., census data), administration data, or a sample from a study with a higher response rate (Olson 2006). Creating postsampling weights, and modeling the nonresponse in your analyses, are additional ways to deal with or understand nonresponse bias and how it affects the ability to generalize.

ATTRITION IN PANEL STUDIES

Attrition is defined as the loss in follow-up responses in a longitudinal study. Attrition and nonresponse are two distinct problems. In longitudinal studies, the goal is to analyze change over time within individuals rather than differences at one point in time across a group, which is the goal of cross-sectional research. Typically there is attrition due to death or disability, and that is inevitable. Other forms of attrition may be due to losing track of respondents over time as they move or change their names as they marry or divorce. Most often, however, attrition occurs as participants refuse to continue participating.

Attrition can compromise the generalizability of longitudinal surveys, which, in turn, may lead to **attrition bias** (Deeg 2002). If attrition becomes a big enough problem, a loss of power to detect effects can occur that is similar to that of nonresponse. Attrition should be examined in much the same way that nonresponse is examined to determine if there are patterns to the attrition that could compromise representativeness. The problem of lack of power may be addressed through statistical methods of dealing with missing data. (See Chapter 15 for a brief discussion of missing data imputation.)

METHODS TO INCREASE PARTICIPANT CONTACT AND COOPERATION

Contact

There are two steps in the recruitment process for sample members, and thus two places to intervene to increase response rates. The first step is contacting the chosen participants, and the second step is convincing them to cooperate with the survey. Prior to contacting participants, research shows that an advance letter, which is routine in mailed surveys and face-to-face surveys, increases response rates (de Leeuw et al. 2007). Using university letterhead also increases participation, while using marketing firm letterhead does not. Advance letters in random-digit-dial telephone surveys can increase response rates if there are associated mail addresses.

For web and Internet surveys, an advance letter can be distributed through e-mail rather than postal mail—if e-mail access is possible. Many people have spam guards on their computers to filter out unsolicited bulk e-mails. Be sure not to use spam language in the subject line or body of the e-mail (refer back to Chapter 3) and to have e-mails sent individually, not with suppressed distribution lists. Posting advance letters to pertinent social media and chat rooms may also increase awareness and support for the study.

Once sufficient time has elapsed after the advance letter is sent, it is time to mail (e-mail) out the survey or to call (visit) the participants to conduct the actual survey. How often will you mail, e-mail, call, or visit with participants in order to gain contact with them? Persistence is important, as are varying the timing and types of contacts when possible.

- Send an advance letter announcing the study.
- Use university letterhead.
- Create a pamphlet explaining your study—the more professional looking, the better.
- Include a self-addressed, stamped postcard for respondents to set the time of the survey.
- Maintain professional standards while personalizing your contacts.
- Attempt multiple contacts.
- Create a study webpage with additional information, means of contacting investigators, and investigator biographies.
- For web-based surveys, make sure to use an organization-based or university-affiliated e-mail address whenever possible.
- For e-mails, use a trustworthy and legitimate subject line.
- Do not include video, pictures, flash, or JavaScript in the e-mail.

What should be included in the advance letters? In other words, what can be included that would encourage or excite participants to respond? Discuss the study, both the content (if possible) and the logistics of participating. Explain the goals of the study and why it is important to society and also to the participants. If the study is designed specifically to target and change a policy, this may be important information to include. What will the study findings add to our world? Pamphlets, especially if they are professionally printed, will increase the confidence of participants in the authenticity of your study. Also, having a webpage that can provide greater detail as well as investigator contact information will increase confidence in the study and, therefore, contact.

Gaining Cooperation

Persistence in attempting to contact respondents is the first step to gaining cooperation. If a respondent refuses to cooperate one time, call again and ask why. Ask what the respondent's concerns are, and attempt to assuage them. If there is a gatekeeper of some sort, a trusted person or community group that you can get to support your study will go a long way toward increasing trust in the study and, consequently, cooperation. Follow-up reminders can help in gaining the cooperation of many who plan to cooperate but may have forgotten due to their busy schedules. If you use a number of follow-up letters or contacts, change the type of contact or the appearance of the follow-up or final contact. Plan the follow-up contacts strategically so that respondents are not inundated with a barrage of contacts—that could end up turning participants off rather than encouraging them to participate. Decide on how many contacts are appropriate prior to survey implementation (more on this in Chapter 11). Appropriately used follow-ups have been effective in increasing response rates (Dillman et al. 1974).

- Attempt multiple contacts—be persistent—evaluate refusals for how determined they are—maybe take two no's before refusal is accepted.
- Use a gatekeeper to help with trust and importance.
- Use follow-ups reminders.
- Brand your study.
- Use incentives—cash or swag.
- Tailor your approach specifically to your population where appropriate.

Branding the study may increase recognition of it and gain trust. Branding is a market term used to attach an identity to a product that has symbolic meaning for the targeted consumers. This is a time-consuming endeavor, but for longitudinal studies, it may have large payoffs in terms of reduced attrition. Figure 9.1 presents two bags that have been branded as part of a public housing relocation study. The larger bag was given to respondents after they completed the postrelocation survey. Its states proudly, "I have told my housing story." The blue color, the reference to the sponsoring university, and the name of the study with contact phone number allows participants to contact the research team, but the bag may also be noticed by missing participants, who may then contact the research team in order to tell their own housing stories. The smaller change purse bears the words "tracking housing change" and is useful for holding change for laundry machines. These bags actually are incentives that double as a means to promote the study.

Incentives are one of the best ways to increase survey response rates. Prepaid incentives appear to be more effective than postinterview incentives. James and Bolstein (1992) increased their response rate by almost 14% through the use of prepaid incentives over post-paid incentives. Participants tend to view post-interview incentives as payment for work whereas they tend to view pre-paid incentives as more of a social contract (Dillman, Smyth, and Christian 2009).

Incentives clearly are quite persuasive, then, at encouraging cooperation with a survey. For this reason, institutional review boards (IRBs) tend to restrict the value of incentives that can be offered to ensure that cooperation with the survey is voluntary and that participants do not feel compelled to cooperate. Sometimes, cash cannot be offered due to university rules, the location where the study is conducted, or other constraints. Gifts such as chocolate, pens, et cetera, are another alternative. These are also effective at increasing response rates, though not as effective as cash. In the housing study example mentioned in the previous section, a cash incentive was provided, but food was also very important. The subgroup being studied expects to be fed when volunteering their time to be interviewed. It is important to get to know the sample well in order to tailor incentives, letters, and brochures to target them.

Figure 9.1 Branding the Study to Improve Connections and Locate Nonresponders

Georgia State University, School of Public Health Urban Health Initiative Program. Photo by Erin E. Ruel.

Retention of Participation in Longitudinal Studies

For longitudinal studies, contact needs to be maintained for future data collections. Set up a means of staying in touch and learning if respondents' contact information has changed. You may want to ask for emergency contact information at the onset of the study to ensure you can contact participants later for future interviews. Send out a yearly holiday card with some study findings, so that the sample will know how important their study contributions have been. The holiday card has two purposes. First, it will create good will among those who receive it. Second, if it is returned because it is undeliverable, it's a signal that a participant needs to be located. There are also services, such as LexisNexis, that for a small monthly fee can help to locate respondents, as long as they are living and not institutionalized. To determine if respondents are no longer living, it is now possible to search obituaries online, or, if you have a social security number, to get death information from the US Social Security Administration.

AN EXAMPLE: THE WISCONSIN LONGITUDINAL STUDY

A remarkable, ongoing, social science study is the Wisconsin Longitudinal Study (WLS 1957–2005). This study began in 1957, over 50 years ago, with a survey sample that included one third of all Wisconsin high school graduates (n = 10,317). This study has not maintained contact with the participants and interviewed them over short time intervals, which would make tracking participants slightly easier. Rather, large time intervals have passed between waves of data collection. Data were collected in 1957, 1964 (interview with parents), 1975, 1992, 2005, and 2011. In 1975, the response rate, almost 20 years after the initial survey was conducted, was 89%. In 1992, the response rate was 85% of the surviving sample, and in 2003 the response rate was 81%.

How did the WLS manage to maintain such consistently high response rates over such a long period of time? First, they maintained a rigorous participant database. They hired and trained staff to focus on retention and maintain the database. They branded the study as the "Happy Days" study. For those old enough to remember, or who like to watch vintage 1980s TV shows, *Happy Days* was a show about teenagers coming of age in Milwaukee, Wisconsin, in 1957. Some of the incentives the study provided were magnets with pictures of juke boxes, girls in poodle skirts, and a 1957 Chevy—all reminiscent of the 1950s.

For the 2003 wave of data collection, 10 years after the prior wave, the WLS staff geared up to make initial contact. A glossy brochure was designed to send out with an advance letter. Included also was the 1950s era magnet. Investigators went on the radio to announce the data collection wave so that participants could contact the study in order to participate. Investigators also attended high school reunions in order to spread the word that another wave of data collection was about to take place. The 2003 WLS survey included, first, a phone interview that lasted over an hour and for which respondents received $50.00. After the phone survey, a 50-page pen-and-paper survey was mailed to participants along with a self-addressed, stamped envelope and two crisp $5.00 bills. Reminder letters were sent out to participants who did not return the mail survey. If this letter did not elicit a response, a final contact with another copy of the mail survey was sent with a new incentive: a CD of the best hits of 1957. Figure 9.2 shows the brochure and the magnets used as incentives to improve response rates.

Figure 9.2 Wisconsin Longitudinal Survey Materials from 2003

Photo by Erin E. Ruel.

ETHICS CORNER

Participation in research should be voluntary, not coerced. There is no clear-cut demarcation between what is coercive and what is not. It may vary based on the characteristics of the population under study, and it depends on the methods employed to increase participation. In this chapter we extensively document ways to encourage and increase participation. For each research study, methods to increase participation should be examined for whether or not they become coercive. For example, giving $100.00 to very poor individuals may be coercive because they really need the money, but this amount would not be coercive to middle class individuals. As researchers develop plans to engage a sample and provide incentives to participate, they should have their plans reviewed by their IRBs to ensure that none of the methods used can be construed as coercive.

CONCLUSION

An important but often glossed over aspect of survey research is how to implement the survey and obtain high response rates. High response rates mitigate the problem that nonresponse bias can introduce and allow for external validation—or allow researchers to generalize their findings to the population. In this chapter we discussed response rates, nonresponse rates, attrition, and bias. If response rates are low or biases are high, then generalizability can become compromised. We highlight ways to contact respondents, gain their cooperation, and, for longitudinal studies, retain their cooperation over time. A few easy-to-implement strategies to get participants to buy into the research process will improve response rates dramatically.

KEY TERMS

CRITICAL THINKING QUESTIONS

Below you will find three questions that ask you to think critically about core concepts addressed in this chapter. Be sure you understand each one; if you don't, this is a good time to review the relevant sections of this chapter.

1. In what ways do nonresponse and attrition compromise generalizability?
2. You are a conducting a study of middle class working families in which both the mother and father are working professionals. Will this be a difficult group to get to volunteer to participate in your survey study? What methods might you employ to increase participation among this group?
3. When do methods employed to improve response rates become coercive?

10

Technologies to Develop and Implement Surveys

INTRODUCTION

There are a variety of different technologies that can be employed to streamline the survey process; however, survey technology is changing at a rapid pace. This can make it difficult to learn about the various technologies. It can be confusing, perhaps even intimidating, trying to keep up with the innovations in technology. This chapter provides a great deal of information that, unfortunately, may quickly become less than state of the art. The chapter will, however, demystify the technology and provide a sense of familiarity that will lend itself to the exploration of newer technologies as they emerge. Therefore, this chapter should be used as a starting point, to determine the types of technology that will be needed and to identify the technology available as of this publication date; then a search can be made online for new innovations.

MAIL SURVEY ADMINISTRATION

Generally speaking, a mail survey uses a very low level of technology. A word processor, a printer/copier, envelopes, and stamps or other postage are all that is needed to get this survey underway. The researcher creates the survey, prints it out, makes enough copies to send to the sample members, and mails it to the respondents (with a self-addressed, stamped return envelope). Once questionnaires are returned, however, a data entry program is necessary. For those with few financial resources, a spreadsheet program such as Microsoft Excel can be used to enter the survey data, although this is not ideal. The survey data can more easily be imported into a statistical program.

IBM SPSS® Statistics* has a specially designed data entry program that can be used if the survey data will be analyzed using this software. In addition, SPSS has software designed specifically for the entire data collection process, taking the researcher from designing the survey through data reporting. It is not cheap, but given all that it can do, it may be well worth the price, depending on the nature of the research project.

COMPUTER-ASSISTED INTERVIEWING

If resources are few, a phone or in-person interview study using a paper version of the survey may be an excellent option. In this case, technology needs are again minimal; follow the advice in the previous section. The interviewer will call the respondents, ask them the questions from the survey instrument, and mark the correct answers on the questionnaires. The survey data will need to be entered into a data entry software program in order to be analyzed.

However, to make the best use of interviewer-administered surveys, use of survey software is highly desirable. Depending on resources, very simple, relatively inexpensive software is available to easily program the survey. This software allows you to develop highly complex surveys with multiple and/or long skip patterns. Some software programs are more user friendly than others, but they are also less flexible. Figuring out the right tradeoff in terms of flexibility and ease will help you choose the best software for each purpose. Expect to spend some time learning how to program survey instruments. For some, the learning curve may be steep. It is always good to assume a steeper learning curve so that enough time is available to learn the appropriate software. Programming surveys, especially if they are complex and have multiple or complex skip patterns, is subject to typing and programming errors. Pretest the survey extensively to assess and correct these types of errors. You can do this by self-administering the survey multiple times, choosing different answers to the same questions to see if and how the skip patterns work. One programming mistake could create a situation where the data are worthless, and the entire survey is a failure. Once you have tested the programming and eliminated all the programming errors, you can test the survey content on a subgroup of your intended population.

Another major benefit of using a computer assisted software program is that data entry happens at the time of the interview. The interviewer will enter each response directly into the computer. This saves both the time and the expense of using data entry personnel and a separate data entry program. A good computer assisted program will

**SPSS is a registered trademark of International Business Machines Corporation.*

interface with one or more statistical data analysis software programs; thus, data are ready to be cleaned and analyzed immediately.

QDS is a company that makes an extremely affordable computer assisted survey program that can be used with many different types of devices. A web-based survey program, however, can also be used with an interviewer-administered survey (either by phone or face-to-face). However, access to the Internet is required, and it may be expensive unless your university provides access to such a program.

Choosing the Right Hardware and Software

These days, computer assisted interviews can be conducted on a computer, on a tablet, and even on a smaller mobile device. Laptops are easy to use, but they are cumbersome and may too quickly run out of power. Thus, they are best used for telephone interviews, but they may be limited for taking into the field for face-to-face interviews. Apple iPads or similar tablets may have longer battery time and be less cumbersome, but they may not sync as well with many available data analysis software programs or with desktop computer systems. There are survey programs available, though, just for the iPad, such as *Snap*, a free survey app available on iTunes. Tablets may be ideal for face-to-face interviewing. Other mobile devices are especially great for built environment audits or time-based calendar surveys. For example, if you want to know what people eat and when they eat it, a mobile device (e.g., smart phone) might be the easiest way to get the best compliance, as many people keep their mobile devices with them and are on them regularly, and the devices can be programmed to sound an alarm to remind participants to comply with the survey. As a caveat, it is very expensive to have a custom app developed, so many researchers will instead need to use available specialized software if this is the desired mode of computer assistance. Make sure to test how each technology interfaces with all the other technology components you will use in your study, both hardware and software, prior to starting the survey. This will minimize problems that arise during the survey process.

Decisions about which software program to use depend on several criteria, only one of which is cost. Software support is important. If the software is supported by a company that is very responsive, that might be really beneficial in programming the survey or managing the data once it is collected. The size and spatial needs of the study also are important considerations for choosing a software program. For a very long survey, does the software allow respondents to start and stop multiple times? For national or international studies, look for a program that can handle different languages, that can provide site licenses in multiple sites, or that can be used by multiple people at the same time.

Below is a list of some popular **computer assisted personal interviewing** (CAPI) and **computer assisted telephone interviewing** (CATI) software programs that are affordable for research projects. It is not an exhaustive list and is not intended to suggest that any of these software packages are better or worse than the others, or better or worse than any software packages not listed. It probably goes without saying, though, that free software and free versions of software that is also available for purchase or license will have limitations and access to fewer features.

Questionnaire Development System (QDS) http://www.novaresearch.com/QDS/

Audio Computer-Assisted Self-Interview (ACASI)(software)http://acasi.tufts.edu/acasi.htm

Computer Assisted Survey Execution System (CASES) http://cases.berkeley.edu/software.html

Web-Based Surveys

Developers of **web server software** have introduced numerous new tools and innovations to increase the accuracy and efficiency of data collection. The possibilities are wide ranging, depending on the level of complexity and size of the questionnaire as well as the nature of the concepts being measured. Widespread access to the Internet now allows access to a greater number of respondents in their homes (or elsewhere) via computer, tablet, or smartphone.

For web-based surveys, the respondent must go to the URL (i.e., website) where the survey is maintained. An e-mail containing a link to the questionnaire can be sent to potential respondents, and/or other traditional or more modern recruitment vehicles can be used. There are many commercial software packages (as well as CASES, described earlier in this chapter) that can be used to develop and program a web-based survey.

Due to advances in technology, web-based surveys can be designed to be interactive, nimble, and attractive. Skillful survey programming can reduce survey fatigue and increase the accuracy of data collection. Web-based surveys are unmatched in terms of the possibilities they offer for use of graphics along with consistency of design across questions. A web questionnaire can incorporate interactive question mapping, photographs, videos, and other media where appropriate. It can also include a considerable amount of information without seeming cumbersome; this is particularly useful in battling survey fatigue. One way this is made possible is through the use of drop-down menus for fixed-response questions, particularly those with numerous answer choices. Additional information, such as definitions or proper noun descriptions (which can be provided typed as well as graphically), can be made available so that they are only provided when requested—this might be designed so that information is shared when a term is either moused over or clicked on. Beyond that, web surveys tend to be less expensive than more traditional surveys. To that end, as with most electronically designed questionnaires, a noteworthy advantage of a web-based survey is that data collected are stored electronically on the server and therefore there is no need to enter data or to hire and train staff to enter data.

So, what is the downside to web-based surveys? While technology is spreading quickly, not everyone has access to the web, and access is not uniform across the population in the United States. For some target populations, a web-based survey may not be feasible. For instance, if the target population consists of individuals who generally do not have access to the Internet or who have access but do not use the Internet, then a web-based survey should not be considered, since the accessible population will not be even remotely representative of the target population.

Recruitment for web-based surveys still needs to be done through traditional methods for most types of social science research. In addition, it might be necessary to bring mobile devices (laptops, tablets, etc.) to some respondents or to reach them by phone and enter information for them. It will be necessary to verify that those respondents have a questionnaire that is equivalent to the questionnaire that web-based respondents are using, since this effectively becomes a **multimode survey**, combining two or more different types of survey methodologies into one complex implementation.

Below is a list of some popular web server survey software programs. It is not an exhaustive list and is not intended to suggest that any of these software packages is better or worse than the others, or better or worse than any software packages that have not be named. It probably goes without saying, though, that the free software, and the free versions of software available for purchase or license, will have limitations and access to fewer features. In this chapter, we will focus on Qualtrics, in part because of its comprehensive features that can be used to implement the techniques that have been introduced throughout this book.

Wufoo	www.wufoo.com
ReMark	www.gravic.com/remark/Web-Survey-Software/
Snap Survey	www.snapsurveys.com
Survey Monkey	www.surveymonkey.com
Qualtrics	www.qualtrics.com

POSTSURVEY DATA ENTRY AND DATA CLEANING TECHNOLOGY

One reason CAPI surveys and web-based surveys are less expensive than traditional surveys is that the responses to the questions are "warehoused" directly into a database. It is easy to use this database to audit your data collection efforts. By audit, we mean keeping track of who has completed the survey and who has not, and of the reasons participants have not completed the survey (e.g., refusals, lack of contact, not eligible). Also, once data collection has ended, most of these programs can easily transform your collected data into an SPSS, SAS, or STATA dataset. This makes the costs of data entry negligible. Most of these programs do not develop true codebooks, however. To create a codebook (see Chapter 12) that will describe the data, the universe for each question, et cetera, the software program will only be the starting point. The research team needs to develop a useable, comprehensive codebook.

As noted earlier, SPSS has a program that will facilitate data entry for pen-and-paper surveys. It is worth the expense to buy a program or have a programmer create a data entry form for you. While Excel can be used for data entry, it is very easy to make a data entry mistake with this program. For example, if the letter *O* is entered in a cell rather than the numeral *0*, Excel will automatically format that row or column as text. Then, when data are transferred from Excel to a statistics program, the variable will remain a string variable. These types of problems, while not serious, will soak up time and resources.

Another software program that may be beneficial is SDA (Survey Documentation and Analysis, http://sda.berkeley.edu/). This is a program designed to assist with documenting data, creating codebooks, and making data publically available. It has two options for publicly available data. One option allows users to download the data and have access to all de-identified details. The other option allows users to analyze the data online without allowing them to download the actual data. For analysis purposes, public users of the data can use SDA's "quick tables" function, which allows users to obtain analysis results online without downloading data.

CONTRACTING WITH A RESEARCH CENTER TO CONDUCT THE SURVEY

For research projects that are well funded or extremely large, there are organizations that can assist with the data collection process. Some software comes with access to consultants and programmers that, for a price, will program the survey instrument for you. Often, these software companies will also provide sampling services and data-cleaning services. There are many universities with telephone survey centers that can be hired to conduct a survey. Look at local research universities to see if they have a survey center; locality is particularly important, as most universities limit the scope of their survey centers to projects within their state. Following is a list of university-based survey centers that includes at least one or two options from each region of the United States.

Again, this is not an exhaustive list and is not intended to suggest that any of these survey centers are better or worse than the others not included. The centers listed are intended as examples; their names can be used as keywords to search for other, more local survey centers.

West

Washington State University Social and Economic Sciences Research Center
http://www.sesrc.wsu.edu/sesrcsite/

Office of Survey Research, University of Texas–Austin
http://moody.utexas.edu/strauss/osr/

California State University, Sacramento, Institute for Social Research
http://www.csus.edu/isr/

Midwest

University of Illinois at Chicago, Survey Research Laboratory
http://www.srl.uic.edu/

Kent State University, The Survey Research Lab
http://www.kent.edu/about/centersinstitutes/SurveyResearchLab.cfm

South

University of Kentucky Survey Research Center
http://www.research.uky.edu/survey/

University of North Carolina at Chapel Hill, Odum Institute for Research in Social Science
http://www.odum.unc.edu/odum/home2.jsp

The Carolina Survey Research Laboratory
http://csrl.sph.unc.edu/

East

Baruch College Survey Research
http://www.baruch.cuny.edu/spa/researchcenters/surveyresearch/

Cornell University, Survey Research Institute
https://www.sri.cornell.edu/sri/

Rutgers University, Bloustein Center for Survey Research
http://policy.rutgers.edu/bcsr/index.php

University of Massachusetts–Boston, Center for Survey Research
http://www.csr.umb.edu/

Additionally, there are commercial survey consulting firms. Again, we list a few, but there are many, many more. Start your search for other firms by going to the website of the American Association for Public Opinion Research (AAPOR, https://www.aapor.org//AM/Template.cfm?Section=Home) or the Association of Academic Survey Research Organizations (AASRO, http://www.aasro.org).

ABT SRBI
http://www.srbi.com/

Battelle's Centers for Public Health Research and Evaluation
http://www.battelle.org/about-us/office-locations

RTI International
http://www.rti.org/page.cfm/Survey_Research_and_Services

Westat
https://www.westat.com/

ETHICS CORNER

The main ethical issues that arise with technology are confidentiality and anonymity. **Confidentiality** means that a respondent is not associated with his or her responses. This could be very important for an online work survey where, for instance, a respondent may complain about her boss. If the survey is not confidential, respondents might not be honest, which is bad for the research. More important, though, if confidentiality is not maintained, there could be repercussions for the respondent, such as being fired for criticizing the boss. Thus, researchers need to think carefully about what sort of security measures are needed to maintain the confidentiality of the research participants. For example, could e-mailing a response code to respondents, so that they can take an online survey, be secure in all circumstances or in only some circumstances? Researchers need to plan for the best possible security to ensure confidentiality.

Anonymity is one of the easier ethical requirements for surveys to meet. **Anonymity** requires hiding a respondent's identity so that no one knows that the respondent participated in the study. Measures of identity such as names or social security numbers are often easily replaced with a random identity number. Given that online survey programs, such as Qualtrics, include software both for recruitment of respondents and for administration of the survey tasks, researchers need to be assured that anonymity will be maintained.

CONCLUSION

Technology has made survey research more affordable in many cases. It has reduced the time required to code data, and therefore the expense of hiring coders; it has reduced administrative costs; and it has reduced the possibility of errors, which used to be a major issue in survey data collection. Technology does not actually replace much of the human element in survey design, though it can ease some of the more burdensome tasks, such data entry and data auditing. Web-based surveys, like pen-and-paper surveys, have low interviewer expenses; but unlike pen-and-paper surveys, they also have low data entry expenses. There is, however, an increase in costs for programming the survey. Web-based surveys tend to increase the costs up front and decrease the postsurvey administration costs. It is usually considerably less expensive to hire one person to program a survey than to hire 10 people to enter and clean the data. Furthermore, administration errors and data entry errors are reduced. Thus, technology use is one more factor to include in the series of decisions researchers make to ensure they are collecting data of the highest possible quality.

KEY TERMS

Computer assisted interviewing 173
Computer assisted personal interviewing (CAPI) 174
Computer assisted telephone interviewing (CATI) 174
Web server software 175
Multimode survey 176
Confidentiality 179
Anonymity 179

CRITICAL THINKING QUESTIONS

Below you will find two questions that ask you to think critically about core concepts addressed in this chapter. Be sure you understand each one; if you don't, this is a good time to review the relevant sections of this chapter.

1. What factors are important in deciding what type of survey administration to use?
2. What role does technology play in researchers' survey administration decisions?

11

Data Collection

INTRODUCTION

So far, topics have included developing good survey questions, designing the survey, pretesting it, and drawing an appropriate sample. This chapter focuses on the actual data collection process. What you need to successfully collect quality data will depend on several things. First, it will depend on how you are administering the survey: self-administered versus interviewer administered. Next, it will depend on whether you are administering a longitudinal or cross-sectional survey. Also, there are decisions to be made about how often to contact sample members; how to handle refusals, ineligibles, and deaths; and how to audit data collection efforts. You will need to measure the final response rate you have achieved at the conclusion of the survey administration, organize data storage, and determine how often to back up the data.

In this chapter we will discuss all of these issues by survey administration type, considering how to address issues that often arise in the collection of data. Addressing as many of these issues as possible prior to entering the field to collect data will minimize potential problems and errors, ensuring the collection of higher quality data.

THE SELF-ADMINISTERED CROSS-SECTIONAL MAILED SURVEY

As previously mentioned, the cross-sectional survey is conducted at one point in time only. The cross-sectional mailed survey is a low-technology survey that depends almost entirely on human labor. Few resources are needed for this type of survey, particularly when the questionnaire is mailed to the respondent. It is best to mail the survey to the respondent with a self-addressed postage-paid return envelope to increase the likelihood of receiving a response. Before you mail the survey, create a list of all the sample participants, and assign to each of them an anonymous identification number that can be stamped onto the individual questionnaire. This way, once the survey is separated from the envelope, the researcher will still know who the respondent is, yet the respondent's identity will be held confidential and anonymous; no one outside the study team will be able to determine the identity of the participant. This is a very important step that will allow all participant responses to be confidential while also allowing the researcher to **audit** the data collection, that is, to account for who has responded to the survey and who still needs to respond. Auditing will be addressed thoroughly in the next section.

The researcher and perhaps one or two assistants can do most of the work. It involves creating and maintaining a list that includes all the participants, the random identification number for each, and the outcome of each attempt to contact the participant and collect the completed survey questionnaire. This is known as the **disposition and audit trail.**

AUDITING THE DATA COLLECTION PROCESS

This list of sample participants is very important, and putting it on a computer will facilitate keeping track of the entire data collection process. For a cross-sectional, mailed survey, a spreadsheet program, such as Excel, should be sufficient for auditing the survey. The word *audit* is used deliberately, as, to some extent, managing the survey will benefit greatly from engaging in the very detail oriented world of accounting. On this spreadsheet include the name, address, additional contact information, and the anonymous identification number assigned to each participant. Make sure only institutional review board (IRB) approved staff can access this spreadsheet, since it has confidential information on it. Additional columns may be used to track or audit the mailing out of the survey, including the date of each mail out as well as the return and date of the return. This is information that may be important when assessing the quality of the final data. Data from those who returned the survey only after multiple mailings may be of lower quality than data from those who returned the survey promptly after the first mailing. Additional columns in the spreadsheet can be used for unforeseen problems encountered during survey administration. A final column can be used for each respondent's **final disposition**—(i.e., completed, partially completed, not returned, bad contact information—never contacted).

Part of the auditing process involves some a priori decisions about how many contact attempts to make with each participant before concluding that he or she is a nonrespondent (Dillman, Smyth, and Christian 2009). Will it be 2 contacts, or 30? At what point does contact become harassment and coercion? How much of the project resources will each contact attempt expend? Two contact attempts is certainly noninvasive and utilizes very little in terms of resources, while 30 attempts might begin to feel like harassment for the would-be respondent. With a mail survey, postage can be a considerable expense, and therefore, fewer contacts are likely. For a web-based survey, contact is virtually cost free. For a phone survey, there is a cost, but it is much less than for a mailed survey, thus more contacts are possible. Whatever you decide is an appropriate number of contacts (e.g. 30 calls), be consistent and stick to it. Make sure contacts are being made at different hours of the day and on different days to increase the likelihood of a "hit." Again, keep track of all of this information on the audit spreadsheet for future analysis of data quality.

Also, a priori, the investigator should decide the potential outcome categories for the contact procedure, so that handling can be standardized by protocol. Of course, a completed survey is the most desired outcome, but what if a participant has died or is mentally incapable of completing the survey? Would these two cases be considered ineligibles or nonresponses? Deciding on what constitutes ineligibility up front will save headaches later when determining the response rate. Generally, the response rate is based on the **eligible sample;** thus, declaring cases ineligible due to death, poor health, or incarceration yields a higher and more realistic response rate. Make certain to carefully document and define the circumstances under which potential participants will be identified as ineligible rather than as noncontact or incomplete. Perhaps all institutionalized participants will be declared ineligible, while those who cannot be found will be considered nonresponses due to "no contact." The more of these types of decisions you make ahead of time, the easier it will be to handle situations automatically by protocol as they arise.

Figure 11.1 provides an example of a simple spreadsheet for a cross-sectional mailed survey. As the figure shows, the researchers have decided to make three attempts to get respondents to fill out the survey. They have decided to wait six weeks after each mailing before sending out the next mailing. Therefore, six weeks after the third mailing, the survey period is over, and the researchers can determine final disposition of each respondent. Because the researchers made these decisions ahead of time, all respondents will be treated in a standardized fashion.

In Figure 11.1, the first respondent completed the survey and returned it after the first mailing. The second respondent completed the survey as well, but not until after the second mailing. Likewise, the third respondent did not complete and return the survey until after the third mailing. A nice feature of the spreadsheet is the ability to sort the lines in order to focus only on those respondents who have not yet completed the survey. The fourth respondent, Carl Shepard, did not complete the survey and return it by the end of the data collection period (six weeks after the final mailing); therefore, his final disposition is marked as incomplete.

The next respondent, Amy Brooks, was listed with a bad address. The post office returned the survey. In order to make sure this respondent has a chance to respond, and to make sure their response rate is good, researchers need to do some investigative work to find a correct address for Amy Brooks. There are address-locating services, such as LexisNexis, that, for a fee, will search out addresses. But in this computerized world,

Figure 11.1 Sample Data Auditing Spreadsheet

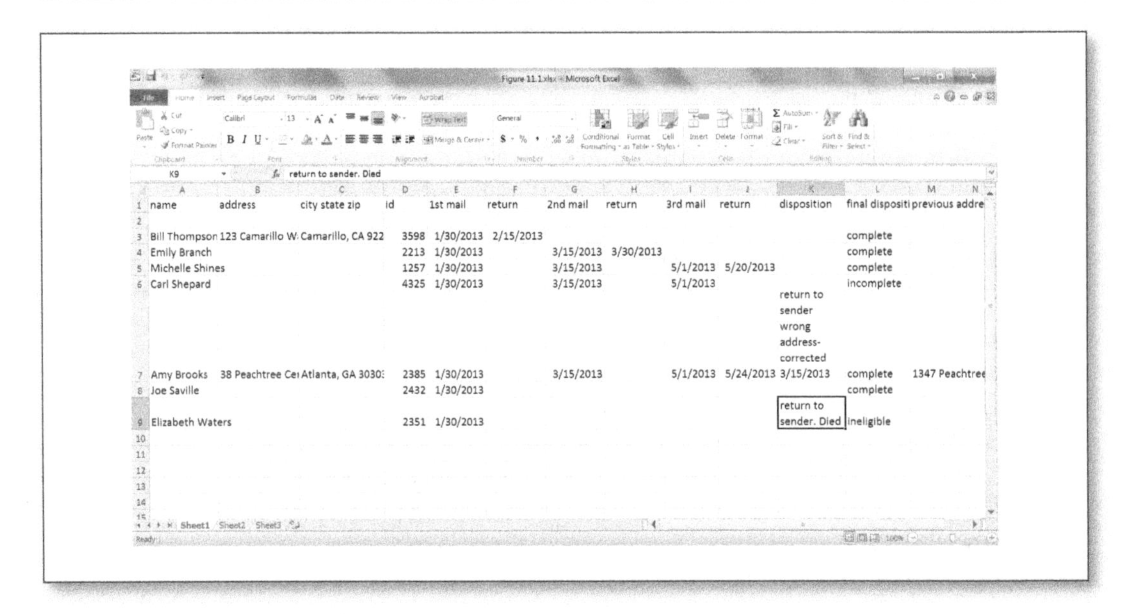

name	address	city state zip	id	1st mail	return	2nd mail	return	3rd mail	return	disposition	final dispositi	previous addre
Bill Thompson	123 Camarillo W	Camarillo, CA 922	3598	1/30/2013	2/15/2013						complete	
Emily Branch			2213	1/30/2013		3/15/2013	3/30/2013				complete	
Michelle Shines			1257	1/30/2013		3/15/2013		5/1/2013	5/20/2013		complete	
Carl Shepard			4325	1/30/2013		3/15/2013		5/1/2013			incomplete	
Amy Brooks	38 Peachtree Ce	Atlanta, GA 3030	2385	1/30/2013		3/15/2013		5/1/2013	5/24/2013	return to sender wrong address-corrected 3/15/2013	complete	1347 Peachtree
Joe Saville			2432	1/30/2013							complete	
Elizabeth Waters			2351	1/30/2013						return to sender. Died	ineligible	

there are also less expensive ways for researchers to do the searching themselves. In the case of Amy Brooks, the researchers found a new address for her and sent the second survey to her corrected address. The respondent filled out the survey and returned it, so her final disposition is complete. The bad address was saved in order to have complete documentation of all steps. Additionally, this information can be used to distinguish those who responded only to the second or third mail attempt due to bad information on the researchers' end from those respondents who simply waited until the second or third mailing to complete the survey. Data quality may differ based on these details.

The survey for the final respondent, Elizabeth Waters, was returned by the post office. In this case however, there was a handwritten note on the envelope stating that the addressee had died. In this case, the respondent is marked as ineligible, and this lack of response will not harm the response rate.

Most of the work takes place prior to mailing out the surveys. Managing the surveys as they come in, auditing the data as they are collected, and searching out wrong addresses are ongoing efforts. Depending on how large the sample is, hiring staff to help with these tasks may be necessary. Resources, such as staff, will also be needed to enter the survey responses into a statistical package. Well-written survey instructions will be clear enough to the respondents so that they respond to the questions such that their true response can be captured. Set up a procedure ahead of time to make it clear to data entry personnel how to handle each potential issue as it arises. For example, if respondents are asked to circle the response that best fits the statement, such as on a five-category Likert scale, it should be easy to enter the responses. Occasionally, however, a respondent may draw a sloppy circle that encompasses two numbers; what should data entry personnel do in this situation? If the answers do not include choices for responses such as "don't know" and "refuse to answer," some questions may end up not being answered. While it is true that a nonresponse is a nonresponse, there are questions to which a "don't know" response provides valuable information. Thus, providing these options on the survey, along with separate responses categories for "don't know" and "refuse to answer," may ease the data entry process.

THE SELF-ADMINISTERED LONGITUDINAL PANEL MAILED SURVEY

With a panel design, the same participants are interviewed at multiple points in time. The questionnaire itself may be exactly the same as one that would be used in a cross-sectional survey. However, the need to keep in touch with the participants over an extended period of time adds complexity to the participant list. People move, change their names, and, these days, change their phone numbers frequently. Thus, keeping in contact with the participants becomes challenging. Auditing the data also may become more complicated, necessitating a new spreadsheet page for each wave of data collection. A relational database such as Microsoft Access (discussed below) may work better to track participants over time and to track the response rates and eligibility for each wave of survey data collected. Otherwise, the same resources and procedures for the cross-sectional mailed survey apply here, just over a longer period of time.

Additional information about the participants will be needed, however, in order to audit or keep track of them over time. In this day and age, few people are willing to share their social security numbers. Depending on the population, in this era of mobile phones, phone numbers may change rapidly, especially among those who opt for prepaid mobile phones. Asking respondents for emergency contact information is one good strategy to help with finding participants. Establishing a contact procedure that involves regularly calling the participant to verify that he or she is still at the same address and phone number is a good way to keep track of participants between waves of data collection. This will add to expenses, as additional labor is needed to conduct these calls. It is not a very efficient use of resources for a study with a large sample size. There are services such as LexisNexis that, for a relatively inexpensive monthly fee, can help locate participants who move. Creating a study webpage or social media page that your participants can follow confidentially may also be a good way to keep in contact with your sample.

Panel studies require much more record keeping than cross-sectional studies require. While one spreadsheet can be used for contact information, and another can be used to audit each wave of data collection, it gets messy very quickly. Spreadsheets are wonderful programs and are very easy to use, but if the dataset is very large and complicated, they quickly become unwieldy. A relational database easily allows you to handle the mess of tracking down participants over time and auditing data each time you go into the field. For each wave of data collection, you need to determine who is eligible. Perhaps a respondent was in a nursing home at Wave 2 and thus was considered ineligible. At Wave 3, however, the respondent is back at home. This participant can be declared eligible for Wave 3.

Figure 11.2 provides an example of a relational database one of the authors used with a longitudinal study of public housing relocations in Atlanta (Oakley, Ruel, and Wilson 2008; Ruel, Oakley, Wilson, and Maddox 2010). To protect confidentiality, no data are shown. However, on the left hand side are the names of some of the data input tables and some of the data auditing queries used. One tracking device we used was to send birthday cards to the participants. This not only helped to determine if the participant still lived at the address provided, but it also created some good will, which may have been beneficial for retention purposes and may have contributed to the high response rates of the study.

INTERVIEWER-ADMINISTERED SURVEYS

Interviewers can administer surveys by phone, in person one-on-one, or in person one-on-group. More resources are needed for this type of survey administration, as interviewers will need to be trained to ask the questions consistently across participants

Figure 11.2 Example of a Relational Database Used to Track Participants and Audit Data Collection

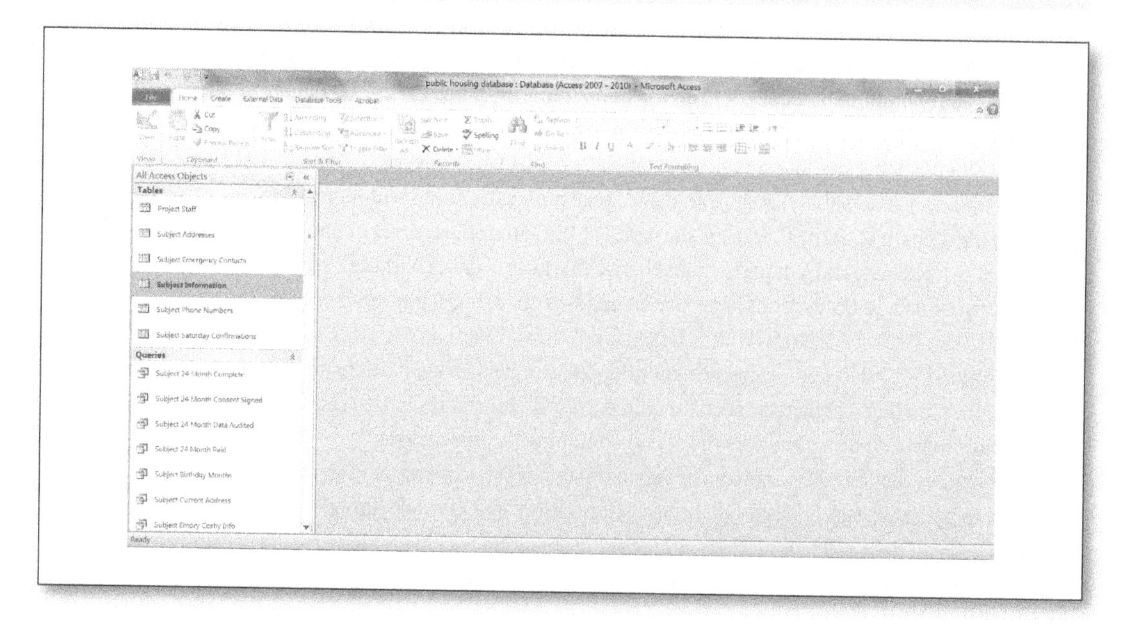

and to respond to participant queries consistently. It is advisable to use some form of computer assisted interviewing technology to assist with this process. While resources are needed up front to purchase the software and to code the survey into the computer, a major benefit of using computer assisted technology is that the data are automatically stored in a database that can easily be transferred into a statistical software program, eliminating the need for data entry workers. Thus, resources will be spent upfront on programming the survey instrument and training and paying interviewers so that the administration of the survey will be standardized across all interviewers. Contacts with participants often take place over the phone. This is fast and inexpensive compared to mailing surveys to participants; thus researchers can plan on many contact attempts before declaring a participant to be a nonrespondent. Mini Case 11.1 describes the preparation of interviewers for the Wisconsin Longitudinal Survey.

MINI CASE 11.1

Implementing the 2003–2005 Wisconsin Longitudinal Study

In 2003, the Wisconsin Longitudinal Study (WLS) implemented the sixth wave of data collection on a sample of one third of all Wisconsin's 1957 high school graduates. They planned on computer assisted telephone interviews to conduct the survey. The eligible sample size, almost 50 years after the study began, was over 7,000 cases. The WLS hired the survey center at the University of Wisconsin to conduct the actual survey. A special software program was used by the survey center to program the survey. It is an extremely complicated and long survey—lasting over 60 minutes. WLS staff created an interviewing instructional manual and spent two weeks training approximately 80 interviewers how to read the questions and respond to various situations in as standardized a manner as possible. Interviewers were expected to practice several times prior to being released into the field. Interviewers were taped and were sporadically and randomly checked for compliance with the interviewing protocol as described in the interviewing instruction manual. If interviewers were not doing a good job, they were asked to attend a retraining. Additionally, since the sample size was very large, the survey was in the field for a long period of time. Interviewers, who were university undergraduate students, turned over frequently. Thus, training was an ongoing activity throughout the two years of data collection as new interviewers joined the project.

Source: WLS 1957–2005.

Regardless of how well survey questions are developed, respondents may still not understand a question, or they may not know one or more words included in the question. If this is going to be a problem, it should show up during the piloting phase of the survey process. If problems arise with a question that researchers do not want to change for some reason (e.g., the question is used in surveys that the current study is replicating), then the interviewing instructional manual can be used to train interviewers how to handle the question. Interviewers can be given definitions to use with participants who do not recognize a word, for example. Or, particular desired responses can be scripted, and the interviewers can be trained to use them with questions participants do not understand.

Given how much diversity there is among individuals, however, it is highly unlikely that all potential question problems will be caught in the piloting process. For problems that arise unexpectedly, the instructional manual should teach interviewers to respond to queries about the meaning of a word only with provided definitions. If there is no provided definition, interviewers should be trained to say, "whatever it means to you."

SELF-ADMINISTERED WEB SURVEYS

This type of survey also requires few resources. The survey needs to be encoded for use on the computer. As you learned in the previous chapter, there are several excellent software programs available to assist with this; thus, researchers no longer need to be computer programmers to create good surveys. Like they do for mail surveys, researchers will need to determine ahead of time the number of contact attempts to make. Unlike the mail survey administration, cost of contact attempts is cheap, and thus the researcher can plan on multiple contact attempts. Auditing and tracking are built into some web design programs, and for programs without these features, the methods listed in previous sections can be used to keep track of participants, contact attempts, and participation. Data will not need to be input into a data entry program, as the responses provided by the participants are automatically saved to the server and can be transferred easily into a statistical program.

Conducting a longitudinal web survey may require a few additional sources. Often researchers will have even less information about the respondents than they have with a phone-based survey, and thus tracking respondents may be more difficult. E-mail addresses change frequently. Having a web presence for the study and inviting participants to view it may help maintain contact with the sample. Instituting regular contact may be even more important for a web-based study than it is when other types of data collection are used.

COMPARING SURVEY TYPES

A great deal of information has been presented so far. How do we evaluate all this information? Table 11.1 attempts to summarize all of it and evaluate each survey administration type in terms of resources needed. It seems that the two survey types that require the fewest resources are mail surveys and web-based surveys. With mail surveys, most of the resources are needed at the end, and with web-based surveys, more resources are needed up front. Face-to-face interviews using CAPI software need many resources, and the face-to-face interview without CAPI software is an even more resource-heavy survey type. Surveys administered to groups or to individuals over the telephone require resource amounts somewhere in the middle.

Adding a longitudinal component to any of the above administration types adds a need for additional resources to track participants and to pay increased auditing costs. But this does not change the comparisons between the types unduly. Also be aware that we are comparing survey types based only on resource needs, not on response rates or access to the participants. Choosing the best administration type depends not only on resources but also on identifying the type that will provide the best access to the population under study and that will minimize nonresponse. Table 11.1 provides a breakout of each survey administration type and the resource needs of each.

DATA STORAGE NEEDS

Data storage space is not the issue it was even 10 years ago. Most universities have servers with ample storage space set aside for university-based research. For very large projects or for multisite projects, however, an investigator might need more space than the university will allow. Currently, there are a number of companies that, for a small fee, will provide cloud storage space. How safe the data are that are stored in the cloud may be an issue. Separating the data from any identifying information is critical, in case the server is hacked and there is unauthorized access to the data. Understanding the security of your data storage is essential.

In addition to cloud storage, **data backup** services are important in order to keep the data from being lost due to computer failure. Backup services are readily available and inexpensive and can back up data on a daily, weekly, or monthly basis. The more frequent the backups, the less likely you are to lose any data or work. Again, security protocols should be developed for any situation where data are available on a connected server for storage or backup.

Table 11.1 Comparison of Resource Needs by Administration Type

	Interviewers	*Programming of Survey*	*Auditing*	*Data Entry*	*Total Resource Needs*
Mail survey	not needed	not needed	limited need	needed	low resources on the back end
Telephone survey without CAPI	needed	not needed	needed	needed	high resource needs
CAPI telephone survey	needed	needed	needed	not needed	medium resource needs on front end
Group interview without CAPI	limited need	not needed	needed	needed	medium high resource needs
Group interview with CAPI	limited need	needed	needed	not needed	medium low resource needs
Face-to-face survey with CAPI	needed	needed	needed	not needed	high resource needs
Web-based survey	not needed	needed	needed—may be handled by program	not needed	low resources on the front end

Researchers with plentiful resources may want to purchase a dedicated server, firewall, and backup system. This requires a great deal of resources in terms of money, knowledgeable IT staff, and temperature-controlled space to hold the equipment, but for large or sensitive projects, it may be feasible, and it is certainly the most secure option.

ETHICS CORNER

Before going into the field to collect the data, but after the study and survey questionnaire have been finalized, it is time to submit the study to the **institutional review board** (IRB). An IRB is part of the university research system. It is a committee of faculty, administrators, and even local community members who have the power to approve, monitor, and review all research involving human subjects spearheaded by university personnel. Surveys generally involve human subjects and therefore must receive approval by the IRB prior to implementation. The purposes of the IRB are to ensure the rights and well-being of all human subjects participating in research, and to see that the research being conducted is both scientific and ethical.

IRBs are empowered by the Food and Drug Administration and the Department of Health and Human Services and are governed by Title 45 of the Code of Federal Regulations, Part 46. All institutions that receive federal support are required to create IRBs and to follow the regulations for institutional review of all research involving human subjects, though many IRBs follow these guidelines for research whether or not the studies they review involve human subjects.

Most of the egregious problems with past research on human subjects have surfaced in health-related or medical studies, such as the Tuskegee Syphilis Study (http://www.cdc.gov/tuskegee/timeline.htm). This study began in 1932 and was designed to chart the natural history of syphilis in black men in order to determine the best treatments for this disease (National Center for HIV/AIDS, Viral Hepatitis, STD, and TB Prevention 2013). Six-hundred extremely poor black men were recruited for the sample. There was no informed consent, and participation was considered coercive because of the benefits provided the men who participated. The study lasted for 40 years, even though a cure was found for syphilis in the mid-1940s.

The social sciences have some examples of research that has not protected the welfare of human subjects as well. For example, the Stanford Prison Experiment (Zimbardo 1973) included 24 students, some of whom became prisoners, while others were prison guards. The premise of the study was to determine what would happen to good people if they were put in a bad situation—jail. The two-week experiment was ended after only six days, because the prison guards quickly became sadistic, and the prisoners experienced extreme stress and depression. (For the full story, see http://www.prisonexp.org/.)

It behooves researchers to support their IRBs as research partners, rather than considering IRBs to be entities that interfere with or frustrate research. IRB approval means that the research is being conducted both correctly and ethically.

CONCLUSION

After you have spent a great deal of time developing good questions, creating the survey, piloting the survey, programming the survey, selecting the sample, training interviewers, and connecting with the sample, entering the field may feel anticlimactic. There is still much work to do, however, such as contacting participants and convincing them to participate, and documenting and auditing who has completed the survey and who has refused to complete the survey, not to mention actually implementing the survey.

Remember that there are decisions that should be made a priori about the number and types of contacts to make before treating a participant as a nonresponse, and about who will be considered eligible and who ineligible and why. This will keep an investigator from introducing bias into the data. Researchers who plan ahead will find they have enough resources for each task. Researchers who do not plan ahead may end up without a backup plan, and data could potentially be lost.

Additionally, survey administration decisions are based, in part, on the amount of resources needed to conduct a survey. Web-based surveys have become very popular, because the programming has been made simple and easy to operate. Resources needed are few compared to other types of survey administration, such as the interviewer-led survey.

KEY TERMS

Data audit 182
Final disposition 182
Eligible sample 183
Data storage 189
Data backup 189
Institutional review board 190

CRITICAL THINKING QUESTIONS

Below you will find three questions that ask you to think critically about core concepts addressed in this chapter. Be sure you understand each one; if you don't, this is a good time to review the relevant sections of this chapter.

1. How does implementing a web-based survey differ from implementing a phone-based survey in terms of resources needed and procedures?
2. Why is it necessary to store contact and personal information separately from survey data?
3. What are the decisions investigators need to make prior to implementing the survey?

SECTION IV

Postsurvey Data Management and Analysis

The survey instrument has been successfully administered. What's next? For studies that have not been conducted with software that enters data as they are collected, the next step is entering the data into a database using a statistical software package. Next, the focus turns to cleaning the data, analyzing the data to answer the research questions that started this process, and finally, making the data publicly available. This completes the process of conducting a survey.

In Chapter 12, we address data entry issues and the strengths and weakness of data entry for each type of survey administration. In addition, we discuss how to handle three unusual types of questions: (1) multiple-response questions, (2) questions that allow for other-specify responses and (3) open-ended questions. Finally, we discuss documenting data entry and a priori decisions that will ease the data entry process.

In Chapter 13, we address post–data collection activities, such as cleaning the data. Additionally, we introduce a variety of techniques to address different data-cleaning issues, including cosmetic issues, missing data, skip patterns, diagnostics, and longitudinal data issues. All of these terms are carefully explained. Last, we discuss the creation of a codebook and what that entails.

Chapter 14 introduces data analysis. We start by examining descriptive analyses suitable for a policy report. These are very basic statistical techniques. For readers, it would certainly help to have taken one statistical course prior to reading this chapter, but familiarity with statistics is not necessary to benefit from reading the chapter. In addition, this chapter demonstrates how to write a policy report using the evidence provided by the basic statistical analysis of the data.

Chapter 15 continues to focus on data analysis. In this chapter we address multivariate regression analyses suitable for a journal article. We stop along the way to discuss creation of dummy variables and scales. These are advanced statistical techniques that assume the student has taken a basic course in statistics.

Chapter 16 discusses archiving data for both private and public use. As federal funding agencies now require that funded projects make data publically available and have a data management plan, it is important to understand the archiving process. We discuss what to archive, how to archive, and where to archive.

We end with an epilogue that summarizes how to conduct a survey study from start to finish, with an easy-to-follow checklist of steps in the process.

12

Data Entry

INTRODUCTION

In research methods courses, students are introduced to the many ways in which social scientists collect their observations, including the use of surveys. Great care is taken to ensure that students understand how to structure the questionnaire, how to write excellent research questions, and how to administer the survey instrument. At the other end of the research process, students take statistics courses in which they learn how to analyze secondary data often collected through surveys. In order for students to learn the important statistical techniques, they practice on very clean data. This leaves an important link out of the equation: Most students do not learn how to enter, manage, and clean data. How do we get from the data collection process to the clean data used for statistical analyses?

The goal of this chapter is to fill that gap with an introduction to data entry and some quick and easy data management guidelines. Data management, in this case, refers to decision-making protocols that researchers should create prior to collecting the data. Do not confuse this with the data management plan required by federal funding agencies that details how the analyzed data will be made publicly available (see Chapter 15). What is meant by data management is planning how data will be entered into a statistics program (if they are not automatically entered by a computer assisted survey tool) and how data will be cleaned.

DATA ENTRY

Data entry is the process whereby the responses to questions captured on the survey are transformed into variables in a statistical database. For surveys administered with pen and paper, data from completed questionnaires are entered manually into a data entry program. Figure 12.1 provides an example of a raw dataset that was created through manual entry of data into SPSS Statistics. While the figure exhibits the screen on a Windows-based computer, the Macintosh screen will look nearly identical. Across the top of the columns are the variable names. Each variable represents a question or part of a complex question (e.g., "check all that apply") from the survey. Each row represents a single respondent or case. Inside the cells are the response values (numbers mostly) given by individual participants for each question on the survey. As can be seen, there can be one and only one value entered in each cell. It is a fairly straightforward task for most survey question types. If a respondent (#519) chooses Response 4 to Question V3, then the value "4" is entered into the corresponding cell for Participant 519 and Question

Figure 12.1 Raw Data Shown in SPSS Statistics (Windows version)

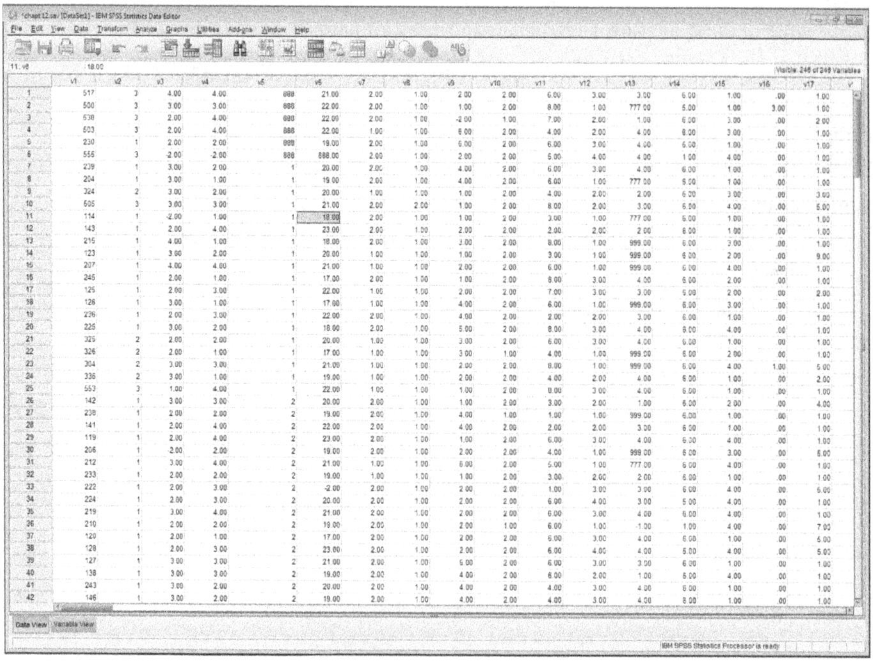

	v1	v2	v3	v4	v5	v6	v7	v8	v9	v10	v11	v12	v13	v14	v15	v16	v17
1	517	3	4.00	4.00	888	21.00	2.00	1.00	2.00	2.00	6.00	3.00	3.00	6.00	1.00	.00	1.00
2	500	3	3.00	3.00	888	22.00	2.00	1.00	1.00	2.00	8.00	1.00	777.00	5.00	1.00	3.00	1.00
3	538	3	2.00	4.00	888	22.00	2.00	1.00	-2.00	1.00	7.00	2.00	1.00	6.00	3.00	.00	2.00
4	503	3	2.00	4.00	888	22.00	1.00	1.00	6.00	2.00	4.00	2.00	4.00	6.00	3.00	.00	1.00
5	230	1	2.00	2.00	888	19.00	2.00	1.00	6.00	2.00	6.00	3.00	4.00	6.00	1.00	.00	1.00
6	555	3	-2.00	-2.00	888	888.00	2.00	1.00	2.00	2.00	5.00	4.00	4.00	1.00	4.00	.00	1.00
7	239	1	3.00	2.00	1	20.00	2.00	1.00	4.00	2.00	6.00	3.00	4.00	6.00	1.00	.00	1.00
8	204	1	3.00	1.00	1	19.00	2.00	1.00	4.00	2.00	6.00	1.00	777.00	5.00	1.00	.00	1.00
9	324	2	3.00	2.00	1	20.00	1.00	1.00	1.00	2.00	4.00	2.00	2.00	6.00	3.00	.00	3.00
10	505	3	3.00	3.00	1	21.00	2.00	2.00	1.00	2.00	8.00	2.00	3.00	6.00	4.00	.00	5.00
11	114	1	-2.00	1.00	1	18.00	2.00	1.00	1.00	2.00	3.00	1.00	777.00	5.00	1.00	.00	1.00
12	143	1	2.00	4.00	1	23.00	2.00	1.00	2.00	2.00	2.00	2.00	2.00	6.00	1.00	.00	1.00
13	215	1	4.00	1.00	1	18.00	2.00	1.00	3.00	2.00	8.00	1.00	999.00	6.00	3.00	.00	1.00
14	123	1	3.00	2.00	1	20.00	1.00	1.00	1.00	2.00	3.00	1.00	999.00	6.00	2.00	.00	9.00
15	207	1	4.00	4.00	1	21.00	1.00	1.00	2.00	2.00	6.00	1.00	999.00	6.00	4.00	.00	1.00
16	245	1	2.00	1.00	1	17.00	2.00	1.00	1.00	2.00	8.00	3.00	4.00	6.00	2.00	.00	1.00
17	125	1	2.00	3.00	1	22.00	1.00	1.00	2.00	2.00	7.00	3.00	3.00	5.00	2.00	.00	2.00
18	126	1	3.00	1.00	1	17.00	1.00	1.00	4.00	2.00	6.00	1.00	999.00	6.00	3.00	.00	1.00
19	236	1	2.00	3.00	1	22.00	2.00	1.00	4.00	2.00	2.00	2.00	3.00	6.00	1.00	.00	1.00
20	225	1	3.00	2.00	1	18.00	2.00	1.00	5.00	2.00	8.00	3.00	4.00	6.00	4.00	.00	1.00
21	325	2	2.00	2.00	1	20.00	1.00	1.00	3.00	2.00	6.00	3.00	4.00	6.00	1.00	.00	1.00
22	326	2	2.00	1.00	1	17.00	1.00	1.00	3.00	1.00	4.00	1.00	999.00	6.00	2.00	.00	1.00
23	304	2	3.00	3.00	1	21.00	1.00	1.00	2.00	2.00	8.00	1.00	999.00	6.00	4.00	1.00	5.00
24	336	2	3.00	1.00	1	19.00	1.00	1.00	2.00	2.00	4.00	2.00	4.00	6.00	1.00	.00	2.00
25	553	3	1.00	4.00	1	22.00	1.00	1.00	1.00	2.00	8.00	3.00	4.00	6.00	1.00	.00	1.00
26	142	1	3.00	3.00	2	20.00	2.00	1.00	1.00	2.00	3.00	2.00	1.00	6.00	2.00	.00	4.00
27	238	1	2.00	2.00	2	19.00	2.00	1.00	4.00	1.00	1.00	1.00	999.00	6.00	1.00	.00	1.00
28	141	1	2.00	4.00	2	22.00	2.00	1.00	4.00	2.00	2.00	2.00	3.00	6.00	1.00	.00	1.00
29	119	1	2.00	4.00	2	23.00	2.00	1.00	1.00	2.00	6.00	3.00	4.00	6.00	4.00	.00	1.00
30	206	1	-2.00	2.00	2	19.00	2.00	1.00	2.00	2.00	4.00	1.00	999.00	6.00	3.00	.00	5.00
31	212	1	3.00	4.00	2	21.00	1.00	1.00	6.00	2.00	5.00	1.00	777.00	6.00	4.00	.00	1.00
32	233	1	2.00	2.00	2	19.00	1.00	1.00	1.00	2.00	3.00	2.00	2.00	6.00	1.00	.00	1.00
33	222	1	2.00	3.00	2	-2.00	2.00	1.00	2.00	2.00	1.00	3.00	3.00	6.00	4.00	.00	6.00
34	224	1	2.00	3.00	2	20.00	2.00	1.00	2.00	2.00	6.00	4.00	3.00	5.00	4.00	.00	1.00
35	219	1	3.00	4.00	2	21.00	2.00	1.00	2.00	2.00	6.00	3.00	4.00	6.00	4.00	.00	1.00
36	210	1	2.00	2.00	2	19.00	2.00	1.00	2.00	1.00	6.00	1.00	-1.00	1.00	4.00	.00	7.00
37	120	1	2.00	1.00	2	17.00	2.00	1.00	2.00	2.00	6.00	3.00	4.00	6.00	1.00	.00	6.00
38	128	1	2.00	3.00	2	23.00	2.00	1.00	2.00	2.00	6.00	4.00	4.00	5.00	4.00	.00	5.00
39	127	1	3.00	3.00	2	21.00	2.00	1.00	5.00	2.00	6.00	3.00	3.00	6.00	1.00	.00	1.00
40	138	1	3.00	3.00	2	19.00	2.00	1.00	4.00	2.00	6.00	2.00	1.00	6.00	4.00	.00	1.00
41	243	1	3.00	2.00	2	20.00	2.00	1.00	4.00	2.00	4.00	3.00	4.00	6.00	1.00	.00	1.00
42	146	1	3.00	2.00	2	19.00	2.00	1.00	4.00	2.00	4.00	3.00	4.00	8.00	1.00	.00	1.00

V3. Some question types generate response data that are more difficult to enter, and we will introduce these question types separately at the end of this section.

Given that there are some variable types that make data entry complicated, it is a good idea to create a **data entry skeleton** of the database first before entering any data. In a data entry skeleton, all the **variables names** that will be associated with each question are set up along the columns of either a data entry program or an Excel spreadsheet.

Each respondent's unique identifier is placed in a cell of the first column. In order to match the data entry skeleton to the survey questionnaire, write the variable number next to each question on a blank copy of the questionnaire. By doing this, in essence, you are creating a data management plan. An important feature of the data entry skeleton is the unique identifier for each participant.

Unique Identifier

In the example in Figure 12.1, the first column shows variable V1, the unique identifier. The **unique identifier** is a randomly assigned number that replaces the respondent's name or social security number so as to identify the respondent without betraying the goal of confidentiality or anonymity. Thus, it is a crucial variable to create. No two participants should have the same unique identifier. It assists with data entry as well. The unique identifier does not come from a question. Researchers assign identifiers to participants ahead of time. The unique identifier is often included on mail surveys, perhaps as a footer with a note that indicates the space is for the use of study personnel only. Data entry personnel will need to be instructed to add the unique identifier variable to the database. Researchers will benefit from programming a unique identifier into a survey even if it is a cross-sectional small survey and the researcher has no intention of asking for any identifying information.

The purpose of the unique identifier is manifold—it is helpful when auditing data collection to determine whether some respondents need to be approached again to fill out the questionnaire, and it's useful for assessing the response rate. Without identifying the participants, it also allows for the tracing of problem cases, such as outliers or duplicate entries, when cleaning or analyzing the data.

Variable Naming Conventions

In Figure 12.1 the variable names are simply numbers with the letter *V*, from V1 through V250. The *V* stands for *variable,* and each number refers the user to the question number on the survey. Thus, *V1* refers to the variable from the first question on the survey questionnaire; in some cases *V1* would contain the unique identifier information described above, though that is sometimes assigned a different sort of variable name such as "ID." This is a simple and effective variable naming procedure, but the variable names provide little information on the content of each question. It is very important to be able to tie the data to the questionnaire, but data with these types of variable names are not very user friendly. There are many other ways to name variables. In order to ensure that the data are entered correctly, choose a label for each variable that ties the column in the data entry program to the question on the survey. Variable labels can provide more detail than variable names. Consistency in variable labeling procedures is good, because it teaches the user what to expect from the variables in the dataset (ICPSR 2009). This is an excellent strategy for a cross-sectional study. Because *Q1* or *V1* does not let the researcher know the content of the variable, use the **variable label** (see data cleaning) to describe the observations the variable represents. During cleaning of the data, variables can be renamed, and variable labels can be added.

Some researchers like to create variable names that reflect the question asked. For example, the question, "Have you given help with child care to one or more of your neighbors?" could be reduced to *supgvchc* or to *helpchld*. The first variable name reflects the construct of "support given for child care," which this question is designed to measure. The second name reflects the single question more directly by including two words from the question. Neither variable name is obvious, nor does it directly remind the researcher of the question it came from. Most likely, six months after creating the variable name, the researcher may no longer know what it means. For some researchers, however, this is the preferred way to name variables. If this is the preferred method, it is a good idea to put the survey question number into the variable label (discussed in next section) to tie the variable directly to the survey questionnaire.

Either naming convention works fine for a small, cross-sectional survey. However, it might not be adequate for a longitudinal study. For a longitudinal study, the survey software programs do not automatically adjust variable names temporally. In other words, the software programs typically are not able to automatically link the same question across different waves of a survey if it is asked at a different position in the questionnaire. This means variable names will be repeated for the questions that are repeated during each wave of the questionnaire administration. The first question asked in Wave 2 may not be the first question asked in Wave 1. Thus, *V1* will be a different variable in Waves 1 and 2. This can be very confusing when trying to analyze the data. This may lead researchers to think the phonetic naming system is better, but that also has issues.

More important, it has a serious negative effect on the ability to merge the panels or waves of data together. We merge each wave of data using the unique identifier, thus the identifier must exist within each panel. When two waves of data are merged using the unique identifier, the resultant dataset will have only one unique identifier. Likewise any other variables that share a name across the two datasets will end up with just one variable with that name; one of the duplicate variables will be overwritten by the first wave of data. This means we have lost information on that variable from one of the waves. Therefore, with longitudinal data, it behooves the researcher to decide on a consistent naming convention.

Often suffixes or prefixes are used for each wave of data in a longitudinal study. For example, for a three-wave longitudinal survey study, a prefix-driven variable naming convention might look like this: "W1Q1", "W2Q1", and "W3Q1", where "W1", "W2" and "W3" indicate which wave the data comes from, and "Q1" indicates the question on the survey. A suffix-driven naming convention would be reversed: "Q1W1", "Q1W2", and "Q1W3." In this case, the wave indicators are used as suffixes. Choose a naming convention based on personal preferences or whatever is best for a given statistical software program.

In the past, statistical software programs limited variable names to only eight characters. A character is a single letter in a word. So the variable name "V1" has a character length of 2. They also limited variable labels to a length of 40 characters. A variable name distinguishes one variable from the rest. But an 8-character variable name may not be very descriptive; thus, the longer variable label gave a better clue or definition of the information captured by the variable. Today, these same programs allow 40 characters for the variable name and 255 characters for variable labels. This seems much more user friendly; however, if we have a long variable name, every time we wish to analyze that variable, we will have to type in that long name (or locate it from a list in a point-and-click dialog box). It is also harder to find spelling mistakes in longer variable names, thus, syntax errors are likely to increase and be harder to locate. Additionally, long variable labels will take up much of the output space, and for some software programs, such as SAS and SPSS Statistics, the results end up being spread over multiple pages, making it difficult to associate the statistics with the variable with which they are associated. We recommend keeping variable names and labels as short as possible while maintaining utility.

Missing Data Codes

Response categories may include "don't know" as an option or, due to a skip pattern, a "not applicable" option might be chosen for a particular question. Respondents may simply leave a question blank—refusing to answer. All of these are examples of **missing values**. Researchers will want to decide how to handle potential nonresponse categories up front and be consistent throughout the survey. Figure 12.1 shows several respondents with values such as "777" or "999." These are the codes for missing values; they are used to designate "don't know" and "nonresponse" respectively. Deciding how to handle missing values and what codes to use for them upfront will make responding to the survey easier for the participants and data entry easier for personnel. We discuss this in more detail in Chapter 13.

Entering Responses From Atypical Questions

Once the data entry skeleton of participants' unique identifiers and variables' names has been created in a data entry program, it is simple to go through each paper survey and enter the response values into the appropriate cells. However, there are three types of questions for which answers are not easy to enter into the data program. They are multiple-response variables, other-specify variables, and open-ended questions. If you are entering data manually, it makes sense to code these variables at the time of data entry. While we discuss coding these variables here in data entry, note that if the data are entered through a web-based or CAPI program, then it makes sense to code these variables during data cleaning.

Multiple-response questions are questions in which participants are asked to "check all that apply." That is, multiple responses are allowed. The question below is an example:

Q12. What tobacco products have you ever tried or smoked? (Choose all that apply.)

1) Cigarettes (a)
2) Cigars (b)
3) Pipes (c)
4) Dip/Chew (d)
5) Cigarillos (e)

Given that in a statistical software program, a question can have one and only one **value**, how do we turn responses to this type of question into a single value that we can enter into the data entry program? There are two ways of doing this. The first is the method used by web-based and CAPI programs, which suggests it is the more flexible. It involves creating a separate variable for each response. Thus, Q12 will have five variables with yes/no response options. Variable Q12a would have a value of 2 for all respondents who indicated they had smoked cigarettes. For respondents who had not smoked cigarettes, the value of Q12a would be 1, for no. The process is repeated for each response option. Thus, a respondent who has tried cigarettes and chew would have the value of 2 for variables Q12a and Q12d and 1 for variables Q12b, Q12c, and Q12e. In the skeleton created to use for data entry, the variable Q12 would not be included. Instead, variables Q12a through Q12e would be included.

The second way of coding is useful if the researcher is interested in learning about the number of different tobacco products individuals try. For this use, a single variable with multiple response categories can be created. So, for example, once the responses are in, we can create new codes for each possible coupling of responses.

1. Cigarettes
2. Cigars
3. Pipes
4. Dip/chew
5. Cigarillos
6. Cigarettes and cigars
7. Cigarettes and pipes
8. Cigarettes and chew
9. Cigarettes and Cigarillos
10. Cigarettes, cigars and pipes
11. ……

N. Cigarettes, cigars, pipes, chew, and Cigarillos

Decide on how the variable will be used and choose the alternative that makes the most sense given how the variable will be analyzed.

In order to be exhaustive, the list of possible responses to some questions may include an "other" possibility and allow the participant to specify exactly what that "other" is. These are called **other-specify responses**. For example, the following question asks about race:

Q5 Would you say you are... (race)

(1) White

(2) Black

(3) Asian

(4) Hispanic

(5) Other (please specify ____________________)

The "please specify" is a separate variable from the race variable. For respondents who choose option #5, we will want to be able to recode the original race variable with values specific to their other-specify responses. Some respondents may fit into the existing categories 1–4, but for others we may need to create new categories. For example, if a participant chooses the value 5 for "other" on Q5 and then writes in the word "Caucasian," for the sake of analysis, this participant can be recoded from a value of 5 to a value of 1, "white." Respondents who give responses such as Korean, African American, Latina, et cetera, can also be recoded into existing categories. Respondents who write in something like "Italian and African American," "Korean and Mexican," or "multiracial," can all be recoded from 5 to a new **response category** of 6 for "multiracial." Respondents who write in "human" cannot be recoded into any category, and they can be left in the "other" response category. Create new categories only if enough respondents can be recoded into that category to make it viable in statistical analysis. We recommend a minimum of five cases in order to create a new category.

In order for data entry personnel to correctly enter the data for this variable, the other-specify variable should be recoded before data entry begins, and new categories should be created and the rules and definitions included in a data entry code book. When creating the data entry skeleton, the researcher will include only the first variable (Q5). The other-specify variable has been used for its purpose and does not need to be entered into the data set. Those two variables are collapsed into a single variable. This is not an easy task—despite the easy example. People can use many ways to say the exact same thing. So you must *read the responses carefully several times* and pay close attention to the *wording* of the original question.

We include **open-ended questions** in our surveys for a couple of reasons. First, sometimes we do not have enough information to create categories ourselves, and this is a good way to allow the categories to evolve out of the mouths of respondents. However, we cannot use text variables in our quantitative analyses; therefore, we will have to code the variable, meaning turn it into a numerical variable. The codes we create have to be able to be used quantitatively—that means thinking about how the variable should be measured. Possibly we will create a nominal or ordinal variable—rarely do we get continuous variables.

Survey coding is the process of taking the open-ended responses and categorizing them into groups (Popping 1992, 2012). The coding process can be very tedious, but careful, consistent coding is necessary in order to ensure reliable results. This should be done by pairs of coders, in order to assess the **reliability** of the codes. This process is described in the following section.

THE CODING PROCESS

1. Read through all the open-ended responses carefully at least twice. As coders read through the responses, they may see some common themes emerging. This allows coders to get a feel for the themes that are occurring and reoccurring, and it also helps coders understand how the population is responding to each specific survey question.

2. Develop the coding categories.

a. Codes or **coding** categories are a means of sorting or grouping the responses so that the material bearing on a given topic can be physically separated from other data.

b. Write down words or phrases to represent these patterns or themes.

c. We like to use Excel for the coding process. It is easy to bring text codes into Excel and use additional columns for themes. Create a column on the Excel spreadsheet labeled "text code," and type in the words or phrases that describe the theme or pattern for each response. If none of the codes apply to a particular response, skip it for the time being.

d. Once you have completed the first run through the coding process, sort the coding spreadsheet by the column labeled "text code." This will physically separate the codes. Just remember to sort the entire codebook—otherwise the code will accidentally be separated from the text data used to create the codes.

3. Assess the resulting codes.

a. Look at all the responses that have been given the same code, and verify that they all belong together. If one or more do not belong, remove the code.

b. Some responses simply cannot be coded, because they are not real responses. Code clear nonresponses as "nonresponse." Responses that are not codeable, but that clearly are not nonresponses, should be coded as "uncodeable."

4. Sort the spreadsheet again, making sure to include the entire sheet, so the responses do not get separated from the code.

a. Read the remaining uncoded responses to determine what themes emerge.

b. Write words or phrases to represent these patterns or themes.

c. Type in the words or phrases that describe the theme or pattern for each uncoded response into the code column. If none of the codes apply to a particular response, skip it for the time being.

d. Once the second run through of the coding process has been completed, sort the spreadsheet by the column labeled "text code" again. This will physically separate the codes. Just remember to sort the entire codebook!

5. Repeat Steps 3 and 4 until you are satisfied that you have given a code to every response.

6. Make a list of the codes you have created, and number them from 1 to n (e.g., $n = 10$ if you have come up with 10 codes). Start with the code that occurs most frequently and proceed to the code that occurs least frequently (except for the nonresponse and uncodeable categories—they should be the last codes in the list).

7. Create a definition for each code and substantiate it with a couple of responses. This list is the **category definition document**.

THE RELIABILITY PROCESS

8. In the coding process just described, coders have worked independently. Now, meet with a coding partner, compare category definition documents, discuss the definitions of each code, and come to a consensus for a final set of categories. Do the two of you have the same number of codes? Can you agree on names for the codes you have? For example, one coder might label a code "financial," and the other might call it "money." Clearly they are related, but, in order to have interrater reliability, we need the same names and attached numeric codes. This means you should not be wedded to the labels you have given to codes or definitions. Code labels are to be used as tools to help you dialogue with one another. Discuss each definition document and set of codes until both of you feel comfortable with the final codes and that there is a clear definition for each code.

9. Once the final set of codes is hashed out, start the whole coding process over—with an uncoded Excel spreadsheet. But this time, code with a clear category definition document. Code all of the responses again using the final codes. This time, give a numeric code rather than a text code.

    a. Delete the information out of the column labeled "text codes."

    b. Create a new column called "number code," and put the number associated with the text code into this column for each response.

10. Once each coder has completed this step, it is time to assess reliability. The first step is to create a crosstab of both coders' codes in Excel. Compare the percentage of codes that are similar or concordant. A reliability of 80% is a good goal—higher is even better. This is difficult to achieve without the two coders working together, coming to consensus on what the codes should be, and creating strong, clear definitions of the codes in the previous steps in this process.

    a. If you and your partner do not reach the correct level of reliability, together look over the responses that are discordant, and work on refining the coding definitions, so that next time you will choose similar codes.

b. If interrater reliability is low, repeat steps 8 and 9 until a reliability percentage of .80 is achieved.

c. As you approach 80% reliability, simply code the last remaining differences together.

11. Once 80% reliability has been reached, the new quantitative variable can be entered into the data entry program.

The data entry skeleton should include only the numerically coded versions of open-ended items; it would take data entry personnel too long to enter all the different text responses. Additionally, the text items may contain some sorts of identifying information. Thus, it makes sense to not retain the text items in the data set.

If there are plenty of resources, SPSS is an excellent program to use for data entry, because it provides a variable view screen. Using this screen, it will be easy to create a variable name and label, to identify the type of variable—either numeric or string (text)—and to enter a width of the variable (meaning how many characters it will need), as well as to enter other important characteristics that can be assigned ahead of time.

If there are few resources, a spreadsheet program such as Excel can be used for data entry. The data can then be imported into almost any statistical program. Excel can be set up ahead of time by creating variable names across the columns and entering cases (unique identifiers) along the rows. The cells cannot be formatted in Excel as well as they can in SPSS; thus, it is possible that more data entry mistakes will occur.

Mistakes are ubiquitous when data are entered manually regardless of the data entry program used. It is very easy to accidentally hit a 5 on the keypad when a 2 should have been hit. This is called **data entry error**, and it is quite common. Therefore, it is important to check over the data entered. This can be done by taking a random sample (see Chapter 7) of surveys and checking each response. If errors are found, then they can be corrected easily. This means, however, that there may be more mistakes. A better solution, if there are enough resources, would be to have all the data entered twice—by two independent persons. Then, each set of data can be compared across each variable, and only where there are different answers do the original surveys need to be consulted and the correct response entered. This will minimize errors in the data due to data entry and increase the data quality.

If a survey was administered using either a web-based program or a CAPI program, then the data will not need to be entered. Rather, the program will save the data in a "warehouse" that can be translated and imported into a statistical database. This will save on resources needed for data entry and reduce data entry errors. It will not reduce interviewer input errors, however. And, in fact, if the interviewer makes an error entering a response, the error will not be found, because there is no original paper questionnaire by which to check it. Thus, it pays to make sure interviewers are well trained on the questionnaire and have practiced using it extensively prior to entering the field.

Another issue to keep in mind is that the web or CAPI program will automatically create multiple variables for the multiple-response questions, will create an other-specify variable, and will include the text responses of the open-ended questions. In these cases, coding other-specify and open-ended items will take place when the data are cleaned.

Once all of these decisions are made, create a data entry manual with rules and definitions to assist the data entry personnel. Use the manual to train data entry and data cleaning staff. When the manual is followed, multiple data entry workers can enter data consistently. This will ensure that the data quality is high.

DOCUMENTATION

At the same time a data entry skeleton is created, the data entry procedures should be documented (ICPSR 2009). **Documentation** should include variable naming procedures as well as all the data entry rules and definitions needed to assist the data entry personnel. The three special types of variables should be located, and instructions on how to handle them need to be included.

ETHICS CORNER

Documentation is an important part of a researchers' ethical obligation. In order for the research process to be transparent, researchers should document each step, process, decision, and outcome of the collection process, data entry process, cleaning process, and analysis process. This allows other researchers to replicate the work, and therefore replicate the findings. When other researchers cannot replicate a study, it makes a study's findings suspicious, and by association, it puts suspicion on the researchers themselves. Therefore, for the sake of transparency and reputation, it is important to document the entire process.

CONCLUSION

Data entry is fairly rare in these days of web-based surveys. However, understanding the principles of data entry can facilitate the creation of the survey. If you are using a web-based program, think very carefully about the variable names being created by the survey. Think about how the response categories will look in the final data set. Think about the types of questions included on the survey.

The types of questions included have consequences for how the data can be included in the dataset and how it can be analyzed. The responses to open-ended questions, for example, cannot be used like qualitative data. Rather, they need to be turned into quantitative data, or they are simply unusable. In addition, they are burdensome for respondents to answer and burdensome to code. Therefore, limit the number of open-ended items in your survey. The other-specify option is a nice alternative when there is some information on how respondents will answer but not complete information. These are much less burdensome on both respondents and data entry staff.

Last, document even the small decisions as they are made. It is very easy to forget the many decisions that researchers make on a daily basis. Documentation is an important step in this process and is far too often neglected.

KEY TERMS

Data entry skeleton 197
Variable name 197
Unique identifier 197
Variable label 198
Missing values 199
Multiple-response questions 200
Value 200
Other-specify responses 201
Response category 202
Open-ended questions 202
Reliability 202
Coding 203
Category definition document 204
Data entry error 205
Documentation 206

CRITICAL THINKING QUESTIONS

Below you will find three questions that ask you to think critically about core concepts addressed in this chapter. Be sure you understand each one; if you don't, this is a good time to review the relevant sections of this chapter.

1. What data issues should we consider prior to fielding our survey?
2. What are the strengths and weaknesses of manual data entry as compared to those of automatic data entry from a web-based survey program?
3. How do we train a staff of four or five people to enter the data? What do we need to think about to ensure the data are entered consistently?

13

Data Cleaning

INTRODUCTION

This chapter furthers our goal of reducing the gap between the raw data students usually collect in a research methods course and the pristine data usually analyzed in statistics courses. We began the demystification of the gap between collecting and analyzing data in the last chapter with our discussion of data entry. In this chapter we move on to data cleaning. Some elements of data cleaning, such as cosmetic cleaning, are very much related to comparable elements of data entry. The same types of decisions must be made, and there are the same documentation goals. However, in this chapter we extend data cleaning to include examining diagnostics, interviewer or mode effects, and longitudinal attrition. Data cleaning involves simple and effective steps that will ensure the highest quality data for analysis purposes.

This chapter assumes that, regardless of how the survey was administered, we now have a raw data file in a statistical software format. It also assumes that some sort of prior planning and setting of protocols were used to enter the data, create variable names, and handle response values and missing values. This next step, data cleaning, ranges from simple cosmetic fixes that make the dataset easier to analyze to diagnostics to assess the quality of the variables and the suitability of the dataset for regression analysis.

We advise all data cleaners to do their cleaning work in **syntax** (statistical software language). Using syntax, which is sometimes called computer coding or programming, simply means to write out the cleaning commands in the statistical software language rather than using a mouse to point and click through dialog boxes. Certainly the point-and-click method can be simpler (because the cleaner doesn't have to remember programming codes), but it usually does not leave a trail of changes made to the dataset. There is no record of what has been done. SPSS Statistics, however, does allow a user to paste syntax from a point-and-click dialog box into a record of the executed procedures. In fact, recent versions of SPSS Statistics automatically paste syntax to the output window whenever a command is executed from a point-and-click dialog box. Syntax can be saved permanently to a file, and therefore there is a record of all data manipulations. This way, errors in data cleaning, when found during analysis, can be easily fixed.

We also advise not directly correcting the data, even though programs like SPSS make it so convenient (and tempting!) to do so. Again, there will be no record of the correction, so documentation will be incorrect. Mistakes are very easy to make (even for experts), and we often have to revert back to the raw data. This means that any fixes made directly to the data will have to be reentered. With syntax, we simply fix the mistake in the syntax and rerun it on the original dataset. In addition to leaving a visible record of all changes made to the dataset, writing in syntax will save much time and energy in the long run and ensure higher quality data.

The first section will discuss the basics of data cleaning for a simple cross-sectional survey. Next, additions for diagnostic cleaning and then longitudinal data will be addressed.

SIMPLE CROSS-SECTIONAL DATA CLEANING

Before cleaning the data, it is good to think through the process first and come up with some consistent practices that make the whole procedure easy to do and easy to understand. Figure 13.1 provides a checklist of all the data-cleaning items needed to properly clean a cross-sectional dataset. We start and end by examining each variable using a frequency procedure. Note which variables are string variables, which are scale items, and which are open-ended. This is important, because we cannot include string values and numeric variables in the same syntax code. Take notes on what each variable needs, and organize the variables by what they need. Starting with the cosmetics, make sure each variable has a variable label that links it to the questionnaire. Make sure that each response value has a value label. Determine whether the formatting of the variables needs to be changed. Note whether the variable has missing values and what those missing values are. Create a list of all the skip patterns, and note which are the gateway variables and which variables they skip. Similarly, create a list of all the variables that have an other-specify option as part of the question. Additional lists of any multiple-response variables and open-ended questions should be created in order to systematically ensure all variables are cleaned.

Start with a frequency of the unique identifier. If there is an identifier with a frequency of more than 1, then it is not unique. Either it was created wrong, it's a data entry mistake, or something went wrong in the syntax. Checking the unique identifier in the beginning and at the end of the syntax or any time datasets are merged is one way to

Figure 13.1 Cleaning Raw Cross-Sectional Data

1. Unique identifier
2. Cosmetics
   a. Value labels
   b. Variable labels
   c. Formats
3. Missing values
4. Skip patterns
5. Multiple-response questions
6. Other-specify responses
7. Open-ended questions
8. Notes
9. Multiple records

determine if any data manipulations have had a negative impact on the dataset being cleaned or analyzed. Mini Case 13.1 provides a frequency of a unique identifier called "Subject" with the variable label "respondent's ID number." If we scroll down the column labeled "Frequency," we want to see all 1s. This indicates uniqueness. Unfortunately, subject 1122 has a frequency of 2. This means two subjects were given the same identifier. Now we cannot distinguish between them. If this frequency were run prior to data cleaning, then we know we have to look to data entry to find this error. We may find that two interviewers used this same number. In fact, we may find that one interviewer transposed the unique identifier number, entering 1122 when he meant to enter 2211.

MINI CASE 13.1

Partial Frequency of a Unique Identifier

We start with the syntax to first access the data and then call for a frequency table to be run. Below the syntax we show the SPSS output the syntax generates. In SPSS, the syntax would look like this:

```
Get file "c:\my documents\survey\data.sav".
Frequency variables=subject.
```

The output is as follows:

Respondent's ID Number				
SUBJECT	**Frequency**	**Percent**	**Cumulative Frequency**	**Cumulative Percent**
1029	1	0.26	1	0.26
1040	1	0.26	2	0.52
1101	1	0.26	3	0.79
1104	1	0.26	4	1.05
1106	1	0.26	5	1.31
1107	1	0.26	6	1.57
1112	1	0.26	7	1.83
1113	1	0.26	8	2.09
1115	1	0.26	9	2.36
1117	1	0.26	10	2.62
1118	1	0.26	11	2.88
1121	1	0.26	12	3.14
1122	2	0.52	14	3.66
....	...	...	...	...
9612	1	0.26	382	100.00

Alternatively, if this frequency were run at the end of data cleaning and we knew the unique identifier was fine prior to running the data cleaning syntax, we would then know that there is a mistake in the syntax that needs to be found and rectified. The first step is to search for all syntax that involves the unique identifier 1122 and examine it for mistakes. If we find a mistake, we can fix it, rerun the syntax on the original data, and then rerun the frequency of the identifier. If the frequency shows one case with the identifier 1122 then we are done. If, however, there are still two cases with the identifier 1122, then the next step is to look for any places in the syntax in which data are merged. Again, check the syntax for mistakes, correct any found, and, after rerunning the syntax, check a new frequency of the unique identifier. If the problem still has not been resolved, run the syntax piecemeal, rerunning the frequency of the identifier after each small piece of syntax that has been run. Eventually the problematic piece of syntax will be isolated, and it can be corrected; then the identifier will once again become unique.

Now, this may seem like a lot of work. Why not just delete the extra 1122 case? Often the problem is not in the identifier—the identifier just lets us know there may be a deeper problem in the data. If we just delete the extra case, we will not know that there is another data error that has not been resolved.

COSMETIC CLEANING

Cosmetic cleaning takes place on each and every variable. As we did with the unique identifier, we run a frequency of each variable before and after any cosmetic cleaning is done. This allows us to see exactly how our syntax affected the variable and if the syntax did what we wanted it to do to the variable. Note that we cannot include string values and numeric variables in the same syntax code.

Variable Labels

In order to have a clear understanding of each variable, give each a variable name and variable label that make sense and that link it to the question on the questionnaire from which it originated. (See Chapter 12 for variable naming conventions.) The variable label is a title that is associated with a given variable name. It can describe the content of the variable. Some survey software will adapt the survey question into a variable label. If the software does not create a label, or if a pen-and-paper survey is used, researchers will have to create a label themselves. Once created, the variable label will appear in statistical output, making the output easy to interpret. The variable label will also appear in the variable view screen on SPSS. Figure 12.2 (Chapter 12) shows the variable view screen, and the variable label is visible.

Response Category Values

In Figure 13.2, in the column just to the right of the column showing labels, is a column headed "Values." *Values* here means value labels, which are the definitions given to each possible response category available for a given question. Value labels assign the wording found in the questionnaire for each response to the value or number found in the data. Each question on the survey will have response options. For example the question, "Have you given help with child care to one or more of your neighbors?" could have several possible response options. We could ask respondents to circle a 1 if the answer

Figure 13.2 SPSS Variable View of the Data

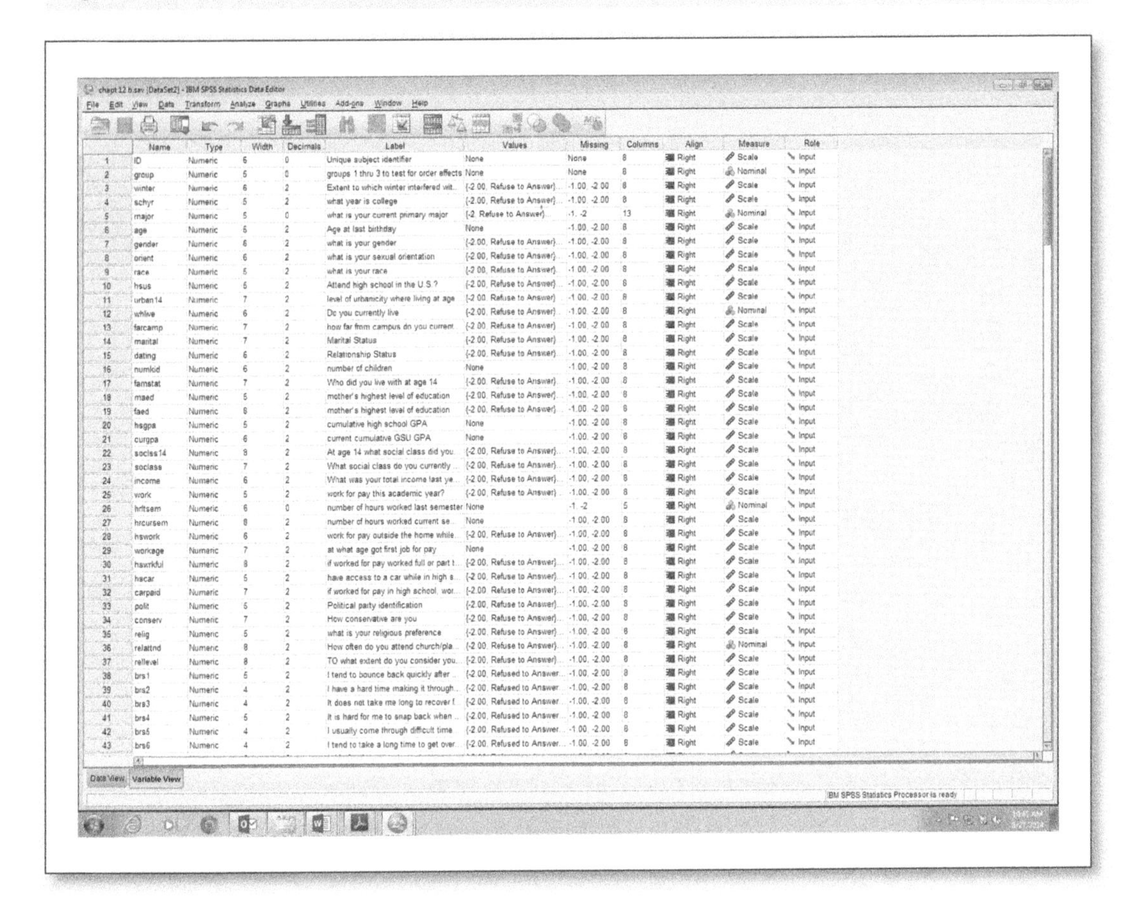

	Name	Type	Width	Decimals	Label	Values	Missing	Columns	Align	Measure	Role
1	ID	Numeric	6	0	Unique subject identifier	None	None	8	Right	Scale	Input
2	group	Numeric	5	0	groups 1 thru 3 to test for order effects	None	None	8	Right	Nominal	Input
3	winter	Numeric	6	2	Extent to which winter interfered wit...	{-2.00, Refuse to Answer}	-1.00, -2.00	8	Right	Scale	Input
4	schyr	Numeric	5	2	what year is college	{-2.00, Refuse to Answer}	-1.00, -2.00	8	Right	Scale	Input
5	major	Numeric	5	0	what is your current primary major	{-2, Refuse to Answer}	-1, -2	13	Right	Nominal	Input
6	age	Numeric	6	2	Age at last birthday	None	-1.00, -2.00	8	Right	Scale	Input
7	gender	Numeric	6	2	what is your gender	{-2.00, Refuse to Answer}	-1.00, -2.00	8	Right	Scale	Input
8	orient	Numeric	6	2	what is your sexual orientation	{-2.00, Refuse to Answer}	-1.00, -2.00	8	Right	Scale	Input
9	race	Numeric	5	2	what is your race	{-2.00, Refuse to Answer}	-1.00, -2.00	8	Right	Scale	Input
10	hsus	Numeric	5	2	Attend high school in the U.S.?	{-2.00, Refuse to Answer}	-1.00, -2.00	8	Right	Scale	Input
11	urban14	Numeric	7	2	level of urbanicity where living at age	{-2.00, Refuse to Answer}	-1.00, -2.00	8	Right	Scale	Input
12	whlive	Numeric	6	2	Do you currently live	{-2.00, Refuse to Answer}	-1.00, -2.00	8	Right	Nominal	Input
13	farcamp	Numeric	7	2	how far from campus do you current...	{-2.00, Refuse to Answer}	-1.00, -2.00	8	Right	Scale	Input
14	marital	Numeric	7	2	Marital Status	{-2.00, Refuse to Answer}	-1.00, -2.00	8	Right	Scale	Input
15	dating	Numeric	6	2	Relationship Status	{-2.00, Refuse to Answer}	-1.00, -2.00	8	Right	Scale	Input
16	numkid	Numeric	6	2	number of children	None	-1.00, -2.00	8	Right	Scale	Input
17	famstat	Numeric	7	2	Who did you live with at age 14	{-2.00, Refuse to Answer}	-1.00, -2.00	8	Right	Scale	Input
18	maed	Numeric	5	2	mother's highest level of education	{-2.00, Refuse to Answer}	-1.00, -2.00	8	Right	Scale	Input
19	faed	Numeric	6	2	mother's highest level of education	{-2.00, Refuse to Answer}	-1.00, -2.00	8	Right	Scale	Input
20	hsgpa	Numeric	5	2	cumulative high school GPA	None	-1.00, -2.00	8	Right	Scale	Input
21	curgpa	Numeric	6	2	current cumulative GSU GPA	None	-1.00, -2.00	8	Right	Scale	Input
22	soclss14	Numeric	8	2	At age 14 what social class did you...	{-2.00, Refuse to Answer}	-1.00, -2.00	8	Right	Scale	Input
23	soclass	Numeric	7	2	What social class do you currently ...	{-2.00, Refuse to Answer}	-1.00, -2.00	8	Right	Scale	Input
24	income	Numeric	6	2	What was your total income last ye...	{-2.00, Refuse to Answer}	-1.00, -2.00	8	Right	Scale	Input
25	work	Numeric	5	2	work for pay this academic year?	{-2.00, Refuse to Answer}	-1.00, -2.00	8	Right	Scale	Input
26	hrltsem	Numeric	6	0	number of hours worked last semester	None	-1, -2	5	Right	Nominal	Input
27	hrcursem	Numeric	8	2	number of hours worked current se...	None	-1.00, -2.00	8	Right	Scale	Input
28	hswork	Numeric	6	2	work for pay outside the home while...	{-2.00, Refuse to Answer}	-1.00, -2.00	8	Right	Scale	Input
29	workage	Numeric	7	2	at what age got first job for pay	None	-1.00, -2.00	8	Right	Scale	Input
30	hswrkful	Numeric	8	2	if worked for pay worked full or part t...	{-2.00, Refuse to Answer}	-1.00, -2.00	8	Right	Scale	Input
31	hscar	Numeric	5	2	have access to a car while in high s...	{-2.00, Refuse to Answer}	-1.00, -2.00	8	Right	Scale	Input
32	carpaid	Numeric	7	2	if worked for pay in high school, wor...	{-2.00, Refuse to Answer}	-1.00, -2.00	8	Right	Scale	Input
33	polit	Numeric	5	2	Political party identification	{-2.00, Refuse to Answer}	-1.00, -2.00	8	Right	Scale	Input
34	conserv	Numeric	7	2	How conservative are you	{-2.00, Refuse to Answer}	-1.00, -2.00	8	Right	Scale	Input
35	relig	Numeric	5	2	what is your religious preference	{-2.00, Refuse to Answer}	-1.00, -2.00	8	Right	Scale	Input
36	relattnd	Numeric	8	2	How often do you attend church/pla...	{-2.00, Refuse to Answer}	-1.00, -2.00	8	Right	Nominal	Input
37	rellevel	Numeric	8	2	TO what extent do you consider you...	{-2.00, Refuse to Answer}	-1.00, -2.00	8	Right	Scale	Input
38	brs1	Numeric	5	2	I tend to bounce back quickly after ...	{-2.00, Refused to Answer	-1.00, -2.00	8	Right	Scale	Input
39	brs2	Numeric	4	2	I have a hard time making it through...	{-2.00, Refused to Answer	-1.00, -2.00	8	Right	Scale	Input
40	brs3	Numeric	4	2	It does not take me long to recover f...	{-2.00, Refused to Answer	-1.00, -2.00	8	Right	Scale	Input
41	brs4	Numeric	5	2	It is hard for me to snap back when ...	{-2.00, Refused to Answer	-1.00, -2.00	8	Right	Scale	Input
42	brs5	Numeric	4	2	I usually come through difficult time	{-2.00, Refused to Answer	-1.00, -2.00	8	Right	Scale	Input
43	brs6	Numeric	4	2	I tend to take a long time to get over...	{-2.00, Refused to Answer	-1.00, -2.00	8	Right	Scale	Input

is yes, or a 2 if it is no. In the data, we would see only 1s and 2s. In order to make sense of the 1s and 2s, we would assign a value label of yes to the 1s and no to the 2. Once these have been assigned, make sure that all yes/no questions have the same values and value labels—document it thus, and even include a rule for this in a data cleaning manual. Consistency in setting up response category values such as no and yes is one way to make the dataset more user friendly.

Formatting Variables

Formatting variables is an important step in cosmetic cleaning. The *type* of variable should be designated ahead of time. The most basic format is the type of variable—string,

Figure 13.3 Types of Variables

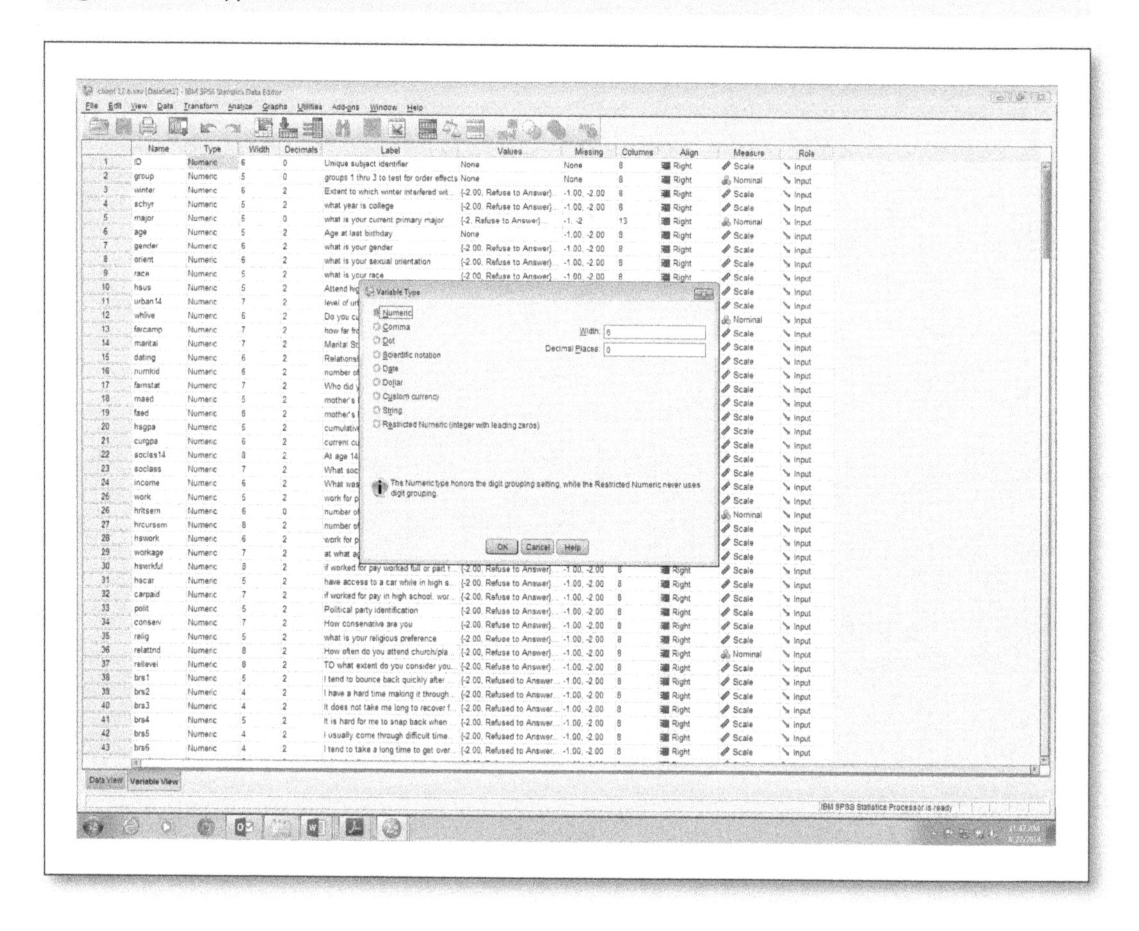

numeric, or date. If it is designated as numeric, then no letters can be included in the values during data entry, only numbers. If it is a string variable, then all values—even numbers—will be treated like text and cannot be analyzed statistically without additional manipulation (being turned into a numeric variable). There are other types of variables, as can be seen in Figure 13.3. Date variables like string variables will need additional manipulation prior to being usable by a statistical program. The other types simply make understanding the numeric data easier. Choosing a particular type restricts the data being entered to that type. By restricting ahead of time, errors may be less likely to happen or may be more easily discovered.

Along with choosing the type of variable, the researcher must choose the width (known as length in some programs), and if necessary, allow for decimal places. In the past, when data storage was expensive, it was important to limit the width of variables to as small as possible. A question with a yes-or-no response really needs a width of only

1 character space. Reducing the width of variables reduces the file size of the overall dataset. If storage space is not a problem, allowing the software program to use the default setting is fine. If space is a problem, reduce the width of variables where possible.

Mini Case 13.2 provides a demonstration of cosmetic cleaning using three questions from a survey. In the data, we find that the corresponding variables are named Q1, Q2, and Q3. None of the variables has a variable label or value label, and all have a width of 8 characters with 2 decimal places. Given that these are not continuous variables, the decimal places do not make much sense. Given that Questions 1 and 2 are related (both are about smoking), our first decision is to better link these two questions through their variables names. We choose to rename Q2 to be Q1a, and note in the variable label that Q1a is Q2 on the questionnaire. The SPSS syntax for making these changes is shown below Mini Case 13.2. Note that comparable syntax for SAS and STATA are included in Table 13.5 at the end of the chapter.

MINI CASE 13.2

Examples of Survey Questions

This example assumes questions are being asked of 14- to 16-year-old high school students.

1. Have you ever smoked a cigarette, even just a puff, in your whole life?
    1. No (go to Question 3)
    2. Yes
2. How many packs of cigarettes have you smoked in the last week?
    3. None
    4. Less than 1 pack
    5. 1–2 packs
    6. 3–4 packs
    7. 5–6 packs
    8. 7 or more packs
    9. Don't know
    10. Not applicable
    11. Refuse to answer

(Continued)

(Continued)

3. Do you plan to go to college?

   12. No
   13. Yes
   14. Undecided
   15. Don't know
   16. Not applicable
   17. Refuse to answer

We start by taking a frequency of each variable. Table 13.1 shows a frequency of each variable. All we see is the question number and values. Thus, we have little information in the table. If we do not cosmetically clean the variables, we will have to go back and forth between output and survey in order to interpret our findings.

The first step is to rename variable Q2 as Q1a:

```
RECODE Q2 (MISSING=SYSMIS) (ELSE=Copy) INTO Q1a.

EXECUTE.
```

This code creates a new variable called Q1a and copies all the values from Q2 to Q1a exactly as they were. Next, we create variable labels for each of the three variables making sure to note that variable Q1a refers to Q2 on the questionnaire:

```
VARIABLE LABELS Q1 "Have you ever smoked a cigarette"

Q1a "(Old Q2) How many packs of cigarettes have you smoked in the last week"

Q3 "Do you plan to go to college?"

EXECUTE.
```

The next step is to assign value labels to the response values found in each question.

```
VALUE LABELS Q1

1 "No"

2 "Yes"
```

Table 13.1 Precleaning Frequencies of Variables

Q1

		Frequency	Percent	Valid Percent	Cumulative Percent
Valid	1	55	24.2	24.2	24.2
	2	172	75.8	75.8	100.0
	Total	227	100.0	100.0	
Total		227	100.0		

Q2

		Frequency	Percent	Valid Percent	Cumulative Percent
Valid	1	4	1.8	1.8	1.8
	2	145	63.9	63.9	65.7
	3	19	8.4	8.4	74.1
	4	3	1.3	1.3	75.4
	5	0	0	0	75.4
	6	1	.4	.4	75.8
	777	55	24.2	24.2	100.0
Total		227	100.0	100.0	100.0

Q3

		Frequency	Percent	Valid Percent	Cumulative Percent
Valid	1	38	16.7	16.7	16.7
	2	132	58.1	58.1	74.8
	3	14	6.2	6.2	81.0
	888	17	7.5	7.5	88.5
	999	26	11.5	11.5	100.0
	Total	227			
Total		227	100.0	100.0	100.0

```
VALUE LABELS Q1a
1 "None"
2 "Less than 1 pack"
3 "1–2 packs"
4 "3–4 packs"
5 "5–6 packs"
6 “More than 7 packs"
777 "Don't know"
VALUE LABELS Q3
1 "No"
2 "Yes"
3 “Undecided”
888 "Don't know"
999 "Refuse to answer"
```

Last, we format the type and width of the variables:

```
FORMATS Q1 Q1a Q3 ( f2.0).
```

This syntax is assigning a numeric format with 2 character spaces for each variable and zero character spaces after the decimal, meaning no decimal places. Table 13.2 shows the postcleaning frequencies. Now, there are descriptive variable labels and value labels that help us to interpret the data without having to go back to the survey.

For the most part, the numbers in the tables match up. However, there is one difference, and that is this: In the postcleaning frequencies, missing values have been assigned to the nonresponses. The next section will discuss missing values.

Missing Values

Being able to distinguish between a refusal, a “don't know,” and a “not applicable” response may provide interesting information both about the respondents and about your questionnaire. For data analysis purposes, each type of missing response may be handled differently. For example, a “don't know” response (coded as 888 in Table 13.1) could end up being a valid and usable response. A “not applicable” (coded as 777) is missing for a valid reason and also may be useable. But a refusal (coded as 999) is not ever usable, and a

Table 13.2 Postcleaning Frequencies of Variables

Ever Smoked a Cigarette

		Frequency	Percent	Valid Percent	Cumulative Percent
Valid	No	55	24.2	24.2	24.2
	Yes	172	25.8	75.8	100.0
	Total	227	100.0	100.0	
Total		227	100.0		

(old Q2) Packs of Cigarettes Smoked in Past Week

		Frequency	Percent	Valid Percent	Cumulative Percent
Valid	None	4	1.8	2.3	1.8
	Less than 1 pack	145	63.9	84.3	65.7
	1–2 packs	19	8.4	11.1	74.1
	3–4 packs	3	1.3	1.7	75.4
	5–6 packs	0	0	0	75.4
	More than 7 packs	1	.4	. 6	75.8
	Total	172	75.8	100.0	
Missing	Not applicable	55	24.2		100.0
Total		227	100.0	100.0	100.0

Plan to Attend College

		Frequency	Percent	Valid Percent	Cumulative Percent
Valid	No	38	16.7	20.7	16.7
	Yes	132	58.1	71.7	74.8
	Undecided	14	6.2	7.6	
	Total	184	81.0	100.0	81.0
Missing	Don't know	17	7.5		88.5
	Refused to answer	26	11.5		100.0
	Total				
Total		227	100.0	100.0	100.0

participant may have refused for any number of reasons. Therefore it is important to keep the various types of missing responses distinguished with a separate code for each. Variables with a single character (e.g. response options 1–5) can use a single-digit code for a missing value. For example, you might use 7 for a Likert scale item with five valid responses. But you might need 77 or even 777 for a variable like age (77 could be a valid age). The researcher must make sure for each question that the missing value assigned is not also a valid response. What codes are assigned to missing values may depend upon the survey software used, and missing value codes will have to be adjusted to fit with the statistical analysis software program used when cleaning the data.

How we handle **missing data** codes also depends on which statistical program is being used. Most statistical programs have a default "system missing" category for string variables, which is a blank space " ", and a dot " . " for numerical variables. SPSS Statistics, in addition, allows the researcher to specify up to three additional codes as missing *per variable,* meaning that different values can be assigned as missing codes for each variable. SAS and STATA allow an additional 26 missing value codes in addition to " . " Theirs include ".a" through ".z". SAS reads the missing codes as low values (less than zero), whereas STATA treats the missing codes as very large numbers—larger than your largest code. This information can be used to your advantage. In SAS, to avoid missing values on a variable, simply use the phrase "greater than or equal to zero" in your syntax. In STATA, the comparable code would specify "less than or equal to" the highest valid response value. If there are multiple users of the data who work with different software packages, handling the missing codes might be tedious.

If multiple people will be using the data with different statistical packages, you may want to create simple-to-use missing data codes that can be adjusted once they are translated into whichever statistical software package will be used. Negative numbers may be an excellent solution, because they are never used as real values in surveys, and they solve the SPSS Statistics problem of needing different values to mean a refusal for variables with large and small numbers of response categories. If you use negative numbers, -1 (-2, -3) can signify refusal ("don't know," "not applicable") for a Likert scale item, a yes/no item and an income item with up to 7 characters. Since the values will be consistent, the syntax to convert into "system missing" is very simple regardless of which software package is used.

Recall the three questions from Mini Case 13.2. For Question 1, those who have never smoked a cigarette will answer no. If they answered no to the first question, there is little point in asking them Question 1a (old Q2). Thus, nonsmokers will automatically be entered in the "not applicable" category for Question 1a. The syntax below assigns missing values in SPSS. Comparable SAS and STATA syntax can be found in Table 13.5 at the end of the chapter.

Question 3 from Mini Case 13.2 asks if the students plan to go to college. There is a valid "undecided" category, and there is a missing code "don't know" available to respondents. How is "don't know" different from "undecided"? Perhaps it is used by students who might like to go to college but are not sure they will have the funds. In other words, they have decided yes, but do not know if it is possible. Perhaps 14-year-olds haven't even thought about college yet, so "undecided" does not quite fit for them. However, we do not know all the reasons older students may be "undecided" either. How much speculation do we want to do? Depending on the research interest, an investigator may decide that "don't know" and "undecided" are essentially the same category and lump the two categories together as valid. Or, the investigator may decide that "don't know" is a valid response and keep it as a valid category that is separate from the "undecided" category. We have no flexibility, however, if we simply lump all missing categories into the same code. Plan to spend some time thinking through what response values may mean to respondents and how to handle them. In general, if separate categories were used in the question, at cleaning it makes sense to keep them separate.

Since there were no missing values in Q1, below we write the syntax to assign missing values and then ask SPSS Statistics to treat them as missing codes. The first piece of syntax simply recodes the original 777, 888, and 999 codes used to capture nonresponse to the more user friendly -1, -2, and -3 codes respectively. The second line of syntax tells SPSS that for the variables Q1a and Q3, values of -1, -2, and -3 should be treated as missing response values. What is nice about this syntax is that it does not matter if each variable has all three types of missing values. It will not hurt the variable to assign a code that doesn't exist in the variable. Thus, in cleaning we can be consistent.

Recode *Q1a Q3* (777 = -1) (888 = -2) (999 = -3).

Missing values *Q1a* Q3 (-1,-2,-3).

SKIP PATTERNS

In the example provided in Mini Case 13.2, there was a **skip pattern**. In a skip pattern, one question acts as a gateway to answering future questions. So, Question 1 acted as a gateway to Question 2 (Q1a) and allowed only those who answered yes to Question 1 to see Question 2. In a web-based survey or interviewer-administered computer assisted survey, the participant will not see the skip. The programmed survey will automatically skip Question 2 if the participant says no to Question 1 (and the survey was programmed correctly). If the survey is in a self-administered pen-and-paper format, participants will see the skip pattern and may or may not follow it. Therefore, a researcher should check to see if skip patterns were handled correctly. This can be checked by running crosstabs on the gateway variable and any skipped variables. For a computer assisted survey or online survey, the skip pattern programming should have been verified to work correctly, and thus the data should reflect a skip program that has been followed correctly.

Table 13.3 Cross-Tabulation of Ever Smoked a Cigarette by Number of Packs Smoked in Last Week

Ever Smoked a Cigarette * Packs of Cigarettes Smoked in Past Week Cross-Tabulation

Count

		Packs of Cigarettes Smoked in Past Week							Total
		None	Less Than One	One to Two	Three to Four	Five to Six	More Than Seven	Not Applicable	
Ever smoked a cigarette	No	0	0	0	0	0	0	55	55
	Yes	4	145	19	3	0	1	0	171
Total		4	145	19	3	0	1	55	227

If skip patterns were not followed correctly, the researcher can manually skip all nonsmokers who did not follow the skip pattern by assigning the "not applicable" code to all the smoking items. First, run a crosstab on Q1 and Q1a. Syntax and output for SPSS Statistics are shown in this example, while SAS and STATA syntax can be found in Table 13.5 at the end of the chapter. The results are displayed in Table 13.3.

```
CROSSTABS
/TABLES=Q1 BY Q1a
/FORMAT=AVALUE TABLES
/CELLS=COUNT
/COUNT ROUND CELL.
```

As can be seen, the skip pattern worked perfectly. All 55 respondents who claimed never to have smoked a cigarette skipped Question 1a and are located in a missing value labeled "not applicable." If we are interested in explaining the smoking patterns of smokers, then we would be done. If, however, we are interested in explaining the smoking patterns of teenagers, then we would have to recode the 55 "not applicable" respondents into "none" respondents. We would use the following SPSS syntax:

```
IF (Q1 = 1) Q1a = 1.
```

MULTIPLE-RESPONSE, OTHER-SPECIFY, AND OPEN-ENDED QUESTIONS

Multiple-response, other-specify, and open-ended questions were discussed in depth in the data discussion in the previous chapter. If the data were entered into a statistical program through a web-based or CAPI program, then these variables need to be addressed in cleaning. Multiple-response variables will need no further work. Simply clean them cosmetically and check for missing values.

Other-specify options will be included in the data as separate variables. The example given in the data entry section was:

Q5 Would you say you are... (race)

(1) White

(2) Black

(3) Asian

(4) Hispanic

(5) Other (please specify ____________________)

All the respondents who chose 5 will have a valid text response to the variable "raceothr." But, what we want is a single variable that includes everyone from Q5 and everyone from raceothr. Therefore, the responses on raceothr will need to be recoded into Q5. First we read through the responses to determine if they belong in an existing Q5 category, if a new category needs to be added to the values and value labels of Q5, or if they should stay in "other." Respondents who write in "human" cannot be recoded into any category, and they can be left in the "other" response category. But responses of "Caucasian" or "multiracial," for example, can be coded. This is not an easy task—despite the easy example. People can use many ways to say the exact same thing. Therefore, you must *read the responses carefully several times* and pay careful attention to the *wording* of the original question.

The syntax below recodes cases of participants who chose Response 5 into an existing category and a new category. Remember that the value labels will have to be updated if new categories are added.

The SPSS syntax to recode is quite simple:

If (*raceothr* = "Caucasian") *Q5* = 1.

If (*raceothr* = "Multiracial") *Q5* = 6.

VALUE LABELS Q5

1. "White"
2. "Black"
3. "Asian"
4. "Hispanic"
5. "Other"
6. "Multiracial"

Finally, run a crosstab of the recoded original variable with the other-specify variable, and make sure there are no mistakes in the recoding syntax. Once you are sure the syntax worked correctly, then the other-specify variable can be deleted from the dataset (not from the raw data, however, just in case).

Open-ended questions will exist in the dataset in text form as well. Follow the instructions in Chapter 12 on how to code an open-ended item. Once it is recoded, the open-ended question can be recoded from the text to the new numeric codes. Again, run a crosstab of the recoded variable with the open-ended variable, and make sure there are no mistakes in the recoding syntax. Once you are confident the new recoded variable is correct, the original open-ended variable can be deleted from the dataset.

Notes: In some cases, respondents provide additional information. They will write comments in the margins of a pen-and-paper questionnaire, or an interviewer will take notes on additional spoken comments. About 20% of the time, the note or comment will provide information that requires us to change the original response. Consider this skip pattern example from the smoking question: A participant responds no and skips all the smoking questions. But in a side note the participant writes, "I haven't smoked in 20 years." This comment lets us know that the participant is a former smoker. We may want to change the response to the gateway question from no to yes. If our original question were worded, "Have you ever quit smoking?" we would change the response to yes. Or if it were worded "Do you currently smoke?" we would leave the answer as no. In the majority of cases, however, the notes or comments simply provide interesting context, and participants' answers do not need to be changed.

A problem with changing information or creating new variables based on the contextual information provided is that it is not standardized. Not everyone provided a comment, and therefore the information provided cannot apply to all respondents. While researchers may want to use the comments like they use open-ended question items, they simply cannot do justice to a new variable created from notes—the results will be biased.

What do we do when our syntax is complete? After all the issues are checked, and our syntax file is created, we run the syntax. We would like to think we are done at this point, but now we need to check and see what additional problems our syntax has created. To check, simply run a frequency on each variable, and compare it to the frequency run on the raw, precleaned data. Frequencies of responses shouldn't change much, unless a variable was recoded. If we ran frequencies on the three variables from Mini Case 13.2, we would find a problem. Since we recoded our missing values from 777, 888, and 999 to -1, -2, and -3 in SPSS, we need to recreate our value labels to reflect that. The value labels do not include these new values. Once we are sure all the variables look exactly how we want them, it is time to turn to examining the variables diagnostically.

CLEANING FOR DIAGNOSTICS

Figure 13.4 provides a list of the issues you may want to examine diagnostically. This is called **diagnostic cleaning**. Here we are assessing the quality of the data, rather than making the data easy to use and understand.

We start with **implausible values**, which are values that simply cannot possibly exist in the data. This is a problem with noncomputerized surveys more than computerized surveys, because programmed surveys often will not allow responses that do not fit within a specified range. For example, consider a self-administered mailed survey in which respondents are asked a question with 5-point Likert scale response categories. In order to show a response that is "off the charts," a respondent puts a 7 into the scale and circles it. The data entry personnel do not notice this and simply type in a 7. When the frequency is run, and a sole 7 shows up without a value label for a question with 5 possible responses, the researcher has an implausible value. This example assumes the participant wanted to place emphasis on the response. But in reality, we cannot make such assumptions. Perhaps no missing values were allowed on this question, but earlier questions may have had a 7 for a "don't know" response. In general, implausible values must be turned into missing values, because we simply cannot know what the participant intended. We also want to handle all issues as consistently as possible.

Figure 13.4 Diagnostic Cleaning

1. Implausible values
2. Variation
3. Finding bad data through scale items
4. Mode of administration or interviewer effects

Variation

In order to statistically analyze our variables, there must be variation within each variable. Variables that produce minimal variation may not be validly measured and may need to be dropped. At a minimum, the lack of variation should be remarked upon in the codebook (see last section of this chapter).

Along with frequencies, the means and standard deviations of all the continuous, ordinal, and dummy variables should be assessed to determine the level of variation. The mean is an average or measure of central tendency. The standard deviation is a measure of the amount of dispersion about the mean. If we wanted to know if there was variation by age in a sample, we could run a mean on the age variable and ask for the standard deviation. These two statistics tell us everything we want to know about how much variation is in a variable. If the data about age collected in the 2003 wave of the Wisconsin Longitudinal Study (1957–2005) were analyzed in this way, they would give a mean of age 65 with a standard deviation of less than 1 year. These statistics show there is little variation by age in this study. In the Atlanta Public Housing Study (Oakley, Ruel, and Wilson 2008; Ruel, Oakley, Wilson, and Maddox 2010), the sample ranges in age from 18 to 96. The mean or average age for the sample is 51 years, and the standard deviation is 17.3 years. There is a great deal of variation in age in this sample. Thus, age could be used in analyses of the Atlanta study but not the Wisconsin study.

Bar charts are useful for visualizing the distribution of ordinal and nominal variables. They help the researcher to determine how to handle these variables later in analyses. Ordinal variables may show little variation across the responses. Rather than using all 5 options in a Likert scale, the majority of users may have only used two categories—the "agree" and "disagree" options, for example. If it's not part of a multi-item scale, it may make sense to transform the variable into a dichotomous variable by collapsing categories. Or, if only one or two respondents chose the "strongly disagree" option, it may be an outlier response. Then it may make sense to turn the variable into a four-category variable by top coding the ordinal variable to a "disagree" maximum allowed response. Figure 13.5 provides a bar chart of a Likert scale item that asks respondents to agree or disagree with the statement, "This neighborhood is a good place to raise kids." While most respondents either agree or disagree, there are quite a few who strongly disagree, suggesting that there is good variation across this variable.

Finding Bad Data Through Scale Items

These are a series of questions that together represent a single unobservable construct. Respondents might complete the survey but will not necessarily answer truthfully. If it's a long survey, they may get bored and just mark the same response for all variables. For example, they may choose option 2 as a response option for every variable after the 20th

Figure 13.5 Bar Chart of an Ordinal Variable

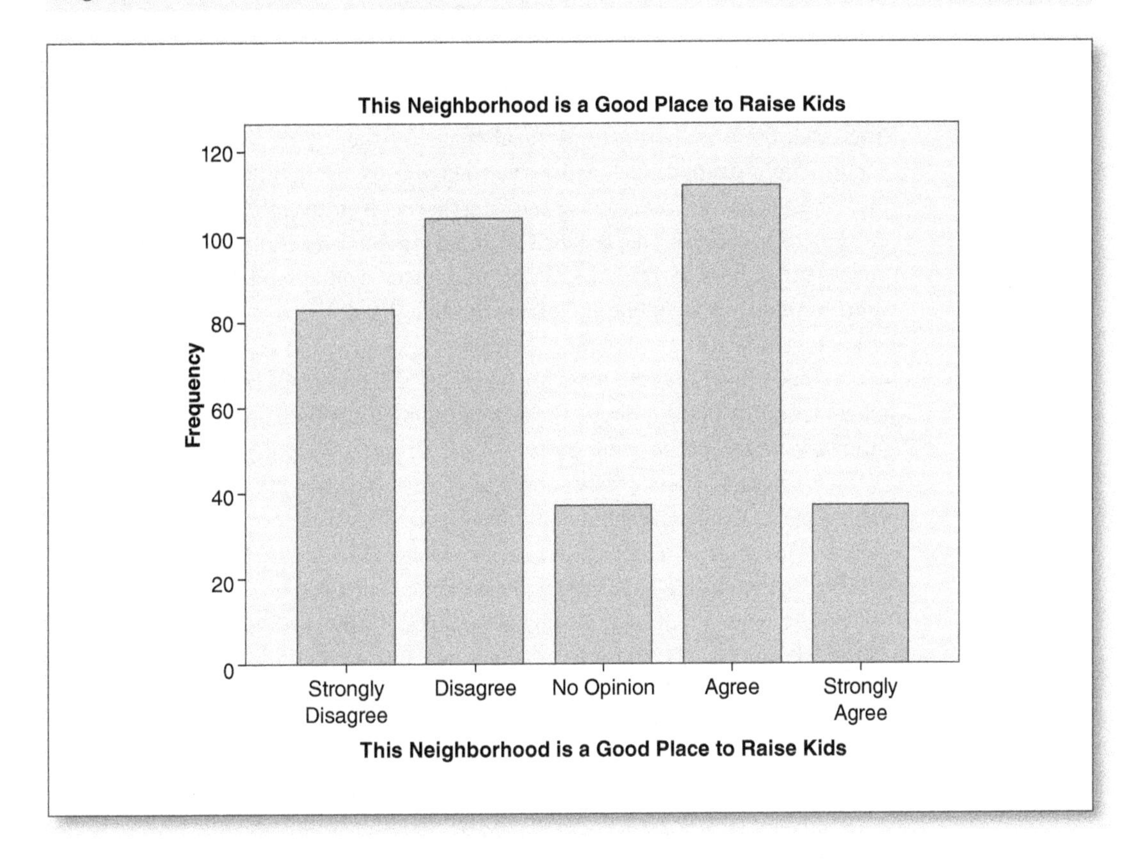

question. Scale items are useful for locating these respondents, particularly if some of the questions in the set of scale items are reverse coded. **Reverse coding** refers to inserting a positively worded item in among negatively worded items, or vice versa. For example, if most of the items in a questionnaire mention positive things about a neighborhood, such as it's a good place to raise kids, reverse-coded items would focus on negative neighborhood aspects. An example of such an item would be, "People in this neighborhood do not share the same values." Thus, if 2 usually means "agree" on the reverse-coded item, a consistent response would be 4, for "disagree." The reverse-coded item will capture inconsistent cases. You will want to create a crosstab of all items in the scale to search for these types of inconsistencies. SPSS will not allow you to do this, so if you are working in SPSS, copy the scale items into Excel, sort by each item, and examine which cases or respondents give the same responses throughout the scale. Once you locate them, you can assess their entire answer set to determine if they gave bad data. If they did, it makes sense to delete them from the dataset.

INTERVIEWER EFFECTS AND MODE EFFECTS

A major benefit of surveys is that they are standardized; all participants receive the same question in the same way. Thus, the only thing that distinguishes participants from each other is their own personal characteristics. If we use a single mode of survey administration, such as interviewing, but we use multiple interviewers, we may find that differences among the interviewers lead to significant differences in answers to questions. This is called an **interviewer effect**. Another way of introducing differences in responses is to administer a multimodal survey—reaching some respondents by phone and others through the Internet, for example. If there is a statistically significant difference in responses to questions administered by different methods, then the responses are no longer standardized. There is now another difference between the groups—the mode of administration is added to the potential interviewer effect of the phone portion of the survey. This is called the **mode effect**.

It is simple to assess whether or not there are interviewer effects. First, in the same way we create a unique identifier for each respondent, we can create an identifier variable for each interviewer. Then, test each variable in the dataset by either running an **analysis of variance (ANOVA)** with continuous variables, or a **chi-square test** of independence with ordinal and nominal variables. If either test is found to be statistically significant (see Chapter 14), then there are interviewer effects on those variables. If there are interviewer effects on all the variables, it may be that there is an outlier interviewer; in this case, controlling for that interviewer (using a dummy variable) in all regression analyses will solve for that problem.

If there are a large number of interviewers, this is not a practical solution. Instead, think about how characteristics of the interviewers might interact with characteristics of the sample. For example, if the sample consists of older adults, younger interviewers might not build as good rapport with the sample as older interviewers do. For this, we can create a dummy variable that is 1 for older interviewers and 0 for younger interviewers. Then we can conduct *t*-tests for continuous variables and chi-square tests for ordinal and nominal variables in the dataset to determine if the age of the interviewer makes a difference in responses. Again, if the results are statistically significant, there are interviewer age effects in the data.

For mode effects, we can create a dummy variable (1 = mode of administration 1) and 0 = mode of administration 2) and run ANOVA or chi-square tests of independence on all of the variables to see if there are statistically significant differences in responses to questions based on the mode of administration. Again, if we find differences on some variables, we need to control for the mode effects by including the mode of administration dummy variable in our analyses.

In our example we run an ANOVA. The ANOVA tests the hypothesis that the mean effect of each group (of interviewers) on the substantively interesting variables is all the

Table 13.4 Analysis of Variance (ANOVA) to Test for Interviewer Effects

ANOVA

		Sum of Squares	*df*	Mean Square	*F*	Sig.
This neighborhood is a good place to raise kids	Between groups	85.203	46	1.852	1.020	.442
	Within groups	591.880	326	1.816		
	Total	677.083	372			
People around here are willing to help neighbors	Between groups	68.351	46	1.486	1.025	.434
	Within groups	479.860	331	1.450		
	Total	548.212	377			
People in this neighborhood generally don't get along with each other	Between groups	51.263	45	1.139	.789	.833
	Within groups	467.969	324	1.444		
	Total	519.232	369			
People in this neighborhood can be trusted	Between groups	51.420	45	1.143	.797	.822
	Within groups	470.454	328	1.434		
	Total	521.874	373			
People in this neighborhood do not share the same values	Between groups	56.446	45	1.254	.984	.506
	Within groups	411.722	323	1.275		
	Total	468.168	368			

same, that is, that there is no interviewer effect on how respondents answered the questions. Results are presented in Table 13.4 The columns in the figure provide the sum of squares, which tells us how much of the variance in each variable is broken out among the grouping variables and within each grouping variable, in this case the interviewers. The column labeled df refers to degrees of freedom; this tells us how many independent pieces of information exist, that is, how many pieces of information the F test is based on. Generally, there are $n - 1$ degrees of freedom, where n = sample size. The F test is the omnibus test of association or whether or not the mean across the interviewers is the same. The column labeled "Sig" provides the level of significance of the test. Usually we set the significance level at .05, meaning that if significance is .05 or higher, then there are no significant differences among the groups, or in this case, there are no interviewer effects. If the significance level is less than .05, then there are significant differences, we reject the hypothesis, and we have interviewer effects.

The SPSS Statistics syntax for an ANOVA that checks for interviewer effects is presented below. Here we are assessing interviewer effects on five variables representing neighborhood social cohesion in the Atlanta Public Housing Study (Oakley, Ruel, and Wilson 2008; Ruel, Oakley, Wilson, and Maddox 2010). Given that the values in the significance column are much larger than .05, we can conclude that there are no interviewer effects on these variables.

```
ONEWAY Q1aW1 Q1bW1 Q1cW1 Q1dW1 Q1eW1 BY IntID
/MISSING ANALYSIS.
```

CLEANING LONGITUDINAL DATA

For panel data that come from a longitudinal study in which the same respondents are interviewed multiple times, the cross-sectional cleaning and the diagnostic cleaning need to be conducted after each wave of data collection. In addition to that, there are a couple of additional cleaning checks that are needed. These are presented in Figure 13.6. The first is **consistency in coding**, and the second is **attrition effects**. Attrition was introduced in Chapter 9; it is a special case of missing data.

Consistency in Coding

We are including several issues in this one category. First, we need to check if there is consistency in response categories over time (Van den Broeck et al. 2005), meaning, in the creation of the survey, did we change the response categories for any questions? If so, we need to document that, because clearly responses will be different over time due to changes in the questions themselves. Another change that is not substantive—it is simply a formatting-the-survey change—takes place when we assign new values to the same old responses. For example, if in Wave 1 we set yes to be 1 and no to be 0, then we

Figure 13.6 Cleaning Longitudinal Data Files

1. Consistency in coding
2. Attrition effects

must make sure to use the same response categories in all later waves of data. If in the next wave, yes is assigned to 2 and no is assigned to 1, then comparing the mean across waves will show a large difference. If we were to check the means of variables in Wave 1, Wave 2, and Wave 3, for example, we want any change we find in the average value to be due to real change experienced by respondents and not because we changed the numeric values of the response categories.

One of the goals of longitudinal analysis is to examine change over time. To do this, items on the survey need to be repeated exactly. If the question wording is changed or a new response category is added in later waves, this means items are not repeated over time. If new response categories are added in later waves, make sure they are not treated as implausible values. Make sure these changes are clear in the data and in the codebook (see the section below on the codebook).

Compare means and standard deviations on the same items from each wave to see if things make sense in general. If either the mean or standard deviations differ greatly, there may be a problem with one of the variables that should be examined closely. Make sure you have noted which variables have added new response categories, as this will create a change in the mean and possibly the standard deviation between one variable in a pair and the other.

Check to see how respondents handle some gateway questions (skip patterns). Over time respondents learn how to work the survey. If answering yes to a gateway question means having to answer a long set of questions, fatigued respondents may respond with a no in Wave 3 or 4, where they responded yes in earlier waves. For example, a respondent said yes to Question 1 (Have you ever smoked a cigarette?) in Wave 1, and then had to answer a series of questions on smoking behaviors. In Wave 2, the respondent may change the answer no to Question 1, and then skip the series of questions on smoking behaviors. Other gateway questions may not be so cut and dried. People rarely forget they used to smoke, but attitudes can change, and people may not remember having had different attitudes in the past.

Attrition

Attrition refers to data loss that takes place when respondents decide to no longer participate in a panel study; they drop out over time. Respondents may be missing for other reasons that could affect the quality of the data as well. They may die between waves of the study or become institutionalized in prisons or nursing homes. These forms of missing data may make participants ineligible for one or more waves of data collection. In addition, people may move or change residences between waves of data collection. The researcher may not be able to find them for one wave of data collection but may be able to bring them back into the study at a later time. In most longitudinal studies, attrition is quite large, and the dataset quickly loses its representativeness for the population from which it was drawn. In other words, findings from research conducted on the data could be biased if attrition is more likely to occur within some subgroups of the population than within others. In fact, Wood, White, and Thompson (2004) have found that in many clinical trials missing data due to attrition on the dependent variable is typically problematic and often mishandled.

In order to assess how representativeness of the sample has changed over time due to attrition, we can compare descriptive statistics (measures of central tendency and dispersion) of demographic characteristics between the Wave 1 dataset and the remaining sample at some future wave. It may be that in the future wave dataset, some age groups, races, or socioeconomic classes will be overrepresented, while others will be underrepresented. We will explore this in depth in Chapter 15 with an example.

THE CODEBOOK

Most computer assisted survey programs will generate a text document, or **codebook**, that matches variable names to the questions on the survey. This is the most important function of the codebook. However, really good codebooks will provide additional information. Long ago, when most secondary datasets were downloaded, they were in a format called ASCII, which is a format that can be easily read into any statistical software package using syntax. ASCII files take up little space on computers; this was an important issue in the not-too-distant past. To ensure that the syntax created to read in the data worked correctly, a researcher would run frequencies on the variables and compare them to frequencies provided in the codebook. Thus, in the past, codebooks often provided material to help researchers make sure the data they were using was correct. Even today, downloaded data can be corrupted without the researcher knowing it, so comparing downloaded data against a codebook is still a good idea.

Other information that was beneficial to secondary users of data was often included in a codebook as well. An example is a list of all the variables skipped by a gateway variable. For each variable skipped, there would be information on what the gateway variable was and how many items were skipped. Current researchers can replicate this resource by providing, for each item on a survey, an eligible list of respondents.

For longitudinal data, a codebook that provides a cross-walk between waves of data is very helpful to all users. In addition, given the advances in web capacities, there are many interactive searchable online codebooks. Searching them is an extensive undertaking and not efficient unless your study is an ongoing, long-term endeavor. Mini Case 13.3 provides an example of a codebook entry from a very well-documented study, the Wisconsin Longitudinal Study (1957–2005). It is time consuming to create codebooks, so reserve some resources for this purpose.

MINI CASE 13.3

Example of a Codebook Entry

The Wisconsin Longitudinal Study (WLS 1957–2005) has about the best data documentation available. Here is an example of a variable from one of the waves of data collection. It includes the variable name, variable label, the source of data—meaning who responded—the year of data collection, and the mode of survey administration. This is a variable created out of responses to three other variables. This information allows the investigators to examine the original variables if they want or need to. Next, a frequency by sex is provided. Last, a note is provided to explain how the variable was generated from the three source variables. Additionally, a lack of consistency in responses over time has been made clear. See the WLS webpage for more examples: http://www.ssc.wisc.edu/wlsresearch/documentation/.

gb001re: Has graduate attended college?

Data source: Graduate respondent. Collected in: 2004. Mode: phone. Source variables: b3a, rb001re, edexpr

		Frequencies		
Value	*Label*	*Male*	*Female*	*Total*
	System missing - NR	1621	1431	3052
−1		1	7	8
1	Yes	1883	1785	3668
2	No	1486	2103	3589

Note: Respondents who said anything but yes in 1993 and refused (b3a = -3) in 2004 were categorized as refused. Respondents who said anything but a definite yes in 1993 and said "don't know" in 2004 (b3a = -1) were categorized as "don't know." As in 1993, if a respondent said yes in 1993 and changed his/her mind by 2004, the 2004 response was categorized as a yes.

Source: Wisconsin Longitudinal Study.

CONCLUSION

Cleaning data is a time intensive and, occasionally, tedious task. In many ways researchers can be considered social forensic scientists because of how they systematically collect and clean the data. Good cleaning will make the analysis of the data a much easier process. But it also provides an excellent introduction to your data, meaning that it helps you to see what the data look like prior to beginning data analysis.

We introduced three types of data cleaning. The first we called cosmetic cleaning, as its purpose is to make examining each variable easy on the user. If we add good variable names, variable labels, and value labels, we do not need the codebook or survey instrument to remind us what the substance of a particular variable may be. Part of cosmetic cleaning involves coding text variables such as other-specify responses and responses to open-ended questions. Working on the codebook at the same time we are doing the cosmetic cleaning will ensure that the data and the codebook are consistent.

The next two sets of cleaning are about assessing the quality of the data through checking diagnostics and attrition on single variables. The more diagnostics we check, the better we can argue that the quality of the data is high. We will extend this work to examining diagnostics on pairs of variables in the next section.

Give yourself plenty of time and resources for this part of the investigative process. Data entry, cleaning, and documentation are integral to the research process, and time and staff are necessary to complete these steps effectively.

SYNTAX FOR ANALYSES DESCRIBED IN THIS CHAPTER

All the SPSS syntax commands used in this chapter are included in Table 13.5. In addition, it includes syntax for use with SAS and STATA.

Table 13.5 Syntax for Chapter 13 Analyses

	SPSS	*SAS*	*STATA*
Accessing data	Get file "c:\my documents\survey\ data.sav".	Libname **da** "c:\my documents\survey"; Data.data; (temporary dataset name) Set **da**.data; run;	Use "c:\my documents\survey\ data"
Frequency procedure	Frequency variables=subject.	Proc freq data=da. data; Tables subject; run;	Tab subject

	SPSS	*SAS*	*STATA*
Renaming variables	RECODE Q2 (MISSING=SYSMIS) (ELSE=Copy) INTO Q1a.	Data da.newdata; Set da.olddata; Q1a=Q2; Run;	Compute Q1a=Q2.
Assigning variable labels	VARIABLE LABELS Q1 'Have you ever smoked a cigarette'.	Data da.newdata; Set da.olddata; Attribute Q1 Label= 'Have you ever smoked a cigarette'; Run;	Label Q1 "Have you ever smoked a cigarette"
Assigning value labels	VALUE LABELS Q1 1 "No" 2 "Yes"	Proc format library =fmt; Value Q1f 1 "No" 2 "Yes"; Data da.newdata; Set da.data; Format Q1 Q1f. Run;	Label define Q1f 1 "No" 2 "Yes" Label values Q1 Q1f
Formatting variables	FORMATS Q1 Q1a Q3 (f2.0).	Data da.newdata; Set da.olddata; Attribute Q1 length=2; format=2.0; Q1a length=2; format=2.0; Q3 length=2; format=2.0; Run;	Format Q1 2.0 Format Q1a 2.0 Format Q3 2.0

(Continued)

Table 13.5 (Continued)

	SPSS	*SAS*	*STATA*
Assigning missing values	Recode *Q1a Q3* (777=-1) (888=-2) (999=-3). Missing values *Q1a* Q3 (-1,-2,-3).	If Q1a=777 then Q1a=.n; If Q3=888 then Q3=.d; If Q3=999 then Q3=.r;	Replace *Q1a*=.n if *Q1*==1 Replace *Q3*=.d if *Q3*==888 Replace *Q3*=.d if *Q3*==999
Crosstabs procedure	CROSSTABS/ TABLES=Q1 BY Q1a /FORMAT=AVALUE TABLES /CELLS=COUNT /COUNT ROUND CELL.	Proc freq data=da. newdata; Tables Q1*Q1a/ list; Run;	Tab Q1 Q1a, all
Recoding variables	If (Q1=1) Q1a=1.	If Q1=1 then Q1a=1;	Replace Q1a=1 if Q1==1
ANOVA	ONEWAY Q1aW1 Q1bW1 Q1cW1 Q1dW1 Q1eW1 BY IntID /MISSING ANALYSIS.	Proc anova data=da. newdata; Class intid; Model Q1aw1 q1bw1 q1cw1 q1dw1 q1ew1 = intid; Run;	Oneway Q1aw1 q1bw1 q1cw1 q1dw1 q1ew1 by intid / statistics homogeneity /missing analysis.

KEY TERMS

CRITICAL THINKING QUESTIONS

Below you will find three questions that ask you to think critically about core concepts addressed in this chapter. Be sure you understand each one; if you don't, this is a good time to review the relevant sections of this chapter.

1. Why is it important to clean the data using syntax?
2. How might our data-cleaning needs change if we are doing a multicountry survey?
3. How do we train a staff of four to five people to clean the data? What do we need to think about to ensure the data are cleaned consistently?

14

Data Analysis for a Policy Report

INTRODUCTION

There are very lengthy textbooks devoted to single aspects of data analysis. We include only two chapters. This chapter examines basic descriptive and associational statistics with accompanying tests. Two chapters in this small survey book will not cover everything on this topic that budding social scientists need to know. While this chapter can serve as a springboard for understanding these matters, we advise readers to obtain a good statistics textbook and not depend solely upon the information in this chapter to analyze their data. One excellent statistical textbook we recommend is *Applied Statistics* by Rebecca Warner (2009). This chapter provides a solid introduction to basic statistical analyses and is sufficient to get any project started.

In addition, we present statistical procedures in a practical manner, teaching how to include analyses in a policy report. Often students are unclear about how to apply the tests and statistics they learn in class to real research activities. By the end of this chapter, students should know how to run several basic statistical procedures, how to turn the data into charts and figures, and how to write up the findings for a policy report.

Again, we encourage the creation and use of an analysis syntax file that can be reused and checked later for possible errors. Some of the syntax covered in Chapter 13 for cleaning the data is also the most commonly used syntax for data manipulation and basic analysis to answer a research question. In this chapter we go beyond simply cleaning the data and begin to examine the data substantively.

POLICY REPORTS

Policy reports are intended to provide information to individuals who need to make a decision. Reports can be advocacy oriented, meaning that they are written to persuade readers to take a particular side, or they can be framed objectively and provide balanced information on alternative sides of whatever issue is being studied. Regardless of the type of report desired, the statistical analyses included in a report tend to be limited to answering descriptive research questions. If your research question is descriptive, then you are asking how much or how often an event occurs, or what the level is of agreement or disagreement with an attitude that Americans express. Essentially, you are summarizing information found in the sample. Figure 14.1 provides examples of typical descriptive research questions.

DESCRIPTIVE STATISTICS

There are two general categories of statistical procedures that are commonly used: point estimates and association analyses, better known as regressions (the subject of Chapter 15). Point estimates tend to be measures of central tendency (i.e., a mean or proportion) calculated on the sample that are used to estimate the population parameters or the central tendency of the population for a given characteristic. We will discuss this in more detail later in the chapter, but first we will provide some background information.

Point estimates tend to use **univariate analysis,** using statistics calculated on one variable at a time. To answer Question 1 in Figure 14.1, we would use univariate statistics, because there is only a single variable included in the question: obesity.

Figure 14.1 Examples of Descriptive Research Questions

	Questions
1	How many adults are obese in America?
2	Has the risk of HIV contraction in the United States changed since the introduction of the HIV drug cocktail?
3	Are attitudes toward gay marriage becoming more liberal over time?
4	How much wealth is accumulated by men and women over the life course?
5	What are retention and graduation rates for standard public high schools versus charter, magnet, and religious high schools?

Question 2 involves examining two variables: risk of HIV contraction and time. Time is measured as a dummy variable (2 categories) with 0 = time prior to introduction of the HIV cocktail and 1 = time after introduction of the HIV cocktail. Essentially, this type of analysis is examining a variable univariately, but at two different time points. The third question examines change in attitudes over time. While there are two variables included in the analysis, attitudes toward gay marriage and time, we actually estimate the attitude variable only at several specific points in time. Thus, the attitude variable is measured univariately at many points in time.

If the point estimate research uses two variables, we describe it as a **bivariate analysis.** The above two examples demonstrate a simplified version of a bivariate analysis, as time is not interesting in and of itself. Another type of bivariate analysis examines a variable univariately across a categorical or grouping variable. For example, Question 4 in Figure 14.1 examines wealth grouped by subpopulations differentiated by gender. Question 4 appears to be very complicated, but it too consists of bivariate analyses: The first examines retention rates across types of high schools, and the second analysis examines graduation across types of high schools.

There is a dependent variable that is the focus of each question found in Figure 14.1, and there is an independent variable in some of the questions. A **dependent variable** is one whose variation *depends* upon the variation in another variable. An **independent variable** *causes* the variation in another variable. In Question 5, the type-of-school variable is thought to cause the variation in retention rates; thus it is an independent variable. The retention rate variable is a dependent variable, because its variation depends upon the type of school.

While we are interested in causation, it is very difficult to demonstrate causation. Thus for the rest of this chapter we will talk about associations between variables, though we will suggest that the variable in one variable probably happens first. **Association** is simply a relationship between two variables such that they vary together. If they vary together positively, then we say there is a positive association between them. If one variable gets higher and higher values as the other variable gets lower and lower values, we say they have an inverse or negative association.

Now we will return to the idea of point estimates. What is meant by point estimates? Essentially, the analyses are attempting to summarize information from the sample using measures of central tendency (i.e. mean, median, and mode) and dispersion (i.e. standard deviation, variance, interquartile range). The **mean** is defined as the arithmetic center of a variable's distribution. The formula to find the mean is shown in Equation 1; it simply states that if we sum each respondent's value on a variable and divide by the total sample size, we will get the mean or average value.

$$\text{Formula for the mean: } \bar{Y} = \frac{\Sigma_{i=1}^{n} y_i}{n} \qquad (1)$$

The **median** is defined as the value at the 50th percentile of a variable's distribution—the absolute center of the distribution. The **mode** is defined as the most frequently occurring value for a variable. In determining the appropriate measure of central tendency, it is important to know the level of measurement for the variable(s) for which you intend to provide descriptive statistics. If the variable is measured at the nominal level, then the mode is the only measure of central tendency that can be used. At the ordinal level of measurement, either the mode or the median may be used. At the interval/ratio level of measurement, any measure may be used, but it's usually best to use the mean, since it incorporates the most information from the data. The exception to this is when the distribution of the variable is notably skewed—does not fit the normal bell curve shape; in that instance, the median would be a better measure, since it is not impacted by outliers to the extent that the mean can be impacted.

Dispersion tells us about the level of variation in responses that exist for a given variable. For continuous variables, such as age or income, we use the variance or standard deviation to describe dispersion. Equation 2 provides the formula for standard deviation. The mean is subtracted from each respondent's value on the variable and divided by the total sample size n less 1. That gives us the **variance.** Take the square root of that, and we get the **standard deviation.** For nominal or qualitative variables, we use the interquartile range to describe dispersion.

$$\text{Formula for standard deviation: } s_y = \sqrt{\frac{\Sigma(Y - \bar{Y})^2}{n-1}} \qquad (2)$$

The appropriate measure of variation (dispersion) should also be selected based on the level of measurement of the variable(s) for which you are preparing descriptive statistics. The variance and standard deviation are appropriate for interval/ratio level variables. The IQR (interquartile range = 75th percentile – 25th percentile) is appropriate for either ordinal or interval/ratio variables. When dealing with nominal variables, the above mentioned measures of variation are not appropriate. The IQV (index of qualitative variation) provides dispersion information for nominal variables.

We are most interested to know, however, if our sample findings accurately represent the population from which we sampled. Therefore, we want our sample point estimates to reflect the central tendency in the population. The distribution of a continuous variable has what is called a **normal distribution**, a bell shaped curve with the mean at the very center. We can use the normal distribution to determine how far away from the mean a given sample's estimate is. Sampling theory (see Chapter 7) tells us that, because 95% of an infinite number of samples drawn from our population (the sampling distribution) will be within two standard deviations of the population mean, our one sample is most likely within two standard deviations of the population mean. All samples will have some level of random sampling error (see Chapter 9). Thus, the sample mean or median will not exactly reflect the population mean or median. The central limit theorem also reminds us we must have a large sample size—at least 200 cases—for the distribution to approach normal. The larger the sample is, the better the distribution of any given variable will be, and the smaller the variance around the population mean.

Since our sample mean will not exactly match the population mean, we like to estimate a range of potential values around the sample mean that should include the population mean. This is called a **confidence interval**. If we are interested in how much wealth ordinary people are able to accumulate over the life course, we would calculate the mean of wealth, as it is a continuous variable. Using 2004 data from the Wisconsin Longitudinal Study (1957–2005), we find that mean wealth for white families nearing retirement age is $768,290 on a sample size of 6,082. While the mean provides information about the central value, it tells us nothing about the dispersion of wealth. We need to calculate the standard deviation. The standard deviation about mean wealth is $1,620,902.

Our estimate of the average wealth levels in the sample should be within two standard deviations of the population average wealth level. We can calculate the average in the sample, and then create a confidence interval around that sample point estimate that is two standard deviations wide and that encompasses the population average. The confidence interval is $727,546 – $809,035. We have 95% confidence that the mean wealth of the population falls between $727,546 and $809,035. This calculation is shown in Equation 3.

$$\text{Formula for a confidence interval: } \bar{Y} \pm 1.96 * \frac{s_y}{\sqrt{n}} \tag{3}$$

ANALYSIS FOR A POLICY REPORT

The data we use for the sample policy report in this chapter come from a study of public housing relocations that occurred in Atlanta (Oakley, Ruel, and Wilson 2008; Ruel, Oakley, Wilson, and Maddox 2010). The study was initiated in a meeting with the jurisdiction-wide board of resident presidents. These resident presidents were against the relocations and asserted that most residents were against the relocations. The study includes three waves of data collection, but only the first wave of data will be used for this policy report example. The first wave took place approximately one year before relocation took place, while respondents still lived in public housing. The sample size included 311 public housing residents from six public housing projects, two of which were high rise buildings for seniors and individuals with disabilities, and four of which were for families. One section of the Wave 1 face-to-face survey included questions on whether or not respondents wanted to relocate, and it asked their opinions on the relocation process, the opportunities they were given to provide input on the relocations, and why they thought the relocations were happening. Understanding public housing residents' opinions about the relocation process makes an excellent policy report topic, because these residents are the ones most affected by this policy, and their voices are seldom heard.

Table 14.1 A Policy Report Example: Sample Demographics by Housing Type

	Family Housing	*Senior Housing*
Number of projects	4	2
Number of respondents	187 (60%)	124 (40%)
Female	180 (96%)	63 (51%)
Black	181 (97%)	111 (90%)
Married	9 (5%)	6 (5%)
Have high school degree	101 (54%)	66 (53%)
Age (mean)	40.3 years	62 years
Tenure in public housing (mean)	6.0 years	7.5 years

Interpretation of Table 14.1

The leaseholders of family housing are primarily female (96%), while there are almost as many male as female leaseholders in senior housing communities. Across both types of housing communities, the residents are primarily African American. Very few residents of either housing type are married (5%). Average age of residents living in family housing is 40.3 years, while average age of residents living in senior housing is almost 62. On average, residents of senior housing have lived in their public housing community for approximately 7 years, which is about 1 year longer than residents of family housing.

In writing a policy report, it is good to begin the "story" as if it were a play and to introduce the players. In this case, we will introduce the sample members by the type of public housing project from which they come. See Table 14.1 for a sample table and write-up.

How did we create this table? This step involves a great deal of exploratory descriptive data analysis. The majority of the variables are nominal, and the counts and percentages come directly from a frequency table or cross-tabulation table. Age and tenure in public housing come from a means procedure, because these are continuous variables. Example frequency and means procedure syntax for SPSS, SAS, and STATA can be found in Table 14.17 at the end of this chapter..

To determine who lived in family versus senior housing, we run a frequency in SPSS:

```
FREQUENCIES VARIABLES = houstype /ORDER = ANALYSIS.
```

Sample output used to create the descriptive statistics table is provided in Table 14.2. As you can see by comparing the output in Table 14.2 to the policy report descriptive

Table 14.2 Univariate and Bivariate SPSS Output

Indicator for Living in Family Housing Versus Senior Housing

		Frequency	Percent	Valid Percent	Cumulative Percent
Valid	Senior housing	124	39.9	39.9	39.9
	Family housing	187	60.1	60.1	100.0
	Total	311	100.0	100.0	

Male * Indicator for Living in Family Housing Versus Senior Housing Cross Tabulation

Count

		Indicator for Living in Family Housing Versus Senior Housing		
		Senior Housing	Family Housing	Total
Male	.00	63	180	243
	1.00	61	7	68
Total		124	187	311

Report

Indicator for Living in Family Housing Versus Senior Housing		Age of Respondent	Tenure in Public Housing in Years
Senior housing	Mean	62.0484	7.4778
	N	124	124
	Std. Deviation	13.21545	6.39578
Family housing	Mean	40.2834	5.9750
	N	187	187
	Std. Deviation	15.01862	7.13782
Total	Mean	48.9614	6.5742
	N	311	311
	Std. Deviation	17.84842	6.88060

statistics in Table 14.1, the count and percentage of respondents living in family housing versus senior high rise housing comes directly from the frequency of the variable houstype. This is a univariate descriptive analysis. The crosstab of male (value of 1) by housing type is simply a count of females and males within senior and family housing projects. We can calculate the percentages by dividing the counts by the total for each housing type. The percentage of females in senior housing is 63/124 = 51%. The mean age and tenure in public housing comes from a bivariate means procedure that provides the means separately by housing type. The means can be drawn directly from the output and entered into the descriptive policy table. Here is the SPSS syntax for these operations:

```
CROSSTABS
/TABLES=gender BY houstype
/FORMAT=AVALUE TABLES
/CELLS=COUNT
/COUNT ROUND CELL.
```

We are now ready to start examining the substantively interesting variables. We start by creating a text document that lists all the variables we plan to use (see Table 14.3). In the table we include the variable name, variable label, and value labels, and we indicate whether the variable is nominal, ordinal, or continuous. It is important to note how each variable is measured and how the variable will be modified, because the statistical techniques and tests used depend upon the measurement of the variables used. The first two variables are nominal dichotomous variables, the third is an ordinal variable, and the last four items are ordinal items that will be combined into an interval-level scale variable.

A **scale variable** is created to represent a complicated concept that cannot be measured well with a single variable. Rather, we ask several questions to capture all the concept's dimensions and then sum them together into the scale.

Creating the scale takes some manipulation, so we will start with that. The items are ordinal, and thus, before we create the scale, it is helpful to examine the items to determine whether the response categories of all four have been coded in the same way (direction). That is, does a high value on each question have the same meaning—in this case, a positive attitude toward the relocations? For the first two questions, the high value is positive, but for the last two questions, the high value is negative. We can check this by running a bivariate **correlation.** All items in the same direction will have positive correlations, but items in opposite direction will have negative correlations. If there are negative correlations, we have to determine the best order, or direction of coding the variables, that fits our story and then reverse code any items not

Table 14.3 Variables to Use in Policy Report

Variable Name	*Variable Label*	*Response Categories*	*Measurement Type*
Q132W1	Are the buildings in your public housing community physically run down beyond repair?	1 = yes 2 = no	nominal
Q134W1	Which would you prefer, to fix up your public housing community or to relocate?	1 = fix up 2 = relocate	nominal
Q137W1	How confident are you that, after the relocations, residents will have a place to live that is as good as or better than their current home?	1 = very confident 2 = somewhat confident 3 = somewhat unconfident 4 = not at all confident	ordinal
Q139AW1-Q139DW1	(1) Since hearing of relocations, my future feels uncertain (2) Been having trouble sleeping since hearing of relocations (3) I am excited to relocate (4) I feel AHA has done a very good job of planning the relocations	1 = strongly agree 2 = agree 3 = neutral 4 = disagree 5 = strongly disagree	ordinal—create an interval-level scale by summing four items

headed in that direction. In other words, if we are interested in positive attitudes toward the relocation process, we want the higher values to mean positive attitudes. Therefore, we would have to reverse code the two questions for which the higher values signify negative attitudes.

Here is the syntax to run the correlation in SPSS (note that comparable SAS and STATA syntax can be found in Table 14.17):

```
CORRELATIONS

/VARIABLES=Q139aW1 Q139bW1 Q139cW1 Q139dW1

/PRINT=TWOTAIL NOSIG

/MISSING=PAIRWISE.
```

Table 14.4 presents the bivariate correlation table for all four variables. Since there are negative correlations, we will have to reverse code two items. For this report, we want higher values to be positive; therefore, the bottom two items found in Table 14.4 will be reverse coded as currently, higher values reflect more-negative attitudes.

Next, we run the syntax to reverse code the two variables. The syntax is fairly straightforward. It is always good practice to run a frequency on the items being recoded before and after the recode to make sure there are no mistakes in the recoding syntax. Table 14.5 presents frequencies of one of the reverse-coded variables before and after running the syntax to demonstrate what reverse coding looks like. The syntax here is for SPSS:

```
RECODE Q139dW1 (SYSMIS=SYSMIS) (1=5) (2=4)
(3=3) (4=2) (5=1) INTO q139dw1_r.
Frequencies q139dw1 q139dw1_r.
```

In the frequencies shown in Table 14.5, the categories of the original variable have been reversed. The original variable category 1 has a frequency of 24 respondents; the recoded variable category 5 has a frequency of 24 respondents. The recode was successful.

Another check to see if reverse coding worked correctly would be to rerun the correlation procedure to make sure all correlations are now positive. Be sure to use the recoded variables rather than the original variables. Table 14.6 presents the new correlation output.

The output shown in Table 14.6 demonstrates that the correlation estimates are now all positive, and the values are essentially the same given rounding error; thus there are no errors in the reverse-coding syntax.

Given that the scale is intended to represent a single concept, we like to ensure that all four variables reliably represent the same concept. We use Cronbach's alpha

Table 14.4 Correlation Table

Correlations	*Q139AW1*	*Q139BW1*	*Q139CW1*	*Q139DW1*
Q139AW1	1.0			
Q139BW1	0.46*	1.0		
Q139CW1	-0.36*	-0.25*	1.0	
Q139DW1	-0.29*	-0.15*	0.42*	1.0

* $p < .01$

Table 14.5 Frequencies of Q139dW1 and Q139dW1_r

I Feel Very Excited About Moving to Subsidized Housing

		Frequency	Percent	Valid Percent	Cumulative Percent
Valid	Strongly agree	24	7.7	7.7	7.7
	Agree	62	19.9	19.9	27.7
	No opinion	52	16.7	16.7	44.4
	Disagree	95	30.5	30.5	74.9
	Strongly disagree	78	25.1	25.1	100.0
	Total	311	100.0	100.0	

I Feel Very Excited About Moving to Subsidized Housing. Reverse Coded

		Frequency	Percent	Valid Percent	Cumulative Percent
Valid	1.00	78	25.1	25.1	25.1
	2.00	95	30.5	30.5	55.6
	3.00	52	16.7	16.7	72.3
	4.00	62	19.9	19.9	92.3
	5.00	24	7.7	7.7	100.0
	Total	311	100.0	100.0	

Table 14.6 Correlation Procedure Including Reverse-Coded Items

Correlations	*Q139AW1*	*Q139bw1*	*Q139cw1_r*	*Q139dw1_r*
Q139AW1	1.0			
Q139BW1	0.46*	1.0		
Q139CW1	0.36*	0.25*	1.0	
Q139DW1	0.29*	0.15*	0.43*	1.0

*$p < .01$

Table 14.7 Cronbach's Alpha: Measure of Reliability

Reliability Statistics	
Cronbach's Alpha	Number of Items
.690	4

because it is a commonly used indicator of measurement reliability. It ranges from 0 to 1, with 1 indicating strong reliability. We hope for a reliability of .70 or higher. The SPSS syntax to run a Cronbach's alpha is presented followed by Table 14.7, which presents the Cronbach's alpha output.

```
RELIABILITY
/VARIABLES=Q139aW1 Q139bW1 Q139cW1_r Q139dW1_r
/SCALE ('ALL VARIABLES') ALL
/MODEL=ALPHA.
```

As can be seen in Table 14.7, in the case of attitude toward relocation out of public housing into subsidized housing, we have a reliability coefficient of .69 using our four items. While this is a little bit low, it is very close to .70, and thus we decide it is appropriate to make the scale. As reliability gets smaller, there is greater noise or measurement error in the scale, and this reduces our likelihood of finding a significant effect if there is an effect to be found in bivariate or multivariate analyses (Type I error).

Finally, we are ready to create the scale. We simply sum the four items into a single, new variable. The SPSS syntax is below, followed by descriptive statistics of the new scale variable in Table 14.8.

```
Compute scale= (q139aw1+q139bw1+q139cw1_r+q139dw1_r).
EXAMINE VARIABLES scale
/STATISTICS DESCRIPTIVES EXTREME
/CINTERVAL 95
/MISSING LISTWISE
/NOTOTAL.
```

Table 14.8 presents descriptive statistics of the new scale variable so that we can assess it diagnostically to determine if it is normally distributed (shaped like a

Table 14.8 Descriptive Statistics of New Scale Variable

Descriptives

			Statistic	Standard Error
Scale	Mean		10.8007	.20750
	95% confidence interval for mean	lower bound	10.3923	
		upper bound	11.2090	
	5% trimmed mean		10.7231	
	Median		11.0000	
	Variance		12.960	
	Standard deviation		3.60002	
	Minimum		4.00	
	Maximum		20.00	
	Range		16.00	
	Interquartile range		5.00	
	Skewness		.293	.140
	Kurtosis		-.404	.280

bell curve). We can see that the scale variable ranges from 4 to 20, with a mean of 10.8 and median of 11. The kurtosis and skew are pretty low, thus we can be confident that the scale is approaching a normal distribution.

Now that our scale is complete, we can return to data analysis. Recall that Table 14.3 lists several nominal and ordinal items and the continuous scale items to be used in the analysis. It may be that not all variables will make it into the report, but we will not know that until we examine the variables univariately and bivariately. We choose to examine two important independent variables from Table 14.1 to use for bivariate analyses with our substantively interesting dependent variables. They are housing type (nominal, if lived in senior or family housing) and housing tenure (ratio, number of years lived in public housing). These two variables will provide a good range of examples and opportunities to use common statistical techniques used in descriptive analysis. In sum, we will first analyze each of the variables in Table 14.3 univariately, and then we will examine the bivariate associations among them by housing type and tenure.

Before we can analyze the data, we need to know which statistical techniques to use. The statistical techniques always depend upon the measurement of the variables. In the case of univariate statistics, we are concerned with only the one variable. We begin the univariate analyses simply by running frequencies of each of the nominal and ordinal variables, and a means procedure on the continuous scale variable. This syntax is not new; we have used it earlier in this book.

Table 14.9 provides a table of descriptive statistics based on the univariate procedures. The first column provides the question from the survey with response categories. The next column presents the frequency or count of respondents in each category, followed by the percentage of the total in that response category. The last two columns are

Table 14.9 Descriptive Table of Public Housing Relocation

	N	Percentage	Cumulative *N*	Cumulative Percentage
Are the buildings in your public housing community run down beyond compare?				
Yes	72	23	72	23
No	239	77	311	100
Would you prefer to fix up your public housing community or relocate?				
Fix it up	149	48	149	48
Relocate	164	52	313	100
How confident are you that after the relocation residents will have a place to live that is as good or better than public housing?				
Very confident	130	44	130	44
Somewhat confident	84	28	214	72
Somewhat unconfident	45	15	259	87
Very doubtful	37	13	296	100
	Mean	**Standard Deviation**	**Minimum**	**Maximum**
Relocation attitude scale	11.2	3.6	4	20

cumulative frequencies and percentages. For a report, it makes better sense to use the percentages with nominal and ordinal variables (usually in graphical form) for the interpretation. Thus, we would interpret the first two variables as indicating that 23% of public housing residents agreed that the buildings in their community were run down beyond repair. Despite this, 52% of public housing residents preferred to relocate rather than fix up public housing. As for relocation attitude scale, it is presented at the bottom of the table. The mean value is 11.2 on a scale that ranges from 4 to 20 with a standard deviation of 3.6. A mean close to 20 would suggest very positive attitudes, and a mean close to 4 would suggest very negative attitudes. This is just the start of the analyses, however, and we will want to compare values on these variables by housing type and housing tenure prior to finalizing our interpretations.

We now have a basic univariate understanding of our variables, and while they are interesting, neither are the findings very exciting nor do we have a story to tell yet. Let's examine some bivariate associations next.

Recall that the univariate technique chosen depended on the measurement of the variable. With bivariate analysis, we must pay attention to the measurement of both variables. In this section we will examine associations with our set of four relocation variables from the previous section with tenure in public housing and with housing type. There are four main types of bivariate analyses that provide tests of association:

(1) A cross tabulation with a chi-square test provides the best description of association in a bivariate analysis between two nominal or ordinal variables.

(2) An analysis of variance procedure (ANOVA) is the best statistical technique to use with a continuous dependent variable associated with a nominal or ordinal independent variable.

(3) A bivariate correlation is the best association technique to use with two continuous variables.

(4) A simple logistic regression is the best technique to use with a nominal (two categories) dependent variable and a continuous independent variable.

We use these tests because we are interested in whether any patterns we find within the sample hold among the population of public housing residents. Therefore, we are making the leap into **inferential statistics.** As we showed with the ANOVA in Chapter 13, each of these tests is testing whether there are associations found between the variables that exist over and above that found purely by chance.

ANOVA partitions the variance of the dependent variable between the groups of a grouping independent variable, and it tests the hypothesis that the mean levels on any given variable are the same for each group. The test statistic is an *F* test, which is a global omnibus test of overall association. If even one group mean is different from the others, then the *F* test statistic will be large and be associated with a significance level, often called a *p* value, of less than .05. If there are no differences in the means between the groups, then the *F* test statistic will be small, and the associated *p* value will be greater than .05.

The chi-square test assesses specifically whether the two nominal variables are independent using a chi-square distribution. The hypothesis it tests is whether variable *X* and variable *Y* are independent of one another. If the association is larger than could be expected purely due to chance, then the chi-square test statistic will be large, and the associated *p* value or probability of finding such an association by random chance will be less than .05. If, however the hypothesis holds and the variables are independent, then the chi-square statistic will be small, and the associated *p* value will be .05 or greater.

The Pearson correlation coefficient provides a statistic that tests the degree of association between two continuous variables. The hypothesis being tested is that there is no association between the two variables, or that the correlation equals zero. Significance is determined by an *F* test, and again degrees of freedom are needed to calculate the test. Again, we use a significance level of .05, so that *p* values less than .05 mean there is an association, and *p* values of .05 or greater means there is no association.

The **logistic regression** procedure is a more advanced technique that can be used to examine whether the relationship between a dichotomous dependent variable and one or more other variables is due to chance or is significantly different from that found merely by chance. It provides both a global test of the whole model and paired tests of association. We will describe this model in more detail in Chapter 15. For now, note that the same *p* values of <.05 or ≥.05 can be used to determine if there is or is not a significant association between two variables.

We will run each of these procedures in the course of analyzing the data. The two independent variables include both nominal and continuous measurement, and the four dependent variables include nominal, ordinal, and continuous measurements. We will start by examining the associations among housing type (nominal independent variable), whether respondents think public housing is run down beyond repair (nominal dependent variable), and whether respondents want to fix up public housing or relocate (nominal dependent variable). The SPSS Statistics syntax is below (see Table 14.17 for SAS and STATA syntax), and note that there is a difference compared to earlier crosstab procedures in that we have added the statistical Pearson chi-square test (CHISQ). This test assumes a large sample is found in each cell of the two by two table (*n* = a minimum of 5). A Fisher's exact test, which is more appropriate for tests with small cell sizes, will also be displayed in the output.

CROSSTABS

/TABLES=**Q132W1 Q134w1** BY **houstype**

```
/FORMAT=AVALUE TABLES
/STATISTICS=CHISQ CMH(1)
/CELLS=COUNT ROW COLUMN TOTAL
/COUNT ROUND CELL.
```

Table 14.10 presents the bivariate output of the chi-square test. In each cell is the count and corresponding percentage of respondents that fit in that particular category. It appears as if only 12% of residents of senior housing say their housing is run down beyond repair, while 31% of residents of family housing feel their housing is run down. Is this pattern statistically significant beyond what we would find purely by chance? The Pearson chi-square test has a p value of < .000. Since this is less than .05, the answer is yes, there is an association between housing type and whether or not the housing stock is run down.

The next crosstab assesses the association between type of housing (senior vs. family) and residents' preference for repairing their housing versus moving to new housing. Sixty-five percent of senior housing residents would prefer to fix up their housing and remain in it, while only 35% of family housing residents have this preference. This association too, is statistically significant, as the p value of <.000 is less than the .05 cut off.

Table 14.10 Chi-Square Test of Association Between Housing Type and Desire to Relocate

Opinion of Building Condition, By Housing Type			
	Senior Housing	*Family Housing*	*Total*
Yes, run down	16 (12.2%)	56 (31.1%)	72
No, not run down	115 (87.8%)	124 (68.9%)	239
Total	131 (100%)	180 (100%)	311
Pearson chi-square test: 15.2. 1 DF, P < .000			
Preference for relocation vs. repair, by housing type			
	Senior Housing	*Family Housing*	*Total*
Fix up	85 (65%)	64 (35%)	149
Relocate	47 (35%)	117 (65%)	164
Total	132 (100%)	181 (100%)	313
Pearson chi-square test: 25.8, 1 DF, P < .000			

For both associations, we find that these patterns of family residents being less satisfied with public housing and wanting to relocate are statistically significant, and therefore, the patterns are systematic and not likely to have occurred by chance. Thus, we can infer that this pattern holds for the population of public housing residents.

The third dependent variable, "confident of finding a good place to live after relocation," is an ordinal variable with four categories. We can examine associations between ordinal variables and nominal variables with the cross-tabulation procedure as well. The appropriate statistical test, however, is different if we wish to take advantage of the additional information an ordinal ranking provides. There are several tests that take advantage of the ordinal nature of variables, but they assume both variables are ordinal. These tests are the gamma, Somers' *d*, and Kendall tau-c and tau-d tests. Alternatively, there are nonparametric tests that can be used with ordinal variables or nonnormally distributed continuous variables, such as the Wilcoxon-Mann-Whitney test or the Whitney test. Please consult a statistics text book for the appropriate test for your needs.

Here we will treat the ordinal dependent variable like a nominal variable and run a chi-square test, because our independent variable is not ordinal. This means we lose some information. The syntax is the same as above. Table 14.11 presents the chi-square test results for this ordinal variable. We find that residents of family housing are significantly very confident (49%) of finding a good place to live after relocation, whereas 37% of residents of senior housing are very confident. The finding, again, is statistically significant ($p < .000$).

Next, we are examining the association between a continuous dependent variable—the relocation attitude scale—and the nominal housing type variable. For this

Table 14.11 Chi-Square Test of Association With Ordinal Dependent Variable

Confident of having a good place to live after relocations, by housing type			
	Senior Housing	*Family Housing*	*Total*
Very confident	43 (37%)	87 (49%)	72
Somewhat confident	34 (29%)	50 (28%)	239
Somewhat unconfident	21 (18%)	24 (14%)	72
Not at all confident	19 (16%)	18 (10%)	239
Total	117 (100%)	179 (100%)	296
Pearson chi-square test: 15.2. 1 DF, P < .000			

Table 14.12 ANOVA Test of Association

ANOVA	*Senior Housing*	*Family Housing*
Relocation attitude scale	11.46(3.6)	10.36 (3.54)
***F* test**	**6.773, p < .010**	

combination of variables, we use the ANOVA procedure to test the association. The SPSS Statistics syntax is below, and the SAS and STATA syntax can be found in Table 14.17. Table 14.12 presents the output of the ANOVA procedure.

```
MEANS TABLES scale BY houstype
/CELLS MEAN COUNT STDDEV
/STATISTICS ANOVA.
```

According to Table 14.12, residents of senior housing appear to hold slightly more positive attitudes toward the relocation process than do residents of family housing, and based on the *F* test and *p* value of < .01, this is a statistically significant difference.

We have examined all associations with the nominal independent variable. Now we move on to examining the associations among the same four dependent variables with the continuous independent variable. Recall that the best test of association for a nominal dependent variable and a continuous independent variable is the logistic regression analysis. Table 14.13 provides SPSS Statistics output of logistic regressions of the two dependent variables, "thinking public housing is run down beyond repair" and

Table 14.13 Logistic Regression Tests of Association

Buildings Run Down, By Tenure	*B (s. e.)*	*Odds Ratio*	*P Value*
Constant	–.946 (.19)		.000
Tenure in public housing	–.044 (.024)	.957	.073
Preference for repair vs. relocation, by tenure	B (s. e.)	Odds Ratio	P Value
Constant	.498 (.162)		.002
Tenure in public housing	–.066 (.019)	.936	.001

"preferring to fix up or relocate," by tenure in public housing (in years). First we will provide the SPSS syntax for running the logistic regressions.

```
LOGISTIC REGRESSION VARIABLES q132w1 Q134W1
/METHOD=ENTER q10year
/CRITERIA=PIN(.05) POUT(.10) ITERATE(20) CUT(.5).
```

Table 14.13 is very difficult to interpret. The first column ("B (s.e.)") provides measures of association between the independent variables and the dependent variable in raw logistic format. In parentheses is the standard error or measure of dispersion about each measure of association. It is very difficult to interpret these measures of association. The odds ratio is a manipulation of the measure of association that is more intuitive and easier to interpret. The *p* value should be a familiar statistic, and we can use it to interpret whether the associations found between housing tenure and the two dependent variables are statistically significant.

In Table 14.13, the first dependent variable, public housing buildings are run down beyond repair (yes/no), is not significantly associated with tenure in public housing ($p = .073$). The second dependent variable, preference for repair versus relocation, is significantly associated with tenure in public housing ($p = .001$). Unlike the cross-tabulation results, these results are not intuitive to interpret. Each additional year of tenure in public housing is associated with a 6.4% (1.0 – .936 * 100%) increase in the probability that a tenant will prefer repair over relocating. Thus, longer tenure is associated with preferring to fix up public housing.

Logistic regression may be the best test of an association under these conditions; however, it may not be appropriate for all audiences. Given that a policy report is designed for politicians, advocates, and/or civil servants rather than other academics, it makes sense to run simpler procedures. We can use the chi-square test if we recode the independent variable into a nominal variable with several categories. When we do this, the results are easy for a lay audience to understand.

As an alternative, we can turn tenure into a categorical variable by grouping all cases within each quartile (a four-category variable ranging from 1 = the 25% of all respondents who have lived the least amount of time in public housing to 4 = the 25% of respondents who have lived in public housing the longest). Then we can compare all associations using the more descriptive two-by two table and chi-square tests or the ANOVA test.

As we have just suggested, we can create a categorical version of tenure in public housing by using quartiles. In the distribution of the continuous tenure variable, the first 25% of residents have lived in public housing for less than two years. The next 25% of residents have lived in public housing for at least two years but less than four years. The third quartile of residents have lived in public housing for four years to eight years, and the fourth quartile of respondents have lived in public housing for more than eight years. First, we create the new categorical tenure variable, and then we run chi-square tests of association. The SPSS Statistics syntax is provided below; it is followed by the output in Table 14.14.

```
compute catten=0.
If (q10year<2) catten=1.
If (q10year>=2 and q10year<4) catten=2.
If (q10year>=4 and q10year<=8) catten=3.
If (q10year>8) catten=4.
CROSSTABS
/TABLES=Q132W1 Q134w1 BY catten
/FORMAT=AVALUE TABLES
/STATISTICS=CHISQ CMH(1)
```

Table 14.14 Chi-Square Tests of Association

By Tenure in Public Housing—Treated Categorically					
Buildings Run Down, by Housing Type	*Tenure Less Than 2 Years*	*Tenure 2–4 Years*	*Tenure 4–8 Years*	*Tenure More Than 8 Years*	*Total*
Yes, run down	18 (24%)	15 (21%)	26 (33%)	13 (15%)	72
No, not run down	58 (76%)	55 (79%)	51 (67%)	75 (85%)	239
Total	76 (100%)	70 (100%)	77 (100%)	88 (100%)	311
Chi-square: 8.478, 3 DF, P = .037					
Preference for Repair vs. Relocation	*Tenure Less Than 2 Years*	*Tenure 2–4 Years*	*Tenure 4–8 Years*	*Tenure More Than 8 Years*	*Total*
Fix up	26 (34%)	36 (50%)	33 (43%)	54 (61%)	149
Relocate	51 (66%)	36 (50%)	43 (57%)	34 (39%)	164
Total	77 (100%)	72 (100%)	77 (100%)	88 (100%)	313
Chi-square: 13.29, 3 DF, P = .004					

```
/CELLS=COUNT ROW COLUMN TOTAL

/COUNT ROUND CELL.
```

It is interesting that, when we do not treat tenure as a linear, continuous variable, we find a significant association between tenure in public housing and thinking public housing buildings are run down beyond repair (p = .037). Tenure has an interesting association with preferring to fix up public housing versus relocate. Those who have been in public housing a short time prefer to relocate, as do those who have lived in public housing for four to eight years. Those who have lived in public housing for two to four years or more than eight years prefer to fix up public housing. The logistic regressions did not provide this interesting finding.

The next dependent variable we will examine is the ordinal variable, level of confidence of finding a good postrelocation home. The best method is, again, a regression method (cumulative logistic regression). This is an even more complicated analysis than logistic regression. We could use a chi-square test with the categorical tenure variable. The problem with this is that we would be reporting a cross-tabulation of a five-by-four table, which may be difficult for the layperson to interpret. Again, we will choose the analysis method most appropriate for the audience, the chi-square test. Not only is the regression method very complicated (cumulative logit model), tenure appears to have a nonlinear association with attitudes toward relocation; thus, we will continue to use the categorical version of tenure. The syntax for chi-square procedures was shown previously. Table 14.15 presents the SPSS Statistics output for this association.

In Table 14.15, it appears that there is little difference in terms of levels of confidence except for those who have lived in public housing more than eight years. Those who have lived in public housing for more than eight years are least likely to say they are very confident of finding a good home and most likely to say they are not at all confident of finding a good home. However, the association is not significant (p = .077), and thus any association we find cannot be distinguished from that found purely by chance.

Last, we will examine the bivariate association between the relocation attitude scale and tenure in public housing. Both are continuous variables, and when the dependent variable and independent variable are both continuous, a simple bivariate Pearson correlation is sufficient to test for an association. Below we present first the SPSS Statistics syntax, and then in Table 14.16 we provide the SPSS Statistics output for the correlation test. We find that longer tenure in public housing is associated with more positive attitudes toward relocation.

```
CORRELATIONS

/VARIABLES= scale q10year /PRINT=TWOTAIL NOSIG

/MISSING=PAIRWISE.
```

Table 14.15 Chi-Square Test of Association, Confidence in Finding a New Home and Categorical Tenure

Confident of Having a Good Place to Live After Relocation	*Tenure Less Than 2 Years*	*Tenure 2–4 Years*	*Tenure 4–8 Years*	*Tenure More Than 8 Years*	*Total*
Very confident	37 (50%)	29 (44%)	35 (49%)	29 (34%)	130
Somewhat confident	20 (27%)	21 (32%)	19 (27%)	24 (28%)	84
Somewhat unconfident	10 (14%)	11 (17%)	12 (17%)	12 (14%)	45
Not at all confident	7 (9%)	5 (8%)	5 (7%)	20 (24%)	239
Total	74 (100%)	66 (100%)	71 (100%)	85 (100%)	296
Pearson chi-square test: 15.563, 9 DF, P = .077					

Table 14.16 Pearson Correlation Test of Relocation Attitude and Tenure in Public Housing

Relocation Attitude Scale	1.0		
Tenure	.120	1.0	
Correlation test P = .037			

The correlation between tenure in public housing and the relocation attitude scale is positive. This means that living in public housing for longer periods is associated with more positive attitudes toward the relocation process. The association is statistically significant ($p = .037$).

SUMMARY

We have examined four variables regarding attitudes public housing residents hold toward being relocated out of public housing and into private market housing. First we examined them univariately, and then we examined their bivariate associations with type of public housing and tenure in public housing. In the process, we introduced several statistical techniques that can be used to run both the univariate and bivariate analyses. In general, we found a lot of significant associations. The association between confidence in finding a good new home and tenure in public housing was the only test that did not provide statistically significant results. Now that we have completed the analyses, we can identify the story found in the numbers and write it up in a policy report.

THE REPORT WRITE-UP

We start with deciding what aspect of the story is most relevant. Given that we examined only four variables, we will include all the results. The next decision is to determine the best way to present the data. Tables and tables of numbers can be mind-numbingly boring. A graph, however, just like a picture, is worth a thousand words. Thus for a report concerning the above findings, we include the important aspects of the story in graphic form. We want to choose statistically significant findings only. We do not want to overstate our case. However, before we discuss the data and interpret the results, we need to set the "story" that we want to include in our policy report. Mini Case 14.1 presents the story we tell prior to introducing the data analysis.

MINI CASE 14.1

The Public Housing Story

Local housing authorities have been demolishing public housing communities that are run down beyond repair under the Housing Opportunities for Everyone (HOPE VI) policy since the early 1990s. It is believed in policy circles that public housing residents will have better opportunities outside of public housing. Thus, since 1994, cities around the United States have been demolishing public housing and relocating tenants into the private market or mixed income communities. The US Department of Housing and Urban Development requires that residents have a say in housing authority decisions regarding public housing. Given that over 200,000 units of public housing have been demolished to date nationally, one would expect that public housing residents universally desire to relocate and agree that public housing is a bad program.

Atlanta is one of the first cities to eliminate all family-based housing projects as well as some high rise projects for seniors and individuals with disabilities. This report provides evidence of Atlanta's public housing residents' experiences and attitudes toward public housing and relocation.

Next, we begin presenting the data. In Figures 14.2, 14.3a, and 14.3b we combine information from several sets of output. The "all" category comes from the univariate analyses, while the housing type columns come from the bivariate cross tabulations. We continue our report by interpreting the graphs in Mini Case 14.2.

Figure 14.2 Percentage Who State Public Housing Is Run Down Beyond Repair, by Housing Type

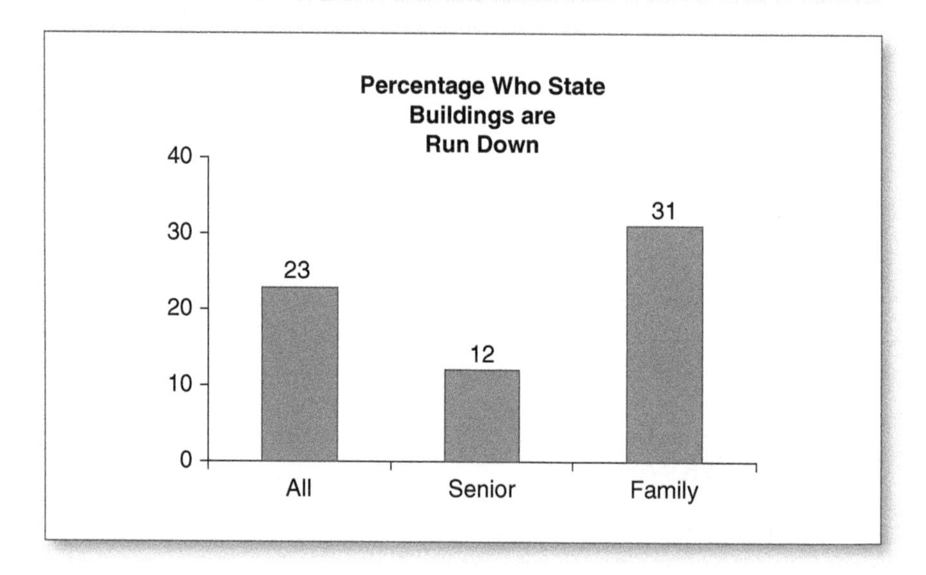

Figure 14.3a & 14.3b Percentage Who Prefer to Relocate, by Housing Type and Tenure in Public Housing

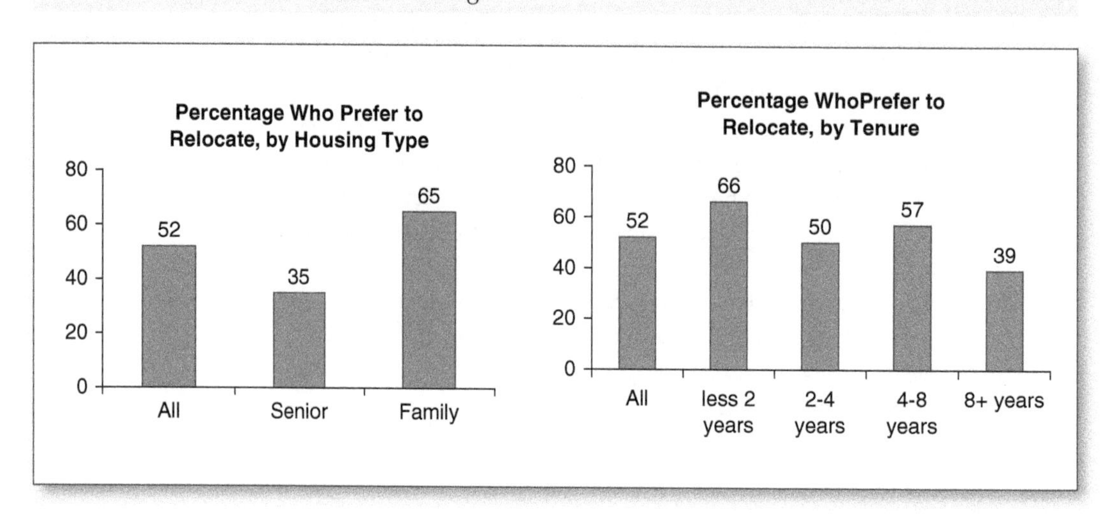

MINI CASE 14.2

Write-Up of First Set of Data

As we can see from Figure 14.2, the majority of residents do not believe that Atlanta's public housing buildings are run down beyond repair. Less than 25% believe this. However, there appears to be a discrepancy between residents of senior housing and residents of family housing, given that 31% of family housing residents state their buildings are run down beyond repair, while only 12% of senior housing residents make this assessment.

Next we turn to residents' preference for either staying in their current public housing (if it is repaired) or relocating (see Figures 14.3a and 14.3b). Despite residents' assertions that in general, buildings are not run down beyond repair, the majority would still prefer to relocate (52%). Again, we find a difference by housing type and tenure in public housing. Approximately two thirds of family housing residents prefer to relocate, compared to just one third of senior housing residents. Residents who have lived in public housing for the shortest amount of time are most likely to prefer to relocate (66%), while residents who have lived in public housing for the longest amount of time are the least likely to prefer to relocate (39%).

The next set of outputs assess an important issue when deciding to demolish units of affordable housing—is there enough market-rate housing available for public housing residents to move into? Mini Case 14.3 provides a write-up of this aspect of the relocation story, as presented in Figures 14.4a and 14.4b.

Figure 14.4a & 14.4b Confident in Finding a Good Home, by Housing Type and Tenure in Public Housing

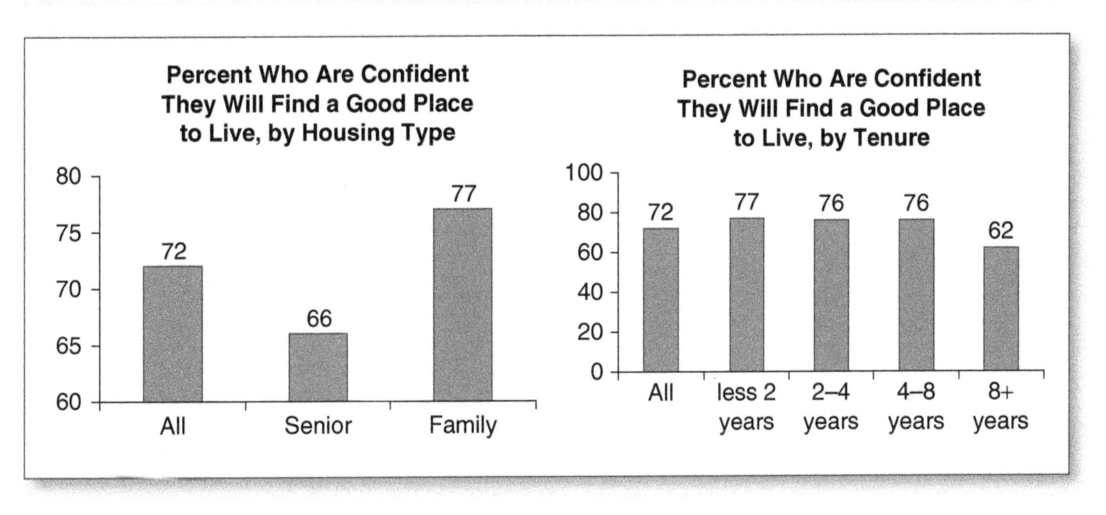

MINI CASE 14.3

Are Good Homes Available for Relocating Public Housing Residents?

It is possible that concern over finding a good home to rent with a housing choice voucher might explain some of the reluctance of public housing residents to relocate. Figures 14.5a and 14.5b show that well over two thirds of all residents feel confident or very confident that, after relocation, they will have homes that are as good as or better than their public housing homes. Once again, residents of senior housing and those who have lived for a long time in public housing show the least confidence. Despite this, a majority of both of these groups are confident or very confident of finding a good home in the private market.

Now, we present findings from the analysis of the final variable. It is the relocation attitude scale that captures (1) stress over moving (and moving is incredibly stressful), (2) how well residents believe the housing authority will handle relocation, and (3) the level of excitement over relocating. The scale ranges from a low value of 4, representing negative attitudes toward relocation, to 20, for very positive attitudes toward relocation. In this piece of the story, we are examining the overall relocation experience to determine how well residents believe it will be handled. The data are presented in Figures 14.5a and 14.5b, and the story is interpreted in Mini Case 14.4.

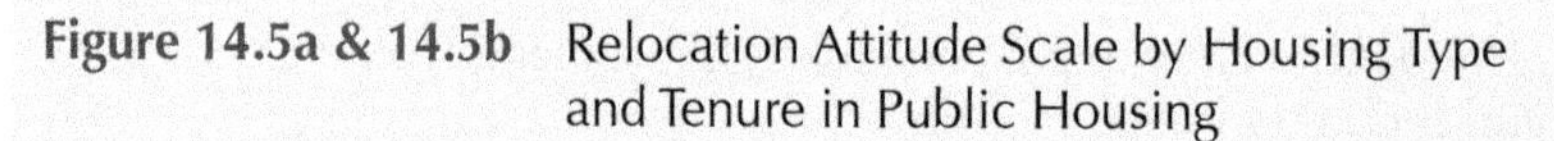

Figure 14.5a & 14.5b Relocation Attitude Scale by Housing Type and Tenure in Public Housing

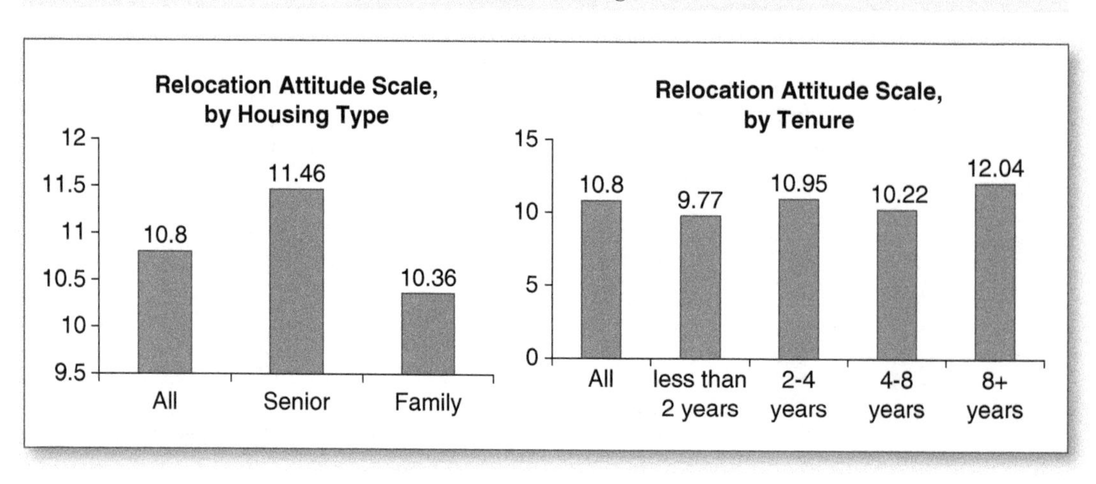

MINI CASE 14.4

Residents' Attitudes Toward Relocation

On average, residents held an attitude with a value of 10.8 points on a scale of 4 (negative attitude toward relocation) to 20 (very positive attitude toward relocation). A neutral attitude would score about 12 points on the scale; thus, residents are slightly negative in their attitudes toward relocation. Residents of senior housing were closer to neutral on the relocation attitude scale, while residents of family housing were slightly more negative in their attitudes. Tenure in public housing appears to generate a similar pattern, with those living there the shortest time and those living there the longest deviating from the norm. Those living in public housing for the shortest period of time held the most negative attitudes toward the relocation, while those living in public housing the longest hold the most positive attitudes toward relocation—though their attitudes were still in the neutral range.

This seems surprising given that the majority of public housing residents would prefer to relocate and believe that they will find a good home in the private market. This suggests that the process of relocation is very hard on public housing residents.

Earlier in the chapter we discussed the two types of policy reports we can write. One is more objective, supplying a balanced view of the issues and data. The alternative is an advocacy-oriented policy report. The date write-ups in Mini Cases 14.1 through 14.4 reflect the objective or balanced viewpoint. However, the questions analyzed are clearly advocacy oriented. We can bring home the advocacy piece of the policy report by providing some policy recommendations. We do this in Mini Case 14.5.

MINI CASE 14.5

Policy Recommendations

Clearly there is a large difference in attitudes and beliefs between residents of family housing and those in senior housing. We recommend that there be separate policies for addressing relocation in each type of housing project.

It is clear that the Atlanta Housing Authority intends to demolish public housing units that residents believe are not run down beyond repair. This

(Continued)

(Continued)

especially holds true for the senior housing units. In addition, the majority of senior housing residents do not want to relocate. We recommend that HUD hold housing authorities to stricter proof that public housing is run down beyond repair—especially for senior housing, because relocating is especially burdensome for older residents.

Despite this, the majority of residents do want to relocate. This suggests that there is something other than disrepair that is wrong with public housing, such as stigma. Given that relocation is a very expensive public program, we recommend determining what this problem might be so as to avoid it in private market housing.

It is important in a report to provide the more savvy readers with a methods section. This can be placed in an appendix, in separate documentation available by request, or online. We did not mark which findings were significant in the figures because most are significant, but if our report were to include nonsignificant findings, we would make sure to highlight the significant ones.

ETHICS CORNER

In presenting findings, we do not want to deviate far from the data. This is an important ethical issue. The policy report example provided in this chapter about public housing relocations began as an advocacy-oriented exercise. The researchers in the example wanted to stop the relocation process and thought respondents would not hold positive attitudes toward relocation, would not want to relocate, and would anticipate having a difficult time finding new homes. This was not the case. In situations such as this, researchers have two options: (1) They can manipulate the findings in order to uphold their original position, rationalizing that in the long run, stopping relocations is good for public housing residents and for taxpayers' wallets; or (2) they can switch to a more balanced viewpoint of the relocation process.

The findings in the data did not support the researchers' original beliefs. Does this mean all findings that don't support the original goal get dropped? Do we only present some findings—the findings that agree with our purpose? Researchers must be ready to be and open to being surprised by their findings. Researchers must be willing to change their minds based on the evidence. How can we expect the public to change their minds based on the evidence if scholars cannot? How can social scientists expect the public to trust social science if researchers are manipulating data to suit their purposes? If social scientists do not present findings as straightforwardly as they can, then they are doing the advancement of social science a grave injustice. They are adding to a situation in which the public will not trust any social science.

CONCLUSION

In this chapter we focused on practical applications of data analysis—analysis for report writing. Everything budding scholars should need to create their own policy reports is included in this section. We showed how to create a scale variable from four ordinal variables, and we showed how to make a single categorical variable out of a continuous variable. Using a practical report writing approach, we covered a variety of univariate and bivariate statistical techniques designed to describe topical characteristics about a sample and to test to see if the patterns hold for the population from which the sample came.

Many of the techniques turn out to be the same for different kinds of variables. Of particular importance is how to choose the correct statistical technique. The statistical technique depends upon the measurement of the variable(s) being analyzed. For univariate analysis and regressions, it is the dependent variable that dictates the statistical technique we choose. For bivariate analysis, the technique chosen depends on both variables.

We discussed that the technique chosen is dependent on how the variables are measured. We use a crosstab procedure and a chi-square test for two variables that are nominally measured. If one or more of the cells has a tiny count, we use the Fisher's exact test. We use the same procedure but a different test (i.e., Somers' *d* or Kendall's tau) for two ordinal variables. We use an ANOVA when one variable is categorical and the other (dependent) variable is continuous, and if the dependent variable is categorical and the independent variable is continuous, we use logistic regression. Finally, if we are examining associations between two continuous variables, a correlation with a Pearson correlation test is appropriate.

Last, we demonstrated how to combine various parts of statistical output into both table and graph format and provided examples of a policy report write-up with interpretation recommendations. Policy reports are an important applied research tool and make important use of the surveys we create. One way of being a "public" sociologist is to write policy reports and widely disseminate findings to the public.

Creating variables that are appropriate for analysis can be time consuming and error prone. Take your time with this task, and remember to always run frequencies and crosstabs on any variables you manipulate before and after the manipulation to make sure your syntax does what you want it to do.

Once again, we caution the reader that we are presenting a conceptual understanding of data analysis. At the same time we are presenting data analysis in a practical outcome manner. As for interpreting findings, we advise staying close to the data while telling a story. This means make sure you include the relevant background information or the social, political, and economic context that is important for your evidence-based story.

SYNTAX FOR ANALYSES DESCRIBED IN THIS CHAPTER

All the SPSS syntax commands used in this chapter are included in Table 14.17. In addition, it includes syntax for use with SAS and STATA.

Table 14.17 Syntax for Chapter 14 Analyses

	SPSS	*SAS*	*STATA*
Frequency procedure	FREQUENCIES VARIABLES= houstype / ORDER=ANALYSIS.	Proc Freq data=da. data; Tables houstype / ; Run;	Tab housetype
Crosstabs procedure	CROSSTABS /TABLES=Q132W1 BY houstype /FORMAT=AVALUE TABLES /CELLS=COUNT /COUNT ROUND CELL.	Proc Freq data=da. data; Tables Q132W1 * houstype / list missing ; Run;	tab q132w1 houstype
Means procedure	MEANS TABLES=Age q10year BY houstype /CELLS MEAN COUNT STDDEV.	Proc means data=da.newdata; Class houstype; Vars age q10year; Run;	summarize age q10year houstype
Bivariate correlation	CORRELATIONS /VARIABLES=Q139aW1 Q139bW1 Q139cW1 Q139dW1 /PRINT=TWOTAIL NOSIG /MISSING=PAIRWISE.	Proc corr data=da. data; Vars Q139aW1 Q139bW1 Q139cW1 Q139dW1; Run;	pwcorr q139aw1 q139bw1 q139cw1 q139dw1

	SPSS	*SAS*	*STATA*
Reverse coding	RECODE q139cw1 Q139dW1 (SYSMIS=SYSMIS) (1=5) (2=4) (3=3) (4=2) (5=1) INTO q139cw1_r q139dw1_r. Frequencies q139cw1_r q139dw1_r.	Data da.olddata; Set da.newdata; Q139cw1_r=6-q139cw1; Q139dw1_r=6-q139dw1; Run;	generate Q139cw1_r=6-q139cw1 Q139dw1_r=6-q139dw1
Cronbach's alpha	RELIABILITY /VARIABLES=Q139aW1 Q139bW1 Q139cW1_r Q139dW1_r /SCALE('ALL VARIABLES') ALL /MODEL=ALPHA.	Proc corr data=da.data alpha; Vars q139aw1 q139bw1 q139cw1_r q139dw1_r ; Run;	Alpha Q139aW1 Q139bW1 Q139cW1_r Q139dW1_r, item
Create scale	compute scale=(q139aw1+q139bw1 +q139cw1_r+q139dw1_r).	Data da.olddata; Set da.newdata; Scale= q139aw1+q139bw1 +q139cw1_r+q139dw1_r ; Run;	Generate scale= q139aw1+q139bw1+ q139cw1_r+q139dw1_r
Assess whether scale is made correctly	EXAMINE VARIABLES scale /STATISTICS DESCRIPTIVES EXTREME /CINTERVAL 95 /MISSING LISTWISE /NOTOTAL.	Proc means data=da.newdata; Var scale; Run;	Sum scale

(Continued)

Table 14.17 (Continued)

	SPSS	SAS	STATA
Chi-square test	CROSSTABS /TABLES=Q132W1 BY houstype /FORMAT=AVALUE TABLES /STATISTICS=CHISQ CMH(1) /CELLS=COUNT ROW COLUMN TOTAL /COUNT ROUND CELL.	Proc Freq data=da. data; Tables Q132W1 *houstype / chisq ; Run;	tab Q132W1 houstype, chi2
ANOVA test	MEANS TABLES scale BY houstype /CELLS MEAN COUNT STDDEV /STATISTICS ANOVA.	Proc anova data=da.data; Class houstype; Model **scale**=houstype ; Run;	oneway scale houstype
Correlation test	CORRELATIONS /VARIABLES= scale Q10year /PRINT=TWOTAIL NOSIG /MISSING=PAIRWISE.	Proc corr data=da. data; Vars scale Q10year; Run;	Pwcorr scale Q10year
Logistic regression	LOGISTIC REGRESSION VARIABLES q132w1 /METHOD=ENTER q10year /CRITERIA=PIN(.05) POUT(.10) ITERATE(20) CUT(.5).	Proc logistic data=da.newdata descending; Model Q132W1=Q10year; Run;	Logit Q132W1 Q10year

Recode tenure in public housing from a ratio	compute catten=0.
	If (q10year<2) catten=1.
	If (q10year>=2 and q10year<4) catten=2.
		Data test4;
		Set test3;
		catten=0;
			generate catten=0
			replace catten=1 if q10year<2

	SPSS	SAS	STATA

variable to an ordinal variable.
 	
Now we can use a crosstab instead of logistic regression.
	If (q10year>=4 and q10year<=8) catten=3.
	
	If (q10year>8) catten=4.
	
	CROSSTABS
	
	/TABLES=Q132W1 Q134w1 BY catten
	
	/FORMAT=AVALUE TABLES
	
	/STATISTICS=CHISQ CMH(1)
	
	/CELLS=COUNT ROW COLUMN TOTAL
	
	/COUNT ROUND CELL.
		if q10year<2 then catten=1;
		
		if 4>q10year>=2 then catten=2;
		
		if 8=>q10year>=4 then catten=3;
		
		if q10year>8 then catten=4;
		
		;
		
		Run;
		
		Proc Freq data=test4;
		
		Tables Q132W1 *catten / chisq ;
		
		Run;
			replace catten=2 if q10year>=2 & catten<4
			
			replace catten=3 if q10year<=8 & q10year>=4
			
			replace catten=4 if q10year>8
			
			tab q132w1 catten, chi2

KEY TERMS

Univariate analysis 239
Bivariate analysis 240
Dependent variable 240
Independent variable 240
Association 240
Mean 240
Median 241
Mode 241
Variance 241
Standard deviation 241
Normal distribution 241
Confidence interval 242
Scale variable 245
Correlation 245
Inferential statistics 252
Logistic regression 253

CRITICAL THINKING QUESTIONS

Below you will find three questions that ask you to think critically about core concepts addressed in this chapter. Be sure you understand each one; if you don't, this is a good time to review the relevant sections of this chapter.

1. What is the goal of a policy report? How do we adapt our statistics to meet those goals?
2. How do we know what statistical test to use for an analysis?
3. What are the ethical considerations when writing up findings and documenting our procedures?

15

More Advanced Data Analysis

INTRODUCTION

In this chapter we turn to analysis of data in order to produce a journal-quality article. Thus, we extend the analysis techniques to multivariate regressions and other advanced techniques suitable for a journal article. We provide a basic understanding of these techniques, but we encourage our readers to consult a dedicated statistics textbook, and we would argue that taking a statistics course is generally needed to effectively use these statistical techniques. One excellent statistical textbook we recommend is *Applied Statistics* by Rebecca Warner (2009). Again, we encourage the creation and use of an analysis syntax file that can be reused and checked later for possible errors. This can be done even while using the point-and-click method in SPSS Statistics, by pasting the syntax into a separate syntax file prior to running commands, or by saving the syntax automatically included in the output windows in the latest versions of SPSS Statistics. For guidance on these methods, we recommend *Using SPSS Statistics for Research Methods and Social Science Statistics* (5th ed.) by William E. Wagner, III (2014).

We start by discussing the importance of asking explanatory research questions that can be addressed using survey methods for data collection; questions of this kind are often found in journal article research. Then, briefly, a journal article and its component parts are described. We then take a big leap and describe the regression analyses often used to answer explanatory questions, including regression assumptions. After the regression models are explained, we begin our analysis example. We start by creating the analysis dataset and addressing variable creation issues and missing data issues as they pertain to regression assumptions. We then present OLS (ordinary least squares) bivariate regression (i.e., linear regression) followed by multivariate regression. We repeat this on a logistic regression example. Finally, we discuss how to write up a results section of a journal article.

EXPLANATORY RESEARCH QUESTIONS

Survey research tends to answer research questions that are predictive or causal. We call these **explanatory research questions**, as we are attempting to explain the relationships between variables: how one variable affects another variable. Figure 15.1 presents a few examples of explanatory questions.

Examining how the type of neighborhood in which one lives is associated with obesity would be a bivariate explanatory analysis, because we are examining how one variable, disadvantaged neighborhoods, affects another variable, likelihood of obesity. The second explanatory research question in Figure 15.1 is an associational analysis involving three variables: HIV contraction, use of HIV testing, and HIV education. The final explanatory research question in Figure 15.1 is multivariate, because we are asking which of a multitude of social factors predict or are associated with men's and women's wealth accumulation, including income, work status, marital status, inheritances, and any other factors we can theorize are related. These analyses are also inferential, and there are many tests within the regression analyses used to determine if findings in the sample are also statistically significant and hold for the population.

Figure 15.1 Explanatory Research Questions

1.	Does living in disadvantaged neighborhoods increase the probability of being obese?
2.	Does the decreased use of HIV testing or lack of HIV education explain the current increase in the likelihood of HIV contraction?
3.	What factors explain why married men may accumulate more wealth than married women?

JOURNAL ARTICLE FORMAT

The audience for a journal article is generally much more statistically sophisticated than the audience for a typical applied research report. Therefore, the analyses and write-up need to be very different. Journal articles have several sections: an introduction, a literature review, a methods write-up, the analysis or findings section, and a conclusion. The introduction explains what the research question is, why it is socially relevant or scientifically important, and what contributions the study is making. The literature review section is used to argue the need for the current study: does it (1) fill a gap in the literature, (2) extend the literature to a new population, or (3) refute some theoretical premise? While there are other arguments, these three are most salient. In general, any hypotheses deduced from the theory will come from the argument presented in the literature review.

The methods section will be far more rigorous and documentation more detailed than what is expected in a policy report. In the methods section, authors need to demonstrate the quality of the data and explain how the dataset is generalizable (if it comes from a survey and uses a probability sampling method). The variables will be presented here alongside the concepts they come from. Issues of reliability and validity and any measurement error should be presented here. Last, the methods of testing the hypotheses will be described in detail.

The results or findings section comes next. The conclusion, or discussion of the findings in relation to the literature included in the literature review, goes last.

The results section is what we focus on here in this chapter. The results section is often based on a form of regression analysis. The most commonly used statistical techniques for journal articles are linear regressions. Regressions are designed to tests directional or causal relationships between sets of variables. We will introduce regressions in the next section.

REGRESSION ANALYSIS

The type of regression method we use depends on how the dependent variable is measured. Table 15.1 lists the regression method suitable for each type of dependent variable. The most used regression method is the **ordinary least squares** (OLS) regression method (i.e., linear regression) used with a continuous (ratio or interval) dependent variable. Logistic regression is used with a nominal binary dependent variable, such as a yes/no variable. Less common regression methods are the Poisson regression for count data, the multinomial regression model for nominal multicategory dependent variables, and the cumulative logit regression method for ordinal dependent variables. In this chapter, we limit our analyses and discussions of regressions to OLS (linear) regression and logistic regression.

Introduction to OLS (Linear) Regression

We start with OLS regression not only because it is the most common but also because it is the easiest of the regressions to understand and interpret. The general regression equation looks like this:

$$DV = a + B_1X_1 + e \quad (1)$$

Table 15.1 Type of Dependent Variable and Applicable Regression Method

Dependent Variable	*Regression Method*
Continuous (income)	Ordinary least squares estimation (OLS)
Binary (yes/no)	Logistic regression
Count (number of cigarettes smoked)	Poisson regression
Multiple categories qualitative (types of tobacco products used)	Multiple logistic regression
Multiple category ordinal (agree to disagree)	Cumulative logit regression

Here, DV is the dependent variable, a is the intercept or value of the DV when $X_i = 0$, X_i is an independent variable associated with DV, B_i is the estimated level of association between the X_i and the DV, and last, e is the error or **residual** term. The residual term includes any measurement error, sampling error, and other predictor variables (X's) that are not directly included in the model. This is a bivariate equation, meaning that we are limiting the analysis to two variables, as we did in Chapter 14.

Regression analyses can have any number of predictor or independent variables included in the model. Equation 2 presents a more typical multivariate regression equation, meaning that there are numerous independent X variables included.

$$DV = a + b_1X_1 + b_2X_2 = b_3X_3 + \ldots b_nX_n + e \tag{2}$$

To do the regression analysis, we use the observed values from our survey data as the dependent variable, and all the X's represent independent variables. When we solve a regression equation, we are solving for both a and all b's. It turns out that there are many possible estimates of a and b that make the equation work. Which is the best set of estimates to use? The least squares criterion is considered the best. Conceptually, the least squares criterion decomposes the total variance in the dependent variable into that which is explained by the X variables in the model and that which is not explained or is residual in the model. It chooses estimates that minimize the residual term and maximize the explained part of the model. We call this ordinary least squares.

In a bivariate regression equation, there is only one b to solve for. We call this model the unconditional relationship between the dependent variable and the independent variable. It is unconditional because the total relationship between DV and X does not depend on any other X variables. We call b in this case the **correlation coefficient**, which is a measure of the strength and direction of the association between X and DV.

Multiple regression is the most widely used statistical technique in the social sciences. That is because it does two very desirable things: First, it combines many variables to produce optimal predictions of the dependent variable, and second, it separates the effects of independent variables on the dependent variable, so you can examine the unique contribution of each variable. This means that each b now represents the unique contribution to the association with the dependent variable rather than the total association with the dependent variable (bivariate regression only). Therefore, in multiple regression, b is no longer the correlation coefficient, but instead is a **partial correlation coefficient**.

There are assumptions that must be met in order to successfully solve the equation and obtain the best solution. The equation itself tells us that the association between the dependent variable and the independent variables is linear and additive. A linear equation is perhaps the simplest way to describe a relationship between two or more variables and still get reasonably accurate predictions. Therefore, we need to make sure that the relationships between the independent variables and the dependent variable meet these assumptions. We can assess this bivariately using scatterplots for two continuous variables. If we do not find linear associations, we can create **dummy variables** out of the independent continuous variable. Recall from Chapter 14 that tenure in public housing and several relocation variables did not have a linear relationship. We created four dummy variables (yes/no) out of tenure, and this resolved the lack of linear association with tenure. If we have multicategory nominal or ordinal variables that cannot be treated as continuous, we can also turn these into dummy variables and include them in our models. Dummy variables do not violate the linear association assumption.

We assume that the distribution of the model is multivariate normal. This means that the joint distribution between the dependent and independent variables creates a shape that is normally distributed. Of course, we cannot visualize it when there are many variables in the model, but it is analogous to the bell shaped normal distribution of a single variable.

Another important assumption is that we have a fully specified model. This means that all the theoretically important predictors are included in the model, and no extraneous variables are included. The literature review is very helpful in helping us to know what the important predictor variables to include may be. If we leave out an important predictor variable, then it is included in the residual term e. This partial correlation coefficient will not be the best estimate, because it will include more than its unique contribution to the association with the dependent variable, and then our conclusions might be wrong. Thus, we do not want our predictor variables to be associated with the residual term.

This leads to the remaining assumptions that all involve the residual term. After estimating the equation, the residual term can be calculated for each respondent by subtracting the estimated DV from the observed DV. If we then sum the residuals across all respondents, it should sum to zero or at least very close to zero. The mean of the residuals should be zero, in which case the residual would be normally distributed. If the summed residual is large, then the model is biased, and the estimated a and b's are wrong. This can happen when the model is not fully specified or if there is measurement error in one or more of the variables included in the analyses.

We have conceptually introduced the OLS regression model, its estimation, and the assumptions needed to be confident that we have estimated the best regression coefficients, a and b(s). We now turn to examining significance and model fit. First, there is the global test of significance. This is an *F* test, and it tests the hypothesis that the model currently being run is the same as the null model. The **null model** is a model predicting the dependent variable with zero independent variables included. If we can reject this hypothesis, it means at least one of our predictor variables is significantly associated with the dependent variable. Again, we reject at a p value of less than .05.

Recall that OLS estimation decomposes the total model variance into that which is explained by the predictor variables and that which is residual. Therefore, total variance = explained variance + residual variance. In the null model, the total variance will be all residual variance. This is important, because it helps us to understand the best measure of model fit, the coefficient of determination.

The **coefficient of determination** (r^2) is the most common measure of model fit used. It is indeed the square of *r*, Pearson's correlation coefficient. It is calculated as follows:

$$r^2 = 1 - \text{Residual error} / \text{ total variance.}$$

Again, we are estimating these concepts conceptually rather than mathematically. Please consult a statistics textbook for the arithmetic calculations. In a bivariate regression model, where the association is the correlation coefficient, the r^2 term is the correlation coefficient squared. We interpret r^2 as the amount of variance in the dependent variable explained by the predictor variables in the model. The range of r^2 is from 0, or none of the variance explained, to 1, or all of the variance explained. If we are examining multiple regression models, we can determine which model fits best by examining which has the largest r^2 or which predicts the largest amount of variance in the dependent variable.

Last, if the *F* test for the global model is significant, meaning at least one of our predictor variables has a significant association with the dependent variable; we can examine a *t*-test of significance for each predictor in the model. The *t*-test is related to the *F* test and operates similarly. It is testing the hypothesis that $b_1 = 0$, meaning there is no association between the predictor variable and the dependent variable. A large *t*-test statistic will be associated with a small *p* value. Again, if the *p* value is less than .05, we reject the null hypothesis, which means there is a statistically significant association between the predictor variable and the dependent variable.

Preparing Variables for Regression Analysis

We run our regression models on a prepared dataset. By prepared, we mean that each variable has been checked to see if its association with the dependent variable fits the assumptions of regression analysis. We start by creating a table of all the concepts and matching variables that will give us a fully specified model. Table 15.2 provides a list of all the variables we will use in this study along with all the manipulations that will be required to each variable to fit the regression assumptions. We created a similar table in Chapter 14 for the policy report. Recall that the statistical technique we choose is based on the measurement of the variables. In the case of regression, we choose based on the measurement of the dependent variable. The relocation attitude scale we first created in Chapter 14 is a continuous variable, and thus we will run OLS regressions to model it.

The dependent variable is a scale. Scale variables are typically not easy to interpret, because they are not in any particularly meaningful set of units. In order to make the interpretation more intuitive, it makes sense to standardize the variable (create z scores). A standardized variable has a mean of 0 and a standard deviation of 1. We can interpret its change now in terms of standard deviations. An increase of 1 means an increase of 1 standard deviation above the mean. Therefore, we write a note to ourselves to fix the scale variable by standardizing it. The standardizing syntax below returns a new variable called Zscale.

```
compute scale=(q139aw1+q139bw1+q139cw1_r+q139dw1_r).

Descriptives variables scale /save.
```

In regression analysis, the intercept is the estimated value of the outcome when the values of all independent variables are zero. So, the next step is to examine all variables and make sure they have a zero value. Often dummy variables will have a 1 = yes, and 2 = no format. In fact, that is how the variable, Q132w1 (Are your public housing buildings run down beyond repair?) is set up. The syntax below is used to modify this variable such that the no value is turned into a 0. While the analyses can be estimated without having that 0 value included, interpretation is much more difficult without it. Therefore, it is advisable to recode all the dichotomous or dummy variables to have values that range from 0 and 1. What would the syntax look like to create a dummy variable called male? How about a variable called female?

```
Recode q132w1 q134w1 (1=0)(2=1).
```

Table 15.2 Variables to Use in Analyses

Variable Name	*Variable Label*	*Response Categories*	*Fixes*
Dependent Variable			
Scale / Zscale	Relocation attitude scale created from Q139aw1-Q139dw1	4–20	standardize
Independent Variables			
Q132w1	Are the buildings in your public housing community physically run down beyond repair?	1 = yes 2 = no	Make 1 = 0 and 2 = 1
Q134w1	Which would you prefer, to fix up your public housing community or to relocate?	1 = fix up 2 = relocate	Make 1 = 0 and 2 = 1
Q137w1	How confident are you that after the relocations, residents will have places to live that are as good as or better than their current homes?	1 = very confident 2 = somewhat confident 3 = somewhat unconfident 4 = not at all confident	Turn into a dummy variable: 1 and 2 = 1, and 3 and 4 = 0
age	Age of respondent	18–93	
gender	Gender of respondent	1 = male 2 = female	Make a dummy variable: male = 1, and female = 0
education	Highest level of education achieved	0–16	Turn into a dummy variable: high school or more = 1, and less than high school = 0
Q10year	Tenure in public housing	.8–33	Make three dummy variables: (1) longten:1 = 8 + years, and 0 = < 8 years (2) shortten: 1 = < 2 years, and 0 ≥ 2 years (3) medten: 1 = 2–8 years, and 0 < 2 and ≥ 8 years

Ordinal variables are sometimes used as if they were continuous variables. Often, they have a minimum of five categories, and their distribution approximates a normal distribution or bell-shaped curve. If they have fewer than five categories or they clearly are not normally distributed, we transform them into dummy variables as well. The variable q137w1 (How confident are you that you will find a home at least as good as your public housing home?) is an ordinal variable with only four categories. While regression can be a robust approach to addressing violations of the continuous variable assumption, that is simply too few categories in a variable to allow such. Therefore, we will turn q137w1 into a dummy variable in which we collapse the two confident categories into one category and the two not confident categories into another single category.

```
Recode q137w1 (1=1) (2=1) (3=0) (4=0).
```

Tenure, meaning years in public housing, is continuous, but its association with the relocation outcomes is not linear. We learned this in Chapter 14. Therefore, we turn it into three dummy variables: (1) those who have lived in public housing for a long time—8 or more years (2), those who have lived there a shorter time—less than 2 years, and (3) those who have lived there a medium amount of time—2 to 8 years. The syntax below demonstrates how to recode this continuous variable into three dummy variables. We also turn education into a dummy variable. What would the syntax look like to create a dummy variable where 1 = has completed high school versus 0 = has not completed high school?

```
compute longten=0.
if (catten=4) longten=1.
compute shortten=0.
if (catten=1) shortten=1.
compute medten=0.
If (catten=0 and shortten=0) medten=1.
```

Once we have recoded all the variables in preparation for analysis, it is time to examine the dataset overall to prepare it for analysis. This specifically means examining the sample size available. This, in turn, means having to address missing data.

Preparing the Analysis Dataset

Essentially, all data analyses for journal articles are inferential, meaning that we are interested in the population from which the sample was chosen rather than the sample itself. Therefore, we need to spend some time examining issues that might compromise generalizability. One issue that may compromise generalizability is **missing data.** This may result when sample members either don't respond to the survey at all or refuse to answer individual questions included in the analysis (item nonresponse). We will want to devote some space in the article's methods section to exploring missing data patterns.

Another issue related to missing data is that we want all analyses to be conducted on the samples of the exact same size. In the analyses for the policy report in Chapter 14, we noted the sample sizes for each two-by-two table, but did not worry that the sample size was different for different variables. Here, for a multivariate analysis, we want the sample size to be exactly the same for all analyses. Why do we need to create an analysis data set that removes all **missingness** on any variables we plan to analyze, when we did not do so in the policy report analysis in Chapter 14? In order to know if the variables in a multivariate analysis have an effect on the dependent variable, we have to eliminate other sources of variation in the dependent variable—such as variations among the samples for each model. If one model includes the whole sample, but the next model includes only a subset of the sample, then we can't know whether the change in the regression coefficients signifies real change or simply the characteristics of a different population. Unfortunately, it might include both, but we cannot decompose the effects. Therefore, we must create an analysis dataset with a permanent sample size based on our decisions on how to handle missing data prior to conducting any analyses.

We can make one or more of several decisions to handle missing data: (1) We can delete any cases with a missing value on any of the variables we will include in the analyses (**listwise deletion**), (2) we can use mean imputation to supply missing values, (3) we can use multiple imputation to supply missing values, or (4) we can use some combination of the above three options depending on the variable and the number of missing values on the variable.

Listwise deletion may reduce the sample size considerably, but certainly it can be a reasonable solution. If the sample size becomes very small, however, we have to question whether or not it is still representative of the population. Also, we need to make sure we have a large enough sample size to estimate the regression equations, and to have enough power to detect an effect if there really is an effect (that is, to avoid a Type 1 error).

Listwise deletion is only one method of handling missing data. In the past, **mean imputation** was a popular method of eliminating missing values. For a given variable with missing values, take the mean of the variable, and then fill all the missing values with the mean. The benefit of this method is that the measure of central tendency will not change. Variance, however, will become smaller, since we've increased the sample size denominator in the formula for the variance, but we have not changed the numerator—the mean.

The US Census uses a method called "hot deck allocation" to impute missing values. This method replaces a missing value on one case by assigning a value from another case matched to it due to its similar characteristics. Age, gender, and race are always used for hot deck matching, but other characteristics may be used as well, such as region or county.

Multiple imputation is a better method of dealing with missing values, though it is more complex. This method adjusts both the mean and the variance, and it brings a certain measure of uncertainty back into the variable by creating several datasets rather than just one, each with a different imputed value to replace the missing values. Thus, the variance will not be artificially reduced. General software packages can now easily multiply impute data, analyze the multiple datasets that multiple imputation creates, and provide a combined single set of regression estimates. However, multiple imputation has some serious assumptions that need to be addressed before using it. At a minimum, data must be missing at random (not missing due to a characteristic of the individuals who didn't respond; this would create bias), and there must not be a large percentage of cases with missing values. See Allison (2002) for a terrific discussion of missing data imputation procedures.

As a rule, then, the first step in any multivariate analysis for an article is to understand the missing data patterns and how they may affect the generalizability of results. The next step is to create an analysis dataset that has a single sample size, either through listwise deletion or imputation of missing values, or some combination of both.

ADDRESSING MISSING DATA

Using the public housing sample and the set of variables listed in Table 15.2, we will analyze missing data patterns and create a final analysis data set. Here we use SPSS syntax to analyze the data, but SAS and STATA syntax are included in Table 15.15 at the end of this chapter. We start by running a frequency on all the relocation variables we plan to use in the analyses. The frequencies can be found in Table 15.3. It turns out there are no missing data on age, gender, and education. But there are missing data on the relocation variables.

```
FREQUENCIES q132w1 q134w1 q137w1

q139aw1 q139bw1 q139cw1_r q139dw1_r.
```

One variable only has 4 missing cases, while another has 17 missing cases. This is a small sample of 311. If each missing case is unique, then we could end up with a sample of 239, which is 76% of the original sample. This could compromise generalizability if we decided to simply delete all the cases with missing values.

Therefore, our next step is to determine whether each missing value is from a separate case, or whether some cases have more than one missing value. If we were to take a crosstab of all the variables, we would find that there is considerable overlap in item nonresponse. That is, the same respondents were likely to have item nonresponse on multiple items—none are unique. This leads to the same concern about generalizability,

Table 15.3 Valid Versus Missing Cases From a Frequency Output

	Valid Cases	*Number of Cases With Missing Values*
Q132w1	299	12
Q134W1	301	10
Q137w1	294	17
Q139aw1	307	4
Q139bw1	305	6
Q139cw1	302	9
Q139dw1	297	14
Total missing		72

but for a slightly different reason, we will introduce bias by listwise deleting the few cases. In other words, are some respondents (cases) more likely to refuse to answer questions than others? We address this below when analyzing missing data patterns.

Four of the items in the frequency we plan to use as a scale. In a crosstab of the four items included in the scale, we find some overlapping missing cases, where respondents skipped all four items (see Table 15.4). This means each missing case is not unique, and thus, with listwise deletion we will have far more than 239 remaining in our sample.

```
CROSSTABS
/TABLES=q139aw1 BY q139bW1 BY Q139cW1_r BY Q139dW1_r
/FORMAT=AVALUE TABLES
/CELLS=COUNT
/COUNT ROUND CELL.
```

However, it makes sense to go ahead and delete all the cases that are missing on all four items—there is no information provided by any of these cases. On a few cases, it looks like respondents answered three of the four items. When we create the scale, the cases with partial information will be dropped due to that one missing case. Is this the best solution, or do we want to take advantage of the partial information we have from the answers to the other three items? It makes sense to impute these missing cases in some way—through either mean imputation or multiple imputation.

Table 15.4 Crosstab of Questions making up a Scale

q139aw1	*q139bw1*	*q139cw1*	*q139dw1*
.	.	.	.
1	1	1	1
1	1	1	3
1	1	2	3
1	1	3	5
1	1	.	2
1	1	4	3
1	.	5	1
1	1	5	.
1	1	5	2
1	1	5	3

Listwise delete these cases using the filter.

Mean impute these cases to retain existing information.

Our next step is to delete all the cases that provide no information. We do this by eliminating through listwise deletion all missing values on all variables except the scale items that have a single missing case. Then we rerun the frequency to see what our sample size looks like. Table 15.5 shows that after listwise deletion, we have a sample size of 283. But there are still seven unique missing cases on the scale variables that need to be mean imputed. Through listwise deletion, our sample dropped from 311 to 283, which means we are retaining 91% of the sample for our analyses.

```
USE ALL.

COMPUTE filter_$=(q132w1>=0) and (q134w1>=0) and (q137w1>=0) and
(q139aw1).

value labels filter_$ 0'Not selected' 1 'Selected'.

Format filter_$ (F1.0).

Filter BY filter_$.
```

Table 15.5 Frequencies After Listwise Deletion

	Valid Cases	*Missing Cases*
Q132w1	283	0
Q134W1	283	0
Q137w1	283	0
Q139aw1	283	0
Q139bw1	282	1
Q139cw1	281	2
Q139dw1	279	4
Total unique		7

Missing Data Analysis

While only 10% of the sample has item nonresponse, it is still important to evaluate whether we will introduce any systematic error into the sample by listwise deleting those cases. We have to back up at this point and bring back the cases we have listwise deleted and imputed. We start by turning the filter off (using SPSS, the syntax is FILTER OFF) or go back to the original dataset and create a dummy variable that has a value of 1 for any cases with any missing data on any of the variables used in the study and a value of 0 if there are valid data for the case.

```
USE ALL.

RECODE filter_$ (1=0) (SYSMIS=1) INTO missing.

VARIABLE LABELS missing 'missing dummy'.

EXECUTE.
```

As can be seen in Table 15.6, a frequency of the missing dummy variable has a value of 0 for the 276 valid cases and a value of 1 for the 35 missing cases. This is correct, and the dummy variable now can be used as a dependent variable in a logistic regression model.

The next step is to run a logistic regression analysis predicting the missing data dummy variable (1 = missing, and 0 = not missing) to determine what, if anything, predicts missingness. We include age, gender, education, income, a dummy variable for living in public housing for 8 years or more, and a dummy variable for living in family

Table 15.6 Frequency of New Missing Data Dummy Variable

Missing Dummy

		Frequency	Percent	Valid Percent	Cumulative Percent
Valid	.00	275	88.7	88.7	88.7
	1.00	36	11.3	11.3	100.0
	Total	311	100.0	100.0	

versus senior housing. (There is little variation by race, so a variable for this was not included). The results of these analyses are presented in Table 15.7. Recall that we introduced logistic regression in Chapter 14. Logistic regression is not easy to interpret, because the raw regression units are logits. The odds ratios, or Exp(B), are easier to interpret. We are looking to see if any variables are significant at the $p < .05$ level. The column labeled Sig (second from the right) provides this information.

```
LOGISTIC REGRESSION VARIABLES missing
/METHOD=ENTER houstype age gender inc_mon longten educ
/CRITERIA=PIN(.05) POUT(.10) ITERATE(20) CUT(.5).
```

In analyses predicting missing values, age is a statistically significant predictor. It is negative, so it can be interpreted as follows: Older adults are less likely to skip questions. Thus, there is a systematic reason that some values are missing. This suggests that, even if we were not planning to, we need to include age in any models we run on this analysis dataset in order to adjust for the age bias in the analysis dataset. We must also report this **limitation** in the methods section of the journal article we are writing. Given that age is important to the story we want to tell about relocations, this association may have a serious impact on our estimates. If we find a significant association between age and the dependent variable in regressions in the next section, we need to ask, does our estimate underestimate—meaning the estimate is too small—the true relationship between age and relocation because we have listwise deleted responses of younger respondents from the dataset? Or does our estimate overestimate, meaning the estimate is too large?

Now that we understand the limitations of our data, we are ready to reduce our sample to the analysis dataset by eliminating the missing cases. To do this, we simply turn the filter back on. Next, we use mean imputation on the few items that still have a couple of missing cases (see Table 15.5) prior to creating the scale in order to preserve the partial information. Table 15.8 shows the SPSS output after running mean

Table 15.7 Logistic Regression of Missing Data

	B	*s. e.*	*Wald*	*DF*	*Sig.*	*Odds Ratio Exp(B)*
Constant	2.92.213	.2.89	3.810.164	1	.001	—
Family housing	−1.302	.989	1.734	1	.188	.272
Age	−.097	.038	6.640	1	.010	.907
Male	−.287	.970	.088	1	.767	.750
Monthly income	.002	.002	1.522	1	.217	1.002
8+ years in public housing	.360	.823	.192	1	.662	1.434
High school degree	−1.430	.892	2.567	1	.109	.239

Reference categories: Senior housing, female, fewer than 8 years in public housing, and less than high school education.

imputation. All missing values on these items have been imputed. The output tells us how many cases were imputed for each variable and what the final valid sample size is after imputation. The analysis data set now has no missing data and has a sample size of 283.

```
RMV /Q139bW1_1=SMEAN(Q139bW1).
RMV /Q139cW1_1=SMEAN(Q139cW1).
RMV /Q139dW1_1=SMEAN(Q139dW1).
```

Table 15.9 presents a piece of frequency output that shows there are no missing cases on any of our important variables. It is also important to note that while we examined only the relocation variables, *all* variables, even control variables, should be included in these analyses, and item nonresponse on control variables needs to be addressed as well. What we did here can be extended very easily to include more variables.

```
Filter BY filter_$.
```

At this point it is a good idea to save both your syntax and your new analysis data-... lick on "save as" and rename your dataset to make sure you do not save it over your original dataset. We now have a final sample size of 283 cases. We are ready to being analyzing the data.

Table 15.8 Mean Imputation Output

Result Variables

	Result Variable	Number of Replaced Missing Values	Case Number of Nonmissing Values		Number of Valid Cases	Creating Function
			First	Last		
1	Q139bW1	1	1	283	283	SMEAN(Q139bW1)

Result Variables

	Result Variable	Number of Replaced Missing Values	Case Number of Nonmissing Values		Number of Valid Cases	Creating Function
			First	Last		
1	Q139cW1_r	2	1	283	283	SMEAN(Q139cW1_r)

Result Variables

	Result Variable	Number of Replaced Missing Values	Case Number of Nonmissing Values		Number of Valid Cases	Creating Function
			First	Last		
1	Q139dW1_r	4	1	283	283	SMEAN(Q139dW1)

Table 15.9 Final Frequency Output Showing No Missing Values

	Valid Cases	*Missing Cases*
Q132w1	283	0
Q134W1	283	0
Q137w1	283	0
Q139aw1	283	0
Q139bw1	283	0
Q139cw1	283	0
Q139dw1	283	0

OLS REGRESSIONS OF THE RELOCATION ATTITUDE SCALE

We are regressing the standardized relocation attitude scale on age. Recall that we are interested in understanding how age is associated with relocations. This first analysis is a bivariate regression, meaning that it will give us the unconditional association or total association between age and relocation attitude. The syntax to run this model is below and is followed by the SPSS Statistics output in Table 15.10. As always, the SAS and STATA syntax are located at the end of the chapter (Table 15.15)

```
REGRESSION
/MISSING LISTWISE
/STATISTICS COEFF OUTS R ANOVA
/CRITERIA=PIN(.05) POUT(.10)
/NOORIGIN
/DEPENDENT zscale
/METHOD=ENTER age.
```

In Table 15.10, the first bit of information provided simply tells us what model is being analyzed. Only age is entered in this model. The second piece of output, the model summary, provides the r^2 or coefficient of determination. This tells us that age explains 6.5% of the total variance in the relocation attitude scale. The next piece of information, titled ANOVA, is the result from the global F test, which shows that this bivariate model does not do a better job of explaining the relocation attitude scale than would the null model with no predictors. It also shows the partitioning of variance into that which is explained (regression) and that which is residual. The F test statistic is large, and the associated p value is less than .05, thus we reject the hypothesis that the bivariate model is no better than the null. That is, the bivariate model does have some predictive value.

The last piece of output, coefficients, solves the regression equation. The constant is the a, and the b is .014, with a t-test statistic of 4.4 and a p value of less than .05. Thus, age is positively and significantly associated with relocation attitude. We interpret this total association between age and positive relocation attitude as follows: Each additional year of life is associated with a .014 standard deviation increase in the relocation attitude scale.

The next model examines the effect of age and gender on the relocation attitude scale. This is a **nested model**. Nested models can be compared for model fit, because they have the same common core of predictors. Thus, we can test for improvements in model fit. I cannot compare a bivariate model with age to a bivariate model with gender

Table 15.10 Bivariate SPSS Regression of Relocation Attitude Scale on Age

Variables Entered/Removed[b]

Model	Variables Entered	Variables Removed	Method
1	Age of Respondent	.	Enter

a. All requested variables entered.
b. Dependent Variable: Zscore(scale)

Model Summary

Model	R	R Square	Adjusted R Square	Std. Error of the Estimate
1	.255[a]	.065	.062	.96876205

a. Predictors: (Constant), Age of Respondent

ANOVA[b]

Model		Sum of Squares	DF	Mean Square	F	Sig.
1	Regression	18.282	1	18.282	19.480	.000[a]
	Residual	263.718	281	.938		
	Total	282.000	282			

a. Predictors: (Constant), Age of Respondent
b. Dependent Variable: Zscore(scale)

Coefficients[a]

Model		Unstandardized Coefficients		Standardized Coefficients	t	Sig.
		B	Std. Error	Beta		
1	(Constant)	-.703	.169		-4.151	.000
	Age of Respondent	.014	.003	.255	4.414	.000

a. Dependent Variable: Zscore(scale)

for improvement in fit, because they are not nested. The trivariate model syntax is below, and the output can be viewed in Table 15.11.

```
REGRESSION
/MISSING LISTWISE
/STATISTICS COEFF OUTS R ANOVA
/CRITERIA=PIN(.05) POUT(.10)
/NOORIGIN
/DEPENDENT zscale
/METHOD=ENTER age gender.
```

The first piece of output, again, provides the r^2. Adding gender to the model changes the r^2 only slightly, to .066. As we add variables into the models, it makes more sense to examine the r^2 adjusted for the degrees of freedom used up by adding more variables into the model. The adjusted r^2 is .059. This is smaller than the r^2 and the adjusted r^2 in the previous model. Thus, this model does not seem to explain more of the variance in the relocation attitude scale. The next piece of output tells us that this model is significantly different from the null, however ($f = 21, p = .000$).

The last piece of output presents the estimated regression equation. This includes the values for the constant as well as the **regression coefficients** in the model for the predicted value of the dependent variable. In multiple regression, the regression coefficients are partial correlation coefficients. The coefficient for age is significant (*t* statistic = 4.4, p =.000) and positively associated with the relocation attitude scale. The association between age and the relocation attitude scale is unchanged despite the fact that the regression coefficient is now a partial correlation coefficient. Thus all the association between age and the relocation attitude scale found in Model 1 is unique. There is no overlap between age, gender, and score on the relocation attitude scale. Being male is not significantly associated with score on the relocation attitude scale (*t* statistic = -.603, $p = .547$). We interpret this to mean that men and women, on average, do not have statistically different attitudes toward relocation.

Next, we present a multiple regression example. The syntax is below and is followed by the SPSS output in Table 15.12. In this example we include several relocation variables as additional predictors of the relocation attitude scale.

```
REGRESSION
/MISSING LISTWISE
/STATISTICS COEFF OUTS R ANOVA
```

Table 15.11 Regressing Relocation Attitude Scale on Two Predictors

Model Summary

Model	R	R Square	Adjusted R Square	Standard Error of the Estimate
1	.257[a]	.066	.059	.96986007

a. Predictors: (constant), are you male or female, age of respondent

ANOVA[b]

	Model	Sum of Squares	DF	Mean Square	F	Sig.
1	Regression	18.624	2	9.312	9.900	.000[a]
	Residual	263.376	280	.941		
	Total	282.000	282			

a. Predictors: (constant), are you male or female, age of respondent
b. Dependent variable: Zscore (scale)

Coefficients[a]

		Unstandardized Coefficients		Standardized Coefficients		
	Model	B	Std. Error	Beta	t	Sig.
1	(Constant)	-.713	.170		-4.186	.000
	Age of Respondent	.015	.003	.266	4.386	.000
	Are you male (yes)	-.087	.144	-.037	-.603	.547

a. Dependent variable: Zscore (scale)

```
/CRITERIA=PIN(.05) POUT(.10)
/NOORIGIN
/DEPENDENT zscale
/METHOD=ENTER age gender educ longten q137w1.
```

The first part of the output again shows the model fit statistics. Here, r^2 has jumped up to .53 but the adjusted r^2 is only .28. Thus, we have explained 28% of the variation in

Table 15.12 Multivariate Regression of Relocation Attitude Scale

Model Summary

Model	R	R Square	Adjusted R Square	Standard Error of the Estimate
1	.530[a]	.281	.268	.85564885

a. Predictors: (constant), how confident are you that after the relocation residents will have a good place to live, are you male or female, educ1, longten, age of respondent

ANOVA[b]

Model		Sum of Squares	DF	Mean Square	F	Sig.
1	Regression	79.199	5	15.840	21.635	.000[a]
	Residual	202.801	277	.732		
	Total	282.000	282			

a. Predictors: (constant), how confident are you that after the relocation residents will have a good place to live, are you male or female, educ1, longten, age of respondent
b. Dependent variable: Zscore (scale)

Coefficients[a]

Model		Unstandardized Coefficients		Standardized Coefficients	t	Sig.
		B	Standard Error	Beta		
1	(Constant)	.411	.206		1.989	.048
	Age of Respondent	.007	.003	.119	2.025	.044
	Are you male or female	.024	.129	.010	.185	.853
	educ1	.023	.107	.011	.216	.829
	longten	.109	.127	.047	.852	.395
	How confident are you that after the relocation residents will have a good place to live (q127w1)	-1.071	.120	-.476	-8.909	.000

a. Dependent variable: Zscore (scale)

the relocation attitude scale with this set of variables. The second piece of output presents the global model fit, and it should be no surprise that we reject the hypothesis that this model is not better than the null model.

The final piece of output presents the estimated regression equation. The intercept, again, is the average relocation attitude when all predictor variables are zero. So, it is the relocation attitude for women without a high school diploma who have not lived in public housing for more than eight years and who are not confident about finding a good postrelocation home.

The regression coefficient for age has decreased in value. It has attenuated. This is a partial correlation coefficient, not the total bivariate association, meaning that of the total association of .014 found in the first model, .007 of it is unique to age, and .007 of it is shared with tenure, with believing buildings are run down, and with confidence in finding a good home and the outcome.

In the final section of this chapter, we show how to pull all these outputs together for a journal article.

CREATING TABLES FOR THE JOURNAL ARTICLE AND WRITING UP THE RESULTS

Writing a journal article has much in common with writing a policy report. Again, we are telling a story. Again, we want to start by introducing the players. The difference between the two written products is in the quantity and type of information provided. Thus, we start our findings with a table of descriptive statistics, but we will add more information to the journal article than we provided in the policy report. We want to be as transparent as possible in the manipulation of our variables so that our study can be replicated. That is, we want others to be able to recreate and confirm our findings.

Creating a Descriptive Statistics Table

Table 15.13 presents a good example of a descriptive table that summarizes all variables that will be included in the multivariate regression analyses in the article. This table provides information on the central tendency (mean or proportion), standard deviation for central tendency, and ranges of the variables, as well as notes that may assist the readers. Dummy variables will have only two values, 0 and 1; hence their ranges are quite small. Dummy variables can be expressed as proportions rather than means, as a proportion is a more descriptive statistic. However, with a two-category variable with values of 0 and 1, a mean procedure will provide the proportion.

To create this table, we use a basic descriptives procedure. Also, note that this table is based on variables that have been cleaned, and final analysis variables have been created. We showed you previously how to clean your variables and make them ready. Note that in Table 15.13, we include the mean and standard deviation in raw units, because the mean and standard deviation of a scale variable provide little information in a descriptive statistics table, because a standardized variable provides very little information about how it is distributed. Mini Case 15.1 demonstrates how to write up the descriptives table in a journal article.

```
Descriptives q132w1 q134w1 q137w1 tenure scale age education
```

Table 15.13 Sample Descriptive Statistics

	Mean/ Proportion	*Standard Deviation*	*Range*	*Special Issues*
Dependent Variable				
Relocation attitude scale	10.7	3.5	4–20	Standardized
Independent Variables				
Age	48.5	17.6	19–98	Age 19 set to 0
Gender (male = 1)	.23	.42	0–1	
Education (received at least a high school diploma)	.52	.50	0–1	
Less than 2 years in public housing	.23	.42	0–1	
Between 2 and 8 years in public housing	.48	.50	0–1	
More than 8 years in public housing	.29	.46	0–1	
Buildings run down beyond repair	.25	.43	0–1	
Prefer to relocate rather than fix up public housing	.53	.50	0–1	
Confident will find a good home	.73	.44	0–1	

MINI CASE 15.2

Writing Up the Descriptive Results for a Journal Article

Table 15.13 presents basic descriptive statistics for the variables included in the models. The dependent variable has an average value of 10.7 with a standard deviation of 3.7. It ranges from 4, which can be interpreted as a negative attitude toward the relocation process, to 20, which can be interpreted as very positive attitude toward the relocation process. The average value of 10.7 is slightly lower than the midpoint value of 12 on the scale. We standardize this variable such that the mean is 0 and the standard deviation is 1. The average age of the sample is 48.5, just under a quarter of the sample is male, and just over half the sample has a high school diploma. Approximately a quarter of the sample has lived in public housing for less than two years, while just under half the sample has lived in public housing for two to eight years, and 29% of the sample has lived in public housing for more than eight years. Just under a quarter of the sample thinks public housing buildings are run down beyond repair, 53% would prefer to relocate rather than fix up public housing, and 73% are confident they will find a good relocation home in the private market.

Creating Regression Tables

Table 15.14 presents three regression models in a single table. All the important information found in the output needs to be included in the table. We include the intercept or estimated a for each model, and all the b's, or associations between the X variables and the dependent variables. We include all the standard errors. We do not need to include the *t*-tests or the significance for each item, as they can be calculated from the regression coefficient and the standard error. We do need to include the sample size, and the adjusted r^2 for each regression model. We use asterisks to denote which regression coefficients are significant. The notes at the bottom of the table allow the reader to see the level of significance and interpret the intercept by knowing what groups are included as the reference categories (where the X's = 0). Mini Case 15.2 provides an interpretation of the results found in Table 15.14.

Table 15.14 OLS Regression on Standardized Relocation Attitude Scale Attitudes

	Model 1	*Model 2*	*Model 3*
Constant	−.709 (.17)***	−.713 (.17)***	.411 (.21)*
Age	.014 (.003) {.255}***	.014 (.003) {.255}***	.007 (.003) {.119}*
Male		−.067 (.14) {−.037}	.024 (.13) {.010}

(Continued)

Table 15.14 (Continued)

	Model 1	*Model 2*	*Model 3*
High school diploma plus		.027 (.11) {.011}	.023 (.11) {.011}
More than 8 years in public housing			.109 (.13) {.047}
Public housing run down beyond repair			−1.011 (.12) {−.049}
Confident will find a good home			−1.071 (.12) {−.476}***
N	283	283	283
r^2	.07	.07	.56
Adjusted r^2	.06	.058	.29

*** $p < .001$ **$p < .01$ *$p < .05$

Note: Columns include raw estimates (b) with standard errors in parentheses, and standardized coefficients (B) in {} brackets.

MINI CASE 15.2

Results Write-Up for a Journal Article

Table 15.14 presents three nested models, one per column. For each variable, we have included the raw regression estimated coefficient b, the standard error (in parentheses), and the standardized regression coefficient (in brackets). Asterisks denote significant associations.

Model 1 in Table 15.14 assesses the bivariate association between age and residents' attitudes toward relocation, as measured by our relocation attitude scale. The raw regression coefficient is .014, and the standardized regression coefficient is .255. We can interpret the association as follows: On average, each additional year of life is associated with a more positive attitude toward relocation amounting to .014 standard deviation. Alternatively we can interpret the standardized coefficient as follows: An additional standard deviation in years of life is associated with a .255 increase in score on the relocation attitude scale, on average. This is the total bivariate association between age and the attitude scale. Age explains about 7% of the variation in the relocation attitude scale.

Model 2 introduces two additional demographic variables, gender and education. Neither gender nor education is significantly associated with the relocation attitude scale. The coefficient of determination (r^2) shows no improvement either, and the adjusted r^2 is lower compared to Model 1. Thus, Model 2 does not improve over Model 1 in explaining variation in scores on the relocation attitude scale.

Model 3 adds additional relocation variables such as tenure in public housing, belief that buildings are run down beyond repair, and confidence in finding a good home postrelocation. We see in Model 3 that the effect of age has been attenuated from .257 to .101, though it remains significant. Net of all the other variables in the model, each additional year of life is associated with a .007 increase in score on the relocation attitude scale, on average. Being confident in finding a good postrelocation home is significantly associated with the relocation attitude scale. Those who are confident that public housing residents will find a good postrelocation home have less positive attitudes toward the relocation process, compared to those who are not confident of finding a new home, by .468 standard deviation.

The main takeaway findings are that older public housing residents hold more positive attitudes toward relocation, and despite being confident of finding a new home, those who were confident held more negative relocation attitudes.

ETHICS CORNER

Recall that age predicted the missing data pattern. Thus, the sample had a slight age bias in that younger respondents were more likely to skip questions included in the analyses. Thus, older adults were overrepresented in the analysis sample. In writing up the findings, if we failed to acknowledge this, we would be misrepresenting our findings. It is important to include all such problems and how they might affect the interpretation so that the readers can decide for themselves how valid the results may be. It is important for us as authors to discuss the age bias, because we have thought about it the longest and have a clearer idea as to how it affects the interpretation. At a minimum, we need to acknowledge how this bias affects representativeness. In the conclusions of the journal article, we need to once again raise the issue of generalizability and caution readers that the bias introduced due to item nonresponse limits generalizability. In this way, we can be assured that we will contribute to the field of study as well as to policy in a thorough way, rather than a deceptive way that might impede progress because we neglected to inform readers of the missing data issue.

CONCLUSION

In this chapter we focused on practical applications of data analysis specifically for the purpose of producing a journal article. We introduced regression methods, which are a pretty sophisticated form of data analysis. Again, we encourage you to take a statistics course and consult with a statistics textbook prior to analyzing your own survey data. The regression method used depends upon the measurement of the dependent variable being analyzed.

Before we can begin conducting regression analyses, it is important to create an analysis dataset, examine issues of missing data, and ensure all variables meet the assumptions of regression analysis. Creating variables that are appropriate for analysis can be time consuming and error prone. Take your time with this task, and remember to always run frequencies and crosstabs on any variables manipulated, before and after the manipulation, to make sure the syntax does what it should do.

Once again, we caution you that we present more of a conceptual understanding of data analysis rather than a rigorous mathematical understanding. At the same time we presented an example of a regression analysis and how to interpret it as well as how to write it up for a journal article. To learn about the math underlying these analyses and the assumptions of regression, please refer to a statistical textbook.

As for interpreting findings, we advise staying close to the data while telling a story. This means making sure you include the relevant background information or the social, political, and economic context that is important for your evidence-based story. And don't forget to include any limitations of your study in your conclusions so as to not overstate the findings.

SYNTAX FOR ANALYSES DESCRIBED IN THIS CHAPTER

All the SPSS syntax commands used in the chapter are included in Table 15.15. In addition, it includes syntax for use with SAS and STATA.

Table 15.15 Syntax for Chapter 15 Analyses

	SPSS	*SAS*	*STATA*
RECODING DUMMY VARIABLES	compute longten=0. if (catten=4) longten=1.	Data da.data1; Set da.data; If catten=4 then longten=1; else longten=0; Run;	Gen longten=catten==4 Tab longten
MULTIPLE VARIABLE CROSSTABS	CROSSTABS /TABLES=q139aw1 BY q139bW1 BY Q139cW1_r BY Q139dW1_r /FORMAT=AVALUE TABLES /CELLS=COUNT /COUNT ROUND CELL.	Proc freq data=da.newdata; Tables Q139aw1*q139bw1* 8Q139CW1_r*q139dw1_r / list missing; Run;	tab1 q139dw1 q139aw1 q139cw1, subpop(q139dw1) nolabel
FILTERING OUT MISSING DATA	USE ALL. COMPUTE filter_$=(q132w1>=0) and (q134w1>=0) and (q137w1>=0) and (q139aw1). value labels filter_$ 0'Not selected' 1 'Selected'. Format filter_$ (F1.0). **Filter BY filter_$.**	Data da.newdata; Set da.olddata; If q132w1<0 then delete; If q134w1<0 then delete; If q137w1<0 then delete; If q139aw1<0 then delete; run;	gen missing = !missing(q132w1, q134w1, q137w1, q139aw1). **include “if miss” in all procedures

(Continued)

Table 15.15 (Continued)

	SPSS	*SAS*	*STATA*
GENERATING A MISSING INDICATOR VARIABLE	USE ALL. RECODE filter_$ (1=0) (SYSMIS=1) INTO missing. VARIABLE LABELS missing 'missing dummy'. EXECUTE.value labels missing 0'Not missing' 1 'missing'. Format filter_$ (F1.0).	Data da.newdata; Set da.olddata; Missing=0; If q132w1<0 then missing=1; If q134w1<0 then missing=1; If q137w1<0 then missing=1; If q139aw1<0 then missing=1; run;	gen missing = !missing(q132w1, q134w1, q137w1, q139aw1, q139cw1_r q139dw1_r).
LOGISTIC REGRESSION	LOGISTIC REGRESSION VARIABLES missing /METHOD=ENTER houstype age gender inc_mon longten educ /CRITERIA=PIN(.05) POUT(.10) ITERATE(20) CUT(.5).	Proc logistic data=da. newdata descending; Model Missing= houstype age gender inc_mon longten educ; Run;	Logit Missing houstype age gender inc_mon longten educ

MEAN IMPUTE	Filter BY filter_$.
	RMV/Q139bW1_1 = SMEAN(Q139bW1).
	RMV /Q139cW1_1 = SMEAN(Q139cW1).
	RMV /Q139dW1_1 = SMEAN(Q139dW1).
		Proc mean data=da.olddata;
		Vars q139bw1;
		Run;
		data da.newdata;
		set da.olddata;
		q139bw1_1=q139bw1;
		if q139bw1_1<0 then q139bw1_1= 2.23;
		q139cw1_1=q139cw1_r;
			sum q139bw1 q139cw1_r q139dw1_r
			gen q139bw1_1=q139bw1 gen q139cw1_1=q139cw1_r
			gen q139dw1_1=q139dw1_r
			replace q139bw1_1=2.24 if q139bw1_1==.
			replace q139cw1_1=2.52 if q139cw1_1==.

	SPSS	*SAS*	*STATA*

		if q139cw1_1<0 then q139cw1_1= 2.52;
		q139dw1_1=q139dw1_r;
		if q139dw1_1<0 then q139dw1_1= 3.01;
		run;
			replace q139dw1_1=3.00 if q139dw1_1==.(mean from above procedure)

STANDARDIZING A VARIABLE	compute scale=(q139aw1+q139bw1 +q139cw1_r+q139dw1_r). Descriptives variables scale /save.	scale= q139aw1+q139bw1_1+q139cw1_1+q139dw1_1; Proc standard mean=0 std=1 data=olddata out=newdata; var scale ; Run;	gen scale= q139aw1+ q139bw1_1+ q139cw1_1+ q139dw1_1 egen zscale = std(scale)
OLS regression	REGRESSION /MISSING LISTWISE /STATISTICS COEFF OUTS R ANOVA /CRITERIA=PIN(.05) POUT(.10) /NOORIGIN /DEPENDENT zscale /METHOD=ENTER age gender educ longten q1332w1 q137w1.	Proc reg data=da.newdata; Model zscale = age gender educ longten q1332w1 q137w1; Run;	Reg zscale age gender educ longten q1 32w1 q137w1, if Miss

KEY TERMS

Ordinary least squares (OLS)
Regression 275
Residual 276
Correlation coefficient 277
Partial correlation coefficient 277
Dummy variable 277
Null model 278
Coefficient of determination 278
Regression coefficient 292
Missing data 282
Missingness 282
Listwise deletion 282
Mean imputation 282
Multiple imputation 283
Limitation 287
Nested model 290

CRITICAL THINKING QUESTIONS

Below you will find three questions that ask you to think critically about core concepts addressed in this chapter. Be sure you understand each one; if you don't, this is a good time to review the relevant sections of this chapter.

1. How do we evaluate a series of nested models for the best fit?
2. Why is it important to think about missing data from nonresponse and item missingness?
3. What are the ethical considerations when writing up findings and documenting your procedures?

16

Data Archiving

INTRODUCTION

There are countless libraries across the United States and elsewhere that archive, among other things, historical documents, oral histories, and artists' papers and journals. Museums archive works of art, historical artifacts, and objects of scientific value. These institutions are saving a form of data for public consumption and enjoyment. **Archiving** means saving the data.

While the data we collect may never be displayed in a museum, they have important scientific value. According to the National Institutes of Health data-sharing guidelines, "Sharing data reinforces open scientific inquiry, encourages diversity of analysis and opinion, promotes new research, makes possible the testing of new or alternative hypotheses and methods of analysis, supports studies on data collection methods and measurement, facilitates the education of new researchers, enables the exploration of topics not envisioned by the initial investigators, and permits the creation of new datasets when data from multiple sources are combined" (NIH 2003). Thus, as social scientists in a community of social scientists, we should all consider very seriously how and when to archive data as we begin each new survey research project.

If researchers collect data in a single US state to answer a single research question and then delete the data once their question is answered, they will almost certainly waste valuable opportunities, not only for themselves but quite possibly for other researchers. First, there may be more questions that can be answered using the data; these may be questions of which the investigators are unaware or questions that they are not interested in answering. If they make the data publicly available, or even allow restricted availability, others have the opportunity to use these data to answer other research questions. This makes the data collection process more efficient and the time respondents spent answering the survey better utilized. In addition, over time the original researchers may derive new questions and wish to collect more data to compare to their first data collection, but if they have not archived it, it no longer exists (see Mini Case 16.1). The more we, as a scientific community, archive data collected from many localities over a broad spectrum of time, the better we will be able to replicate our findings, test our social scientific theories, and validate our constructs.

MINI CASE 16.1

Survey Research Example

The city of Atlanta, Georgia, was the first city in the United States to eliminate all family-based public housing projects as well as the first to demolish senior high rise housing projects. A health researcher, interested in the impact the resulting relocations of residents may have on the health of low-income households in Atlanta, conducts a longitudinal survey to determine the health of public housing residents prior to being relocated out of public housing and again two years after relocation. The investigator writes two papers examining the chronic health conditions of public housing residents, and the changes in their health symptoms and mental health before and after the relocations. Once the papers are published, the scholar deletes the data to make room for the next study. A colleague reads the papers, realizes that some crime measures were included in the study as controls, and wants to address a question on change in victimization before and after relocations and its association with mental health. This topic never entered the original investigator's mind, but now collaboration on this new topic cannot be achieved, as the data are no longer available. Archiving the data would have allowed for continued research opportunities.

SEEKING EXTERNAL FUNDING FOR YOUR SURVEY PROJECT

The National Institutes of Health (NIH) and the National Science Foundation (NSF) are now requiring anyone who receives a federal research grant of $500,000 or more to share the data collected while supported by the grant, unless there is a truly compelling reason not to share it. According to NIH, all data should be considered for data sharing, and the data should be widely and freely accessible—though the privacy of the research subjects should still be carefully protected. Since 2011, NSF has required all proposals to include a supplementary document labeled "**Data Management Plan**." NSF is somewhat vague in defining data and a suitable public data archive. They leave it to the field or community of scientists to determine this. Fortunately, data archiving is well established in social science survey research fields, and there are plenty of publically available archives from which to choose.

Data management requires resources, particularly time and personnel. There are additional costs to archiving data. If you are seeking external funding for a research project, be sure to include in the budget the time and resources to create the best possible (meaning highest quality) dataset and documentation.

ARCHIVING ORIGINAL AND FINAL DATA

So far, archiving has meant sharing data publically by making it available in a data archive. Archiving can also be done for private access only. That might mean saving backup copies of records of all aspects of the data collection process. Therefore, not only should the final data product be archived, but the raw interview material should also be archived privately for personal use. For example, in computer assisted personal interview (CAPI) surveys, all the data are collected on a computer and then warehoused before they are exported into a statistical program. This warehoused record should also be archived so that if anything happens to the exported data, they can be recreated easily. This means having the warehouse saved on a desktop computer but perhaps also writing it to a CD/DVD or USB drive. Or, if the pen-and-paper administration method was used, perhaps all the surveys should be scanned and saved to an electronic file. Alternatively, it is also common to obtain a fireproof lockable file cabinet in which to store them.

Once the dataset is created, prior to being manipulated in any way, it too should be archived. This version of the dataset is called the **original dataset**. To archive it, create a read-only version of it and save it in a couple of places where no one will accidently use it or overwrite it, such as the portable media mentioned above. There are countless stories of years of work disappearing because data were saved to a single hard drive that became corrupted, or because a computer was infected with a virus and the hard drive needed to be reformatted, or because a laptop was accidentally damaged or stolen. It is important to use multiple media and to have a backup plan. Most universities should provide backup services. If not, save to portable media, pay for cloud storage space, or save to a backed-up, separate file folder on a desktop computer. Archiving on portable media can be problematic, since those media have only a relatively short life span. Be prepared to create new copies every year as the backup medium ages and/or technology changes.

EXAMPLE OF EVOLVING DATA STORAGE TECHNOLOGY

Ever heard of a ZIP drive? If not, do an Internet search for iOmega ZIP. If material was backed up on one of those once extremely popular ZIP disks, it might be difficult to access it now, since finding a ZIP drive is a tall order. And one cannot assume the data stored in it have not been corrupted or lost altogether over time.

Archiving the original dataset is really a temporary step; it allows researchers to revert to the original raw data throughout the data cleaning and analysis stages whenever (or if ever) they happen to make a mistake. As researchers work with, manipulate, and analyze the data collected, they are most likely changing that data in such a way that they are eliminating some level of information. For example, suppose a researcher is interested in conducting an analysis using only 20 variables from a large dataset with 2,500 cases and 500 variables. The first thing the researcher *should do* is create a new dataset that is a subset of the original and includes only the variables of interest (hopefully—see Chapter 15 on subsetting). However, most researchers skip that step and find themselves in trouble. Instead, the researcher will simply delete all but the 20 variables from the original clean data and accidentally save over the original dataset. Or, a researcher will delete all missing values on the 20 variables to determine the level of response available. Let's say the researcher ends up dropping 234 respondents, leaving a dataset with 2,500 – 234 = 2,266 cases. If the researcher gets distracted, or takes a break to answer the phone or refresh her coffee, she may forget what she was doing and save over the original dataset. In the first case the researcher has created a new dataset of 20 variables and 2,500 cases, and in the second she has created a new dataset with 500 variables and 2,266 cases—but in both cases she has saved the new dataset with the same old name—overwriting the original dataset of 2,500 cases and 500 variables. If she did not have an archived backup of the original data, or did not archive the raw collected data, she just lost a large amount of work.

Once you have cleaned the data and documented the process, you have a final version of the dataset. Over time, you may make several changes to the dataset. Each time, you should rename the dataset with a new version number (as well as the date), and you should carefully document the changes since the last version. While you can save and back up each version of the dataset, keeping the syntax used to create each version of the dataset is equally important, as you can use it to recreate each version of the dataset. It is especially helpful to insert notes into the syntax to remember the name of the dataset you started with, the name of the newly created dataset, and why you made particular changes.

DATA FORMAT

There are three main, generalist statistical software packages that most social scientists use (SAS, SPSS, and STATA). Saving an original copy of your data in the software package that you use most often is typically fine, but it might cause some problems long term. Given the rapid innovation in computer technology, operating systems, and even within the statistical packages, the data may quickly become obsolete. You will need to make sure, as operating systems and statistical software packages progress or change, that your data remain viable. If you maintain your own archive, you ought to revisit it at least once per year to determine whether you need to migrate to a new storage medium or update your statistical files. This suggests that another factor to consider is how much work it will be to archive the data and maintain them yourself versus sending them to one of the large public dataset archives. You might consider creating a transport/export file or **portable file.** This changes the extension, for example, from .sav in SPSS to .por, and makes the data file easily portable across varying computer domains and software versions. Export or portable files are designed by the software companies to be compatible across differing versions, platforms, and operating systems.

Creating an **ASCII** (American Standard Code for Information Interchange) version of the dataset is probably the most versatile way of saving the data over the long term, though recreating the data later will take some effort. ASCII has been around for a very long time and will most likely continue to be around far into the future. An ASCII file is a raw text (.txt) or data (.dat) file that contains the raw data without formatting such as variable and value labels. You can save the data in a delimited format, with some character such as a comma delineating the distinct variables. Or you can document the columns of each variable in the codebook in a comparable delimited form, for example, "subject ID columns 1–4, gender, 5–5, age, 6–8." It is important when archiving data in ASCII format to document the total record length and total number of cases, and to provide frequencies of the variables so that you (and other users) can accurately recreate the dataset exactly in the statistical package of your choice.

MAKING DATA PUBLICLY AVAILABLE

There are two options for archiving the final dataset. First, you can archive it and make it publically available yourself if you have the funds and resources to do so. Otherwise, you can archive your data with one of the publically available archives. It is pretty rare to have the resources to maintain your own archive. Two examples come to mind: The Wisconsin Longitudinal Study (WLS 1957–2005) housed at the University of Wisconsin (http://www.ssc.wisc.edu/wlsresearch/) and the Integrated Public Use Micro data

(IPUMS) housed at the University of Minnesota (https://www.ipums.org/). If you decide to make the data publically available yourself, you should carefully browse through these two websites to see what types of information are helpful for other users.

If you decide to share your data using an existing archive, you should contact the archive prior to beginning the data management process so that you can use the management and documentation methods preferred by the archive. This will save you much time and effort.

ARCHIVES

The partnership called the Data Preservation Alliance for the Social Sciences (Data-PASS) consists of many local US archives. The mission of Data-PASS is to archive, catalog, and preserve at-risk social science data. Probably the most well-known member of the partnership is the Inter-university Consortium for Political and Social Research (ICPSR) which can be found at www.icpsr.umich.edu. Figure 16.1 shows their home page.

They have an extensive collection of data available to member institutions. They also have a wonderful guide to archiving data, now in its fourth edition (ICPSR 2009). They have an easy-to-follow web page that researchers can search for secondary data.

Figure 16.1 Home Page of Inter-University Consortium of Political and Social Research (ICPSR)

Additionally, they provide instructions for those who wish to deposit data into their archive. Other well-known social science data archives are the Odum Institute, housed at the University of North Carolina; the Murray Research Archive at the Institute for Quantitative Social Science (IQSS), Harvard University; and the Roper Center for Public Opinion Research at the University of Connecticut. These archives also accept data for archiving and have easy-to-follow instructions on their web pages.

ETHICS CORNER

One of the most important aspects to consider when making your data publically available is the confidentiality of your participants. For confidentiality reasons, there are some variables you do not want to make available to the public. Variables that directly identify the research subjects, such as their names and addresses or social security numbers, should be removed from all publically available datasets. The US Census also engages in other steps to restrict the ability of public users to combine variables in order to identify specific individuals. The Census top-codes certain variables, such as income, and limits the geographic specificity of variables to general areas, such as regions of the country, to protect the privacy of research subjects. As you create a publically available dataset, think carefully about what variables you might have to adapt by removing, top-coding, or generalizing to a broader category in the raw data to protect the privacy of your research subjects.

If the integrity of the data is compromised by securing confidentiality, an option may be to make available a **restricted-use dataset.** A restricted-use dataset is made available to researchers under controlled conditions. One type of use is a contract that specifies the conditions under which a researcher is allowed access to the data, often including how the researcher will protect the confidentiality of the subjects, a reason for needing the restricted data, and the time length the data is needed for. Alternatively, the data can be made available at a restricted location, and researchers wanting to use it must go to that location and use the data there.

CONCLUSION

Deciding whether or not to archive data for your personal use or for public use depends on a number of considerations. Financial and time considerations play a key role; they should be figured into any budget and scheduled during the survey planning stage. Using multiple methods of saving the data and saving multiple versions of the data will protect against accidental overwriting and problems of computer crashing, among other things. If you choose to archive, take into account the long-term issues, bearing in mind that most storage media deteriorate over time or become unusable as technology advances.

If your project is federally funded, the decision to archive or not is taken out of your hands; your main decision in this case is about which public archive to approach. Additionally, you need to think about maintaining confidentiality, what variables can be made publically available, and what, if any, manipulations of the data are needed to ensure confidentiality.

KEY TERMS

archiving 305
data management plan 307
original dataset 307
portable file 309
ASCII 309
restricted-use dataset 311

CRITICAL THINKING QUESTIONS

Below you will find three questions that ask you to think critically about core concepts addressed in this chapter. Be sure you understand each one; if you don't, this is a good time to review the relevant sections of this chapter.

1. What are the advantages and challenges of archiving data for private use or public use?
2. Why do the National Institutes of Health and National Science Foundation require their investigators to make data publically available?
3. What are the decisions you need to make to keep your data secure and viable over the long term?

EPILOGUE

In these 16 chapters, we have walked through the survey research process, indeed from start to finish. There are many steps and many decisions to be made throughout this process, and they can become quite overwhelming at times. Here in this epilogue we pull everything together in one large survey-conducting checklist. You can make a copy of it to use for every new survey research project you initiate. We wish you the very best of luck in all your survey endeavors and beyond.

SURVEY ADMINISTRATION CHECKLIST

- ☐ Type of Survey Administration
- ☐ Self-Administered
  - o Mail survey
  - o Online survey
- ☐ Interviewer Administered (with or without CATI)
  - o Telephone survey
  - o One-on-one survey
  - o One-on-group survey
- ☐ Multimode Administered

Four pieces of information are used to decide on the type of administration: what the research question is, who the target population is, what the available resources are, and which type will give the best or highest response rates.

SURVEY DESIGN AND ORGANIZATION CHECKLIST

- ☐ Introduce the survey.
- ☐ Make the design uncluttered.
- ☐ Use **boldface,** *italics,* and underlining consistently and judiciously.

☐ Avoid distracting images and bright colors.

☐ Group questions into logical subsets.

☐ Order questions in intuitive sequence.

☐ Avoid writing separate items that appear similar.

☐ Lead with interesting or intriguing questions.

☐ Locate sensitive questions toward the middle.

☐ Save demographic questions for the end.

☐ Check that all questions are absolutely necessary.

☐ Create a cover letter.

- Introduction of researcher and organization
- General description of the nature of the study (and its importance)
- Statement of time commitment for the survey
- Due date for completion
- Contact information
- Assurance of respondent anonymity/confidentiality
- Thank you!
- Single page
- Web-based surveys: Avoid spam language.
- Pen-and-paper surveys: Use official stationary or departmental letterhead.

What the questionnaire looks like will depend in large part on the administration decision. If an interviewer is used or if it is web based, it can be more complicated than a paper-and-pen questionnaire that respondents must fill out on their own. Organization of the survey instrument will also depend on administration type. Make decisions keeping the well-being of the respondents in mind.

WRITING GOOD QUESTIONS CHECKLIST

☐ Question Wording

- Are the questions short and worded simply?
- Are the questions specific and direct?
- Is only one question posed at a time?
- Are sensitive or private questions worded with maximum respect for the respondent?

- ☐ Time References
  - o Are specific time references included for questions that require recall?
  - o Are longer time periods provided for important milestones?
  - o Are shorter time periods provided for items of low importance?
- ☐ Response Options
  - o Given the social context, are these response options relevant?
  - o Is an "other" category necessary to provide a comprehensive choice of responses?
  - o Are response options mutually exclusive?
  - o Are response options weighted appropriately, with equal numbers of positive and negative responses?
- ☐ Reliability and Validity
  - o Assess the reliability of each question.
  - o Assess the validity of each question.
    - ▫ Face validity
    - ▫ Content validity
    - ▫ Construct or criterion validity

PILOTING OR PRETESTING CHECKLIST

- ☐ Assess administration.
  - o How long does the survey take to complete?
  - o Did the time to complete the survey vary widely among the test participants?
  - o Are the instructions for each section clear and unambiguous?
  - o Were the respondents thanked for their time?
- ☐ Assess organization.
  - o Do the different sections flow reasonably from one to the next?
  - o Are all questions necessary in order to collect information on your topic?
  - o Are the questions within each section logically ordered?
- ☐ Assess content.
  - o Are the questions direct and concise?
  - o Are the questions measuring what they are intended to measure?
  - o Are the questions free of unnecessary technical language and jargon?
  - o Are examples and analogies relevant for individuals of all cultures represented in the sample?

- Are questions unbiased?
- Are there questions that make respondents feel uncomfortable, embarrassed, annoyed, or confused? If so, can these be worded differently to avoid doing so?
- Are the response choices mutually exclusive and exhaustive?
- Are all response options necessary for inclusion?

CHOOSING A SAMPLE CHECKLIST

- ☐ Define the population.
- ☐ Define the target population.
- ☐ Determine the optimal sample size.
- ☐ Create a sampling frame, if possible.
    - With a sampling frame, use a probability sampling method.
        - Simple random sample
        - Systematic random sample
        - Stratified random sample
        - Cluster sample
    - Without a sampling frame, use a nonprobability sampling method.
        - Convenience sample
        - Purposive sample
        - Quota sample
        - Snowball sample
        - Respondent-driven sample

IMPROVING RESPONSE RATES CHECKLIST

- ☐ Minimizing nonresponse
    - Send an advance letter announcing the study.
    - Use university letterhead.
    - Create a study pamphlet—the more professional looking the better.
    - Include a self-addressed, stamped postcard for respondents to set the time of the survey.
    - Maintain professional standards while personalizing your contacts.
    - Attempt multiple contacts.
    - Create a study web page with additional information, means of contacting investigators, and investigator biographies.

- For web-based surveys, use an organization-based or university-affiliated e-mail address whenever possible.
- For e-mails, use a trustworthy and legitimate subject line.
- Use incentives—cash or swag.
- Tailor your approach specifically to your population where appropriate.

☐ Minimizing attrition (in addition to above)

- Remind sample members as the time for follow-up contacts approaches.
- Brand your study.

DATA COLLECTION CHECKLIST

☐ Train staff.

- Develop a training manual.
- Determine whether there is a need for ongoing training.

☐ Create auditing guidelines.

- Determine the number of attempts at contact to be made with each sample member.
- Identify rules to determine who is an eligible participant.
- Predetermine response outcome codes.

☐ Organize all data storage needs.

- Create and institute a data backup procedure.
- Create media for storing used and raw data.

DATA ENTRY AND CLEANING CHECKLIST

☐ Data Entry

- For pen-and-paper surveys,
  - ☐ Create data entry manual.
  - ☐ Train data entry personnel.
  - ☐ Enter data into statistical software package.
  - ☐ Check data entry.
- For web or CATI surveys, import warehoused data into statistical package.
- Create a unique identifier for each respondent.

- ☐ Data Cleaning
    - Create data cleaning manual.
    - Train data cleaning staff.
    - Clean data.
        - Cosmetic cleaning
            - Value labels
            - Variable labels
            - Formats
            - Missing values
        - Skip patterns
        - Other-specify
        - Multiple response questions
        - Open-ended questions
        - Notes
        - Multiple records
        - Diagnostic cleaning
            - Implausible values
            - Variation
            - Finding bad data through scale items
            - Mode of administration or interviewer effects
        - Longitudinal cleaning
            - Consistency in coding
            - Attrition effects
    - Save cleaned dataset, and create a backup of cleaned dataset.
- ☐ Analyze data.
- ☐ Answer research question.

Analyses can begin once data collection and cleaning are both complete. Data analysis is quite unique and will differ dramatically depending upon the research question, the measurement of the dependent and independent variables, and how the research will be written up. Thus, it does not readily avail itself to a checklist.

REFERENCES

Adler, Emily Stier, and Roger Clark. 2015. *An Invitation to Social Research: How It's Done* (5th ed.). Stamford, CT: Cengage.

Allison, Paul D. 2002. *Missing data.* Thousand Oaks, CA: Sage.

Alwin, Duane F., and Jon A. Krosnick. 1991. "The Reliability of Survey Attitude Measurement: The Influence of Question and Respondent Attributes." *Sociological Methods & Research* 20 (1): 139–181.

Babbie, Earl. 2013. *The Practice of Social Research* (13th ed.). Stamford, CT: Cengage.

Babbie, Earl. 2014. *The Basics of Social Research* (6th ed.). Stamford, CT: Cengage.

Bassili, John N., and Stacey B. Scott. 1996. "Response Latency as a Signal to Question Problems in Survey Research." *Public Opinion Quarterly* 60 (3): 390–399.

Bauermeister, J. A., E. Pingel, M. Zimmerman, M. Couper, A. Carballo-Dieguez, and V. J. Strecher. 2012. "Data Quality in HIV/AIDS Web-Based Surveys: Handling Invalid and Suspicious Data." *Field Methods* 24 (3): 272–291.

Bengtson, Vern L. 2000. *Longitudinal Study of Generations,* 1971, 1985, 1988, 1991, 1994, 1997, 2000 [California]. ICPSR22100-v2. Ann Arbor, MI: Inter-university Consortium for Political and Social Research.

Bernard, H. R. 1988. *Research Methods in Cultural Anthropology.* Thousand Oaks, CA: Sage.

Biemer, Paul P. 2001. "Nonresponse Bias and Measurement Bias in a Comparison of Face to Face and Telephone Interviewing." *Journal of Official Statistics* 17: 295–320.

Biemer, Paul P., and L. E. Lyberg. 2003. *Introduction to Survey Quality.* Hoboken, NJ: John Wiley & Sons.

Bradburn, Norman M., Janellen Huttenlocher, and Larry Hedges. 1993. "Telescoping and Temporal Memory." In *Autobiographical Memory and the Validity of Retrospective Reports,* edited by Norbert Schwarz and Seymour Sudman, 203–215. New York: Springer-Verlag.

Bradburn, Norman, Seymour Sudman, and Brian Wansink. 2004. *Asking Questions* (2nd ed.). San Francisco: Jossey-Bass.

Carmines, Edward, G., and Richard A. Zeller. 1979. *Reliability and Validity Assessment.* Beverly Hills, CA: Sage.

Chambliss, Daniel F., and Russell K. Schutt. 2013. *Making Sense of the Social World: Methods of Investigation* (4th ed.). Thousand Oaks, CA: Sage.

Cohen, Jacob. 1992. "Statistical Power Analysis." *Current Directions in Psychological Science* 1, (3): 98–101.

Converse, Jean M., and Stanley Presser. 1986. *Survey Questions: Handcrafting the Standardized Questionnaire.* Thousand Oaks, CA: Sage.

Couper, Mick P. 2008. *Designing Effective Web Surveys*. New York: Cambridge University Press.

Courtenay, Gillian. 1978. "Questionnaire Construction." In *Survey Research Practice*, edited by G. Hoinville and R. Jowell, 27–54. London: Heinemann Educational Books.

Crawford, Scott D., Mick P. Couper, and Mark J. Lamias. 2001. "Web Surveys: Perceptions of Burden." *Social Science Computer Review* 19 (2): 146–162.

Cronbach, L. J. 1951. "Coefficient Alpha and the Internal Structure of Tests." *Psychometrika* 16: 297–334.

Curtin, Richard, Stanley Presser, and Eleanor Singer. 2005. "Changes in Telephone Survey Nonresponse over the Past Quarter Century." *Public Opinion Quarterly* 1: 87–98.

de Leeuw, Edith, Mario Callegaro, Joop Hox, Elli Korendijk, and Gerty Lensvelt-Mulders. 2007. "The Influence of Advance Letters on Response in Telephone Surveys: A Meta-Analysis." *Public Opinion Quarterly* 71 (3): 413–443.

Deeg, Dorly J. 2002. "Attrition in Longitudinal Population Studies: Does It Affect the Generalizability of the Findings? An Introduction to the Series." *Journal of Clinical Epidemiology* 55: 213–215.

DeMaio, Theresa J., Jennifer Rothgeb, and Jennifer Hess. 1998. "Improving Survey Quality Through Pretesting." *Proceedings of the Section on Survey Research Methods, American Statistical Association*, vol. 3, 50–88.

DeVellis, Robert F. 2005. "Inter-rater Reliability." In *Encyclopedia of Social Measurement*, edited by K. Kempf-Leonard, vol. 2, 317–322. San Diego: Elsevier.

DeVellis, Robert F. 2011. *Scale Development Theory and Applications*. Newbury Park, CA: Sage.

Dillman, Don. 2007. *Constructing the Questionnaire: Mail and Internet Surveys* (2nd ed.). New York: John Wiley & Sons.

Dillman, Don A., D. A. Christenson, E. H. Carpenter, and R, Brooks. 1974. "Increasing Mail Questionnaire Response: A Four State Comparison." *American Sociological Review*, 39: 744–756.

Dillman, Don A., Jolene D. Smyth, and Leah M. Christian. 2009. *Internet, Mail, and Mixed-Mode Surveys: The Tailored Design Method* (3rd ed.). Hoboken, NJ: John Wiley & Sons.

Draisma, Stasja, and Wil Dijkstra. 2004. "Response Latency and (Para)Linguistic Expressions as Indicators of Response." In *Methods for Testing and Evaluating Survey Questionnaires*, edited by Stanley Presser et al., 131–148. San Francisco, CA: Wiley.

Ferketich, Sandra, Linda Phillips, and Joyce Verran. 1993. "Development and Administration of a Survey Instrument for Cross-Cultural Research." *Research in Nursing & Health* 16 (3): 227–230.

Finch, Janet. 1987. "The Vignette Technique in Survey Research." *Sociology* 21 (1): 105–114.

Flick, Uwe. 2011. *Introducing Research Methodology: A Beginner's Guide to Doing a Research Project*. Thousand Oaks, CA: Sage.

Graf, Ingrid. 2008. "Respondent Burden." In *Encyclopedia of Survey Research Methods*, edited by Paul J. Lavrakas, 740–740. Thousand Oaks, CA: Sage.

Groves, Robert M. 2006. "Nonresponse Rates and Nonresponse Error in Household Surveys." *Public Opinion Quarterly* 70: 646–675.

Groves, Robert M., and Mick Couper. 1998. *Nonresponse in Household Interview Surveys*. New York: Wiley.

Heckathorn, Douglas, A. 1997. "Respondent-Driven Sampling: A New Approach to the Study of Hidden Populations." *Social Problems* 44: 174–199.

Heckathorn, Douglas, A. 2002. "Respondent-Driven Sampling II: Deriving Valid Population Estimates from Chain-Referral Samples of Hidden Populations." *Social Problems* 49: 11–34.

Heckathorn, Douglas, A. 2007. "Extensions of Respondent-Driven Sampling: Analyzing Continuous Variables and Controlling for Differential Recruitment." *Sociological Methodology* 37 (1): 151–207 .

Heckathorn, Douglas, A. 2011. "Snowball Versus Respondent-Driven Sampling." *Sociological Methodology* 41 (1): 355–366.

Heerwegh, Dirk. 2003. "Explaining Response Latencies and Changing Answers Using Client-Side Paradata from a Web Survey." *Social Science Computer Review* 21 (3): 360–373.

Hox, Joop, and Edith de Leeuw. 1994. "A Comparison of Nonresponse in Mail, Telephone, and Face-to-Face Surveys: Applying Multilevel Modeling to Meta-Analysis. *Quality and Quantity* 28 (4): 329–344.

Inter-University Consortium for Political and Social Research (ICPSR). 2009. *Guide to Social Science Data Preparation and Archiving: Best Practices throughout the Data Life Cycle* (4th ed.). Ann Arbor, MI: Author.

James, Jeannine M., and Richard Bolstein. 1992. "Large Monetary Incentives and Their Effect on Mail Survey Response Rates." *Public Opinion Quarterly* 56: 442–453.

Jansen, Harrie, and Tony Hak. 2005. "The Productivity of the Three-Step Test-Interview (TSTI) Compared to an Expert Review of a Self-Administered Questionnaire on Alcohol Consumption. *Journal of Official Statistics* 21: 103–120.

Kalton, Graham. 1983. *Introduction to Survey Sampling*. Newbury Park, CA: Sage.

Kaye, B. K., and Johnson, T. J. 1999. "Taming the Cyber Frontier: Techniques for Improving Online Surveys." *Social Science Computer Review* 17 (3): 323–337.

Keeter, Scott, Carolyn Miller, Andrew Kohut, Robert M. Groves, and Stanley Presser. 2000. "Consequences of Reducing Nonresponse in a National Telephone Survey." *Public Opinion Quarterly* 64: 125–148.

Kemeny, John G., and J. Laurie Snell. 1960. *Finite Markov Chains*. Princeton, NJ: Van Nostrand.

Kish, Leslie. 1995. *Survey Sampling*. New York: John Wiley & Sons.

Kobrin, Jennifer L., Brian F. Patterson, Emily J. Shaw, Krista D. Mattern, and Sandra M Barbuti. 2008. "Validity of the SAT for Predicting First-Year College Grade Point Average." College Board Report No. 2008–5. New York: College Entrance Examination Board.

Krosnick, Jon A., Allyson L. Holbrook, Matthew K. Berent, Richard T. Carson, W. Michael Hanemann, Raymond J. Kopp, Robert Cameron Mitchell, et al. 2002. "The Impact of 'No Opinion' Response Options on Data Quality: Non-Attitude Reduction or an Invitation to Satisfice?" *Public Opinion Quarterly* 66: 371–403.

Krumpal, Ivar. 2013. "Determinants of Social Desirability Bias in Sensitive Surveys: A Literature Review." *Quality and Quantity* 47 (4): 2025–2047.

Kulas, John T., and Alicia A. Stachowski. 2013. "Respondent Rationale for *Neither Agreeing Nor Disagreeing*: Person and Item Contributors to Middle Category Endorsement Intent on Likert Personality Indicators." *Journal of Research in Personality* 47 (4): 254–262.

Lenth, Russell, V. 2001. "Some Practical Guidelines for Effective Sample Size Determination." *The American Statistician* 55 (3): 187–193.

McKay, Ruth B., Martha J. Breslow, Roberta L. Sangster, Susan M. Gabbard, Robert W. Reynolds, Jorge M. Nakamoto, and John Tarnai. 1996. "Translating Survey Questionnaires: Lessons Learned." *New Directions for Evaluation* 70: 93–104. doi: /10.1002/ev.1037/ abstract.

Merkle, Daniel M., and Murray Edelman. 2002. "Nonresponse in Exit Polls: A Comprehensive Analysis." In *Survey Nonresponse,* edited by Robert Groves, Don Dillman, John Eltinge, and Roderick Little, 243–257. New York: John Wiley & Sons.

National Center for HIV/AIDS, Viral Hepatitis, STD, and TB Prevention. 2013. *U.S. Public Health Service Syphilis Study at Tuskegee: The Tuskegee Timeline.* http://www.cdc.gov/tuskegee/timeline.htm.

National Commission for the Protection of Human Subjects of Biomedical and Behavioral Research. 1979. *Belmont Report.* Washington, DC: US Department of Health and Human Services.

National Institutes of Health. 2003. *NIH Data Sharing Policy and Implementation Guidance.* http://grants.nih.gov/grants/policy/data_sharing/data_sharing_guidance.htm

Newman, W. Lawrence. 2012. "Designing the Face-to-Face Survey." In *Handbook of Survey Methodology for the Social Sciences,* edited by L. Gideon, 227–248. New York: Springer.

Nunnally, Jum C. 1967. *Psychometric Theory.* New York: McGraw-Hill.

Nunnally, Jum C., and Bernstein, Ira. H. 1994. *Psychometric Theory* (3rd ed.). New York: McGraw-Hill.

Oakley, D., E. Ruel, and G. E. Wilson. 2008. *A Choice With No Options: Atlanta Public Housing Residents' Lived Experiences in the Face of Relocation.* Atlanta: Partnership of Urban Health Research, Georgia State University.

Olson, Kristen. 2006. "Survey Participation, Nonresponse Bias, Measurement Error Bias, and Total Bias." *Public Opinion Quarterly* 70 (5): 737–758.

Olson, Kristen. 2010. "An Examination of Questionnaire Evaluation by Expert Reviewers." *Field Methods* 22 (4): 295–318.

Osgood, C. E., G. Suci, and P. Tannenbaum. 1957. *The Measurement of Meaning.* Urbana: University of Illinois Press.

Popping, Roel. 1992. "In Search for One Set of Categories." *Quality and Quantity,* 25 (1): 147–155.

Popping, Roel. 2012. "Qualitative Decisions in Quantitative Text Analysis Research." *Sociological Methodology* 42: 88–90.

Presser, Stanley, and Johnny Blair. 1994. "Survey Pretesting: Do Different Methods Produce Different Results?" *Sociological Methodology* 24 (1): 73–104.

Presser, Stanley, Mick P. Couper, Judith T. Lessler, Elizabeth Martin, Jean Martin, Jennifer Rothgeb, and Eleanor Singer. 2007. "Methods for Testing and Evaluating Survey Questions." In *Methods for Testing and Evaluating Survey Questionnaires,* edited by S. Presser, J. M. Rothgeb, M. P. Couper, J. T. Lessler, E. Martin, J. Martin, and E. Singer, 1–22. San Francisco, CA: Wiley.

Reja, U., K. L. Manfreda, V. Hlebec, and V. Vehovar. 2003. "Open-Ended vs. Close-Ended Questions in Web Questionnaires." *Developments in Applied Statistics* 19: 159–177. http://www.stat-d.si/mz/mz19/reja.pdf

Richland, Lindsey E., Nate Kornell, and Liche Sean Kao. 2009. "The Pretesting Effect: Do Unsuccessful Retrieval Attempts Enhance Learning?" *Journal of Experimental Psychology: Applied* 15 (3): 243–257.

Rothgeb, Jennifer M. 2008. "Pilot Test." In *Encyclopedia of Research Methods,* edited by P. J. Lavrakas, 584–586. Thousand Oaks, CA: Sage.

Rousson, Valentin, Theo Gasser, and Burkhardt Seifert. 2002. Assessing intrarater, interrater, and test-retest reliability of continuous measurements. *Statistics in Medicine* 21: 3431–3446.

Ruel, E., D. Oakley, G. E. Wilson, and R. Maddox. 2010. "Is Public Housing the Cause of Poor Health or a Safety Net for the Unhealthy Poor?" *Journal of Urban Health* 87 (5): 827–838.

Salganik, Matthew, J., and Douglas D. Heckathorn. 2004. "Sampling and Estimation in Hidden Populations Using Respondent-Driven Sampling." *Sociological Methodology* 34 (1): 193–240.

Schuman, Howard, and Stanley Presser. 1981. "The Acquiescence Quagmire." In *Questions and Answers in Attitude Surveys*, edited by Howard Schuman and Stanley Presser, 203–230. New York: Academic Press.

Schwarz, Norbert. 1999. "Self-Reports: How the Questions Shape the Answers." *American Psychologist* 54 (2): 93–105.

Schwartz, Norbert, and Hans J. Hippler. 1995. "Subsequent Questions May Influence Answers to Preceding Questions in Mail Surveys." *Public Opinion Quarterly* 59: 93–97.

Scriven, A., and S. Smith-Ferrier. 2003. "The Application of Online Surveys for Workplace Health Research." *Journal of the Royal Society of Health* 123 (2): 95–101.

Sheatsley, Paul Baker. 1983. "Questionnaire Construction and Item Writing." In *Handbook of Survey Research*, edited by P. H. Rossi, J. D. Wright, and A. B. Anderson, 195–230. San Diego: Academic Press.

Shuttles, Charles D., and Mildred A. Bennett. 2008. "Cover Letter." In *Encyclopedia of Survey Research Methods*, edited by Paul J. Lavrakas, 166–168. Thousand Oaks, CA: Sage.

Singleton, Royce, and Bruce Straits. 2005. *Approaches to Social Research* (4th ed.). New York: Oxford University Press.

Smith, Tom W., Peter V. Marsden, Michael Hout, and Jibum Kim. 2013. General Social Surveys, 1972–2012 [machine-readable data file]. Chicago: National Opinion Research Center [producer]; Storrs, CT: The Roper Center for Public Opinion Research, University of Connecticut [distributor].

Smith, Tom W. 2009. "A Revised Review of Methods to Estimate the Status of Cases with Unknown Eligibility." AAPOR working paper. http://www.aapor.org/AAPORKentico/AAPOR_Main/media/MainSiteFiles/FindingE.pdf

Sudman, Seymour. 1983. "Applied Sampling." In *Handbook of Survey Research*, edited by P. H. Rossi, J. D. Wright, and A. B. Anderson, 145–194. San Diego: Academic Press.

Sudman, Seymour, and Norman M. Bradburn. 1973. "Effects of Time and Memory Factors on Response in Surveys." *Journal of the American Statistical Society* 68 (344): 805–815.

Sue, Valerie, and Lois Ritter. 2007. *Conducting Online Surveys*. Thousand Oaks: Sage.

Tourangeau, Roger, and Ting Yan. 2007. "Sensitive Questions in Surveys." *Psychological Bulletin* 133 (5): 859–883.

U.S. Census Bureau. 2010. *Population and Housing Unit Counts*, Census of Population and Housing, CPH-2-12, Georgia. Washington, DC: Author.

Van den Broeck, Jan, Solveig Argeseanu Cunningham, Roger Eeckels, and Kobous Herbst. 2005. "Data Cleaning: Detecting, Diagnosing, and Editing Data Abnormalities." *PLoS Med* 2 (10): e267.

Vogt, Dawne S., Daniel W. King, and Lynda King. 2004. "Focus Groups in Psychological Assessment: Enhancing Content Validity by Consulting Members of the Target Population. *Psychological Assessment* 16 (3): 231–243.

Wagner, William E. 2014. *Using IBM SPSS Statistics for Research Methods and Social Science Statistics* (5th ed.). Thousand Oaks, CA: Sage.

Warner, Rebecca M. 2009. *Applied Statistics: From Bivariate Through Multivariate Techniques*. Thousand Oaks, CA: Sage.

Wisconsin Longitudinal Study (WLS). 1957–2005. Version 13.01 [machine-readable data file]. Robert M. Hauser and William H. Sewell, principal investigators. Madison: University of Wisconsin. http://www.ssc.wisc.edu/wlsresearch/documentation/

Wood, Angela M., Ian R. White, and Simon G. Thompson. 2004. "Are Missing Outcome Data Adequately Handled? A Review of Published Randomized Controlled Trials in Major Medical Journals." *Clinical Trials* 1 (4): 368–376.

Yammarino, Frances J., Steven J. Skinner, and Terry L. Childers. 1991. "Understanding Mail Survey Response Behavior." *Public Opinion Quarterly* 55: 613–639.

Yzerbyt, Vincent Y., and Jacques-Philippe Leyens. 1991. "Requesting Information to Form an Impression: The Influence of Valence and Confirmatory Status." *Journal of Experimental Social Psychology* 27: 337–356.

Zimbardo, Paul. 1973. "On the Ethics of Intervention in Human Psychological Research: With Special Reference to the Stanford Prison Experiment." *Cognition* 2: 243–256.

NAME INDEX

SUBJECT INDEX

Lightning Source UK Ltd.
Milton Keynes UK
UKHW031533300621
386361UK00005B/175